ANDREAS CAPELLANUS, SCHOLASTICISM, & THE COURTLY TRADITION

Don A. Monson

❦

ANDREAS CAPELLANUS,

SCHOLASTICISM,

& THE COURTLY

TRADITION

The Catholic University of
America Press • Washington, D.C.

The paper used in this publication meets the minimum requirements of
American National Standards for Information Science—Permanence of
Paper for Printed Library Materials, ANSI z39.48–1984.

∞

LIBRARY OF CONGRESS CATALOGING-IN-PUBLICATION DATA

Monson, Don Alfred.

Andreas Capellanus, scholasticism, and the courtly tradition / Don A.
Monson.

p. cm.

Includes bibliographical references and index.

ISBN 13: 978–0–8132–1419–1 (alk. paper)

ISBN 10: 0–8132–1419–x (alk. paper)

1. André, le chapelain. De amore et amoris remedio. 2. Love. 3. Courtly
love. 4. Courtly love in literature. 5. Scholasticism. I. Title.

HQ461.M65 2005

306.7—dc22

2004018273

CONTENTS

ACKNOWLEDGMENTS

In the course of completing this study, I have incurred many debts to individuals and to institutions. The College of William and Mary, the University of Pennsylvania, the National Endowment for the Humanities, Clare Hall, Cambridge, and Kenyon College have all provided financial and other material support for my research, for which I am extremely grateful. I would like to thank the following journals and publishers for permission to reprint my articles in somewhat modified form: *Speculum* for "Andreas Capellanus and the Problem of Irony" (*Speculum* 63 [1988]: 539–72), which became Chapter 4; *Viator* for "Andreas Capellanus's Scholastic Definition of Love" (*Viator* 25 [1994]: 198–214), which provided most of Chapter 5; and Rowman and Littlefield / National Book Network for *"Auctoritas* and Intertextuality in Andreas Capellanus' *De amore"* (*Poetics of Love in the Middle Ages,* ed. Moshé Lazar and Norris J. Lacy [Fairfax, Va.: George Mason University Press, 1989], pp. 69–79), which was used in Chapter 3. Colleagues and friends too numerous to mention have shared their insights with me over the years, contributing to my understanding of a complex subject, for which I offer them my thanks. I owe a special debt of gratitude to Serge Lusignan, who generously shared with me his electronic copy of the *De amore*, and to Elizabeth Schulze-Busacker, who acted as intermediary. I am also very grateful to John W. Baldwin and Douglas Kelly for their careful reading of my manuscript and their helpful comments and suggestions, which have allowed me to avoid many pitfalls and to refine certain aspects of my analysis. I would like to thank David J. McGonagle, Susan Needham, Theresa B. Walker, and the staff of Catholic University of America Press, as well as Carol A. Kennedy, for all their help in getting my text into final form. I gratefully dedicate this labor of love to my beloved wife, Natalia, without whose continuous encouragement and support it would never have come to fruition.

ABBREVIATIONS

AA	Ovid. *Ars amatoria.*
AL	*Aristoteles Latinus.* Ed. Lorenzo Minio Paluello. 33 vols. Bruges: De Brower, 1951–.
DA	Andreas Capellanus. *De amore* (Latin text). All references are to the book, chapter, and paragraph numbers of Walsh (see below), followed by the page numbers of the same edition, in parentheses.
FEW	Wartburg, Walter von. *Französisches Etymologisches Wörterbuch.* 25 vols. Basel: Zbinden, 1928–.
GRLMA	*Grundriss der romanischen Literaturen des Mittelalters,* 6. Ed. Hans Robert Jauss. Heidelberg: Winter, 1970.
Parry	Andreas Capellanus, *The Art of Courtly Love.* Trans. John J. Parry. New York: Columbia University Press, 1941; new ed. 1969.
P.-C.	Pillet, Alfred, and Henry Carstens. *Bibliographie der Troubadours.* Halle: Niemeyer, 1933.
PL	Migne, J.-P., ed. *Patrologiae cursus completus, Series latina.* 221 vols. Paris: Garnier, 1844–1905.
RA	Ovid. *Remedia amoris.*
ST	Thomas Aquinas. *Summa theologiae.*
Trojel	Andreae Capellani Regii Francorum, *De amore libri tres.* Ed. E. Trojel. Copenhagen: Gad, 1892; new ed. Munich: Fink, 1972.
Walsh	Andreas Capellanus, *On Love.* Ed. and trans. P. G. Walsh. London: Duckworth, 1982 (translation, introduction, and notes).

ANDREAS CAPELLANUS, SCHOLASTICISM, & THE COURTLY TRADITION

INTRODUCTION

The medieval treatise on love attributed to Andreas Capellanus has become the subject of seemingly endless controversy. The past forty years have produced several books and numerous articles on the subject, yet we appear to be nowhere near anything like a consensus on the major issues that it raises. The fundamental matters on which no early agreement seems likely include the following: Who was Andreas Capellanus? Where and when did he live and write? What is his book about? Why did he write it? For what public did he intend it? What message did he wish it to convey? Ongoing scholarly controversies on these and related questions have ultimately rendered this complex, baffling work even more difficult of access.

Yet Andreas's *De amore* cannot be ignored, for it plays a key role in a much larger debate, with important implications for the entire field of Western European literature in the Middle Ages: the problem of "courtly love." Long a widely held, comfortable assumption about medieval literature and society, the whole notion of "courtly love" has in recent years come under vigorous attack by scholars who view it as a myth and, indeed, as an impediment to our understanding of the Middle Ages. Even among scholars who accept the historicity of "courtly love," lively discussions have arisen as to its specific content. Whatever meaning they attach to the term, most proponents of "courtly love" see Andreas as an important advocate of this doctrine and thus as a major medieval source for understanding it. Opponents of "courtly love" regard Andreas as condemning ironically the love between the sexes that he seems to advocate, and they attribute to the traditional (mis)interpretation of the work an important role in the perpetuation of the alleged myth. Thus the *De amore* is at the very center of the debate on "courtly love." This fact goes a long way toward explaining not only the interest and passion that the treatise continues to arouse, but also the difficulties experienced by modern scholarship in trying to reach any consensus about it.

Despite the intense scholarly activity, Andreas studies are at something of an impasse. At present most scholars concerned with these matters appear locked into polemical positions admitting of little compromise, and it is doubtful whether additional arguments in favor of well-known theses will persuade an appreciable number on either side. In fact, it may be argued that the controversy itself has become an impediment to understanding. A new approach is clearly needed if substantial progress is to be made.

Most scholarship on Andreas has been and continues to be dominated by the question of meaning: the meaning of the treatise itself and the meaning (if any) of "courtly love." Other matters, such as the identification of the treatise's author or of the public to which it was addressed, tend to be subordinated systematically to this central, overriding concern. Now, it is very true that any work of literature, like linguistic utterances generally, has as its ultimate purpose the communication of a certain meaning. But though meaning is, ideally, the final destination, it is not necessarily the best point of departure for scholarly investigation. Scholars on both sides of the Andreas controversy exhibit a common tendency to begin with a certain theory as to the work's meaning and then to look for arguments to support the theory. Because of the complexity of the *De amore* and the heterogeneity of the material that it contains, support can be found there for widely divergent and, indeed, contradictory meanings. But to assume a given meaning at the outset is to posit, in effect, what remains to be proven. When a predetermined meaning presides over the selection of materials to be examined, the resulting argumentation proves little beyond its own circularity.

It is a well-known principle of linguistics that meaning is intimately connected with form. Abundant recent scholarship has shown that this applies not only to relatively simple utterances, such as sentences, but also to infinitely more complex linguistic configurations, such as works of literature. The various linguistic elements of a sentence or a book do not signify all by themselves, independently of each other. The meaning of each is rather a function of its relationship to all the others. In linguistics or in literature, form is not only an interesting subject of investigation in its own right, it is also the surest path toward meaning.

The formalistic study of medieval literature has been much advanced in recent years, particularly through the application of linguistic theory to literary problems. One need only think of the contributions of scholars such as Pierre Bec, Roger Dragonetti, Robert Guiette, and Paul Zumthor to the study of the vernacular literature in Old French and Old Provençal. But by and large recent formalist critics have avoided thematic questions, such as "courtly love," which smacks of the old scholarship against which they are reacting. Guiette's dictum, "le thème n'est qu'un prétexte," has set the tone for subsequent research in this area. In Zumthor's monumental *Essai de poétique médiévale,* for example, "courtoisie" and *"fin' amors"* are relegated to a short appendix (pp. 466–75), where they are discussed in well-chosen but rather traditional terms. Moreover, the formalists' disdain for the traditional scholarship has generally been reciprocated, with the result that the thematic study of literature has continued to develop largely independently of formal considerations.

The neglect of formal matters is nowhere more evident than in the case of Andreas Capellanus, about whose doctrine so much has been written. It is only very recently that scholars have begun to look seriously at this aspect of his treatise, partly in response to the impasse over its meaning. This long-standing neglect of formal considerations in the *De amore* can be traced in part to the close association between the work and the problem of "courtly love." Insofar as scholars have seen and used the treatise primarily as a repository of thematic material in support of one or another theory of "courtly love," the formal organization of such material within the treatise has been viewed as secondary and, indeed, negligible. A second, related reason for this neglect concerns the critical tools usually brought to the study of the *De amore.* Any consideration of form in Andreas's work must begin from the obvious fact that it is an early scholastic treatise written in Latin, yet it has been studied almost exclusively by specialists in the medieval vernacular literatures, who are not always interested in or informed about the methods and traditions of the Latin schools.

The scholastic organization of the *De amore* is certainly one of its most striking features. It has often been mentioned in passing, but rarely studied in depth, for the reasons previously indicated. In their haste to get at Andreas's meaning, scholars have largely ignored his method. Yet I think it can be argued that an understanding of the scholastic organization of the treatise is essential to any evaluation of its contents. Before we ask whether Andreas wished to promote or condemn the profane love of the troubadours, we must recognize his most obvious and fundamental intention, that of constructing a discourse on love in the new, emerging scholastic mode. This approach probably offers the best hope for finally resolving the controversies that the *De amore* has aroused.

Whatever its debt to Ovid, to the troubadours, or to Christianity, the *De amore* doubtless owes as much to the revival of Latin learning that has come to be known as the Twelfth-Century Renaissance. In the ongoing debate concerning the identity of its author, the only matters on which all scholars can agree are that Andreas was a cleric writing somewhere in Northern France toward the end of the twelfth century or, perhaps, at the beginning of the thirteenth. This means that the *De amore* was written in a time, place, and milieu of intense intellectual activity affecting every sphere of scientific endeavor. The twelfth century saw the reintroduction of Aristotle, including the complete Organon, into the West through the great translations. It witnessed the complete revitalization of the liberal arts, particularly the linguistic arts of the trivium (grammar, rhetoric, and dialectic) which, along with the mathematical arts of the quadrivium, formed the basis for medieval primary education. A concomitant development was the firm establishment of the method of systematic compilation and confrontation of all the authorities on a given subject, which has come to be called the *sic et non* method, from its embodiment in Abelard's famous treatise of that name. Already in the twelfth century, the application of these new methods to the higher studies of theology and jurisprudence produced such monumental works as Peter Lombard's *Sentences* and Gratian's *Decretum*. Thus the twelfth century was responsible for the formation of the scholastic method associated with the great syntheses produced in the following century by the schoolmen of the University of Paris.

It would be surprising indeed if these contemporary developments were not reflected in the *De amore.* In fact, a cursory perusal of the work would suggest that they played a large part in shaping it. In the case of medieval jurisprudence, this has been convincingly demonstrated by Rüdiger Schnell. But the judicial dimension of the work, however important, is far from exhausting its debt to scholasticism. Following Schnell's lead, we would do well to consider the question of form in the *De amore* first of all in terms of the use that it makes of the scholastic method developed in the course of the twelfth century. We shall see that the work's great originality is its more or less systematic application of that method to the literary subject of love.

The cultural context surrounding the *De amore* is no less important to our investigation than its form. According to standard linguistic theory, it is the interplay between form and context that generates the meaning of any linguistic utterance, be it a sentence or a work of literature. In fact, much of the controversy that Andreas's work has elicited stems from the different interpretive contexts in which it is viewed. Should the *De amore* be understood primarily in the light of the practices of the feudal courts and that of the vernacular poetry which they produced? Is it rather a work in the Ovidian tradition, a medieval attempt to rewrite the *Ars amatoria,* with or without an understanding and emulation of Ovid's facetious tone? Is it essentially Christian in inspiration, a work of moral predication aimed at the condemnation of sexual love, albeit through the rhetorical device of irony? The treatise conveys very different meanings when it is examined in the light of these various contexts, all of which can draw support from the text.

Recognition of the scholastic background of the *De amore* will not only yield new insights concerning the work's form, it can also contribute to a better understanding of the cultural context that provided most of its contents. In particular, it encourages us to broaden the interpretive context that we bring to the treatise. One of the few things about which we can be fairly certain concerning Andreas Capellanus is that he was both a cleric and a courtier—"chaplain of the royal court," according to one passage (*DA* 1.6.385 [152]) and the rubrics of some of the manuscripts. This means that he participated in several cultural currents—clerical and lay, Latin and vernacular, pagan and Christian, literary and social—all of which are reflected in his work. Because of his scholastic formation, Andreas must have seen these currents as complementary to each other. Far from reducing his discourse on love to a single, consistent point of view, as scholars have too often been tempted to do, he appears rather to have attempted a synthesis of the insights provided by various competing traditions, in accordance with the dialectical method of twelfth-century scholasticism. Hence the baffling complexity of his treatise and the difficulty that scholars experience in trying to come to grips with it.

There is perhaps no document that illustrates better than the *De amore* the need for an interdisciplinary approach to medieval studies. If this most influential of medieval texts is also among the most controversial, this is at least in part because its generic and cultural complexity has seldom been taken fully into consideration. Ostensibly a Latin treatise in the tradition of medieval philosophy and science, the work has been studied almost exclusively by specialists in the vernacular literatures. It has long been viewed as a ready reference guide to the "courtly love" of the troubadours, and when this interpretation is called into question, it is usually in terms of another eminently literary notion, that of irony. Literary influences form a very real and important element in the *De amore,* but this current alone, however broadly defined, is not sufficient to account for the complexities of the work. It must be supplemented by insights drawn from several other disciplines, all of which contributed to Andreas's inspiration. These include medieval philosophy, theology, psychology, medicine, and jurisprudence, as well as intellectual and social history. More important than the influence of any single discipline is the constant interaction between these various currents observable throughout the treatise.

Despite its advantages, such an interdisciplinary approach is not without difficulties and pitfalls. Chief among these is the impossibility of mastering all the disciplines in question. Literary scholars may find parts of my analysis too technical; specialists in medieval philosophy or theology, intellectual or social history, medicine or law will doubtless find that it is often not technical enough. In general, I have concentrated on basic notions in the non-literary disciplines, neglecting many of the details with which the specialists must be concerned. My aim is merely to introduce a few basic concepts from several other medieval disciplines into a scholarly discourse that has heretofore been almost exclusively literary.

The considerations expounded above have presided over the organization of the present study. Thus the first of two parts is concerned with problems of form, particularly the various ways in which Andreas's scholastic methodology contributes to the formal properties of his work. Chapter 1 explores in terms of scholastic practices and models the baffling generic identity of a work that is both a scientific treatise on a natural phenomenon *(De amore)* and a practical manual on the art of loving *(De arte amandi).* Chapter 2 examines the complex interaction between rhetoric and dialectic, which is particularly apparent in the dialogues but which also informs the work as a whole. Chapter 3 concerns two aspects of the *De amore*'s intertextuality: its innovative use of the scholastic notion of authority, and the complex interweaving in its structure of classical and medieval as well as Latin and vernacular models. Chapter 4 applies insights derived from Andreas's scholastic method to the currently burning question whether his work should be interpreted as humorous or ironic. While examining important aspects of the *De amore* left relatively unexplored, these chapters are also aimed at providing interpretive orientation for the subsequent investigation of Andreas's treatment of the courtly themes.

An outgrowth of the study of form, the study of meaning in the *De amore* applies the earlier findings concerning Andreas's scholastic method to an analysis of the thematic contents of his work, within the broad cultural context that informs it. Part II explores in depth the complex dialectic that Andreas establishes between four main traditions: the commonplaces of vernacular poetry, the practices and prejudices of feudal society, the dictates of Christian theology and canon law, and the classical pagan tradition represented especially by the love writings of Ovid. The courtly themes are grouped in four broad categories corresponding to the final four chapters of the book: (1) the definition of love, which draws on both philosophical and literary sources; (2) questions concerning the psychology and physiology of love, which involve the interaction of vernacular poetry, Ovid, and medieval philosophy and medicine; (3) social questions, such as nobility of birth versus nobility of character, which oppose vernacular poetry and feudal society; and (4) moral questions, such as love and marriage, or carnal love versus spiritual love, which oppose vernacular poetry to Christianity and to Ovid. For each theme, all the references throughout the work are brought together and examined in light of each other, with particular attention to the degree to which Andreas succeeds in achieving a synthesis between conflicting traditions. Thus the final chapters provide a thorough and rigorous study of Andreas's doctrine, shedding new light not only on the *De amore* but also on the entire question of "courtly love."

PART I

PROBLEMS OF FORM

Andreas and the Scholastic Method

1 ❦

THE PROBLEM OF GENRE

Description versus Prescription

What kind of a work is the *De amore?* Leaving aside for the moment the question of its specific content, I believe we can agree that it is, at least ostensibly, a didactic work, one that purports to teach something.[1] That intention is conveyed from the very first sentence of the preface through the use of the word *docere,* "to teach." Andreas feels compelled, as he explains, to teach his disciple Walter all the things that the latter needs to know about love (*DA* 0.1 [30]). This same intention is reinforced throughout the treatise through the repeated use of *docere* and its derivatives, particularly the noun *doctrina* ("teaching, instruction"), which is often used to describe the contents of the work.[2]

To say that the *De amore* is a didactic work does not advance us very much, however, for didactic literature is a broad and varied category, particularly for the Middle Ages, which were much given to this type of writing. Within this very broad class of texts, can we assign the treatise to a particular subgenre? In what sense or senses is it didactic, and what is the general nature of the teaching that it seeks to impart?

1. For the place of didactic literature in relation to the traditional tripartite division of genres, as well as an elementary discussion of didactic subgenres, see Seidler, pp. 438–55.

2. With its participial forms, the verb *docere* occurs 36 times, to which may be added 18 occurrence of derivatives such as *edocere.* We find one occurrence of *documentum,* 49 of *doctrina.* In the dialogues the latter term often refers to the "teaching" of the male suitors by the women being wooed. Elsewhere it often designates the content of the treatise itself (e.g., *DA* 3.117 [322]: *nostra . . . doctrina*). In 11 cases the expression is *amoris doctrina,* which may or may not refer to the treatise.

The question may be viewed in various ways. From a twelfth-century perspective, we may ask, in the terms of the medieval academic prologues *(accessus ad auctores),* "To what branch of learning does it belong?" *(Cui parti philosophiæ supponitur?).* That is, where does it fit into the various schemata for classification of the sciences that were current in the twelfth century?[3] Or, in terms of the modern linguistic science of "pragmatics," which examines the ways in which linguistic utterances interact with the world, we may ask, what is the "illocutionary force" of the treatise? In other words, what general kind of effect can it be expected to produce on the reader?[4]

Manuscript rubrics: *Ars* versus *scientia*

One obvious place to look for indications as to the work's genre is the titles and rubrics that accompany it in the medieval manuscripts. For medieval writers in the *accessus* tradition, the title plays an important role in the elucidation of a text. Remigius of Auxerre sees the title as a "key" to the work that follows. For Gundissalinus, the title enables one to know what the book treats and hence to form an idea of its intention. For Bernard of Utrecht the title indicates, among other things, the "genre of writing" to which the work belongs.[5] More recently Gérard Genette has stressed the importance of what he calls the "paratext," a category that includes titles, for both the pragmatic and the generic dimensions of a work.[6]

Of course, the titles found in the medieval manuscripts of the *De amore* cannot be ascribed to Andreas himself, but rather to the scribes and rubricators responsible for the transmission of the text. The earliest of the extant manuscripts date from the thirteenth century, and most can be assigned to the fourteenth or fifteenth centuries. The rubrics may or may not be older than the extant manuscripts; in any case, they do not prove anything about Andreas's intention. Nevertheless, they

---

3. Minnis, *Medieval Theory,* pp. 23–27; Weisheipl.

4. For a general introduction to pragmatics, see Searle, *Speech Acts.*

5. Remigius, p. 2; Gundissalinus, p. 141; Bernard of Utrecht, *Commentum in Theodolum,* in Huygens, p. 60. Cf. Minnis, *Medieval Theory,* pp. 19–20.

6. Genette, *Palimpsests,* pp. 3–4; idem, *Paratexts,* pp. 55–105.

can provide a suggestive indication of the generic affinities perceived by a medieval clerical audience much closer in time and culture than we to the author and his tradition.[7]

Of the forty-one manuscripts listed by Karnein, fourteen give little or no information of a generic nature (Karnein, nos. 1, 6, 7, 12, 15, 22, 23, 29, 31, 33, 38, 39, 40, 41). The others may be divided roughly into two broad categories: those that announce a subject to be investigated, a phenomenon to be understood, and those that evoke an activity to be learned, a skill to be acquired.

Twelve manuscripts announce a subject to be studied: Karnein, nos. 5, 8, 10, 16, 17, 18, 24, 25, 27, 28, 32 and 36. The rubrics of these manuscripts take one (or both: ms. 8) of two forms: *De amore*, "On Love" (mss. 8, 16, 17, 27, 28, 36), or *Liber amoris*, "Book of Love" (mss. 5, 8, 10, 18, 24, 25, 32). *De amore* is the title adopted by E. Trojel and reaffirmed recently by P. G. Walsh (p. 1). In several of the manuscripts it is reinforced by terms such as *tractatus*, "treatise" (ms. 8), *summa* (ms. 16), or *liber* (mss. 27, 36).[8] These rubrics not only announce the subject of the work, they also situate it in a tradition of scientific and philosophical writing going back to classical antiquity, in which "On whatever . . ." is the standard title for a treatise. This nuance is lacking in the other subgroup of rubrics, which merely state the book's subject: *Liber amoris* or *Liber amoris et curtesie* (mss. 24, 25).

The rubrics evoking an activity substitute for the noun *amor* a verb,

---

7. On the manuscripts and their rubrics, see especially Karnein, *"De amore,"* pp. 267–87. Cf. Trojel, pp. xx–xxxvii; Roy, "A la recherche."

8. The noun *tractatus* occurs 7 times in Andreas's treatise: *DA* 1.0 (32); 1.2.2 (34); 1.4.5 (38); 2.2.2 (228); 2.5.1 (234); 3.119 (322) [twice]. All but one (1.2.2) of these occurrences appear to refer to the work itself or to some part of it. The first and last seem particularly significant: *Accessus ad amoris tractatum* (1.0); *tractatum nostrum* (3.119). There are also 7 occurrences of the verb *tractare* in the sense "to treat a subject scientifically," including 3 in the first person with *de amore* as complement: *DA* 1.7.1, 3 (208–10); 1.11.1 (222). Except for the headings of the three "books," the word *liber* is used only twice, once of Cicero's *De amicitia* (3.12 [290]), and once in an internal reference to Andreas's own work (1.6.269 [116]: *in libro ad Gualterium scripto*, "in the book written to Walter"). Much more frequent is the modest diminutive *libellus*, which occurs 7 times, always referring to the *De amore*. The noun *summa* occurs only twice, in the expression *breviter et in summa notare*, "to resume briefly" (1.6.161 [84]), in which it can hardly be taken as referring to the work itself. There are 8 occurrences of *auctoritas* (see below, n.

usually *amare,* "to love," in the gerund. Their typical formulation is *De arte amandi,* "On the Art of Loving" (mss. 2, 4, 11, 20, 26, 37),[9] generally followed by [*De*] *remedio amoris,* "Love's Remedy" (mss. 4, 20), *De reprobatione amoris,* "The Rejection of Love" (ms. 2), or by both (ms. 26). The first part of this title was loosely adopted by Parry for his translation of the work, *The Art of Courtly Love.* Here the key word is *ars,* which places the work in a long tradition of practical treatises containing advice for exercising one of the arts, be it liberal or mechanical. In particular, one cannot help but think of the *Ars amatoria* of Ovid.[10] Also in the Ovidian tradition are the rubrics designating the third book as *De remedio amoris,* including not only the manuscripts indicated above, but also three others that contain no general title for the treatise (mss. 19, 34, 35). And clearly situated in the same vein, although they do not contain the word *ars,* are the rubrics of one other manuscript, which exhibit the characteristic gerund construction: *Liber acquirendi amoris, Liber remedij seu derelinquendi amorem* (ms. 13).[11]

Finally, a few manuscripts seem to hesitate between the two types of designation. One manuscript calls the work *De arte amandi* at the outset but *Liber de amore* in the explicit (ms. 9). Another combines both types in a single rubric: *De amore et arte amandi et de remediis amoris* (ms. 14). And two others combine a general title of the *Liber amoris* type with an Ovidian title of the *Remedia* type for Book Three (mss. 21, 30).

The rubrics thus seem to indicate two very different perceptions of the Chaplain's work on the part of its late-medieval clerical audience. By some it is seen as a scientific treatise on the natural phenomenon of

---

9), but only one of these (1.6.465 [178]: *amoris . . . auctoritas*) could possibly be understood as a reference to the *De amore.*

9. Mss. 11 and 20 have *De arte amoris.* Another rubric of ms. 11 reads *De arte mundi,* clearly a corruption of *De arte amandi.* Several of these titles are also reinforced with words such as *liber,* "book" (ms. 2); *libellus,* "little book" (ms. 11); *tractatulus,* "little treatise" (ms. 20); and *auctoritates* "authorities" (ms. 37, a florilegium).

10. A second rubric of ms. 2 (f. 119r) reads *De arte amatoria,* as did the rubric of a manuscript now lost (ms. 45).

11. A somewhat similar title, dated 1721, is found in the fourteenth-century manuscript now in Montpellier (ms. 3): *Liber de conciliando amori,* "Book on Acquiring Love."

love. For others it is rather a practical manual on the art of loving. And for a few, perhaps not the least perceptive, it is both.[12]

The rubrics raise the question of the precise relationship of the two concepts *ars* and *scientia* in medieval thought and practice. The answer is not simple, for the two concepts are interrelated, and the terms that designate them are subject to variations in definition or usage from one period to another or even from one author to another. In particular, we observe a marked difference between scholastic writers of the twelfth century, those who were roughly contemporary with Andreas Capellanus, and those who wrote in the thirteenth century, the period that produced the oldest surviving manuscripts of the Chaplain's work.

For the twelfth century there seems to be little or no distinction between *ars* and *scientia*. In his *Didascalicon* Hugh of St. Victor, quoting Isidore of Seville, wrote: "Knowledge [*scientia*] can be called an art [*ars*] 'when it comprises the rules and precepts of an art.'"[13] The term *scientia* was applied with particular frequency to the liberal arts of the trivium and quadrivium. Again quoting Hugh: "dialectic is knowledge [*scientia*], meaning an art [*ars*] or discipline."[14] And a chapter of the *Didascalicon* entitled "Which Arts Are Principally to Be Read" begins with "Out of all the sciences above named . . ."[15]

---

12. Karnein, *"De amore,"* pp. 270–71, argues that the rubrics of the *De arte amandi* type are a later development from the *De amore* type by way of an intermediate *Liber amoris et curtesie* type. But this hypothesis, which appears to stem from Karnein's theory of a "change in paradigm" in the treatise's reception (see below, Chapter 4), is not supported by the evidence. In fact, the chronological distribution of these three rubric types is fairly even: for the *De amore* group there is one manuscript from the fourteenth century (ms. 28), the others being from the fifteenth; for the *Liber amoris* type there is one manuscript from the thirteenth century (ms. 24), one from the fourteenth (ms. 25), and the rest from the fifteenth; the *De arte amandi* type is represented by two fourteenth-century manuscripts (mss. 2, 11), all the others being from the fifteenth century.

13. *Didascalicon* 2.1 (trans. Taylor, p. 61); cf. ibid., p. 196, n. 5; Paré et al., pp. 103–4.

14. *Didascalicon* 2.30 (trans. Taylor, p. 81); cf. ibid., p. 82: "knowledge which is an art or discipline"; Gundissalinus, p. 45: *Grammatica igitur est ars vel scientia,* "Therefore grammar is an art or a science" (my translation).

15. *Didascalicon* 3.3 (trans. Taylor, p. 86); cf. ibid., p. 211, n. 40. John of Salisbury also uses *ars* and *scientia* as more or less equivalent. See *Metalogicon* 1.11.26–33 (ed. Hall, p. 30): *Præcedit enim inuestigatio comprehensionem, examinationem, et custodiam omnium* sciendorum. . . . *Et hæc quidem est omnium origo* artium (my emphasis); trans. McGarry, p. 34: "In our acquisition of [scientific] knowledge, investigation is the first step,

It was only in the thirteenth century, when the influx of Aristotelian ideas had brought greater rigor in scientific terminology, that a clear distinction between *ars* and *scientia* appeared. Aristotle had already laid the foundation for such a distinction in his *Posterior Analytics:* "From experience . . . originated art [τέχνη = *ars*] and knowledge or science [ἐπιστήμη = *scientia*], art in the sphere of coming to be or generation and science in the sphere of being."[16] In the mid-thirteenth century the following formal distinction was established by the anonymous author of the *Summa philosophiæ* formerly attributed to Robert Grosseteste:

> There seems to be this difference between science and art, that science contemplates and examines principally certain causes of its truth, but art considers rather the manner of operating according to the truth transmitted and proposed. Consequently the philosopher and the artist have a common matter but different precepts or principles and ends. . . . And it happens that a certain theoretic and speculative part and a practical or operative part are assigned in almost all matter of science.[17]

This distinction between the speculative and the practical is also clearly discernable in the writings of Thomas Aquinas. He defines *ars* variously as "nothing other than the right judgment about things to be made,"[18] and as "nothing other than a definite and fixed procedure established by reason, whereby human acts reach their due end through appropriate means."[19] And of the verb *scire* he wrote: "To know scientifically seems to be nothing less than to understand the truth of a conclusion through demonstration."[20]

Despite the overlapping of the concepts *ars* and *scientia* and the con-

---

and comes before comprehension, analysis, and retention. . . . This, in short, is how all the arts have originated." The confusion continued into the thirteenth century, at least until Alexander of Hales; see Minnis, *Medieval Theory,* p. 119.

16. Aristotle, *Posterior Analytics* 2.19 (100a6–9), quoted from McKeon, *Selections,* 2:431–32. Cf. ed. Tredennick, p. 259: "art in the world of process and science in the world of facts."

17. The Pseudo-Grosseteste, *Summa of Philosophy* III, vii, quoted from McKeon, *Selections,* 1:312. Cf. Robert Grosseteste, p. 301.

18. *ST* 1a2æ 57.3 (ed. Blackfriars, 23:46–47).

19. Thomas Aquinas, *Commentary* 1.1.1 (trans. Larcher, p. 1).

20. *Commentary* 1.4.9 (trans. Larcher, p. 16).

fusion between them that reigned in the twelfth century, there emerges from thirteenth-century writers a fairly clear distinction. Science or knowledge refers to the understanding or intellectual apprehension of the truth of that which is, whereas art is concerned with a modus operandi designed to "make" something or bring it into being. We may say that the former is essentially descriptive, the latter essentially pre-scriptive. Or, in the terminology of pragmatics, we may say that the "speech acts" to which science gives rise are primarily "representatives," whereas those associated with art are generally "directives."[21] *Scientia* provides a "representative" description of being, in the form of a logical sequence of true propositions. *Ars* offers a "directive" prescription for modifying what is in accordance with certain preestablished ends.

Art does involve knowledge, insofar as the effective completion of a factive operation may depend on the application of certain particular truths. But in the process of making, the artisan relies primarily on the direct apprehension of these necessary truths through experience, rather than on the formal, demonstrative kind of knowledge to which Aquinas refers. Science and art may well deal with a common subject matter; but, like basic research and technology in our day, they treat this com-mon subject matter from very different perspectives, the former being concerned with ascertaining general truths, the latter with applying particular truths to practical problems.

Coming back to Andreas Capellanus, we observe in his work a strange mixture of the speculative and the practical that probably ac-counts for the two types of rubrics contained in the manuscripts. In typical twelfth-century fashion, Andreas seems to confuse these two genres of discourse. But the presumably later rubrics, dating from a time when the distinction was more clearly made, emphasize sometimes one aspect, sometimes the other aspect of this complex work.

21. Searle, "A Classification," distinguishes five major categories of "speech acts": (1) *representatives,* which undertake to represent a state of affairs; (2) *directives,* which are designed to get the addressee to do something; (3) *commissives,* which commit the speaker to something; (4) *expressives,* which express the speaker's psychological state; and (5) *declarations,* which bring about the state of affairs to which they refer. Pratt, pp. 80–85, has argued that this analysis can be applied not only to discreet utterances, but also to larger units of discourse, including works of literature.

Scientia

The scientific, speculative aspect of the Chaplain's enterprise is particularly visible in the early part of the work. Here Andreas calls upon the standard scholastic techniques of definition, distinction, and proof, which were an integral part of the apparatus of dialectical demonstration, in order to arrive at the essence of the phenomenon under discussion.

The first book opens with a short *Accessus* or "Introduction" (*DA* 1.0 [32]). Not only the title but also to a great extent its form are reminiscent of the medieval academic prologues, or *accessus ad auctores,* which served to introduce commentaries on curriculum authors of every discipline.[22] In particular, rubrics such as *quid sit . . .* and *unde dicatur . . .* recall Richard Hunt's "type D" prologue, whose origin goes back apparently to Cicero's *De inventione,* by way of Boethius's *De differentiis topicis.*[23] The particular use to which Andreas puts these traditional *accessus* techniques is in line with the new emphasis on *ordinatio* discernable in medieval bookmaking starting in the second half of the twelfth century, as a concomitant to the rise of the scholastic method. The *Accessus* serves as a *materia operis,* a kind of synoptic introduction indicating the topics dealt with in each section, and it will be relayed by a series of rubrics, or chapter headings, thus permitting easy "access" to the work (as the name implies) for the purpose of citing it as an authority on the various subjects treated.[24]

The function of Andreas's *Accessus* is to separate the object under investigation into its constituent parts. To this end he calls upon the

22. Quain; R. Hunt; Huygens; Minnis, *Medieval Theory,* pp. 9–39.

23. R. Hunt, pp. 86–89, 97; Minnis, *Medieval Theory,* p. 31; p. 231, nn. 136, 137. This, the last and most complex of Hunt's four schemata, is exemplified by the *Summa super rhetoricam* of Thierry of Chartres, the *Glosa super Priscianum* of William of Conches, and the *De divisione philosophiæ* of Gundissalinus. Gundissalinus, p. 43, lists the following heads: *Quid sit ipsa, quid genus eius, que materia, que partes, que species, quod officium, quis finis, quod instrumentum, quis artifex, quare vocetur, et quo ordine docenda et discenda sit,* "What is it? What is its genus, matter, parts, species, function, goal, means? Who is its agent? Why is it so called? And in what order should it be taught and learned?" (my translation).

24. Parkes, esp. pp. 117–19. Cf. Rouse and Rouse, esp. pp. 202–9.

scholastic technique of *divisio*. For thirteenth-century writers such as Alexander of Hales and Robert Kilwardby, the *modus divisivus* was one of the three basic modes of human science, along with the *definitivus* and the *collectivus*.[25] But Andreas's use of *divisio* is not the formal distribution of genus into species practiced in the following century under the influence of Aristotelian logic; it is rather the more informal "division by separation into parts" advocated by Hugh of St. Victor as the method of expounding texts.[26] Despite apparent digressions, the brief outline suggested by the *Accessus* will be followed throughout the *De amore*. The successive treatment of the various parts here distinguished will constitute a total description of the object under examination.

The first five rubrics enumerated by the *Accessus* will constitute, respectively, the chapter headings for Book One, Chapters One, Three, Four, Two, and Six: *quid sit amor; unde dicatur amor; quis sit effectus amoris; inter quos possit esse amor;* and *qualiter acquiratur amor.*[27] The seven remaining chapters of Book One may be seen as "matters arising," necessary clarifications of subjects previously discussed. Chapter Five, "What Persons Are Suited for Love," is an amplification of Chapter One, as we shall see. Chapters Seven, "The Love of Clerics," Eight, "The Love of Nuns," and Eleven, "The Love of Peasants," are necessary to complete the sociological schema around which the dialogues of Chapter Six are organized.[28] Chapters Nine, "Love Obtained by Money," Ten, "The Easy Granting of Requested Favors," and Twelve, "The Love of Prostitutes," provide further elaboration on two of the five ways of acquiring love distinguished at the beginning of the same Chapter Six.

A similar pattern can be observed for Book Two. The six remaining

---

25. Minnis, *Medieval Theory,* pp. 122–23.

26. Hugh of St. Victor, *Didascalicon* 6.12 (trans. Taylor, p. 150); cf. ibid., 3.9 (trans. Taylor, pp. 92); Aristotle, *Posterior Analytics* 2.14 (98a1–12); Paré et al., p. 119.

27. *DA* 1.0 (32). Cf. Walsh, p. 33: "what love is, why it is so called, and its effect; between what persons it can exist, how it can be obtained."

28. This function is made explicit at the beginning of Chapter Seven, where Andreas recalls the three ranks of society previously distinguished before adding a forth, namely the clergy (*DA* 1.7.1 [208]). Likewise, the beginning of Chapter Eleven specifies that the peasants to be discussed in that chapter are not included in the earlier discussion of commoners (*DA* 1.11.1 [222]).

rubrics of the *Accessus* refer, in order, to the first six chapters of the second book: *qualiter . . . amor retineatur* (the general title for Book Two, more or less equivalent to Chapter One, . . . *debeat conservari*); . . . *augmentetur; . . . miniatur; . . . finiatur; de notitia amoris mutui; quid unus amantium agere debeat altero fidum fallente.*[29] The two remaining chapters, Seven, "Various Decisions in Love Cases," and Eight, "The Rules of Love," are devoted, respectively, to resolving outstanding questions and to summarizing the results.

Only Book Three, "The Rejection of Love," is not mentioned in the *Accessus.* But there is a fairly transparent allusion to it in the preceding *Præfatio,* in which, addressing himself to "Walter," Andreas explains his own motives and intentions in writing the treatise. There the Chaplain promises to "teach" *(docere),* in a second phase of his instruction, *qui non amantur, quibus modis sibi cordi affixa valeant veneris iacula declinare.*[30] In fact, there appears to be an explicit reference to this allusion in the beginning words of the *Accessus:* "First we must see" *(est igitur primo videre).* Here *igitur,* "therefore," explains and justifies the program outlined in the *Accessus* through reference back to the motives and intentions enunciated in the *Præfatio,* whereas *primo,* "first," suggests that this program will be followed by a second phase, which can only be that to which Andreas has previously alluded. Thus the entire substance of the *De amore* is outlined, or at least suggested, in the *Accessus.*

Andreas's first chapter, *Quid sit amor,* calls for a definition. Andreas's definition of love is perhaps the most striking example in the treatise of the application of the methods of science to the subject under investigation. Because of its importance, it will be analyzed in detail below (Chapter 5), in terms of both its form and its content. Here a brief sum-

29. *DA* 1.0 (32). Cf. Walsh, p. 33: "how it can be . . . kept, increased, diminished, and ended; how reciprocated love is recognized, and what one lover should do if the other is untrue."

30. *DA* 0.1 (30). Cf. Walsh, p. 31: "to instruct you . . . the means by which those whose love is unrequited can shift Venus's shafts lodged in their hearts." The *Præfatio's* formula for describing the first part of Andreas's instruction, *qualiter inter amantes illæsus possit amoris status conservari,* is very close to the heading of Book Two, Chapter One: *Qualiter status acquisiti amoris debeat conservari.* But it can be seen to refer more generally to all of Book Two *(Qualiter amor retineatur),* which in turn implies the successful application of the instructions on acquiring love contained in Book One.

mary must suffice. Close examination of the definition in the light of Andreas's own commentary on it and of parallels from contemporary scholastic writers reveals that it conforms to Aristotelian requirements for definition and that it makes appropriate use of major concepts of medieval logic and psychology. It also appears to have been formulated implicitly in terms of Aristotelian causality. Despite certain difficulties, probably attributable to fluctuations in terminology in the early scholastic period, it is a carefully constructed, properly scientific definition drawing on a long philosophical tradition.

The definition of love is followed by a discussion of the definition, which occupies the rest of the first chapter. The form that this discussion takes is no less interesting than its contents, for it is based on the eminently scholastic technique known as *glossatio,* or glossing of terms. The "gloss" *(glosa)* is the outgrowth of the standard medieval school exercise, *lectio,* the reading and explanation of the curriculum authors. It is usually distinguished from the freer "commentary" *(commentum)* in that it pays particular attention to the *littera,* that is, the exact words in their literal meaning.[31] Andreas's discussion of his own definition is centered around its key terms: *passio, innata, visio, cogitatio,* and *immoderata.* Each is taken in turn, defined, and analyzed in its own right, expanded and clarified through a process of association and distinction with respect to other terms:

Quod amor sit *passio,* facile est videre. Nam . . .
Quod autem illa passio sit *innata,* manifesta tibi ratione ostendo,
    quia . . .
. . . Est igitur illa passio innata *ex visione et cogitatione.*
Non quælibet cogitatio sufficit ad amoris originem, sed *immoderata*
    exigitur; nam . . .[32]

---

31. Paré, pp. 19–22; Paré et al., pp. 116–19; Hugh of St. Victor, *Didascalicon,* 4, 16, trans. Taylor, p. 119; cf. Taylor, pp. 218–19, n. 55; William of Conches, *In proœmium Calcidii,* § 10 (ed. Jeauneau, p. 67).

32. *DA* 1.1.2 [32], 8, 13 (32–34) [my emphasis]. Cf. Parry, pp. 28–29: "That love is a *suffering* is easy to see, for . . . That this suffering is *inborn* I shall show you clearly, because . . . This inborn suffering comes, therefore, *from seeing and meditating.* Not every kind of meditation can be the cause of love, an *excessive* one is required; for . . ." (my emphasis). Walsh, pp. 33–35, translates this passage somewhat more freely.

Then the words used to explain the key terms of the definition are themselves explained through yet other words, and so on. For example, the word *angustia*, "anguish, torment," with which *passio* is glossed, is itself glossed with *timor*, "fear," and various forms of *timere*, "to fear," after which various types of fear are distinguished according to the circumstances of the lover, who may be "rich" *(dives)* or "poor" *(pauper)*, who may be "base" *(turpis)* or a victim of "rumors" *(rumores)*, whose love may be "requited" *(amor utriusque perficitur)* or "unrequited" *(res imperfectæ, singularis amor)*, and so on. Thus by this process of systematic glossing of terms the original brief definition is progressively expanded into a full description of the phenomenon under investigation.

A similar process of further elaboration of the original definition can be traced throughout the four chapters that follow. Each of these chapters takes up some specific aspect of the definition and draws from it further implications, often with precise repetition of the wording of Chapter One.

Chapter Two, "Between What Persons Love May Exist," is devoted primarily to limiting love relationships to heterosexual situations: "It must first be noted that love cannot exist except between people of the opposite sex" *(DA* 1.2.1 [34]). This pronouncement may be seen as an expansion of the phrase "of the other sex" *(alterius sexus)* in the definition of Chapter One. It in turn will be elaborated and demonstrated through the use of other terms and phrases from the same definition: *cogitatio*, "meditation"; *amplexibus frui/potiri*, "to enjoy the embraces"; *omnia amoris mandata/præcepta compleri*, "to carry out all of Love's mandates/precepts." Thus the restriction deduced from the definition is justified in terms of the final cause of love, the carrying out of "all of Love's mandates," which Andreas sees as requiring participants of different sexes.

Chapter Three, "Whence It Is Called Love," completes the "definition of the thing" *(definitio rei)* with a "definition of the name" *(definitio nominis)*, that is, an etymology. This development is based on the widespread medieval principle that the origin of the name reflects the essence of the thing named. Or, as Dante put it: *Nomina sunt consequentia rerum.*[33] The most important medieval application of this prin-

---

33. Dante Alighieri, *Vita nuova*, § 13: "Names are the consequences of things" (my

ciple is that of Isidore of Seville, who organized an entire encyclopedia of science around the etymologies of words. In fact, Andreas appears to have derived not only the principle but also his etymology from Isidore, who had written: *amicus ab hamo, id est, a catena caritatis; unde et hami quod teneat.*[34] Andreas repeats this false etymology, adapting it somewhat to his own context: *Dicitur autem amor ab amo verbo* ("Love is so called from the word 'hook'"). He then proceeds to analyze this "hook" image in terms of the paradigm *(action)/passion/reaction* established in Chapter One, expressed here primarily through an alternation between the active and passive voices of the verb *capere*, "to catch": *quod significat capere vel capi. Nam qui amat, captus est cupidinis vinculis aliumque desiderat suo capere hamo.*[35] Thus the etymology further expands and completes the original definition, while preparing the way for the development in Chapter Six of how love may be acquired.

In Chapter Four, "What Is the Effect of Love," the overriding desire for the embraces of the other is developed into the principle of chaste fidelity to one woman. There is another aspect of love deserving ample praise, Andreas claims: the fact that it adorns a man, as it were, with the virtue of chastity, since he who shines with the light of one love can hardly think of embracing another, however beautiful (*DA* 1.4.2 [38]).[36] This passage appears to be an elaboration of the phrase *super omnia cupit*, "desires above all else," in the original definition. Once again we encounter key words from the definition, particularly those associated

---

translation). Cf. Curtius, pp. 495–500. On the medieval etymologizing, see also Amsler; Klinck.

34. *Etymologiæ* 10.1.5. Cf. Parry, p. 31, n. 6: "A friend *(amicus)* is so called from the word for hook *(hamus)*, that is, a shackle of affection; therefore they are also called hooks because they hold." For a discussion of the principle of etymologizing, cf. *Etymologiæ* 1.29.

35. *DA* 1.3.1 (36) [my emphasis]. Cf. Walsh, p. 37: "*Amor* is derived from the verb *amo*, meaning catch or be caught, for the lover is caught in the bonds of desire and longs to catch another on his hook *(hamo)*"; Parry, p. 31: "Love gets its name *(amor)* from the word for hook *(amus)*, which means 'to capture' or 'to be captured,' for he who is in love is captured in the chains of desire and wishes to capture someone else with his hook." The wordplay on *amo*, "I love," and *(h)amo*, ablative of *hamus*, "hook," is difficult to render into English.

36. For the use of the word *castitas* to describe the fidelity to one woman in a love relationship, see below, Chapter 8.

with the efficient cause *(cogitatio/cogitare)* and the final cause *(amplexus)* of love.

In Chapter Five, "What Persons Are Apt for Love," the principle of fidelity developed in the previous chapter is further elaborated to exclude from love the "excessively voluptuous," who are unable to confine themselves to one partner. Too much abundance of pleasure is an impediment to love, Andreas argues, for there are some who have so much desire for pleasure that they cannot be caught in Love's snare: after thinking a great deal about one woman or enjoying her favors, when they see another, they immediately desire this other's embraces, ungratefully forgetting the services of the first *(DA* 1.5.7 [40]). Likewise, the blind are excluded from love, owing to the seminal role of sight in love's origin. Blindness is an impediment to love, it is argued, because a blind man cannot see anything from which his mind could conceive immoderate thought, so love cannot develop in him *(DA* 1.5.6 [40])— "as was clearly shown earlier," Andreas adds, an explicit reference to the discussion of this subject in the first chapter *(DA* 1.1.8–9 [34]). Chapter Five also excludes from love—again, apparently, on physiological grounds—the very old and the very young, who by reason of age are incapable of carrying out "all of Love's precepts."

Thus we have seen that in the first five chapters of his work the Chaplain establishes a properly scientific discourse on the phenomenon of love, using all the standard techniques of dialectical argumentation. After first dividing his subject into its constituent parts, he then proceeds to a definition of its essence, which definition he elaborates through further definitions and distinctions into a complete description of the phenomenon. These chapters seem to justify fully the rubric *Tractatus de amore.*

Ars

The other aspect of the Chaplain's treatise, the practical manual on the art of loving, is also present from the beginning. In the "Preface" *(Præfatio),* which precedes the entire work, Andreas evokes a certain Gualterius, whose request for practical advice had supposedly occasioned the work's composition. The subjects that Andreas promises to teach are eminently practical: how a state of love can be preserved intact between lovers, and likewise how those who are not loved in return can get rid of the darts of Venus lodged in their hearts (*DA* 0.1 [30]).

In fact, the entire passage is concerned with what the lover can "achieve by his actions" *(suis actibus operari)*, expressed primarily through a series of conventional metaphors in the Ovidian tradition: to "get rid of the darts of Venus" *(veneris iacula declinare);* to "manage your horse's reins" *(guberare frena caballi);* to "engage in this kind of hunting" *(huiusmodi vacare venatibus);* and the like. The expression used to describe the entire enterprise, *amoris doctrina,* "Love's teaching," is, to be sure, ambiguous, as we have seen; but in the conclusion of the treatise, coming back to Gualterius and the rhetorical frame that he provides, Andreas will use another expression that is quite unambiguous: *ars amatoria.*[37]

After the first five theoretical chapters discussed above, the practical side of Andreas's discourse comes to the fore in Chapter Six, *Qualiter amor acquiratur et quot modis.* This subject is, of course, an important part of any total description of love, and indeed it was listed in the *Accessus* among the subjects to be covered. Yet here we find ourselves on rather different ground, for the question is no longer "what" *(quid),* but rather, as already in the first sentence of the *Præfatio,* "how" *(qualiter, quo modo).* The discourse is no longer concerned with the "quiddity," or essence, of a phenomenon, but rather with the modality of an operation.

We might note in passing a rather surprising shift in the meaning of the word *amor.* Had Andreas stuck to his original definition, "Amor est passio . . .," he would not now have to ask how love may be acquired, for he has already explained that it comes "from the sight of and excessive meditation upon the beauty of the opposite sex." What the Chaplain is now talking about acquiring is clearly not *amor,* as he himself has defined it, but rather what he will subsequently refer to repeatedly as

---

37. *DA* 3.117 (322):*artem amatoriam . . . serie tibi plena dirigimus et competenti ordinatione dispositam delegamus;* cf. Walsh, p. 323: "I chart for you the art of love in its full development, and I send it to you set down in the appropriate order." The expression *amoris ars* also occurs 5 times in the treatise: *DA* 1.6.146 (80), 354 (142); 1.8.5 (212); 2.3.8 (232); 3.1 (286). The word *ars* is used 16 times in all.

"the solaces of love" *(amoris solatia),* that is, the assuagement of the suffering by "carrying out all of Love's precepts in the other's embrace." This rather loose treatment of important technical terms is not unlike that encountered in the definition itself (see below, Chapter 5). Is this the carelessness to be expected from a none too proficient scholastic who mixes so freely *ars* and *scientia?* Is it rather a reflection of the general lack of rigor of the early scholastic age? In any case, the semantic shift in the use of the term *amor* parallels the generic shift in the Chaplain's discourse at this crucial point.

Whereas the speculative part of the work bears the stamp of dialectic, the practical part is dominated by another of the liberal arts of the trivium, rhetoric. Falling back on the technique of *divisio,* Andreas distinguishes five means of acquiring love: physical beauty, virtuous character, eloquence, wealth, and the easy granting of the thing requested (*DA* 1.6.1 [40–42]). He then produces various arguments to show that most of these are not, in fact, valid means to the desired end. On a theoretical level he concludes in favor of virtuous character: "Only good character is worthy of Love's crown" (*DA* 1.6.15 [44]). But in practice it is not always easy to tell when one is in the presence of virtue, so most of the burden falls upon "eloquence of speech" *(sermonis facundia),* whose function is to "create a good impression about the speaker's moral worth" (ibid.).

How love may be won through eloquence is illustrated in a series of eight dialogues between men and women, which constitute more than one-half of the entire treatise. Although rhetoric is the guiding principle throughout the dialogues, dialectic also plays an important role. We shall leave to the next chapter our analysis of the subtle interplay between rhetoric and dialectic in the dialogues and in the treatise as a whole. For the moment we shall content ourselves with the observation that Andreas's conception of *ars amandi* brings together the two kinds of "art" distinguished by Hugh of St. Victor in his classification of the sciences: "the mechanical, which supervises the occupations of this life; and the logical, which provides the knowledge necessary for correct speaking and clear argumentation."[38]

---

38. *Didascalicon* 1.11 (trans. Taylor, p. 60).

The practical thrust of Book One, Chapter Six, is carried over into the second book, *Qualiter amor retineatur* ("How Love Is Retained"). Not only the general book title but also the chapter headings for each of the first four chapters contain the characteristic *qualiter,* indicative of a "how-to" approach to the subject: Chapter One, "How an Acquired Love Should Be Maintained"; Chapter Two, "How Love, Once Consummated, Should Be Increased"; Chapter Three, "How Love Is Diminished"; Chapter Four, "How Love Is Brought to an End." Here there is an important difference, however. In the first book the whole discussion was directed toward a single end, the "acquiring" of love, that is, the carrying out of "all of Love's mandates." The appropriateness of this goal was quite unproblematic, since the impulsion toward it was included in the very definition of the phenomenon. But in Book Two Andreas sets conflicting outcomes in dialectical opposition to each other, opposing love's preservation to its demise, its increase to its decrease. Are we to conclude that, once the main, overriding goal of love's consummation is achieved, the Chaplain envisages that a variety of goals may be set regarding its subsequent development?

There are several indications that Andreas regards the preservation and increase of love as the normal goal of the successful lover, in imitation of Ovid, whose *Ars amatoria,* Book Two is devoted entirely to preserving love. That conclusion emerges from some parts of the discussion in these same chapters, for example in Chapter Three, where the description of the processes by which love decreases is interrupted by advice on how to avoid such a decrease. Love is diminished, the Chaplain claims, if the woman finds the lover to be foolish and indiscrete, or if he seems to go beyond moderation in his demands for love, without respecting the modesty of his partner. A faithful lover should choose the harshest pains of love, Andreas adds, rather than causing his partner shame by his demands, for he who considers only the attainment of his own desires, neglecting the welfare of his partner, should be called a traitor rather than a lover (*DA* 2.3.3 [230]). The same conclusion is also evident from the very formulation of the chapter headings: the construction *debeat* plus passive infinitive in Chapters One and Two indicates what one "should" do to achieve a certain end, whereas the passive construction in the two following chapters merely refers to what sometimes happens.

Despite the use of *qualiter,* Chapters Three and Four are not concerned with dispensing practical advice for achieving the stated outcome. They do have considerable ramifications for the field of action, but these are primarily indirect and negative in nature, consisting in the implication that certain actions must be avoided if one is to avoid a given outcome. The tone of these chapters is for the most part factual and descriptive. Without abandoning entirely the prescriptive thrust of his discourse, Andreas nevertheless reintroduces an element of the theoretical and the speculative. By the dialectical confrontation of opposites he achieves something of the objectivity of science, with each of the outcomes and their corresponding processes contributing to the total description of the phenomenon.

As we have seen in Book Two, neither the speculative discourse characteristic of the early chapters of the treatise nor the practical discourse that dominates the dialogues is limited to these passages. Rather, it is the constant dialectical interweaving of these two strands that contributes in large measure to the complex texture of the word. One further example will perhaps suffice to illustrate this.

The Chaplain's work contains two codifications of the principles governing love: the first is appended to the "Purgatory of Cruel Beauties" episode in the Fifth Dialogue; the other, introduced by an Arthurian adventure, closes Book Two. One may wonder why the work would propose two separate codes, one containing twelve items, the other thirty-one, with little repetition from one list to the other.

In Parry's translation, both of these codes are called "Rules of Love." In the Latin text, however, *præcepta,* "precepts," is used in the Fifth Dialogue, *regulæ,* "rules," in Book Two.[39] The difference between these

---

39. *DA* 1.6.266 (114), 268–69 (116); 2.8.1 (270), 40, 43–50 (280–84). Cf. Parry, pp. 81–82, 184–86. Walsh's translation preserves the distinction: "precepts" (pp. 115–17); "rules" (pp. 281–85). *Regula* occurs another 26 times in the treatise, including 9 times in the expression *amoris regula,* in addition to 10 occurrences (5 of *amoris regula*) in Book Two, Chapter Eight. In Books One and Two *regula* refers most often to the Rules of Love expounded in that chapter. In the third book it is used 9 times, generally in the logical sense, referring to generalizations. *Præceptum* occurs another 20 times, including

terms is slight but significant: whereas *præceptum* is used only of injunctions or admonitions to action, *regula* may also indicate a standard of judgment or a general statement of fact.

This difference in formulation is borne out completely by the contents of the two codes. The *præcepta* of the Fifth Dialogue are all "directives" or prescriptive injunctions, couched in the second person imperative (nos. 5, 6, 10) or an equivalent construction, either optative subjunctive (nos. 1, 3, 4, 7, 11, 12) or paraphrastic *debeo*, "ought," plus infinitive (nos. 2, 8, 9):

I. Avaritiam sicut nocivam pestem effugias et eius contrarium amplectaris.

II. Castitatem servare debes amanti.

. . .

V. Mendacia omnino vitare memento.[40]

On the other hand, the *regula* of Book Two all take the form of "representatives," or declarative statements in the third person indicative. In many cases the descriptive character of these declarations is reinforced through a variety of techniques, including the use of the verbs *solet* (nos. 6, 29) and *consuevit* (nos. 10, 13, 15) expressing habitual action, the use of proverbial turns of phrase (e.g., no. 2) indicating general truths, and the use of the adverb *semper*, "always" (nos. 4, 10, 20, 21; cf. *raro*, "rarely," no. 13), of the negative indefinite pronouns *nemo*, "no one" (nos. 3, 8, 9) and *nil*, "nothing" (nos. 26, 31), and of the indefinite adjectives *omnis*, "all" (no. 15) and *quilibet*, "any" (no. 24), all reinforcing the categorical nature of the statements:

---

14 times in the expression *amoris præceptum*, and in most other cases with the same sense, all in Books One and Two, in addition to 5 occurrences (3 for *amoris præceptum*) in the Fifth Dialogue. *Mandatum*, "mandate," a common synonym for *præceptum*, occurs 32 times, including 9 times as *amoris mandatum* and most others with the same reference. There is also one occurrence each, all in the dialogues, of the expressions *amoris lex, amoris norma*, and *amoris traditio*, "the law . . ./norm . . ./tradition of love."

40. *DA* 1.6.268 (116). Cf. Walsh, p. 117: "1. Avoid miserliness as a harmful disease, and embrace its opposite. 2. You must maintain chastity for your lover. . . . 5. Remember to avoid lying completely." With the exception of no. 8, which has *debet*, "should," all conjugated verbs are in the second person singular.

II. Qui non zelat amare non potest.
III. Nemo duplici potest amore ligari.
IV. Semper amorem crescere vel minui constat.

. . .

VI. Masculus non solet nisi plena pubertate amare.

. . .

XV. Omnis consuevit amans in coamantis aspectu pallescere.[41]

The first of these two codes thus offers practical advice on the art of loving, the second the objective principles of the science of love. There is no redundancy in the two codes because each is attached to one of the two strands of Andreas's dual discourse.

Sapientia

The interplay between the practical and the speculative described above goes a long way toward explaining the generic complexity and ambiguity of the Chaplain's work as reflected in the rubrics of the manuscripts. It does not exhaust the subject, however, for many of Andreas's declarations can be ascribed neither to *scientia* nor to *ars*. This includes the many statements involving a value judgment.

Let us come back for a moment to the rubrics of the manuscripts. The manuscript that Trojel calls *D* (Karnein, no. 2), a fourteenth-century manuscript in the Bibliothèque nationale in Paris, contains the following incipit: *Liber de arte amandi et de reprobatione amoris,* rubric of the *ars* type as we have seen. However, another hand has written above this rubric the words *honeste* and *inhonesti,* so that the amended title now reads: *De arte (honeste) amandi et de reprobatione (inhonesti) amoris.*[42]

---

41. *DA* 2.8.44, 46 (282). Cf. Walsh, p. 283: "2. The person who is not jealous cannot love. 3. No one can be bound by two loves. 4. Love is known to be always waxing or waning. . . . 6. A male usually loves only on reaching manhood. . . . 15. Every lover tends to grow pale when his partner looks at him." All conjugated verbs are in the atemporal present, with the exception of the three occurrences of *consuevit,* "to be customary," which is perfect in form but present in meaning.

42. Trojel, p. xxv; cf. Karnein, *"De amore,"* p. 274: "amoris (inhoneste)"; ibid., p. 270.

This emendation probably dates from the fifteenth or even the sixteenth century. It appears to be an early attempt to resolve the problem posed by the third book, not unlike the distinction between "good" and "bad" women found in the translations of Drouart la Vache and Johann Hartlieb.[43] Its power to "prove" anything about Andreas's intention is even less than that of the rubrics themselves. Nevertheless, it provides a valuable indication of yet another generic dimension of the Chaplain's discourse.

The interpolated adjective *honestus* and its adverbial derivative refer to a concept that is both moral and social; in any case, it is evaluative, it conveys a value judgment. The medieval concept of *honestum* is derived from Cicero's *De officiis* by way of St. Ambrose's *De officiis ministrorum* and the *Moralium dogma philosophorum* attributed to William of Conches. In this tradition, the *honestum* is virtue seen as an end in itself, as opposed to the "useful" *(utile),* which serves as a means to some other end.[44] These words introduce into our consideration a notion of "honor" or "decency" that can be attached neither to the objective observations of science nor to the strategic calculations of art, but that nevertheless constitutes an important aspect of the Chaplain's enterprise.

This revised rubric brings to mind another important medieval distinction, that between *scientia* and *sapientia*. Science or knowledge, as we have seen, is the understanding of the truth, in general. Wisdom, On the other hand, "pertains to divine things," according to Aquinas, and "judges by the highest cause."[45] For Aristotle, wisdom is concerned with first causes and principles.[46] Its domain then, among the sciences, is metaphysics or, in the context of the Christian Middle Ages, theology.

Despite the philosophers' definitions, however, *sapientia* is not only an intellectual concept; it also has important implications for the realm

43. Drouart, vv. 7533–46 (ed. Bossuat, p. 216); Sargent, esp. pp. 536–39; Hartlieb, pp. 18–20, 258; Karnein, "La Réception," pp. 525–26; idem, *"De amore,"* pp. 184–87, 256–60.

44. Klose; Cherchi, *Andreas and the Ambiguity,* pp. 43–47. This concept is also reflected in the rhetorical tradition (Cicero, *De inventione* 2.52.158–55.168; *Rhetorica ad Herennium,* 3.2.3–4.7). Andreas uses *honestus* or its derivatives 17 times.

45. *ST* 1a2æ 62.2 (ed. Blackfriars, 23:140); cf. *ST* 1a2æ 57.2 (ibid., 23:42–47); 66.5 (ibid., 23:212–17).

46. *Metaphysics* 1.1 (981b27–29).

of action, according to a long tradition both classical and biblical. Often associated with the cardinal virtue of prudence *(prudentia)*, it goes beyond ordinary practical prudence to include the ordering of actions in accordance with eternal principles. In this sense its realm is what the scholastics called "praxis," actions or operations considered in their bearing on good and evil. It is concerned with *scientia practica*, or ethics, rather than with *scientia speculativa*. It is "practical" only in the medieval sense, in that it is directed toward the ordering of action, but without the pragmatic, utilitarian, instrumental implications now associated with the term. Indeed, the distinction between wisdom and art is closely related to that which we have seen between the *honestum* and the *utile*. For, unlike art, *sapientia* is directed not toward goals that are specific, finite, other, but rather toward that good which is an end in itself.[47]

References to wisdom occur frequently in the Chaplain's work, either directly through the use of *sapientia* or of the participle *sapiens*, "wise," from which it derives, or indirectly, through the use of terms indicating the opposite quality: *stultus* or *fatuus*, "foolish," and *simplex*, "simple."[48] In some cases the word *sapiens* seems to indicate ordinary practical prudence, as in a passage from Book One, Chapter Two, stating that a "wise lover" *(sapiens amator)* does not throw away riches like a

---

47. Aristotle, *Nicomachean Ethics* 6.3.1 (1139b15–17) enumerates five means by which the mind attains truth: "art" (τέχνη), "science" (ἐπιστήμη), "prudence" (φρόνησις), "wisdom" (σοφία), and "intelligence" (νοῦς). The subsequent discussion distinguishes between "art," which relates to making, and "prudence," which concerns action; between "science," which is deductive, demonstrative knowledge, and "intelligence," which denotes inductive, intuitive reasoning; and between "prudence," which is practical in orientation, and "wisdom," which is theoretical, relating to first causes and principles. Thomas Aquinas, *Commentary on the Posterior Analytics of Aristotle* 1.44.405.11 (trans. Larcher, pp. 161–62:), makes similar distinctions. The predominant role assigned to *prudentia* in moral matters is a result of Aristotle's and St. Thomas's purely intellectual conception of *sapientia*.

48. *Sapiens* and its derivatives occur 89 times in the treatise. There are 14 occurrences of *stultus*, 14 of *simplex*, and 7 of *fatuus*. The semantically closely related *prudens* and its derivatives are also frequent, with 65 occurrences. However, this includes 18 occurrences in the dialogues where *tua prudentia*, or more frequently (14 times) *vestra prudentia*, is used as a polite form of address. Cf. Parry: "Your Prudence." In contrast, *ars* and *scientia* occur only 16 and 12 times, respectively.

wasteful steward, but plans his spending according to the size of his inheritance (*DA* 1.2.5 [36]). In most cases, though, it evokes that higher wisdom described above.

As we might expect, references to wisdom are particularly frequent in Book Three, *De reprobatione amoris:* about two and one-half times as frequent as in the first two books.[49] This is entirely in accordance with the eternal, theological viewpoint adopted in that part of the work. Following the initial, introductory paragraph, the second paragraph of Book Three opens with the word *sapiens.* Any wise man *(sapiens),* the Chaplain asserts, is obliged for many reasons to reject all the deeds of love and always to oppose Love's mandates (*DA* 3.3 [286]). Citing the biblical examples of David and Solomon, Andreas will later argue that love is particularly dangerous for the wise, whom it is likely to drive even more insane than others (*DA* 3.62–64 [304–6]). The condemnation of women includes the accusation that wisdom is completely foreign to them (*DA* 3.77 [310]). Two of the authorities quoted in Book Three, Ovid and Solomon, are referred to respectively as *sapiens* and *sapientissimus,* "most wise."[50] And it is no surprise to find the entire work concluding with an elaborate allusion to the parable of the wise and foolish virgins.[51]

This appeal to wisdom accompanies a discourse that is neither the objective description of science nor the practical prescription of art. The generic focus of Book Three is ethics, the judgment of actions in the light of eternal principles. This discourse is scientific and descriptive in the sense that it is based on eternal truth and that it proceeds by logical deduction from that truth. It is "practical" and prescriptive in that it has as its object actions and operations. In medieval scholastic terminology, it is *scientia practica.*

This type of discourse is eminently suited to Book Three, whose

---

49. For Books One and Two there are 64 occurrences of *sapiens* and its derivatives for 310 pages in Trojel's edition, or about one occurrence for every 5 pages; for Book Three there are 25 occurrences for 49 pages, or about one occurrence for every 2 pages.

50. *DA* 3.89, 94 (314) [Ovid]; 3.109 (318) [Solomon]. Solomon is also cited as an exemplary figure with reference to his *sapientia* (*DA* 1.6.460 [176]), or with the epithet *sapientissimus* (*DA* 3.31 [296]).

51. *DA* 3.120–21 (322–24). Cf. Matt. 25:1–13.

purpose is the condemnation of love on ethical and theological grounds. But it is by no means limited to Book Three, for the notion of wisdom and the moralization that accompanies it occur frequently in the first two books as well, interwoven with the strictly scientific and the purely practical.

If we go back to the beginning of Book One, Chapter Six, "How Love Is Acquired," we find that two of the five methods of acquiring love enumerated in that passage, "abundant riches" and "a readiness to grant what the other seeks," are subsequently eliminated from consideration by preemptive moral judgment. In the Chaplain's opinion, only by the first three means is love acquired, and the last two should be utterly expelled from Love's court (*DA* 1.6.2 [42]). The point is not that these methods are ineffective, but rather that one *ought not* resort to them.

Returning to the subject in Chapter Nine, "On Love Acquired with Money," Andreas will attempt to justify on intellectual grounds *(monstrare)* a moral judgment originally advanced as a personal opinion *(nostra opinio),* as he had promised to do in the above-mentioned passage. This justification will involve him in another shift in semantics. The love acquired by wealth, the Chaplain claims, is not "true love" *(verus amor),* which "comes only from the affection of the heart" (*DA* 1.9.1 [212]). Apparently the goal is no longer to "carry out all of Love's precepts in the other's embrace," but rather to afflict the other with the same suffering.

It is true that Andreas has prepared somewhat for this development through a carefully worded clause in the original definition, of which the present passage is perhaps, once again, an amplification. In his definition, the Chaplain saw the carrying out of "all of Love's precepts" as taking place "by a common desire" *(de utriusque voluntate).* Should this insistence on reciprocity of feeling be taken as forming the basis for a kind of "natural" love ethic, derived from the very definition of the phenomenon, and thus excluding by definition such things as venal love?[52]

---

52. A similar process of deduction from first principles can be observed in Chapter Ten, "The Easy Granting of the Thing Requested," where the principle of reciprocity enunciated in the previous chapter is combined with the principle of fidelity to one

In any case, despite its apparent intellectual content, the force of the word *verus* in this context is ethical. Once again, a semantic shift in the use of terms signals a generic shift in the discourse.[53]

Equally interesting is the Chaplain's treatment of "beauty" *(formæ venustas)* in the same opening passage of Book One, Chapter Six. Although beauty is included among the three acceptable ways of acquiring love, Andreas speaks rather disparagingly of it, as though begrudging its obvious efficacy. Physical beauty acquires love with only a modest effort, he claims, especially if that of a "simple" *(simplex)* lover is sought, for a simple lover does not look for anything except a beautiful face and figure and a well-cared-for appearance (*DA* 1.6.3 [42]). Andreas neither praises nor condemns such lovers, he says, but most of the subsequent discussion is devoted to showing the inadequacy of beauty as a way of acquiring love and the relative superiority of good moral character *(morum probitas)*. This conclusion is contained in a paragraph beginning once again with the word *sapiens*. A wise woman should seek as a lover a man of praiseworthy character, it is argued, not one who anoints himself all over like a woman or make himself shine with the care of the body (*DA* 1.6.8 [42]).[54] In Andreas's original definition, beauty was identified as the ultimate efficient cause of love. If it is now

---

lover developed in Chapters Four and Five, with the result that love too easily obtained is rejected. In particular, the phrases *nimia carnis voluptas,* "excessive pleasure of the flesh" (*DA* 1.10.1 [220]), and *nimia Veneris abundantia,* "excessive abundance of Venus" (*DA* 1.10.2 [220]), recall Chapter Five's *nimia voluptatis abundantia,* "excessive abundance of pleasure" (*DA* 1.5.7 [40]), but here they are applied to the prospective female partner.

53. The word *verus* is used rather frequently in a purely intellectual, logical sense, to distinguish between true and false propositions, in expressions such as *ut vera loquamur,* "to tell the truth" (*DA* 1.1.5 [32]); *hoc verum esse . . . profiteor,* "I admit that this is true" (*DA* 1.5.6 [40]); *Verum est, quod dicitis,* "What you say is true" (*DA* 1.6.492 [186]); etc. For other examples of *verus* with an ethical force, see below, n. 55. This confusion of intellectual and ethical values in the use of the term can perhaps be seen as a reflection of twelfth-century Platonism.

54. The point of choosing a *sapiens mulier* for the purpose of acquiring her love is that lovers who are *minus sapientes* or *incauti* (*DA* 1.6.4 [42]) are not likely to be able to keep a secret, with disastrous results for the love relationship. Throughout the passage Andreas plays on the ambiguity of *sapiens* in order to justify a moral stance in terms of an argument from ordinary practical prudence.

subordinated to excellence of character, a moral category, this can be only for ethical reasons.

The ethical use of the term *verus* encountered in Chapter Nine occurs rather frequently throughout the treatise, especially in connection with the words *amor* and *amans*.[55] A case in point is found in the "Rules of Love" that close Book Two. In three of these rules (nos. 12, 25, 30), Andreas distinguishes the "true lovers" *(verus amans)* from other, presumably false, ones; for example: "XII. A true lover does not desire the embraces of any except his beloved" (*DA* 2.8.45 [282]). Despite the objective, declarative form of the sentence, the force of this statement is scarcely different from that of one of the injunctions contained in the "Precepts" of the Fifth Dialogue: "II. You must maintain chastity for the beloved" (*DA* 1.6.268 [116]). Other rules introduce ethical considerations through the use of verbs indicating an obligation: *debeo,* "ought," (no. 8), also used in certain of the "Precepts," or impersonal *decet,* "it is proper." Thus alongside the truly descriptive statements of the type, "XV. Every lover regularly turns pale in the sight of the beloved" (*DA* 2.8.46 [282]), we find disguised prescriptions such as, "XI. It is not proper to love anyone whom one would be ashamed to marry" (*DA* 2.8.45 [282]), which are, in fact, moral judgments.

One of the best examples of moralization in the first two books is that other codification of love which is the Third Dialogue. There the advice that a woman of the higher nobility gives to a man of the middle class constitutes a systematic reinterpretation of the courtly love ethic in terms of Christian morality. The would-be lover is advised, for example, to turn the other cheek to wrongdoers, to honor the clergy, rather than mock them, and to attend church regularly (*DA* 1.6.159–61 [84]). It is no surprise to encounter, near the end of the passage, a reference to

---

55. *Verus* is used 11 times of *amor,* 9 times of *amans,* "lover," once of *amator,* "lover." Other ethical uses of *verus* occur with *amicus,* "friend" (3 times); *amicitia,* "friendship"; *dilectio,* "love"; *gaudia,* "joy"; *nobilitas,* "nobility"; *virtus,* "virtue"; and perhaps *zelotypia,* "jealousy" (6 times). In one passage *verus amor* is formally opposed to *falsificatus amor,* "feigned love" (*DA* 1.6.513 [192]). The contrary of *verus amans* appears to be *fallax amator,* "deceitful lover," which occurs 3 times; cf. *animi fallacis amator,* "lover of deceitful mind." Like *falsificatus, fallax* appears to underline the moral force of its opposite, *verus.* On the other hand, *falsus* is used with *zelotypia* (*DA* 1.6.382 [150]) to indicate what seems to be an essentially intellectual distinction.

men who "foolishly" *(fatuissime)* believe that women like it if they despise everything connected with the Church (*DA* 1.6.161 [84]).

From the point of view of art, which was that originally adopted in the dialogues, the efficacy of this advice would doubtless depend on the piety of the woman being wooed. The dialogues not only provide rhetorical models for would-be lovers, however, they also offer ethical models for the lovers' ladies. Not content successfully to resist all advances, the women of the dialogues also seize the occasion to impose upon their suitors, in exchange for the slightest glimmer of hope, Christian moral conduct of the highest order. This curious dual function of the discourse is in the best tradition of medieval pedagogy, which freely combined instruction in moral philosophy with the teaching of the trivium, particularly grammar and rhetoric.[56]

As the previous examples illustrate, the ethical thrust of Andreas's work is far from being limited to the third book. Long before calling for the rejection of love, the Chaplain had undertaken a vast project of normalization and neutralization of the secular love ethic, be it Ovidian or troubadouresque, in terms of the dictates of Christian morality. This normalization process also has its social dimension, expressed, for example, in the frequent references to "courtliness" *(urbanitas, curialitas)* and in the numerous appeals to reputation or to public opinion. It can be seen as an extension of the ethical tendencies already observable in the secular vernacular love literature of the period, but it generally goes well beyond them. From the very beginning of the treatise, this ethical stand is interwoven with the speculative and the practical to form the complex texture of the work.

Generic complexity

One of the most striking features of the *De amore* is the constant interplay within it between the three types of didactic discourse that we have labeled with the terms *ars, scientia,* and *sapientia.* The complex interaction between these three tendencies in the treatise goes a long way toward explaining its generic indeterminacy, as well as the heated mod-

56. Delhaye, "L'Enseignement"; idem, "'Grammatica' et 'Ethica.'"

ern controversies that it has aroused. This is not surprising, since the three concepts in question and their relationship to each other were a major problem not only for Andreas but for much of ancient and medieval thought. Indeed, the early vicissitudes of these concepts have played an important role in the development of modern semantics.[57]

Having identified the major generic vectors of Andreas's discourse, we can now come back to the question asked at the outset: "To what branch of learning does it belong?" I believe that the answer must be: to all of them. As William of Conches wrote of Plato's *Timæus,* "It does not belong to only one branch of learning, but something of several of them is contained in it."[58] For if we compare our findings with the most complete and sophisticated of the contemporary classifications of the sciences, that expounded by Hugh of St. Victor in the *Didascalicon,* we see that each of Hugh's main headings corresponds to one dimension of the Chaplain's work.

Hugh establishes the following fourfold distinction among the sciences:

> We have said that there are four branches of knowledge only, and that they contain all the rest: they are the theoretical, which strives for the contemplation of truth; the practical, which considers the regulation of morals; the mechanical, which supervises the occupations of this life; and the logical, which provides the knowledge necessary for correct speaking and clear argumentation.[59]

His "theoretical" science or knowledge *(theoretica)* corresponds to the theoretical or speculative dimension that we found in the *De amore,* especially in the early chapters, and that we called simply *scientia.* In particular, Andreas's speculation on the nature of love would find its place in that branch of theoretical science which Hugh calls *physica,* that is,

57. For Plato's use of τέχνη, ἐπιστήμη, σοφία and related terms, see Lyons. On *wîsheit, kunst, wissen,* and related terms in Middle High German, see Trier, *Der deutsche Wortschatz;* idem, *Aufsätze und Vorträge.*

58. *Glosæ super Platonem,* Prologus, IV (my translation). Cf. ed. Jeauneau, p. 60: *Non uni tantum parti philosophie supponitur sed de pluribus aliquid in eo continetur.*

59. *Didascalicon* 1.11 (trans. Taylor, p. 60). On the importance of Hugh's classification as a culmination of the early medieval tradition and as a synthesis of the Boethian and Stoic strands of that tradition, see Weisheipl, pp. 65–68; trans. Taylor, pp. 7–11.

natural science or philosophy, whose function is to search out and to consider "the causes of things as found in their effects, and the effects as derived from certain causes."[60] The practical (i.e., instrumental) thrust of the Chaplain's discourse, which we have called *ars,* could (albeit at the cost of a regrettable loss of symmetry, not to mention spirituality) take its place beside the seven "mechanical arts" that Hugh distinguishes under the general rubric *mechanica.*[61] At the same time, Andreas's *ars amandi* makes considerable auxiliary use of another of Hugh's branches of knowledge, *logica,* particularly the subdivision of it that he calls *ratio disserendi* and that deals with argumentation.[62] Finally, the evaluative dimension of the treatise that we have called *sapientia* has its foundations in a sub-branch of the theoretical, namely *theologia,* but its chief sphere of activity is the branch of learning that Hugh calls *practica,* that is, ethics or moral philosophy.[63]

But what sort of relationship obtained among the various sciences in the medieval tradition? Can we discern there a principle of organization or hierarchy that would bring *ars, scientia,* and *sapientia* into focus with each other and thus shed light on the essential character of the *De amore?*

In one way the diverse medieval branches of learning may be seen as separate but equal disciplines designed to examine the same object or objects from a variety of independent perspectives. This is the point of view Thomas Aquinas expressed in defending the autonomy of the various sciences: "The diversification of the sciences is brought about by the diversity of aspects under which things can be known."[64] This pro-

---

60. *Didascalicon* 2.16 (trans. Taylor, p. 71). Hugh's insistence on the importance of the principle of causality in natural science is particularly interesting in view of Andreas's use of the Aristotelian system of causality for his definition of love (see below, Chapter 5). An even more striking parallel occurs in Alfarabi's *De ortu scientiarum,* translated from Arabic by Gundissalinus around 1150. Alfarabi also discusses what he calls *ars naturalis* in terms of causality, then goes on to write: *Hæc igitur scientia fuit scientia de naturis, quæ est scientia de actione et passione,* "So this was the knowledge of natures, which is the knowledge of actions and passions" (Alfarabi, 1.5 [p. 20]; my translation). Cf. Weisheipl, pp. 68–69.

61. *Didascalicon* 2.21 (trans. Taylor, p. 74).

62. Ibid. 2.28, 2.30 (pp. 79, 81).

63. Ibid. 2.1 (p. 62).

64. *ST* Ia 1.1, ad secundum (ed. Blackfriars, p. 9).

nouncement reflects the Aristotelian rationalism of the thirteenth century, but something of the same attitude is already discernable in Hugh of St. Victor, who wrote: "But although all the arts tend towards the single end of philosophy, they do not all take the same road, but have each of them their own proper businesses by which they are distinguished from one another."[65]

On the whole, however, the twelfth century was more prone to see the various branches of learning as organized hierarchically, in accordance with a Christian scale of values. This attitude is best expressed, once again, by Hugh of St. Victor, who wrote: "all natural arts are the servants of divine science, and lower wisdom, properly ordered, leads to higher wisdom."[66] Hugh then goes on in the same passage to establish a true hierarchy of disciplines: at the bottom the literal sense *(historia)*, associated with the trivium; then the allegorical and tropological senses, associated with the quadrivium and with *physica;* and above all the rest, "that divine science to which divine Scripture leads" or, according to the chapter title, *divina sapientia* (ibid.). A similarly hierarchical approach can be seen in William of Conches and in Gundissalinus, particularly in the progression that each advocates in the teaching of the various disciplines.[67]

From the medieval perspective, it is fairly easy to see the basis for such an hierarchy of disciplines. Science is superior to art as being is to becoming, as the general is to the particular, as reason is to experience, as the intellect is to the appetite; and wisdom is the highest form of science, since it deals with things eternal and divine, with first causes and principles.

Coming back to the *De amore,* we observe that a similar hierarchy of values is suggested in the *Præfatio* and in the opening and closing paragraphs of Book Three. At the beginning of Book Three, for example, Gualterius is told to read this little book not as one seeking to take up the life of a lover, but so that, refreshed by the theory and trained to excite women's minds to love, he may refrain from doing so, and thus

---

65. *Didascalicon* 2.17 (trans. Taylor, p. 71).

66. Hugh of St. Victor, *Sacraments,* Prologue, vi (trans. Deferrari, p. 5); cf. Minnis, *Medieval Theory,* p. 27.

67. Weisheipl, pp. 67, 70–72.

win an eternal reward and deserve to take pride in greater blessings in God's presence (*DA* 3.2 [286]). The ultimate end of both the theory and the art of love seems to be to have the wisdom not to use either. Such advice would appear to lend support to the opinion of those who see the ultimate thrust of Andreas's work as normative or prescriptive in terms of Christian morality. It does not mean, however, as some would claim, that the whole burden of the *De amore* is contained in the third book, nor that the first two books must be interpreted ironically; for, as we have seen, the interplay between our three main types of didactic discourse is fairly constant throughout the treatise.[68]

From a more modern perspective, there is a sense in which the Chaplain's work may be seen as essentially descriptive. Not so much that it describes what is, but that it describes what has already been written about what is. This is in the best tradition of medieval culture, for which scientific investigation of whatever variety always has as its foundation the written record of those who have gone before. Such statements as "Every lover regularly turns pale in the presence of his beloved" may or may not be true of life, but they are certainly much truer of literature. From this point of view, the strong prescriptive element observable in the Chaplain's work, with its instrumental and moral components, may also be seen as a reflection of the supreme importance that prescription of all sorts assumes in all medieval literature, and particularly in medieval love literature.

The *De amore* is sometimes viewed as a kind of *summa* on love, a compilation of all the pertinent authoritative opinions on the question, in the manner of Abelard's *Sic et non,* Peter Lombard's *Sentences,* or Gratian's *Decretum* (see below, Chapter 3). A similar principle of *compilatio* and of systematic dialectical confrontation of opposites could perhaps be invoked to explain the work's generic complexity and ambiguity. Not content to assemble all the things that have been said about love, Andreas also seems intent upon illustrating, in a single, complex volume, all the ways in which one may speak about it.

68. On ironic interpretations of the *De amore,* see below, Chapter 4. Andreas's suggestions of a hierarchy of values is doubtless more compatible with the "gradualist" interpretation of D. Kelly, "Courtly Love."

2 ❋

LOVE AND THE ARTS

Rhetoric versus Dialectic

I*n the previous chapter we referred* on several occasions to the liberal arts of the trivium. We must now come back to this important subject and explore in some detail the considerable role that two of these arts, rhetoric and dialectic, played in shaping the *De amore*. But first we must say a word about the place of the trivium in medieval culture.

The trivium in the twelfth century

The liberal arts were the foundation of the educational system that the Middle Ages inherited from antiquity. Originally nine in number, they were reduced to seven by the great encyclopedists of the transitional period, who, along with Boethius, were primarily responsible for their transmission to the Middle Ages: Martianus Capella, Cassiodorus, and Isidore of Seville. From the Carolingian period onward, a distinction was made between the three linguistic arts of the trivium, that is, grammar, rhetoric, and dialectic, and the four mathematical arts of the quadrivium, which included arithmetic, geometry, music, and astronomy. The arts of the trivium came before those of the quadrivium in the curriculum, and in practice the latter were often neglected. Together they formed the basis for all the higher studies: theology, natural philosophy, medicine, and law.[1]

---

1. A good general introduction is provided by Wagner. For additional bibliography, particularly on the trivium, see Murphy, *Medieval Rhetoric.*

The three arts of the trivium had in common the fact that all were concerned with the use of language. In theory, the distinction between them was clear: grammar was the art of "speaking correctly," rhetoric that of "speaking well," and dialectic that of "speaking truly"; but in practice they overlapped considerably. Rhetoric, in particular, occupied an intermediate position between grammar and dialectic; and since the political and judicial institutions on which classical rhetoric was based had long since disappeared, this art was in danger of succumbing under the combined weight of the other two. Deprived of the forms appropriate to its former deliberative and forensic functions, rhetoric was often reduced to a matter of style or ornamentation, but the figures of style that formed the substance of the rhetorician's *elocutio* were also discussed by the grammarians under the guise of "permitted faults." As a system of argumentation considered apart from its original context, rhetoric was scarcely distinguishable from dialectic, and the two were often lumped together, as in the *Didascalicon* (2.30) of Hugh of St. Victor, under the rubric "probable argument." Even the distinction between grammar and dialectic was to be blurred somewhat by the rise of speculative grammar in the thirteenth century.[2]

Grammar was the ultimate basis of all intellectual activity; it was, in the words of Isidore (*Etymologiæ* 1.5), "the origin and foundation of liberal letters." Thus it is always mentioned first among the arts of the trivium, though the order of the other two is sometimes inverted, as in Martianus Capella. Its scope was rather broader than what we associate with grammar, for it included, according to Quintilian (1.4.1), "the science of correct speech and the interpretation of the poets." Far from being limited to linguistic analysis, etymology, versification, and the like, it constituted a general repository of literary culture. Its basic exercise was the *lectio,* or close reading of literary texts, in terms not only of grammatical considerations, but also of style and content. It derived its principles from the textbooks of Donatus and Priscian, but most of its substance came from a fixed but flexible canon of curriculum authors, who served not only as models for writing and speaking, but also as

2. On the changing relationship between the arts of the trivium see McKeon, "Rhetoric."

sources of authoritative citation for rhetorical and dialectical argumentation.

The relationship of rhetoric to dialectic is discussed in some detail at the beginning of Book Four of Boethius's *De differentiis topicis,* a standard textbook for the later Middle Ages. According to his analysis, the two disciplines differ in three respects: in subject matter *(in materia),* in methodology *(in usu),* and in goal *(in fine).* They differ in subject matter because dialectic examines *theses,* that is, general questions not involved in circumstances, whereas rhetoric is concerned with *hypotheses,* that is, particular questions surrounded by circumstances. There are two ways in which they are seen to differ in methodology: on the one hand, dialectic uses questions and answers, rhetoric unbroken discourse; on the other hand, dialectic uses complete syllogisms, whereas rhetoric is content with enthymemes, or imperfect, abbreviated syllogisms. Their goals are, respectively, to draw concessions from an adversary and to persuade a judge.[3]

Boethius's criteria are interrelated and can serve as a useful point of departure for distinguishing between the two disciplines. The general propositions, the syllogisms, and the question-and-answer method aimed at drawing concessions from an adversary are all appropriate to the speculative inquiries of philosophers. The particular questions of rhetoric, as well as its use of continuous discourse and of enthymemes to persuade a judge, can all be related to the orator's concern for "political matters" *(res civiles),* especially those subsumed under the three classical genera.[4] Dialectic is essentially a mode of thought, rhetoric a mode

---

3. Boethius, *De differentiis topicis* 4 (*PL* 64:1205–6). Cf. trans. Stump, 1978, pp. 79–80; Leff.

4. Following Aristotle (*Rhetoric* 1.3, 1358a36–b8), Cicero's *De inventione* (1.6.8) and the *Rhetorica ad Herennium* (1.2.2) distinguish three kinds of situations *(genera causarum)* calling for the orator's art: (1) the "deliberative" *(deliberativum),* which involves discussions of policy in public assemblies and persuasion or dissuasion regarding possible future actions; (2) the "judicial" or "forensic" *(iudiciale),* which is concerned with prosecution or defense in courts of law and the establishment of guilt or innocence regarding past actions; and (3) the "demonstrative" or "epideictic" *(demonstrativum),* which is devoted to praise or blame, especially of persons, for example, on ceremonial occasions. See Lausberg, §§ 59–62 (pp. 30–34). Only the last of these three functions survived into the Middle Ages.

of action. Thus the distinction between these two disciplines is closely related to the distinction that we established in Chapter 1 between the theoretical and the practical, between science and art.

Although they were theoretically of equal rank within the medieval curriculum, in fact the arts of the trivium varied considerably in their relative prestige and influence from one period to another. With the "second sophistic" of late antiquity rhetoric was the dominant art, as it would be again for Renaissance humanism, but for most of the Middle Ages it was subordinated to the other two, for the reasons previously mentioned. In the Carolingian Renaissance the efforts to rescue the Latin language from the corruption of barbarism produced an age of grammarians. And the great scholastic movement of the later Middle Ages was dominated by dialectic. But the weight of tradition and the intrinsic value of each of the arts prevented any of them from ever disappearing completely.

The period known as the Twelfth-Century Renaissance, whose roots went back into the eleventh century, was a time of intense intellectual activity affecting all three of the arts of the trivium.[5] New major works of an encyclopedic nature, such as the *Heptateuchon* of Thierry of Chartres and the *Didascalicon* of Hugh of St. Victor, consolidated the legacy of the past and laid the foundations for future developments. Priscian was intensely glossed, and new grammatical treatises were written by Hugh of St. Victor, Evrard of Bethune, and Alexander of Villedieu, the latter two destined to replace Donatus and Priscian as the standard textbooks. The same period saw the beginnings of what was to become "speculative grammar," as well as the rise of treatises on poetry *(ars metrica)* that drew on material common to the grammarian and the rhetorician. The commentaries on Cicero's *De inventione* and the pseudo-Ciceronian *Rhetorica ad Herennium* rose sharply in number, and the increased influence of Quintilian can be seen in John of Salisbury's *Metalogicon*. New, peculiarly medieval branches of rhetoric developed, in accordance with contemporary institutions and needs: the pre-

---

5. On the twelfth-century revival of interest in the trivium see Murphy, *Rhetoric,* pp. 89–132. On the arts of poetry, letter writing, and preaching see ibid., pp. 135–355; D. Kelly, *The Arts;* Camargo; Briscoe and Jaye.

viously mentioned *ars metrica* and the arts of letter writing *(ars dicta-minis)* and preaching *(ars predicandi)*.

It was dialectic, however, that experienced the most spectacular development. In the early part of the twelfth century this was due chiefly to the influence of Abelard, whose *Dialectica* and other logical writings represented the culmination of the tradition of the Old Logic, and whose *Sic et non* gave its name to a new method of confrontation and reconciliation of apparently conflicting authorities, soon to have major ramifications, particularly in theology and canon law. From the second quarter of the century onward, an even greater impetus came from the introduction of the New Logic, the remaining four books of Aristotle's Organon *(Prior* and *Posterior Analytics, Topics, On Sophistical Refutations)*, which were added to the two already available *(Categories, On Interpretation)*, to the *Isagoge* of Porphyry, and to Boethius's logical writings, henceforth known collectively as the Old Logic. By the second half of the century dialectic was already coming to dominate intellectual life, and the foundation was laid for the great scholastic syntheses of the following century.

It was within the intellectual ferment of the Twelfth-Century Renaissance that Andreas Capellanus wrote his treatise on love, and it would be surprising indeed if these developments were not reflected in his treatment of his subject. As a medieval cleric he saw the world through the eyes of a man whose intellectual training was based on the liberal arts of the trivium, at a time when these arts were receiving renewed emphasis and exhibiting new possibilities. Even the flourishing vernacular love literature from which Andreas drew much of his material and inspiration was itself profoundly influenced by the liberal arts, as abundant recent scholarship has shown. By integrating this material into a scholastic treatise in Latin, by applying to it the standard techniques of medieval intellectual discourse, Andreas was, in effect, merely amplifying tendencies that already existed in his vernacular sources. Thus the trivium and its twelfth-century developments inform the *De amore* at two distinct but complementary levels. Their influence is crucial to any attempt to understand the treatise on its own terms.

We can now turn our attention to the ways in which Andreas's treatise reflects the influence of the arts. As this is a very large subject, my comments will, of necessity, be suggestive rather than exhaustive, concentrating particularly on the implications of Andreas's method for our understanding of his doctrine.

The influence of grammar is everywhere present in the *De amore,* but with the exception of a few passages, such as the chapter on etymology (Book One, Chapter Three), it does not appear to have contributed significantly to structuring the discourse beyond the level of individual sentences. Grammar provides the foundation but not the architecture. Consequently, my remarks on this subject will be limited to a few passing comments. Of course, in its larger sense, as a repository of general literary culture, grammar is intimately related to the questions of authority and intertextuality that I shall discuss in the next chapter.

Our primary concern will be the role of rhetoric and dialectic in shaping the *De amore.* It is not easy to separate these two influences, for their complex interaction in the treatise reflects the ambiguity of their relationship in medieval culture, to which I have referred. Nevertheless, for the sake of clarity I shall treat them separately, compensating for any resulting distortion through the use of cross-references and through my concluding remarks. As the dialogues of Book One, Chapter Six, provide a particularly good opportunity for examining the influence of both rhetoric and dialectic, they will serve as our point of departure, but we shall see that the implications of this analysis extend well beyond the dialogues and indeed to the work as a whole.

The rhetoric of love

Among the five ways of acquiring love enumerated at the beginning of Book One, Chapter Six (*DA* 1.6.1 [40–42], 16 [44]), Andreas includes "eloquence of speech" *(sermonis facundia).* Eloquence is, of course, the principal object of the art of rhetoric.[6] References to the use of eloquence to acquire love are scattered throughout the *De amore,* particu-

---

6. Cicero, *De inventione* 1.5.6 (ed. Hubbell, pp. 13, 15): "There is a scientific system of politics which includes many important departments. One of these departments—a large and important one—is eloquence based on the rules of art, which they call rhetoric."

larly the dialogues.[7] In Book Two Andreas will argue that, once love is acquired, it can be increased by eloquence or, conversely, it can decrease owing to a lack of that quality (*DA* 2.2.6 [228]; 2.3.5 [230]).

According to Cicero (*De inventione* 1.5.6), the function and end of eloquence is persuasion. The *De amore*, and especially the dialogues, make numerous references to persuasion,[8] but in the passage in question, Andreas defines the function of *facundia* more narrowly as that of creating "a presumption in favor of the excellence of character of the speaker" (*DA* 1.6.16 [44]). In the preceding discussion, the Chaplain has concluded that "character alone is worthy of the crown of Love" (*DA* 1.6.15 [44]); but one's moral worth is not always immediately apparent to others, hence the role of eloquence in making that worth manifest.

The relationship of eloquence to moral character is an important subject of discussion in the rhetorical tradition. Cicero expounds at length on the necessity of combining eloquence and wisdom (*De inventione* 1.1.1–4.5). Disputing Cicero's emphasis on persuasion as the end of eloquence, Quintilian (*Institutio oratoria* 2.15.34) defines rhetoric as the science of speaking well, then goes on to argue that the notion of "speaking well" implies that the orator must be a good man (ibid. 2.16.11). But, like Aristotle before him, Quintilian also feels obliged to defend rhetoric against the charge that it makes falsehood prevail over truth and that it makes the worse cause seem the better.[9]

This debate among rhetoricians is reflected in the *De amore*. Despite the role that Andreas assigns to eloquence as an ancillary to character, doubts concerning the relationship of these two qualities emerge later in the treatise. In the Second Dialogue the woman accuses the man of trying to defend his errors with such eloquence that it is not easy for her to answer his empty words (*DA* 1.6.107 [70]). In the Eighth Dialogue

---

7. Andreas's *facundia*, the post-classical equivalent of Cicero's *eloquentia*, occurs 9 times in the *De amore*, 7 of them in Book One, Chapter Six: *DA* 1.6.1 (42), 10, 16 (44), 69 (58), 107 (70), 332 (134), 505 (190); 1.8.4 (212); 2.2.6 (228); cf. *DA* 1.6. 422 (164); 1.8.4 (212): *facundus*.

8. Cicero's *persuasio* and *persuadere* are not found in the treatise, but *suadere* occurs 21 times, 15 of them in the dialogues, and *suasio/suadela* occurs 10 times, 7 of them in the dialogues.

9. Quintilian, *Institutio oratoria* 2.16.1–6. Cf. Aristotle, *Rhetoric* 1.1.13 (1355b2–7), 2.24.11 (1402a17–29).

the woman argues that a man who asks for love by his services alone should be preferred to one who puts his faith in eloquence (*DA* 1.6.505 [190]). And in two different passages the Chaplain warns Gualterius to beware of the eloquence of women (*DA* 1.6.10 [44]; 1.8.4 [212]). Although Andreas appears at first to share Quintilian's confidence in the moral value of eloquence, he subsequently admits some of the objections to rhetoric that Quintilian sought to refute.

After this brief theoretical discussion of the role of eloquence in acquiring love, Andreas proposes to illustrate the matter (*DA* 1.6.16 [44]). The result is the eight dialogues. Although Andreas promises to make his illustration "as brief as possible," the dialogues will occupy more than one-half of the entire treatise, thus underlining the importance that the Chaplain ascribes to eloquence.

Andreas's use of illustrative material is based on an important principle of rhetoric, the imitation of models. For the classical rhetorical tradition, *imitatio* referred primarily to the imitation of models.[10] The *Rhetorica ad Herennium* (1.2.3) lists imitation alongside "theory" or "precept" *(ars)* and "practice" *(exercitatio)* as a means to acquire rhetorical skill. A similar distinction is found in the early-thirteenth-century *Poetria nova* of Geoffrey of Vinsauf (vv. 1705–8). Quintilian goes even further: "For there can be no doubt that in art no small portion of our task lies in imitation, since, although invention came first and is all-important, it is expedient to imitate whatever has been invented with success."[11] In the medieval tradition of the *ars dictaminis,* preceptive manuals were supplemented or even replaced by large collections of model letters for every occasion, to be copied with minor adjustments.[12] In the light of this long rhetorical tradition, Andreas's dialogues can be seen as a set of model discourses to be imitated by would-be lovers.

The dialogues are organized according to the social class of the participants, with three classes distinguished for each sex: commoners, the nobility, and the higher nobility (*DA* 1.6.17 [44]).[13] This can also be at-

---

10. McKeon, "Literary Criticism."

11. Quintilian, *Institutio oratoria* 10.2.1 (ed. Butler, 4:75).

12. Murphy, *Rhetoric,* pp. 199–202, 218–19; idem, *Medieval Rhetoric,* pp. 98–102.

13. Normally we would expect to find nine dialogues, corresponding to the number of possible combinations of men and women from various classes. One dialogue has

tributed to a rhetorical principle, the doctrine of the *genera dicendi* or three levels of style. In the Ciceronian tradition, especially the *Rhetorica ad Herennium* (4.8.11), the distinction between the "grand" *(gravis)*, "middle" *(mediocris)*, and "simple" *(extenuata)* styles was merely a matter of elocution; but the Middle Ages, following the Virgilian tradition of Donatus and Servius, associated this stylistic distinction with a distinction in the dignity or rank of the persons or events concerned. This medieval doctrine of style is best expressed in John of Garland's *Parisiana poetria*, which develops it in terms of the "Virgilian Wheel": each of the three styles *(gravis, mediocris, humilis)* is associated, respectively, with one of Virgil's major poetic works *(Æneid, Georgics, Eclogues)*, with the social types corresponding to those works *(miles,* "knight"; *agricola,* "farmer"; *pastor,* "shepherd"), and with the attendant objects and circumstances.[14]

It is not difficult to see in the social organization of Andreas's dialogues an adaptation of this doctrine. The characteristic feature retained is a tripartite distinction of class associated with different ways of speaking. In the introduction to the Sixth Dialogue (*DA* 1.6.281 [120]), the word used to describe this is *stilus,* "style." The introduction to the Eighth Dialogue (*DA* 1.6.401 [158]) advises the use of "pleasant and agreeable words" in addressing women of the higher nobility. In the Second Dialogue the man discusses the appropriateness for noble people of using gentle speech and of avoiding harsh, uncourteous words (*DA* 1.6.89 [64]). The woman of the Eighth Dialogue speaks of the importance of saying "to each one words appropriate to his condition" (*DA* 1.6.410 [160]). All such remarks indicate on the part of Andreas an awareness of and concern for the appropriateness of different levels of style based on distinctions of class.

---

been left out, however, that which should have come sixth, opposing a nobleman and a woman of the higher nobility, so the actual number is eight. For men there is a fourth class, the "most noble," i.e., the clergy (*DA* 1.6.20 [46]), but with the exception of a passage in the Eighth Dialogue (*DA* 1.6.478–99 [182–88]), no rhetorical model is offered for clerics, presumably because it is later stipulated that in pursuing love, they must abandon their clerical nobility and court according to the rank of their birth (*DA* 1.7.4 [210]).

14. Faral, pp. 86–89; cf. John of Garland (ed. Lawler, pp. 38–41).

Andreas's social classification is not a simple reproduction of the traditional doctrine, but rather an adaptation of it to fit the needs of his particular context. Here there is no mention of the "farmer" *(agricola)* or the "shepherd" *(pastor)* of the Virgilian Wheel; indeed, in Chapter Eleven, which functions as a kind of appendix to the sociological schema of the dialogues, Andreas will subsequently banish all "peasants" *(rustici)* from "Love's court."

The idea of adapting the levels of style to later circumstances can be seen in John of Garland, for alongside the traditional, Virgilian distinction of classes we find an updated, medieval version that distinguishes "courtiers" *(curiales),* "city dwellers" *(civiles),* and "peasants" *(rurales).*[15] Andreas's adaptation goes even further, restricting the classification to those social classes having some degree of access to the feudal courts, and hence to the "courtliness" that the Chaplain sees as a prerequisite for love. Nevertheless, by making a distinction within the nobility, Andreas manages to maintain the tripartite schema of his model. In fact, a contemporary of John of Garland, the German *ars dictaminis* writer Ludolf of Hildesheim, presents a classification quite similar to that of Andreas: the highest class *(persone sublimes)* includes emperors, kings, princes, dukes, and marquises; the middle class *(medii ordinis persone)* includes counts, barons, and city magistrates; the lowest class *(infimi ordinis persone)* includes simple knights, city dwellers, and merchants.[16] Peasants are again excluded, presumably because they neither sent nor received letters.

The doctrine of levels of style is adapted in another way in the dialogues, in that it is reduplicated by being applied to both sexes. This can probably be attributed to yet another rhetorical principle: the fact that rhetorical persuasion depends on the nature of both the speaker and the audience. Aristotle *(Rhetoric* 1.2.3–6, 1356a1–20) distinguishes three means to achieve persuasion: the moral character of the speaker (ἦθος), the emotions of the audience (πάθος), and the demonstrative power of the speech itself (λόγος). Aristotle's *Rhetoric* was not widely known in the West until the thirteenth century, but something of this

---

15. Ed. Lawler, pp. 10–11, 36–39.
16. Ludolf of Hildesheim, *Summa dictaminum,* in Rockinger 1:361.

part of his doctrine was transmitted by the Roman rhetorical tradition. In his discussion of the exordium, Cicero (*De inventione* 1.16.22) distinguishes four ways of securing goodwill: from our own person, from the person of the opponents, from the person of the judges, and from the case itself. The *Rhetorica ad Herennium* (1.4–5.8) presents a nearly identical distinction. Quintilian (6.2.8–24) retains the Greek terms ἦθος and πάθος in discussing the arousal of emotion in the peroration.

Similar considerations can be seen in the medieval *ars dictaminis* tradition. In the eleventh-century *Flores rhetorici* of Alberic of Monte Cassino, we read: "First we must consider the identity of the sender and of the person to whom the letter is sent; we must consider whether he is noble or common in rank."[17] Significantly, in this medieval formulation of the doctrine, the notion of social class figures prominently. It is not difficult to see how Andreas could combine the rhetorical principle of persuasion based on the nature of the speaker and the audience with the medieval interpretation of the three levels of style, thus concluding that the social class of both participants in a given dialogue is relevant in determining the appropriate manner of expression.

Despite the organization of the dialogues in terms of the *genera dicendi,* there appears to be very little actual stylistic difference observable from one dialogue to the other. The use of rhetorical figures and tropes, for example, which lies at the heart of the classical and medieval doctrine of *elocutio,* does not appear to be correlated in any way with the social standing of the dialogues' participants. Even such a socially pertinent stylistic feature as the use of second-person singular or plural pronouns and verb forms *(tu/vos)* offers no clear-cut correlation, for in three of the dialogues the men change from the formal to the familiar style, in one case several times.[18] Moreover, the introductions to five of the eight dialogues (the Second, Third, Sixth, Seventh, and Eighth) contain remarks to the effect that in this situation one may also speak in

17. Alberic of Monte Cassino, *Flowers of Rhetoric,* in Miller et al., p. 138.

18. In the Second and Fourth Dialogues the man starts with *vos* then switches to *tu* (*DA* 1.6.96 [66], 173 [88]). In the Fifth Dialogue the man changes back and forth four times (*DA* 1.6.211 [100], 219 [102], 229 [104], 274 [118]). The man uses *tu* throughout in the First Dialogue, *vos* throughout in the last three. The women use *tu* consistently in the first five dialogues, *vos* consistently in the last three.

the manner of one or more of the preceding dialogues. It is one such passage, in the introduction to the Sixth Dialogue, that uses the word *stilus* (*DA* 1.6.281 [120]).[19]

It is true that Andreas has placed himself in a difficult position, stylistically speaking, by the adaptations that he makes to the doctrine of levels of style. Any medieval rhetorician would have been hard-put to distinguish nine different styles corresponding to Andreas's nine social situations. Perhaps the most we can expect is a rudimentary stylistic differentiation based on the *relative* social standing of the participants, as in C. Julius Victor's brief discussion of the tone to adopt in writing to a superior, an equal, or an inferior.[20] But even such a distinction, which three dialogues would probably have sufficed to illustrate, is difficult to discern in the stylistic practice of the dialogues.

The solution to this enigma lies, apparently, in the peculiarly medieval conception of style. Franz Quadlbauer has shown that, in the context of the *genera dicendi,* the word *stilus* meant for the Middle Ages not what we normally think of as style, but rather the actual subject matter. The expression used by Geoffrey of Vinsauf is, significantly, *stilus materiæ.*[21] This very material conception of style means that stylistic unity is achieved if the matters discussed are in keeping with the dignity of the persons involved.

Stylistic appropriateness depends on choosing words, especially nouns, that designate objects and activities conventionally associated with the social class in question. This is made clear in John of Garland's *Rota Virgilii,* where each of the genres is associated with particular animals (horse/cow/sheep), objects (sword/plow/staff), places (city, castle/

---

19. It is perhaps this notion of the interchangeability of styles that accounts for the omission of one of the nine dialogues. This hypothesis is reinforced by a comment in the introduction to the Eighth Dialogue, which equates, for rhetorical purposes, the noblewoman with the woman of the higher nobility: women of both classes are especially prompt in censuring the words and deeds of noblemen, hence the care that must be exercised in addressing them (*DA* 1.6.401 [158]). Thus, by implication, the Fifth Dialogue, between the nobleman and the noblewoman, can perhaps also stand for the missing dialogue between the nobleman and the woman of the higher nobility.

20. C. Julius Victor, *Ars rhetorica* § 27, in Halm, p. 448.

21. Quadlbauer; Geoffrey of Vinsauf, *Documentum de modo et arte dictandi et versificandi* 2.157, in Faral, p. 315; ibid. 2.161 (p. 316).

field/pasture), and trees (laurel, cedar/apple, pear/beech). Thus "style" is not really concerned with expression, but rather with invention, the securing of appropriate arguments. The effect of the medieval doctrine of the three levels of style is to limit the scope of topical invention in terms of a socially based notion of decorum.

There is abundant evidence to suggest that this is the conception of style that Andreas applies in the dialogues. The introductions to several of them contain advice on the subject matter appropriate to the given situation. In the First Dialogue Andreas suggests that the man begin with praise of the woman's country or family or person, subjects particularly appropriate for women of the middle class (DA 1.6.24–25 [46]). Two of the introductory passages suggesting the use of material from other dialogues qualify that suggestion in terms of differences in the subject matter appropriate in each case. In the Second Dialogue the man is advised to use the same arguments with that noblewoman as were used with the commoner, except that now praise of the woman's noble ancestry can be included (DA 1.6.68 [58]). The introduction to the Seventh Dialogue makes essentially the same observation, adding, however, that the praise of the noblewoman herself should be reduced (DA 1.6.322 [132]).

The social class of the participants is also reflected in various ways in the matters actually discussed in the dialogues. An obvious example is the question raised in the Second Dialogue, between a commoner and a noblewoman, whether a person who practices a trade should also seek to engage in love. The exemplary piety exhibited in the speeches by the women of the higher nobility in Dialogues Three and Eight may well be interpreted along the same lines. The best example of this comes from the Third Dialogue: in the introduction the author stresses the notion that a commoner who wishes to woo a woman of the higher nobility must possess the highest possible character *(morum probitas)*, to compensate for the difference in station; subsequently the entire dialogue is devoted to the various ramifications of the question of *probitas.*

As is clear from the preceding examples, not only the existence and the organization of the dialogues are dependent upon rhetoric, but also a great deal of their content. Fairly explicit references are made in the dialogues to several of the five "parts" or operations of rhetoric distinguished by Cicero (*De inventione* 1.7.9; cf. *Rhetorica ad Herennium* 1.2.3): *inventio,* "invention"; *dispositio,* "arrangement"; *elocutio,* "expression"; *memoria,* "memory"; and *pronuntiatio,* "delivery." The introduction to the First Dialogue (*DA* 1.6.23 [46]) refers quite clearly to invention *(concepta),* to arrangement *(disposita),* and to (a lack of) memory *(perdunt).* The woman of the Eighth Dialogue cites a passage from the *Rhetorica ad Herennium* (3.10.18) concerning memory in justification of her own *dispositio* (*DA* 1.6.409 [160]), falsely attributing her source to Cicero. A further reference to *dispositio* occurs near the end of the treatise (*DA* 3.117 [322]), in connection with the arrangement of Andreas's own discourse.

Despite occasional references to other matters, the main emphasis throughout the dialogues is on *inventio,* the securing of arguments. This most critical aspect of rhetoric was the main subject of the earliest and the latest of Cicero's rhetorical works, the *De inventione* and the *Topica.* In the twelfth century Hugh of St. Victor, echoing Cicero and Boethius, saw invention and judgment as the two main integral parts running through the whole theory of argumentation.[22] Following this tradition, Andreas's dialogues may be seen as a kind of specialized *topica* presenting, mainly by example rather than by precept, the "places of argumentation" *(loci)* appropriate to love. It thus constitutes a collection of what Aristotle calls "proper" or "specific" topics, those appropriate to a particular science, as opposed to "common topics," applicable to any science.[23]

In the introductions that precede the various dialogues, the main emphasis is on how to begin. There is nothing surprising in this. Quintilian stresses the importance of the *exordium* in gaining access to the audience: "I need hardly say that these aims have to be kept in view throughout the whole speech, but they are especially necessary at the commencement, where we gain admission to the mind of the judge."[24] In the introduction to the First Dialogue, Andreas suggests another reason why advice on how to begin is particularly important, the fact that

22. *Didascalicon* 2.30 (ed. Buttimer, pp. 46–47); cf. trans. Taylor, pp. 81–82; Cicero, *Topica* 2.6.
23. Aristotle, *Rhetoric* 1.2.21–22 (1358a10–35). Cf. Stump, p. 22.
24. *Institutio oratoria* 4.1.5 (ed. Butler, 2:9).

later in the dialogue the words of the woman will provide a subject for discussion (*DA* 1.6.22 [46]).

In the introduction to the Seventh Dialogue (*DA* 1.6.322 [132]), the word for "to begin speaking" is *exordiri,* whose derivative *exordium* is the technical rhetorical term for the beginning of a speech. The introduction to the First Dialogue advises that a subtle, indirect opening be adopted, not only in this situation, but by all lovers (*DA* 1.6.21–24 [46]). This is a fairly clear reference to the Ciceronian distinction between the two species of *exordia* (*De inventione* 1.15.20; *Rhetorica ad Herennium* 1.4.6): the direct "introduction" *(principium)* and the subtle "insinuation" *(insinuatio),* the latter particularly appropriate for hostile audiences.

More than Roman rhetoric, it is the medieval *ars dictaminis* that appears to have influenced Andreas's approach to the opening. In twelfth-century treatises on letter writing, the Ciceronian *exordium* is broken down into two components: the "greeting" *(salutatio)* and the "securing of good will" *(captatio benevolentiæ).*[25] Under the rubric *salutatio* the theoreticians of *dictamen* developed an elaborate system of formulae for addressing people of various ranks and stations. Andreas's introductions to Dialogues One and Four advise the lover to begin by greeting the lady (*DA* 1.6.21 [46], 166 [86]), in the first case using the word *salutatio.* This part of the theory of letter writing is perhaps also reflected within the dialogues by the men's use of honorific titles such as "Your Prudence" *(Prudentia Vestra)* or "Your Grace" *(Gratia Vestra)* to address the ladies.[26]

From the *captatio benevolentiæ* comes Andreas's stress on "praise" *(laus, laudatio),* which is mentioned in the introductions to the First, Second, and Seventh Dialogues (*DA* 1.6.24–25 [46], 68–69 [58], 322 [132]), and which recurs frequently within the dialogues, both as a

25. Murphy, *Rhetoric,* pp. 224–25.

26. *Vestra/tua Prudentia* appears to be used 18 times as a form of address; *vestra/tua Gratia,* 8 times; *vestra Celsitudo,* twice; *vestra Altitudo/Clementia/Dignitas/Excellentia/Serenitas,* each once. These honorific titles are scattered throughout the eight dialogues in no apparent pattern. Elsewhere the same expressions can be taken in their proper sense, designating the qualities of the persons addressed; in some cases the interpretation is doubtful.

rhetorical practice and as a subject of discussion.[27] In Roman rhetoric praise is not discussed in connection with the *exordium,* being relegated to the epideictic branch, but in the medieval *ars dictaminis* praise plays an important role in the securing of goodwill. Lavish praise is used by the men at the beginning of several of the dialogues. In the First Dialogue it takes the form of a hyperbolic description of the lady's beauty (*DA* 1.6.26 [46]). In the Third Dialogue it is accomplished through preterition to avoid the suspicion of flattery, in keeping with the lady's high social standing (*DA* 1.6.124 [74]). In both cases, the ornate style of the opening sentences is prolonged throughout most of the first speech through the use of additional figurative language: an allegorical image of Love's army in the First Dialogue; a metaphor of shipwreck in the Third Dialogue. Such openings illustrate an aspect of medieval style to which Marbury Ogle has called attention: the fact that the use of the tropes and schemata of the *ornatus difficilior* is generally concentrated in certain parts of the discourse, notably the prologue or *exordium,* where it is often combined with praise or blame.[28]

Not limited to the opening speeches, the influence of the medieval theory of letter writing can be seen throughout the dialogues. In the *ars dictaminis,* the Ciceronian six parts of an oration are reduced to five, the first two corresponding to the classical *exordium.* The three remaining parts include the narration of circumstances supporting a petition (*narratio*), the presentation of requests (*petitio*), and the conclusion (*conclusio*).[29] The petitionary structure and function of medieval letter writing is well suited to Andreas's purposes in the dialogues, and he took full advantage of that circumstance.

That Andreas was very familiar with the methods of the *ars dictaminis* is clear from the letter addressed to the Countess of Champagne at the end of the Seventh Dialogue. It begins with a standard medieval

---

27. The word *laus* and its derivatives (*laudare, laudatio, laudabilis,* etc.) occur 134 times in the treatise, including 85 times in the dialogues.

28. Ogle. Medieval arts of poetry such as the *Poetria nova* of Geoffrey of Vinsauf distinguish an "easy" and a "difficult" style of ornamentation, the latter characterized by the use of "tropes," figures of speech (such as metaphor) involving a change of meaning. See Faral, pp. 89–97.

29. Murphy, *Rhetoric,* pp. 224–25.

salutation, with the recipient in the dative, the senders in the nominative, and *salutem* in the accusative (*DA* 1.6.390 [154]). The laudative epithets *illustris,* "distinguished," and *sapiens,* "wise," as well as the wish for "whatever is most pleasing in the world," are standard embellishments for a recipient of this rank; they lead already into the *captatio benevolentiæ.* This will continue throughout the second paragraph, where it is developed in sententious style through an aphorism on the importance of seeking wisdom and truth at their source, by implicating the countess herself (ibid.). The third paragraph presents the narration, in past time, of the events and circumstances leading up to the present request (*DA* 1.6.392 [154]). This is followed by the request that the countess settle the dispute; then a brief conclusion repeats the petition while renewing the praise of the recipient (*DA* 1.6.393–94 [154]).

The verb *petere,* "to request," occurs in the introductions to the Fourth, Sixth, and Eighth Dialogues (*DA* 1.6.167 [86], 281 [120], 401 [158]); in the latter two, the expression is *amorem petere.* The verb *petere* and its derivatives are found one hundred times in the dialogues, typically in the expression *amorem petere* or *petere amari,* "to ask for love/to be loved," including seventeen examples of the noun, *petitio.* Likewise, the verb *narrare* occurs in the introduction to the Second Dialogue (*DA* 1.6.69 [58]), referring to the lover's arguments. This is the reference for most of the thirty attestations of the verb *narrare* in the dialogues and for the one attestation of *narratio* (*DA* 1.6.558 [206]).

This use of the technical vocabulary of letter writing is a reflection of the fact that much of the men's discourse in the dialogues is structured on the epistolary model: the securing of goodwill, especially through praise, followed by a narrative justification and a request. This can be illustrated by the first speech of the Second Dialogue. The man begins with a modified preterition formula, which functions as a variant of the "affected-modesty" topos (*DA* 1.6.70 [58]). He asks the woman's indulgence, then he proceeds with a narration in past time (*DA* 1.6.73–74 [60]). Finally he arrives at his only slightly veiled request (*DA* 1.6.77 [60]), thus bringing to an end a short speech that is structured very much like a letter.

Despite the influence of the *ars dictaminis,* the dialogues present not letters, but the oral discourse of oration and debate. Thus the epistolary model of the medieval theory of letter writing is constantly intertwined with the oratorical models of classical rhetoric. We have seen that for Boethius the end or goal of rhetoric was to persuade a judge, reflecting the preponderance of forensic oratory in Roman rhetorical theory. Although Roman judicial institutions no longer existed, the forensic model of oratory continued to influence rhetorical thinking throughout the Middle Ages. Not surprisingly, it is reflected in Andreas's dialogues, for which it is well suited. The dialogues are strewn with legal concepts and arguments conveyed by a properly juridical vocabulary relating to the "law" *(lex, legalis),* to "right" and "justice" *(ius, iustus, iustitia),* to "equity" *(æquus, æqualis, iniquus),* to "judgment" *(iudex, iudicium, iudicare),* and the like. The same tendency will carry over into the "Love Cases" of Book Two.

The forensic flavor of the dialogues can be illustrated by the following examples. In the Second Dialogue (*DA* 1.6.85–86 [62–64]) the woman takes up again from Book One, Chapter Four (*DA* 1.4.3–4 [38]) the question whether Love is a just or unjust judge *(iustus/iniquus iudex).* A similar image is evoked by the woman of the Third Dialogue (*DA* 1.6.161 [84]), who speaks of "pleading in Love's court" *(in amoris curia perorare).* In the Sixth Dialogue (*DA* 1.6.296 [124]) the man speaks of the "lawfulness" of his love *(legalitas amoris),* which he opposes to any possible "just suspicion" *(iusta suspicio)* on the lady's part concerning his worth. He goes on to suggest (*DA* 1.6.297 [124], 300 [126]) that if his deeds are "by right" *(de iure)* worthy, an adverse "decision" *(iudicium)* by the lady would constitute an "injury" *(iniuria)* to him and would "defraud" *(defraudare)* him of his deserts, to which the woman answers (*DA* 1.6.302 [126]) with a reference to "law" *(amoris lex)* and to "custom" *(consuetudo amantium).* In the Seventh Dialogue (*DA* 1.6.356 [142]) the man pleads a "just cause" *(iusta causa)* and "just necessity" *(iusta necessitas)* to override the "rule of law" *(iuris regula).* In the Eighth Dialogue (*DA* 1.6.449–51 [172–74]) the entire discussion of widowhood centers upon the question whether continuing mourning beyond the minimum time set by law *(legalis observatio, tempus legibus præstitutum)* is not to "show contempt for the law" *(legalia iura contemnere)* and to risk doing "legal injury" *(de iure nocere)* to a potential suitor. In the Forth Dialogue (*DA* 1.6.170 [86–88]) and in the Seventh Dialogue (*DA*

1.6.387 [152]) the woman refuses to pass judgment, invoking the rule prohibiting anyone from "judging his own case" *(in propria causa iudicare)*. In two passages of the Eighth Dialogue (*DA* 1.6.427 [166], 506 [190]) there is a question of the "rights of a litigant" *(litigatoris iura)*: if they are "unknown to the judge" *(indici incognita)*, he will "bring back adverse decisions" *(contrarii calculi statuta reportat)*; if the litigant is "unaided by a lawyer" *(nullius advoctione iuvatur)*, the "judge" *(iudex)* is obliged to give him special consideration.

The abundant use of legal terminology in the dialogues creates a quasi-juridical situation, the dynamics of which can be analyzed in terms of Cicero's four *loci* for securing goodwill. From the point of view of the male lovers being instructed in the rhetoric of love, the women occupy simultaneously two of the four functions: they are both adversary and judge. This de facto dual function is underlined, in the very process of denial, by the two women who refuse to pass judgment in particular cases on the grounds that they are implicated in the proceedings. In both of the references to "litigants" in the Eighth Dialogue, the "judge" mentioned is, by implication, the woman. The tension between these two functions is often visible in the cautious replies of the men. Their problem is to refute the adversary without offending the judge.

The two other *loci* are occupied by the men, for they are not only the pleaders, but also to a great extent the subject of the plea. Insofar as the dialogues are concerned with the particular questions that are the subject of rhetoric, they are concerned primarily with the men themselves: their rank, age, marital status, character, deeds, sentiments, and so on. Thus a large part of the material of the dialogues can be analyzed in terms of the Ciceronian doctrine of "personal attributes" *(attributa personis)*.

Cicero (*De inventione* 1.24.34) lists eleven attributes of persons: "name" *(nomen)*, "nature" *(natura)*, "manner of life" *(victus)*, "fortune" *(fortuna)*, "habit" *(habitus)*, "feeling" *(affectio)*, "interests" *(studia)*, "purposes" *(concilia)*, "achievements" *(facta)*, "accidents" *(casus)*, and "speeches made" *(orationes)*. Along with the attributes of actions *(attributa negotiis)*, they constitute the basic topics of proof *(confirmatio)*; in addition, they play a central role in the praise and blame that form the substance of epideictic oratory (ibid. 2.59.177). In the twelfth century

Matthew of Vendôme (*Ars versificatoria* 1.77–92) repeats the same list of eleven attributes of persons, adding his own examples and commentary, in the course of a discussion of the invention appropriate to description.[30]

In Andreas's dialogues we find several of the Ciceronian attributes of persons used repeatedly as an integral part of the argumentation. In many cases it is Cicero's very term that is used, though often with a more restricted, medieval meaning; in other cases Cicero's term is not to be found, but the idea is clearly present. *Natura* is used regularly in the dialogues to designate social class or origin, thus corresponding more or less to Cicero's *cognatio*, a subcategory of *natura;* another such subclass, "age" *(ætas)* also figures prominently in the dialogues. Neither Cicero's *victus* nor Matthew's *convictus* is attested in the *De amore*, but two important subjects of discussion in the dialogues could be subsumed under this category: marital status and the distinction between the clergy and the laity. *Fortuna* occurs three times in the dialogues in the specialized sense of success in love. *Habitus* is for Cicero an acquired, more or less permanent physical or mental condition, such as a skill or a state of knowledge; in the dialogues *habitus* is used only in the very restricted sense of external appearance and especially dress, but one of the most important topics discussed, "character" *(morum probitas)*, would be included in Cicero's original conception. *Affectio* occurs frequently in one of two restricted meanings, both of which are intimately connected with the subject at hand: it is used either as a synonym for *amor* or else in the expression *affectio maritalis*, "marital affection," which is distinguished from and even opposed to *amor. Facta* is used repeatedly in a narrow, feudal sense, referring to the "deeds" by which the lover hopes to gain the recompense of love. *Studium*, along with the adjective *studiosus* and especially the verb *studere*, indicates the intensity of commitment, the "zeal" with which the lover seeks to serve the lady and merit her love. *Orationes* does not occur in the dialogues, but it is illustrated on every page.

Whether they be used to praise the lady or to bolster the claims of

30. For the development of the Ciceronian attributes into the medieval doctrine of "circumstances" *(circumstantiæ)*, with considerable ramifications for medieval theology and jurisprudence, see Gründel. Cf. below, Chapter 8, n. 7.

the man, the *attributa personis* constitute the main "places of argument" throughout the dialogues, thus substantiating the view that the latter serve as a kind of specialized *topica* for lovers. It is probably also this "topical" function that explains one curious feature, the fact that no attempt is made to maintain consistency of characterization for the participants. In the First Dialogue Andreas switches in mid-stream from the arguments appropriate to an older man to those that pertain to a younger man, formally announcing the transition and linking the two types of discourse to the corresponding circumstances (*DA* 1.6.46 [52]). Thus the arguments supplied cover roughly the ages enumerated by Cicero under *natura* (*De inventione* 1.24.35): *ætate, puer an adulescens, natu grandior an senex* ("as to age, boy, youth, of middle age, or an old man"); except that the extremes have already been eliminated from consideration in Chapter Five. In the Eighth Dialogue the process is carried much further, though without authorial commentary. Early in the dialogue the woman objects that the man is married, which he acknowledges (*DA* 1.6.443–44 [170]); later it is similarly objected and acknowledged that he is a cleric (*DA* 1.6.478–81 [182]). This state of affairs is surprising, though not impossible, but with the woman's status the situation is more complex. First she claims to be bound by a previously established relationship with another suitor (*DA* 1.6.434 [168]); then she argues that she is advanced in age and a widow in mourning for her deceased husband (*DA* 1.6.445 [172]); finally she portrays herself as too young for love and totally lacking in experience, with a desire to keep her virginity intact for some future husband (*DA* 1.6.452 [174], 466–67 [178]). Once again, Andreas has manipulated the discourse to cover the major *loci,* not only for age but also for "manner of life."

From the preceding analysis it is clear that rhetoric plays a crucial role in the dialogues. Not only their existence and their organization but also much of their substance must be viewed first of all in terms of their rhetorical function, the illustration of the winning of love through the use of eloquence. From this observation we can draw an important conclusion for the interpretation of the text: the various assertions advanced in the dialogues cannot be taken at face value as a straightforward exposition of doctrine, for they are first and foremost rhetorical arguments designed to persuade. Thus for over one-half of the treatise no evaluation of the doctrine is possible until rhetorical analysis has been carried out, a principle too often forgotten in practice.

No better example can be found to illustrate this than the passage from the Eighth Dialogue concerning the distinction between "pure" and "mixed" love (*DA* 1.6.470–75 [180]), which will be analyzed in detail in Chapter 8. This passage is frequently viewed as a central document for the understanding of "courtly love," but when it is viewed in its rhetorical context, it takes on a very different light. Based on the classical and medieval commonplace of the five "stages of love," the doctrine advanced by the man in this passage is a deft rhetorical ploy aimed at advancing his own case while assuaging various fears expressed by the woman earlier in the dialogue. This interpretation is confirmed by the woman's reaction, as well as by several remarks Andreas makes later in the treatise.[31]

Although the dialogues provide the most striking illustrations of the influence of rhetoric on the *De amore,* this influence is by no means limited to them. There is another kind of rhetoric in evidence throughout the treatise, that by which the author seeks to persuade his public. Introduced in the Preface, this other rhetorical thrust is relayed by numerous later references, forming what we may call a "rhetorical frame" for the treatise as a whole.

In the Preface, which precedes Book One, Andreas explains the circumstances leading him to compose the treatise. He is impelled to write, he claims, by his concern for one "Walter" *(Gualterius),* a "revered friend" who has recently fallen in love and is in need of advice on this subject (*DA* 0.1 [30]). A fair amount of scholarly effort has been expended toward identifying Walter, but the results are so far inconclusive.[32] The attribution of a literary work's origin to the request of a patron or friend is a medieval commonplace. It constitutes a variation of the "affected modesty" topos, a standard rhetorical device of the *exordium.* Its function is to justify the discourse that will follow: the author has not taken it upon himself to write, he is merely acceding to anoth-

---

31. See below, Chapter 8. Cf. Monson, "L' 'amour pur.'"

32. The latest hypothesis is that of Karnein, "Auf der Suche," who identifies Gualterius with Gautier le Jeune, a courtier at the Parisian court of Philip II ("Philip Augustus") of France.

er's request. Of this device Ernst Robert Curtius has written: "Innumerable medieval authors assert that they write by command. Histories of literature accept this as gospel truth. Yet it is usually a mere topos."[33]

The effect of Andreas's Preface is to establish a rhetorical context for the entire treatise. It presents, inscribed within the text, the principal actors of the rhetorical transaction, each with his own pertinent characteristics. Walter is described as inexperienced and as having trouble containing his newly discovered emotions; this contrasts sharply with the author, who invokes his own experience (*DA* 0.2–3 [30]). Walter is established as a person in need of advice, the author as one competent to dispense it. The Preface not only explains and justifies the author's temerity in presuming to teach, it also prepares the audience to accept his teaching by showing that his is an authoritative voice.[34]

The rhetorical context established in the Preface is evoked and extended by numerous later references scattered throughout the treatise. This is accomplished most obviously by the use of some twenty forms of address in the vocative to command Walter's attention: *Gualteri, amice,* or both.[35] In addition, many first- or second-person pronouns, verb forms, or possessives are used to reintroduce the author or his addressee. Often Andreas seizes the occasion to express his personal opinion, for example his mistrust of Love's tendency to "carry unequal weights" (*DA* 1.4.3 [38]), or to recount his personal experiences, as in the chapter on nuns (*DA* 1.8.4–6 [212]). All these later references combine with the Preface to form what we may call a "rhetorical frame" for the treatise as a whole.

This rhetorical frame is closely associated throughout with an ideo-

33. Curtius, p. 85. "*Usually* a mere topos" is doubtless an exaggeration. For recent work on medieval patronage, particularly of German literature, see Bumke; Jaeger, "Patrons."

34. This rhetorical effect is reinforced by the use of several conventional metaphors—to "get rid of the darts of Venus," "manage one's horses reins," "engage in this kind of hunting," etc.—illustrating once again the medieval predilection for using the tropes of the *ornatus difficilior* in the *exordium.*

35. *Gualteri amice: DA* 1.4.3 (38); 3.1 (286). *Gualteri: DA* 1.6.10 (44), 167 (86); 1.8.6 (212); 1.9.20 (218); 2.6.26 (246), 38 (248); 3.6 (286), 23 (292), 109 (320), 120 (322), 121 (322), 121 (324). *Amice: DA* 1.2.8 (36); 1.8.6 (212); 1.9.16 (218); 2.4.5 (234); 3.48 (300) [*carissime a.*], 3.114 (320) [*venerande a.*].

logical message of which the author seeks to persuade his pupil: the in-advisability of engaging in love. In the Preface the author expresses great reluctance to give advice on this subject, claiming that he does so only in the hope that it might encourage Walter to use greater caution (*DA* 0.4 [30]). With few exceptions, that is also the burden of the later passages. In several cases these interventions are accompanied by the use of imperatives or optative subjunctives indicating what Walter should do, especially *cave,* "beware," introducing warnings on what he should avoid.[36] Not surprisingly, nearly one-half of all such passages, nine out of twenty, are found in Book Three, "The Rejection of Love." This in-cludes the introductory paragraph, where Walter is advised to use his new knowledge to refrain from loving and thus increase his reward in Heaven (*DA* 3.2 [286]). It also includes the closing lines of the treatise, where Gualterius's name is mentioned three times in a final warning to follow the example of the Wise Virgins of the gospel parable (*DA* 3.120–21 [322–24]).

The use that Andreas makes of rhetoric in the Preface and the rhetorical frame is closely related to the generic vector of the treatise that we have called *sapientia.* While instructing Walter in the art of ac-quiring love through eloquence, the Chaplain deploys his own elo-quence to persuade his putative pupil, and through him his wider audi-ence, to have the wisdom not to use that knowledge. His discourse thus embodies that combination of rhetoric and wisdom that St. Augustine recommends to the Christian orator in *De doctrina christiana.*[37] Perhaps even more than the interaction between rhetoric and dialectic, it is the tension established between this divine rhetoric of Christian teaching and the human rhetoric of sexual love that determines the fundamental structure of the treatise.

---

36. *Cave: DA* 1.6.10 (44), 1.8.6 (212), 3.121 (324); *cernas:* 3.6 (286), *discas:* 3.48 (300); *relinquas:* 3.23 (292), *studeas:* 3.121 (322), *summas:* 3.120 (322).

37. Aurelius Augustinus, *De doctrina christiana* 4.5–6. Cf. Murphy, *Rhetoric,* pp. 68–69.

The dialectic of love

In the course of the Twelfth-Century Renaissance, dialectic assumed a dominant role in the intellectual life of Western Europe. We can distinguish two complementary aspects of this development: on the one hand, the reintroduction of the remaining books of Aristotle's Organon led to marked improvements in the techniques of intellectual analysis and argumentation; at the same time, the need to rationalize the "topics" of argumentation led to a generalization of the method of confrontation and reconciliation of conflicting authorities known as the *sic et non* method. These two developments of the twelfth century would pave the way for the great scholastic syntheses of the thirteenth.

Written near the end of the twelfth century, the *De amore* reflects the strong emphasis on dialectic that was prevalent in the ambient scholastic culture. We saw in the previous chapter the considerable role played by several of the techniques of dialectic in shaping the first five chapters of the *De amore.* We must now explore the influence of this art on the dialogues and on the treatise as a whole. We shall see that Andreas was very much aware of the major new techniques of intellectual discourse, though he does not always use them with the same degree of adroitness that will become usual in the following century. Even more important in shaping the treatise is his concern for confronting and reconciling divergent points of view on a given subject.[38]

As with rhetoric, the eight dialogues of Book One are an appropriate place to begin our discussion of dialectic, for nowhere in the treatise is its influence more apparent. Although rhetoric provided the point of departure for the dialogues, as well as their overall structure and a fair amount of their material, much of their methodology and tone is dependent on dialectic. This is probably a reflection of the subordination of rhetoric to dialectic in medieval culture. In fact, the methods of argumentation used in the dialogues present a constant interaction, a dialectical interweaving, between rhetoric and dialectic.

According to Boethius, the aims of dialectic and rhetoric are, respec-

38. For a stimulating discussion of the influence of dialectic on the *De amore,* see Brown, pp. 91–115.

tively, to draw concessions from an adversary and to persuade a judge. We have seen that the dialogues make considerable use of the judicial language of forensic rhetoric, but also that, in this scenario, the ladies are obliged to assume simultaneously two distinct roles, that of adversary and that of judge. In fact, this state of affairs corresponds rather closely with the situation of the dialectician as it is described by Boethius:

> The rhetorician has as judge someone other than his opponent, someone who decides between them. But for the dialectician, the one who is the opponent also gives the decision because a reply [which is], as it were, a decision is elicited from the opponent by the cunning of the questioning.[39]

It is only in the Love Cases of Book Two, Chapter Seven, that a properly judicial situation will be achieved, with a third party providing the decisions, though even there the influence of dialectic is very much apparent.

Much more than a judicial case, the dialogues resemble that form of public debate which the Middle Ages called "disputation" *(disputatio)*. Introduced into the curriculum in the course of the twelfth century, *disputatio* took its place beside *lectio* as one of the two main school exercises. Carefully integrated with each other in the course of instruction, *lectio* and *disputatio* provided practical training, respectively, for grammar and for dialectic, and both were carried over into higher studies such as theology. The principles of disputation were contained in two of the logical works of Aristotle, the *Topics* and the *De sophisticis elenchis,* whose reintroduction in the mid-twelfth century provided much of the impetus for the development of the exercise.

Andreas's dialogues contain seven attestations of the noun *disputatio* as well as two of the verb *disputare*. Neither appears elsewhere in the treatise. Having received a categorical refusal from the lady, the man in the Sixth Dialogue refers to their exchange as a "disputation," vowing to redouble his efforts and to resolve the matter by "disputing" (*DA* 1.6.304 [126]). The word *disputatio* occurs three times in the letter ad-

---

39. Trans. Stump, p. 80. Cf. PL 64:1206.

dressed to the Countess of Champagne at the end of the Seventh Dialogue, referring to a dispute that she is asked to resolve (*DA* 1.6.392–93 [154]). In the Eighth Dialogue the discussants use the expression alternatively to refer to their own discussion (*DA* 1.6.423 [164], 503 [190], 528 [198], 560 [206]). It is perhaps significant that all these references occur in the last three dialogues and are placed in the mouths of representatives of the higher nobility, who were presumably more conscious of the procedures they were following. It is also in these same dialogues that we find the most striking examples of the new techniques of argumentation.

The subjects for debate that served as the point of departure for the exercise of disputation were known as "questions" *(quæstiones)* and later as "disputed questions" *(quæstiones disputatæ).* These questions grew out of difficulties or obscurities encountered in commenting on the standard authors in the *lectio.* A *quæstio* consisted of an affirmation and its contradictory negation, as we read in Gilbert de la Porée; not all contradictions are *quæstiones,* however, only those for which arguments can be adduced on either side. The *quæstio* thus corresponds to what Aristotle calls a "dialectical problem" *(problema dialecticum).*[40]

Disputed questions abound in the dialogues of the *De amore,* providing much of the matter for discussion. Not infrequently they take the form of dilemmas proposed for discussion by one of the disputants, particularly in the later dialogues. In one such case the term *quæstio* is used (*DA* 1.6.554 [206]). The same term also introduces one of the cases discussed in Book Two, Chapter Seven (*DA* 2.7.13 [254]). Perhaps even more significant is Andreas's repeated use of the standard scholastic introduction to a disputed question, the disjunctive interrogative *utrum,* "whether." In her letter of the Seventh Dialogue, for example, the Countess of Champagne resumes thus the dispute presented to her for resolution: "Whether *(utrum)* love can have a place between spouses" (*DA* 1.6.396 [156]). *Utrum* occurs nine times in the dialogues and three times in Book Two.

At the beginning of the Fourth Dialogue, the nobleman asks the

---

40. Gilbert of Poitiers, *Boecii prologus* § 3 (ed. Häring, p. 63); Aristotle, *Topics* 1.11 (104b1–17).

woman of the middle class to resolve a certain "doubt," whether good character is more to be praised in a noblewoman or in a commoner (*DA* 1.6.169 [86]). In the Sixth Dialogue the woman of the middle class asks the man of the higher nobility to decide whether she should follow her heart or her will (*DA* 1.6.310 [128]). The last part of the Eighth Dialogue, between a man and a woman of the higher nobility, contains a series of disputed questions that the disputants propose alternatively for discussion. The man begins by asking the woman to choose between "pure" and "mixed" love (*DA* 1.6.475 [180]). She later takes up the same question in another form, proposing to debate whether the solaces of the upper or the lower part of the body are to be preferred (*DA* 1.6.533–34 [198–200]). After considerable discussion, she accedes to the position defended by the man, but then proposes immediately another dilemma: which of two lovers should a woman retain, an earlier one who has returned after being presumed dead, or a second whom she has taken in the absence of the first (*DA* 1.6.550–53 [204]). It is to this dilemma that the man applies the term *quæstio*. At the very end of the dialogue the man proposes, in two slightly different formulations, yet another disputed question: should a man lose the love of a woman for courting another, although unsuccessfully or, indeed, with no intention of being unfaithful (*DA* 1.6.561, 563 [208]). This dilemma, like the preceding one, anticipates those that will be taken up among the cases of Book Two, Chapter Seven.[41]

With the reintroduction of the complete Aristotelian corpus, the hallmark of dialectic became the application of human reason *(ratio)* to all intellectual discourse. In the late twelfth century an otherwise unknown Magister Radulfus gave the following definition of disputation: *Disputatio est rationis inductio ad aliquid probandum vel contradicendum* ("Disputation is the introduction of reasoning for the purpose of proving or disproving something").[42] The term *ratio* occurs fifty-eight times in the dialogues of the *De amore,* generally in the sense "argument." The man of the Second Dialogue, for example, boasts that he is "forti-

41. The dilemma proposed by the woman is related to Case XIV (*DA* 2.7.31–34 [262]); those proposed by the man have analogues in Cases II and XII (*DA* 2.7.6–8 [252], 25–27 [260]).

42. Grabmann, 2:19–20; my translation.

fied by [an] incontrovertible argument *(ratio)*" (*DA* 1.6.72 [60]). All these references to "reason" confer upon the dialogues a tone of rationality hardly in keeping with the emotional subject of love being discussed. This paradox again reflects the subordination of rhetoric to dialectic in twelfth-century culture. Theoretically the lovers set out to "persuade" the ladies, but in practice they seem primarily bent on "drawing concessions" from them.

To illustrate Andreas's use of the new techniques of argumentation in the application of reason to love, we shall concentrate on three of the most important: division, definition, and syllogism. These correspond to the three "modes" distinguished by thirteenth-century scholastics such as Alexander of Hales in the *forma tractandi* appropriate to human science: the *modus divisivus,* the *modus definitivus,* and the *modus collectivus* (i.e., ratiocination).[43] We have seen that both definition and division figure prominently in the early chapters of the *De amore.* They also play an important role in the dialogues, where they are joined by syllogistic reasoning.

In the early chapters of the *De amore* we encountered *divisio* primarily as "division into parts," in which sense it is also known as *partitio.* In its more properly logical sense it refers to the distribution of genus into species through the application of differences. In this sense division is closely related to definition, although the latter is concerned with determining the essence of a given species, the former with classifying the relationship between related species. In yet another use, division distinguishes the various meanings of a word, in which sense it is synonymous with *distinctio.*

The term *divisio* does not occur in the *De amore;* the verb, *dividere,* is found only once, in Book Two (*DA* 2.7.23 [258], Case X), referring to the "separation" of married couples. *Distinctio* and related terms *(distinguere, distinctus)* are more frequent, with twenty attestations in the treatise, sixteen of them in the dialogues. With the exception of *distinctus,* however, these occurrences refer to social distinctions of class, rather than to logical distinctions. Nevertheless, the latter do occur without the corresponding terms in the dialogues and elsewhere, taking

---

43. Minnis, *Medieval Theory,* pp. 119ff.

the form either of divisions into parts or of distinctions in the meaning of terms.

In discussing the relationship between deeds and the granting of love, the man of the First Dialogue distinguishes four stages of love, applying to them the adjective *distinctus* (*DA* 1.6.60 [56]). Love should be granted by way of encouragement to those who have not yet done any deeds, he argues, but only for the first three stages. His argument depends on *partitio*. In the Seventh Dialogue the man distinguishes three *species* in jealousy (*DA* 1.6.378–79 [150]). Although one might be tempted to see in this passage the scholastics' division of genus into species, the translation of John J. Parry and P. G. Walsh, "aspects," is doubtless more appropriate. The man subsequently refers to them as "parts" *(partes),* claiming that all three must be present for true jealousy to exist. Once again, the division is into parts.

In the Fourth Dialogue the woman of the middle class turns against the nobleman his own argument that virtue is more to be praised in a commonwoman than in a noblewoman; by the same reasoning, she argues, she should prefer the love of an commoner. The man replies by making a distinction concerning the word "more" *(magis).* Virtue in a commoner is perhaps more to be praised but not to be automatically preferred (*DA* 1.6.185 [92]). The man has got himself into a tight position with his excessive flattery, and his cavil about the meaning of *magis* is just a graceful way to make a partial retraction. Learning that the woman already has a lover, the man of the Eighth Dialogue combats Love's injunction against wooing suitably paired women (*DA* 1.6.268 [116], Precept III) by means of a distinction concerning "suitably" *(idonee).* This word may imply, according to his argument, not only that the lovers are of equal worth, but also that they are equally fond of each other (*DA* 1.6.528–29 [198]). The man hopes by this quibble to keep his chances open, but the woman successfully counters: as to the suitability of her established relationship, the man must take her word for it, for the law of secrecy prevents her from revealing any more details.[44]

44. A similar cavil is introduced by the man later in the same dialogue concerning the rule that no one should be deprived of his love "without blame" *(sine culpa)* on his

Distinctions in the meaning of terms are a response to the problem posed by the existence of ambiguous or "equivocal" terms, those with more than one meaning. Aristotle discusses this problem extensively in the *Topics* and the *Sophistic Refutation*. Abelard alludes to it near the beginning of the Prologue to *Sic et non,* identifying it as one of the major obstacles to the interpretation of texts.[45]

In Case IX of Book Two, Chapter Seven, Ermengarde of Narbonne refuses to decide whether the affection felt by lovers is greater than that of married couples, on the grounds that the term *affectio* is used equivocally of two incomparable objects (*DA* 2.7.21–22 [258]). Her use of the term *species* to designate the two related but distinct classes of affection subsumed under a common name illustrates the close relationship between distinctions in the meanings of terms and the division of genus into species. Ermengarde's pronouncement is loosely based on a passage from Aristotle's *Topics* (1.15, 107b13–18). This surprisingly learned reply from a lady of the court, made according to Andreas "after philosophical meditation," constitutes the most sophisticated use of *divisio* found in the *De amore*.

Definition also figures prominently in the early part of the treatise, whose first chapter is devoted to a definition of love. Definition, which is of species, proceeds by joining *genus,* or general class, to *differentiæ,* the characteristics that distinguish the species being defined from other species of the same genus, in order to arrive at the essence of the species in question (see below, Chapter 5).

The term *definitio* occurs eleven times in the *De amore,* including ten times in the dialogues. There are also nine attestations of the verb *definire,* four of them in the dialogues. *Definire* is used generally in the sense of "passing judgment," particularly in the expression *iudicio definire.* This is also the meaning of *definitio* near the beginning of the

---

part (cf. *DA* 2.8.45 [282], Rule VIII): "without blame" should be interpreted, he argues, as meaning "without any other just reason" *(sine alia iusta causa),* to which the woman subsequently agrees (*DA* 1.6.557–560 [206]).

45. Aristotle, *Topics* 1.15 (106a1–107b37), 1.18 (108a18–37), 2.3 (110a23–111a7); idem, *De sophisticis elenchis* 4 (165b23–166a23), 17 (175a31–176b28), 19 (177a9–32), 22 (178a24–28), 23 (179a15–25), 32 (182b13–31); Abelard, *Sic et non* (ed. Boyer and McKeon, p. 89); cf. Minnis and Scott, p. 87.

Fourth Dialogue (*DA* 1.6.170 [86–88]). In the Seventh Dialogue, however, the entire discussion turns upon definition, in the proper sense of the term. It is punctuated by the repetition of the term *definitio* as well as the scholastic phrase typically used for defining: *nihil aliud esse quam/nisi . . .* ("X is nothing other than . . .").

The woman argues that she cannot love the man because she already loves her husband, and the laws of Love forbid loving more than one person at a time. To this the man replies by accusing the woman of misusing the term "love," adding that the marital affection one feels for a husband does not come under the "true definition" of love. He then provides a definition of love, seen as a passionate desire to receive a furtive, secret embrace (*DA* 1.6.368 [146]). He will later argue that the embraces between husband and wife, being perfectly licit, cannot be furtive, and so do not fit the definition.

This definition of love is rather different from that given by Andreas in the first chapter of the *De amore,* although the words *immoderata* and *amplexus* are clearly echoes of it. Of that definition this one reproduces only the last part, dealing with the final cause of love. Even that part is modified, especially with the addition of the "furtive and secret" clause, upon which the man's argument depends. Surprisingly, the woman appears to accept this definition, however, at least at first, being content to quibble with its implications. If the definition is correctly understood, she says, "furtive" and "secret" will be seen to be more or less equivalent, and nothing prevents spouses from exchanging secret embraces. Near the end of her speech she proposes her own definition, modifying only slightly that of the man by removing the crucial "furtive and secret" clause (*DA* 1.6.374–76 [148]). On the basis of this new definition she then again claims that nothing prevents love from existing between man and wife.

Interwoven with this discussion on the definition of love is another on the definition of jealousy. At the end of his earlier speech the man has given, as it were, an alternative definition of love, claiming that jealousy is of love's very substance (*DA* 1.6.371 [146–48]). In one sense "substance" is synonymous with "essence," that is with definition, as we read in Aquinas: "In another way, that is said to be substance which signifies the essence of all things, as we say that the definition signifies the substance of a thing."[46] Thus the man has redefined love to include jealousy in its essence. He then combines syllogistically this "definition" with an ethical argument to the effect that jealousy between husband and wife is universally condemned, drawing the conclusion that husbands and wives are excluded from love.

To this the woman replies by defining jealousy as a shameful, malevolent suspicion of a woman, unworthy of any lover, married or not (DA 1.6.373 [148]). Thereupon the man produces his own "description" *(descriptio)* of jealousy, which is very much like a definition.[47] Jealousy is an true emotion, he claims, whereby we greatly fear that the substance of our love may be diminished by some defect in serving the wishes of the beloved, and an anxiety that one's love is not returned, and suspicion of the beloved, but without shameful thoughts (DA 1.6.378 [148–50]). This "description" of jealousy clearly echoes Andreas's definition of love in the first chapter of the treatise: it has at its core the expression *animi passio,* corresponding to the Chaplain's *passio innata,* and it emphasizes "fear" *(tememus, trepidatio)* as a constituent part of the emotion, as does Andreas in the discussion immediately following his definition. Thus it reinforces the man's contention that jealousy is an essential part of love. At the same time, the last clause, with yet another echo of Andreas's definition *(cogitatio),* rejects the woman's contention that jealousy is base or shameful *(turpis).* People often mistake shameful suspicion for jealousy, the man continues, being ignorant of the latter's "description" (DA 1.6.381–82 [150]). This point is crucial to the man's argument, for he contends that the suspicion associated with jealousy is shameful only in the case of husband and wife, and in their case necessarily so.

In his summation the man stresses the importance of the proper use of definition, taking the woman to task for her failures in this regard, but his argument is neither clear nor convincing. He accuses the

46. Thomas Aquinas, *In lib. II Sent.* 37.1.1, in McKeon, *Selections,* 2:500. Cf. Aquinas, *Opera omnia,* ed. Busa, 1:233.

47. Cf. McKeon, *Selections,* 2:444: "DESCRIPTIO, *description:* names a characteristic or property of a thing (unlike definition which names its genus and differentia); description may, therefore, demarcate the species unambiguously, but it can not state its essence."

woman of "going beyond" the definition of love, citing "very old authorities" against adding "explanatory language" to definitions (*DA* 1.6.384 [150–52]). This apparently refers to the woman's contention that love with a spouse may be practiced without sin, for this is the subject currently being discussed. If the "very old authority" invoked refers to Aristotle's injunction against definitions that are too long (i.e., include language not pertaining to the essence of the thing being defined),[48] it is rather the man who has exceeded the definition of love with his "furtive and secret" clause. It is not at all clear whence he derives the idea that definitions are not to be glossed, a principle belied by Andreas's extensive glossing of his own definition in the first chapter. The objection also is rather unfair, for the woman "glossed" her definition by combining a moral judgment with it, much as the man himself did with respect to jealousy. Nevertheless, the man claims to have invalidated the woman's interpretation, showing it to be contrary to the spirit of the definition. Moreover, the woman's definition of love is itself unsustainable, the man declares, citing the teachings of Andreas Capellanus, who excludes the blind and the insane from loving (*DA* 1.6.384–85 [152]). The woman remains unconvinced, but rather than advancing any further arguments, she suggests that the matter be submitted to the opinion of a third party. The joint letter sent to the Countess of Champagne asks that she settle the debate by a *justa definitio* (*DA* 1.6.393 [154]), that is, of course, a "judgment" first of all, but also, in the context of the dialogue, a definition. The countess takes up the challenge with a judgment that finds in favor of the man on all counts but that "defines" love and jealousy only by implication.

Although the "definitions" of love and jealousy advanced in the Seventh Dialogue draw upon Andreas's definition in the first chapter of the treatise, the use both disputants make of this technique is much less rigorous than that of the Chaplain himself. Particularly striking is the fact that the man advances two different "definitions" of love in the same speech, whereas a given species can have only one true definition. Even by twelfth-century standards the overall performance is certainly not distinguished. Rather than an example of the dialectical technique of

---

48. Aristotle, *Topics* 6.1 (139b15–18), 6.3 (140a23–141a22).

definition, we should probably see in this passage an adaptation of that technique to the particular circumstances of a rhetorical situation.

The influence of Aristotelian rationality is most visible in "ratiocination," the formal logic of syllogistic reasoning. Aristotle defines dialectic as reasoning or syllogizing from probable arguments.[49] One index of Andreas's rationality is the frequency with which he uses the term *ergo,* "therefore," to draw a conclusion: it occurs seventy-five times in the dialogues alone, and another forty times in the rest of the treatise. Another such index is the frequency of the verbs *monstrare* and *demonstrare,* "to demonstrate," found twenty-four times in the dialogues and another seventeen times elsewhere.

According to Boethius, dialectic differs from rhetoric in its tendency to use complete syllogisms, as opposed to enthymemes, or imperfect, abbreviated syllogisms. In the dialogues of the *De amore* we encounter both forms. The man of the Third Dialogue, for example, argues that since good character alone makes a man worthy of ennoblement, and since only nobility is considered worthy of the love of a noblewoman, only good character deserves the crown of a noblewoman's love (*DA* 1.6.141 [78]). Propositions involving the term *solus,* "only," are not examined in the *Prior Analytics,* but they are discussed by thirteenth-century scholastics under the rubric of "exclusive propositions" *(dictio exclusiva).*[50] To put them into correct logical form, the usual procedure is to "convert" them, transposing subject and predicate, to get universal affirmative propositions:

All nobility comes from good character.
All love of noblewomen is earned by nobility.
All love of noble women must be earned by good character.

In this form we have a nearly perfect first-figure syllogism in Barbara.[51] This is essentially the argument used by the man of the Second Dia-

---

49. Aristotle, *Topics* 1.1 (100a18–20, 29–30).
50. Prior, pp. 133–34.
51. Syllogisms are classified according to "figure," which is determined by the way the middle term functions in the premises, and "mood," which concerns the quantity and quality of the premises and conclusion. See Prior, pp. 110–114. In the first figure, of which our syllogism is an example, the middle term is subject of the major premise and

logue, who claims that if only good character deserves to adorn men with the qualities of nobility, then good character alone should impel the woman to love (*DA* 1.6. 91 [64–66]). Here, however, it is presented as an enthymeme, with the minor premise suppressed.

Not only the men but also the women of the dialogues engage in syllogistic reasoning. The woman of the Fifth Dialogue, for example, argues that once he has entered Love's court, a lover has no will to do or not do anything except what Love's table sets before him and that which pleases the other lover; from this she concludes that one should not go near such a court, for one should utterly avoid entering a place that one cannot leave freely (*DA* 1.6.213–14 [100]). This argument is constructed entirely with indefinite propositions, although it is reasonable to assume that universal affirmatives are intended, and the major premise has been tacked on at the end. If we reorder the argument and assume universals we get:

(All) places that one cannot leave freely should be avoided.
(All) courts of Love are places that one cannot leave freely.
(All) courts of Love should be avoided.

Once again we have a first-figure syllogism in Barbara.[52]

The Sixth Dialogue offers a particularly dense passage of formal rea-

---

predicate of the minor. In terms of mood our syllogism is *AAA* or, according to a medieval mnemonic device, in *Barbara,* since the three propositions are all universal affirmatives. Strictly speaking, however, the syllogism is not valid, because of a slight shift in the crucial middle term: to be "worthy of ennoblement" is not the same as to possess nobility. *Nobilitas* must be taken in a figurative sense, with *nobilitatem* [*habere*] as equivalent to *dignus nobilitari* [*esse*], which resolves the problem. *Nobilis* is used literally, however, in the expression *nobilis amor,* so the entire argument depends on the ambiguity of this term.

52. This syllogism is also not without problems. The difference in formulation of the major term is not terribly important, as *fugiendum esse* ("ought to be avoided") in the major premise subsumes *non appetendum esse* ("ought not to be sought") in the conclusion. More troubling is the difference in the middle term: *nihil potest . . . velle vel nolle* ("can neither wish nor not wish") refers to a limitation on *psychological* freedom, whereas *libere non patet egressus* ("the exit does not lie freely open") appears to be a more physical limitation. The difficulty is perhaps more apparent than real, however, since *ingressus curiæ amoris* ("the entrance to Love's court") is a figurative expression referring to an essentially psychological commitment.

soning involving a chain of syllogisms interspersed with enthymemes. It follows immediately the passage in which the man vows to resolve the issue at hand by "disputing." He will "prove" (*probare*) his contention, he asserts, that he cannot rightly be deprived of love. First he tries to show that love is a good thing, using a disjunctive syllogism in the *modus tollendo ponens*.[53] Love is either good or bad, he argues. It is not prudent to assert that it is a bad thing, since it is clear to all that neither woman nor man can be regarded as happy or do any good in this world unless inspired by Love. Therefore, one must conclude that love is a good and desirable thing (*DA* 1.6.304–5 [126]). On this conclusion he constructs an enthymeme, assuming a major premise of the type "people who wish to enhance their reputation must do good things," to prove that such people must necessarily love (*DA* 1.6.306 [126–28]).[54] Apparently assuming that all people would like to have a good reputation, he then uses a hypothetical clause to pass from the universal to the particular by means of a deftly ambiguous first person plural (*tenemini,* "we are required"), thus leading into another disjunctive syllogism in the *modus tollendo ponens*. If we are required to love, he continues, we must love either evil men or those of good character. To love evil men is against Love's precepts; therefore it follows that the lady's love should be given only to good men (*DA* 1.6.306 [128]). Finally, building on the conclusion of the second syllogism, that the woman must give her love only to good men, the lover produces an enthymeme to show that, if he is good, she must love him (*DA* 1.6.306 [128]).

If this final conclusion were accepted, it could become the major premise of a hypothetical syllogism whereby the man would have only to prove his own worth to earn an automatic right to the lady's love.

53. A disjunctive syllogism is one that presents an alternative (either/or). The *modus tolendo ponens* is the "mood" in which one "asserts" (*ponere*) one thing while "denying" (*tolere*) its contrary. Cf. Prior, pp. 7–8, 48.

54. The argument is defective, for the man has shown only that "love is a good thing," not that "love is the only good thing," or that "all good things are love," although the latter proposition would be required as a minor premise to arrive at the conclusion "people who wish to enhance their reputation must love." Such a proposition could be derived, not from the conclusion of the previous syllogism, but from the arguments presented in support of its minor premise: "nor can any woman . . . do any good thing in this world unless Love inspires it."

The argument is unacceptable, however, for the man has committed the same error in distribution of terms as in the previous enthymeme: the fact that one must love *some* good man does not mean that one must love *every* good man, which is what would be required for the argument to be valid. The woman is quick to seize upon this point. Conceding the conclusions of the two syllogisms, that love is a good thing and that one should love only good people, she nevertheless reserves the right to love *some other* good man in place of the disputant (*DA* 1.6.307 [128]). The man has allowed for this possibility in his initial statement, declaring that he will show "whether it is right or not for you to refuse me your love, assuming that you have bestowed it on no other suitor" (*DA* 1.6.304 [126]), although he neglects it entirely in the subsequent reasoning. It is doubtless significant that the errors in reasoning occur in the enthymemes, where they are less likely to be detected, whereas the syllogisms are logically sound, as the woman's acquiescence indicates.

As with division and definition, the use of syllogism in the dialogues shows complete familiarity with the technique, although the execution itself often leaves something to be desired. This is not the *disputatio in forma* that became current following the introduction of the *logica nova*, but rather the much freer *disputatio extra formam*.[55] Throughout the dialogues, the formal techniques of dialectic are interspersed with those of rhetoric and adapted to the informal requirements of a rhetorical situation.

Dialectic is concerned not only with the construction of arguments but also with the detection of fallacies in the arguments of an opponent. The latter was the subject of the last of Aristotle's logical works, *De sophisticis elenchis*, whose reintroduction in the twelfth century provided new impetus for the development of the discipline. The dialogues of the *De amore* contain two references to sophistic reasoning. In the First Dialogue the man expresses surprise that the woman should debate in such a "sophistic" manner (*sophistice; DA* 1.6.56 [54]). In the Sixth Dialogue the man accuses the woman of covering her words in a cloak of "sophistry" (*sophistica; DA* 1.6.319 [130]). It is interesting to

55. Grabmann, 2:20.

note that it is the man who makes this accusation in both cases, although the women of the dialogues are certainly no less adept in exposing sophistry, as is clear from several of the examples examined above. Indeed, it is possible that the weaknesses in argumentation observable in the dialogues were put there to illustrate the detection and exposure of fallacious reasoning.

More often than *sophisticus,* it is *fallax,* "false," and its derivatives *fallaciter,* "falsely," and *fallacia,* "fallacy," that are used in the *De amore* to designate fallacy. These occur eight times in the dialogues and thirteen times elsewhere in the treatise. The semantic content of *fallax* wavers, however, between the intellectual sense of "fallacious" and the moral sense of "deceitful." The former meaning dominates in expressions such as *regula fallax* (*DA* 1.6. 363 [144]; 3.72 [308], 106 [318]), the latter in phrases such as *fallax amator.*[56] Andreas apparently considers it obvious that insincere lovers will be prone to use fallacious arguments. The ambiguity of the term provides one of the bridges that the Chaplain builds between science and wisdom.

Much more than the technical mastery of the procedures of debate, it is the constant opposition of contrary ideas that marks the influence of dialectic on the dialogues. The organization of the discourse around a series of disputed questions, the ongoing alternation between disputants defending one or the other side in the controversy, the promptness of the adversaries to detect fallacies in each other's reasoning and to oppose their own distinctions, definitions, and syllogisms to those of their opponents, the continuous striving of each to draw concessions from the other while making a minimum of concessions, are all a reflection of twelfth-century advances in dialectic and of the new emphasis accorded to this art. This same confrontational technique is also applied to conflicting authorities on love, as we shall see in the next chapter. Through it Andreas is able to explore, in the form of debate that was the current scientific idiom of his day, most of the major questions and controversies surrounding his subject.

The general lack of resolution in the dialogues has frequently been remarked. On specific questions there is occasional agreement, as when

---

56. See above, Chapter I, n. 55.

the woman of the Eighth Dialogue accedes, somewhat grudgingly, to the man's preference for the solaces of the upper part of the body (*DA* 1.6.550 [204]). But most of the time the disputants simply agree to disagree and then move on to the next subject (e.g., *DA* 1.6.503 [190]). Nor is there any resolution at the end of the various dialogues: with the exception of the seventh, in which the Countess of Champagne adjudicates the question of love and marriage, they remain open-ended and indeterminate. Some have seen in this state of affairs an ironic reflection on the male lovers, whose lack of tangible success is interpreted as a subtle condemnation of their enterprise.[57] It is perhaps better viewed, however, as an extension of the basic indeterminacy of the dialectical situation. Disputed questions are by definition those for which arguments can be adduced on either side, those for which there are no easy solutions. Theoretically, the confrontation of thesis and antithesis should produce a synthesis, but in practice such a resolution often proves elusive. In *Sic et non,* for example, Abelard was content to juxtapose conflicting authorities on various questions of theology, leaving to his students the task of trying to reconcile them.[58] His procedure can perhaps be seen as a model for the open-endedness of Andreas's dialogues.

Although the dialogues provide the best illustration in the *De amore* of the dialectical confrontation of opposing opinions, this phenomenon is by no means limited to them. Indeed, it extends well beyond the dialogues to form much of the texture of the entire treatise. The most striking use of dialectic outside the dialogues can be seen in the Love Cases of Book Two, Chapter Seven. Each of these cases presents a dialectical structure of opposition of ideas, embodied in the brief summary of a forensic debate, although they differ from the dialogues in that a

---

57. Robertson, *Preface*, pp. 442–43.

58. Abelard, Prologue to *Sic et non,* in Minnis and Scott, p. 99: "This having been said by way of preliminary, it is my purpose, according to my original intention, to gather together various sayings of the holy Fathers which have occurred to me as being surrounded by some degree of uncertainty because of their seeming incompatibility. These may encourage inexperienced readers to engage in that most important exercise, inquiry into truth, and as a result of that inquiry give an edge to their critical faculty." Cf. ed. Boyer and McKeon, p. 103.

resolution is achieved through the intervention of a third party who pronounces a judgment. Moreover, we have seen that several of the cases (II, XII, XIV) develop disputed questions already discussed in the Eighth Dialogue, and that another (IX) makes significant use of the dialectical technique of *divisio*. In many respects the Love Cases of Book Two are simply an extension of the debate of the dialogues.

Beyond the dialogues and the cases, the dialectical mode of thinking is often evident even in passages where Andreas speaks with a single, authoritative voice. This tendency is already apparent early in the treatise, for example in the dialectic established at the beginning of Book One, Chapter Six (*DA* 1.6. 3–15 [42–44]) between physical beauty and worth of character as means of acquiring love. It is even more apparent in passages in which the Chaplain himself again takes up disputed questions previously discussed, as in the following examples.

In the authorial commentary introducing the Third Dialogue, Andreas returns to the question of nobility that has provided much of the material for discussion in the first two dialogues (*DA* 1.6.28–39 [48–50], 71–113 [60–72]). He places in dialectical opposition the theme of nobility of merit, defended by the men, and the class consciousness of the northern French aristocracy, represented by the women, reaching the conclusion that, if a woman of the higher nobility finds a man of equal or greater worth among the higher classes, she ought to prefer him; otherwise, a worthy commoner should not be rejected (*DA* 1.6.120 [74]). Thus merit receives its due, but only after the requirements of caste have been satisfied. The solution proposed by Andreas is clearly an attempt to synthesize the antithetical positions defended by the disputants of the dialogues.

In Book One, Chapter Seven, the Chaplain takes up again the love of the clergy, a major subject of discussion in the Eighth Dialogue (*DA* 1.6.478–99 [182–88]). Here the dialectical chain of reasoning is more complex, requiring several steps to reach a synthesis. First Andreas recalls that highest nobility that he claimed for the clergy at the very beginning of the dialogues (*DA* 1.7.1 [208]; cf. *DA* 1.6.20 [46]). To this he opposes the objection, raised by the woman of the Eighth Dialogue, that such "nobility" excludes the pursuit of love (*DA* 1.7.2 [210]). The objection is then countered by the "weakness of the flesh" argument, invoked by the man in the same dialogue. Andreas concludes that clerics are not required to renounce love, but only the use of their "higher nobility" in the pursuit of it (*DA* 1.7.4 [210]). Once again the desire to reach a synthesis is clearly evident.

Such passages illustrate a phenomenon widespread throughout the treatise and in large measure determinate of its basic structure and texture: the written adaptation and transposition of the techniques of oral debate. It is the same procedure that will produce the great scholastic *summæ* of the thirteenth century. Through it Andreas is able to bring together a great many conflicting opinions on the complex subject of love and to attempt to synthesize them, with more or less success according to the subject. For some disputed questions at least a provisional synthesis is achieved in the Love Cases of Book Two or in the Chaplain's authorial comments. For others such a resolution remains elusive. Nevertheless, the intention to synthesize whenever possible is everywhere apparent. Consequently, it is possible to see in the *De amore* a kind of twelfth-century *summa* on love, not unlike Abelard's *Sic et non* or Peter Lombard's *Sentences* for theology, or Gratian's *Decretum* for canon law.

It is in the light of this dialectical method apparent throughout the *De amore* that one should examine the most controversial aspect of the treatise: the relationship of Book Three to the first two books. The third book stands in sharp contrast and opposition to the main thrust of the two preceding books, hence the difficulty and the controversy. This relationship is precisely the antithetical relationship of dialectic, which thus can be seen to inform the treatise as a whole.

Not only does the third book respond in a general way to the two earlier books, but many of its specific arguments take up again matters already discussed, particularly in the dialogues, offering propositions antithetical to those previously presented. The argument developed near the beginning of the Book Three, for example, that loving is odious to God (*DA* 3.3–7 [286–88]), continues the discussion of this subject in the Eighth Dialogue, adopting the position defended there by the woman (*DA* 1.6.411 [160]) and refuting the contrary opinions of the man (*DA* 1.6. 415–17 [162]). The argument that follows immediately in Book Three, that love harms one's neighbors (*DA* 3.8 [288]), also develops the subject that follows immediately in the corresponding passage of the Eighth Dialogue (*DA* 1.6.411 [160], 418–19 [162]), thus underlining the fact that the later passage is a conscious reply to the earlier discussion. The contention put forward later in Book Three that love is the source of all evil (*DA* 3.33 [296]) is obviously an antithetical response to the assertion of Book One, Chapter Four, that love is the source of all virtue (*DA* 1.4.1 [38]), an argument frequently advanced by the men of the dialogues (e.g., *DA* 1.6.211 [100], 305 [126]). Even the question of the love of the clergy, which was apparently resolved in Book One, Chapter Seven, is reintroduced in the third book, with new arguments that cast doubt on the earlier conclusion (*DA* 3.34 [296]). Like the Love Cases of Book Two and the passages of authorial commentary in the first two books, Book Three is simply a continuation of the debate.

Recognition of the role of dialectic in the structuring of the *De amore* renders unnecessary the recourse to the Averroist doctrine of the "two truths" to explain the relationship between Book Three and the two previous books.[59] It is possible, of course, that, influenced by the Latin Averroism that was current in his day, Bishop Tempier saw such a doctrine as implicit in Andreas's treatise, and therefore condemned the treatise, along with a number of other works that definitely did participate in that tendency. It would be entirely anachronistic, however, to imagine that the Chaplain himself could have been influenced by a doctrine that had barely been formulated in his day and that penetrated into the West only much later. Nor is there the slightest hint of the enunciation of such a doctrine anywhere in the *De amore*. The relationship of the third book to the rest of the treatise is a matter not of doctrine but of method, of a method that had very ancient antecedents in the West and that reached its culmination in the northern France in the Twelfth-Century Renaissance.

Unlike many earlier passages where Andreas speaks with a single, authorial voice, the third book makes no attempt to synthesize. On the contrary, here the Chaplain seems intent on polarizing the discussion

---

59. Denomy. For a recent critique of this hypothesis, see Hissette, "André le Chapelain"; idem, "Une *duplex sententia*."

by adopting the most extreme positions imaginable. It is in that spirit that he asserts that all evil comes from love, echoing the equally exaggerated claim that love is the source of all good, or that he punctuates his virulent anti-feminist diatribes with statements to the effect that the rules which he is enunciating admit of no exception (*DA* 3.72, 73–74 [308], 79 [310], 106 [318]). Adhering strictly to the rules of debate, Andreas makes no concessions. The unmediated juxtaposition of antithetical discourses renders the entire treatise, like the dialogues, open-ended and indeterminate. It is especially this lack of resolution that has disconcerted the critics.

The elaborate disputed question that Andreas has constructed in the *De amore*, that which opposes the conflicting claims of human love and divine law, cannot be resolved at the level of human science, but only at that of divine wisdom. That fact is reflected in the uncompromising stance that the Chaplain adopts in the final book of his treatise. Despairing of finding a viable synthesis by means of human reasoning and argumentation, Andreas resorts to the ultimate authority of Holy Scripture to provide a kind of resolution. That is why, at the very end of the treatise, he abandons dialectic and returns to the rhetorical frame established in the Preface, substituting for the impossible synthesis the divine rhetoric of Christian exhortation.

3 ❀

THE INTERTEXTUALITY
OF LOVE

Authorities and Models

Having examined in Chapter 2 the use that Andreas makes of the liberal arts of the trivium, we must now take a closer look at his relationship to his sources. The two subjects are closely related, for it is the application of the liberal arts, especially dialectic, to textual material inherited from the past that constitutes the core of medieval scholasticism. Andreas's relationship to his sources comprises two distinct but related aspects: the citation of authoritative opinions in support of arguments and the use of earlier texts as models for his own discourse. In the interest of clarity, we shall treat them separately, while keeping in mind their interrelatedness. But first a word about the medieval notion of *auctoritas.*

Auctoritas and intertextuality

The concept of *auctoritas* played an important role in the medieval liberal-arts curriculum. An established but flexible canon of author-authorities *(auctores)* served as the basis for grammatical studies. They were also one of the chief sources of topical invention for rhetorical and dialectical argumentation.[1]

At least as early as Quintilian (1.4.2), grammar was defined as com-

1. Curtius, pp. 48–54, 247–64.

prising two parts: the science of speaking correctly and the art of interpreting the poets. This is because the poets to be interpreted also served as models to be imitated in matters of usage and style. In the twelfth century John of Salisbury invokes Quintilian in his *Metalogicon* (1.24) in describing one of the basic medieval school exercises, *lectio,* as practiced by Bernard of Chartres. *Lectio* was the reading of and commentary upon the curriculum authors, who were also committed to memory, recited, and imitated in original compositions. In his *Didascalicon* (6.8–11), Hugh of St. Victor also describes the exercise of *lectio,* which progressed in three steps from the *littera* to the *sensus* and finally to the *sententia,* that is from analysis of the grammatical construction to the literal meaning and from there to the deeper moral or mystical meaning.

In the *Topics* (1.1, 100a30–b17; 100b21–23), Aristotle defines dialectic as reasoning from generally accepted opinions, that is, from the opinions of all or of the majority or of the wise. Cicero, in his rhetorical *Topica* (2.8), distinguishes between "intrinsic arguments," which are inherent in the nature of the subject under discussion, and "extrinsic arguments," which depend principally on authority. Boethius synthesized the Aristotelian and Ciceronian doctrines in his *De differentiis topicis,* incorporating in particular the distinction between intrinsic and extrinsic arguments. It was in this form that the classical doctrine of authority was transmitted to the Middle Ages, where it would thus play an important role in the other basic school exercise, *disputatio,* as well as in the specifically medieval forms of rhetoric, namely the arts of preaching, letter writing, and poetry.

The literary tradition of medieval schools was strengthened by two other sources of authority: the religious tradition of the theologians and the juridical tradition of canonists and lawyers. Christianity was a religion of written authority, a religion of the Book. All speculation in theology had as its point of departure the Bible and its authorized interpretation by the Fathers. Despite the ambivalence toward classical pagan authors that emerged periodically, medieval Christianity ultimately strengthened the notion of authority as applied to them by viewing them as a secular dispensation of divine wisdom and by allegorizing the incompatible elements. Like theology, jurisprudence depended upon an authoritative text, the *Corpus juris civilis,* the decretals, and the like, which the medieval commentator merely interpreted. From Quintilian (8.5.3) on, the term most often used for quotations of authority is a legal term, *sententia,* which originally designated the judgment or decision of a public body.

Beginning in the mid-twelfth century, literary studies suffered a decline owing to the rise of dialectic. It was in part this tendency that John of Salisbury decried in attacking the Cornificians in Book I of the *Metalogicon.*[2] This development did not signal the end of the *auctores,* but rather their transformation, for if they were no longer studied as authors, they were increasingly cited as authorities. This explains the semantic evolution of the term *auctoritas:* originally designating the prestige of the author or, by metonymy, the author himself, it came to mean a passage quoted from the author's works.[3] A concomitant movement inseparable from the rise of dialectic was the development of the *sic et non* method, the systematic compilation and confrontation of all the various existing authorities on a given subject. Another related development was the rise of *florilegia* or *flores auctorum,* compilations of excerpts from the authors, arranged by subject or by author or alphabetically, that flourished particularly in France in the late-twelfth and thirteenth centuries, providing a shortcut to grammatical and moral studies and a ready source of quotable quotes from the classics.

The authors were put to various uses in the Middle Ages, beyond being models of usage and style. Many served as technical authorities for particular disciplines: Donatus and Priscian for grammar, Cicero for rhetoric, Aristotle for logic, Galen for medicine, Vegetius for warfare, Vitruvius for architecture, Palladius for agriculture, and so on. But they were especially a source of worldly wisdom and general philosophy, expressed in the form of *sententiæ* and *exempla,* hence the close relationship between the study of the trivium, particularly grammar, and the teaching of ethics in the twelfth century.[4]

The concept of authority implies the establishment of a canon, a selection of those writers held to be most authoritative. This is already implicit in Aristotle's reference to "the wise." The prestige and popular-

---

2. Tacchella.
3. Chenu; Minnis, *Medieval Theory,* pp. 10–12.
4. Curtius, pp. 57–61; Delhaye, "L'Enseignement"; idem, "'Grammatica.'"

ity of different authors varied greatly in the Middle Ages and were sometimes subject to changes in fashion, but such was the prestige of the written word that any author was, ipso facto, potentially an authority. The lists of curriculum authors that have come down to us reproduce certain names with great regularity, but no two such lists are exactly alike. In general, the lists tend to grow longer as time goes on and to include more and more contemporary medieval authors alongside the standard classical and patristic sources. Medieval distinctions between authors tend to be more generic than qualitative. Some writers do rank them qualitatively, but much more common is the distinction that takes *auctor* as a synonym of *poeta,* opposing it to *philosophus,* that is, any prose writer. Another distinction opposes the ancients and the moderns: only the former are *auctores;* the latter are called *magistri,* and though their opinions carry authority, it is not *authentica.* But many medieval writers put ancient and medieval, pagan and Christian, authors side by side, as if all participated in the same timeless, undifferentiated authority.[5]

In the Middle Ages all intellectual activity, whether speculative, practical, or esthetic, had as its point of departure a previous text or texts. Medieval science has as its aim not the making of new discoveries but rather the re-elaboration of traditional, inherited knowledge. Far from expressing pride in their own originality, medieval poets often ground their discourse in some authoritative source. Medieval literature is thus an ideal ground for the study of "intertextuality." It is probably not by chance that this concept was first developed in connection with the study of a medieval work, *Le Petit Jehan de Saintré* of Antoine de la Sale.[6] Medieval literature is intertextual literature *par excellence.*

The notion of "intertextuality" has several advantages with respect to the traditional study of sources. It recognizes that, beyond concrete, conscious contacts between authors, all texts are produced within a given intellectual climate that includes many other texts as well as the generic and cultural norms and expectations that they embody. It envisages a much more dynamic relationship between text and source, including critical reaction as well as imitation, the stretching of bound-

5. Curtius, pp. 251–64, 464–67.   6. Kristeva.

aries, and the violation of norms. It sees a similar dynamic obtaining between texts and non-textual systems of meaning in the ambient culture, including other art forms as well as social institutions. All these features are pertinent to the assessment of Andreas's relationship to his sources, to which we can now turn.

Andreas and authority

The sources used by Andreas in composing the *De amore* have long constituted a subject of interest and investigation for scholars. Beginning with the limited suggestions of E. Trojel (pp. liv–lvi) and Max Manitius (3:285–86), our knowledge of the subject has been advanced especially by John J. Parry and P. G. Walsh, in the copious annotation accompanying their respective translations. Other studies have identified possible sources for particular passages of the treatise. The purpose of the present study is neither to assemble nor to critique all the various suggestions that have been made concerning Andreas's sources, much less to add to them. Rather, taking as my point of departure the identifications made by earlier scholars, particularly Parry and Walsh, I shall attempt to synthesize their findings and draw some conclusions concerning the use that the Chaplain makes of his sources.[7]

Andreas's concern for authority is illustrated by his use of the term *auctoritas* in eight passages to introduce an opinion, such as the expression *Iacobi apostoli auctoritas* referring to the Epistle of St. James (*DA* 3.56 [302]) or *physicalis auctoritas* introducing a medical opinion (*DA* 3.57 [304]).[8] *Auctor* also occurs nine times, usually with the same function.[9] *Sententia,* often a synonym of *auctoritas,* is found thirty-three times, but only in a few cases does it introduce citations of authority, as in the expression *Pauli sententia* (*DA* 1.6.415 [162]).[10]

In assessing the use to which authority is put in the *De amore,* we

---

7. For an earlier version of this section, see Monson, *"Auctoritas."*

8. *DA* 1.6.345 (140), 465 (178), 486 (184), 563 (208); 2.6.23 (244); 3.13 (290), 56–57 (302–4).

9. *DA* 1.6.384 (152), 425 (166), 494 (186), 508 (190), 515 (192); 3.38 [3 times], 39 (298). The four occurrences in Book Three are metaphorical, naming the devil as the "author" (i.e., source) of evil and God as the "author" of good.

10. The most common meaning in the treatise for *sententia* is that of "opinion" or

must first determine what constitutes an invocation of authority for Andreas, beyond these most obvious examples. Laurent Jenny has addressed this problem in general terms in his fundamental article on intertextuality. According to Jenny, intertextuality in the truest sense is characterized by the presence within a text of previously structured elements beyond the lexeme level. This he opposes to simple allusions or reminiscences, which constitute cases of "weak" intertextuality.[11] Elaborating somewhat on this distinction, we can identify six different types of references in the *De amore* that might be included as citations of authority, with some overlap between certain categories.

The first type involves the use of personal proper names to identify the source of authoritative opinions. The most obvious examples in this category are references to the standard classical and Christian authors, such as Ovid or St. Paul. These may introduce either a direct quotation or only a general allusion. In only one case is the work invoked, Cicero's *De amicitia*, also cited by name. In some cases the attributions are erroneous (Iohannicius; Marcianus [Capella]), but this in no way affects the mechanism of the reference. A related but distinct phenomenon is the use of the names of historical or literary personages, such as the Old Testament king David or the Trojan prince Paris, who become exemplary figures in support of a particular argument. One personage, Solomon, is invoked sometimes as an author and sometimes as an exemplary figure.

The second category is the use of a generic common name to indicate an authoritative source. In many cases this involves the figure of antonomasia, the substitution of a general term for the proper name of an author. For example, *regula logicorum,* "the rule of the logicians," introduces a quotation derived either from Aristotle or from Boethius (*DA* 1.6.118 [72]). Ovid is twice referred to as *sapiens,* "the wise man"

"contention," referring to the positions defended by the disputants in the dialogues. In the Love Cases of Book Two it has the juridical meaning of "sentence" or "judgment." However, the man of the Eighth Dialogue cites one such judgment, called *sententia,* as an authoritative opinion (*DA* 1.6.444 [170]). Andreas reinforces the authority of one opinion cited by stressing its antiquity: *antiqua sententia* (*DA* 2.6.15 [242]). Elsewhere *sententia* means "meaning," as it *proverbii sententia* (*DA* 1.6.30 [48]; cf. 1.6.59 [56]; 3.12 [290], 117 [322]).

11. Jenny, pp. 40–41.

(*DA* 3.89, 94 [314]), St. Paul is called *apostolus,* "the apostle," and a passage from Psalms is attributed to *propheta,* "the prophet." It is to this category that we can ascribe the frequent use of the words *proverbium* or *sententia* to introduce quotations, only some of which are genuine popular sayings, as well as the many paraphrases used to refer to the Bible: *evangelica veritas, divina auctoritas, sacra scriptura,* and the like. In some cases a passive verb form such as *legitur,* "we read," is used to refer to a literary source (e.g., *DA* 1.6.499 [188]; cf. Gen. 3.6).

The third category includes verbatim quotations from literary sources that are in no way identified as such. Often these quotations are introduced simply by the conjunction *quia,* "because," indicating their demonstrative function with respect to an argument. A number of them are familiar biblical passages that would be recognizable to many readers even today. Many others are in verse, such as the elegiac verse of Ovid's love poetry, a fact that contributes both to their recognizability and to their authority.

The fourth category comprises non-verbatim quotations, general allusions, and vague reminiscences based on literary sources. Even more than for the preceding group, the identification of these passages depends almost entirely upon the general culture of the reader. For medieval clerics, schooled in the authors and conversant with the *florilegia,* many such references would have been immediately recognizable. For most modern readers the annotation provided by editors and translators such as Parry and Walsh constitutes an indispensable aid.

The fifth category is that of commonplaces referring not to a particular work or author, but rather to an entire genre or tradition. These allusions will generally be recognized by anyone familiar with the tradition from which they derive. In some cases it may be difficult to decide whether we are dealing with a vague allusion to a particular author or with a commonplace from the author's tradition.

The last category is that of references to non-literary and perhaps even non-verbal traditions such as social "reality." This kind of reference can be introduced in a variety of ways, most of which closely parallel the traditional citation of literary authority. Some opinions are supported by the use of proper names referring not to authors in the traditional sense but rather to prominent social figures. Some are introduced by generic common names, such as *vulgus,* "the crowd," *vulgares,* "common people," *sapientes,* "wise people," or *consuetudo,* "custom." Others are introduced by indefinite pronouns: *multi,* "many people," *quidam,* "certain people," or *quilibet,* "anyone." Finally, a number of such opinions are introduced by passive verb form: *videtur,* "it seems"; *reputator* or *præsumitur,* "it is thought"; *invenitur,* "we find"; *dicitur* or *fertur,* "it is said"; and so on.

The six types of authoritative reference that we have delineated are obviously not of equal weight. The first three types, proper names or generic terms indicating a source and unannounced verbatim quotations, are strongly intertextual and constitute authorities of the classic variety. The last three, vague allusions to particular literary source, commonplaces derived from entire traditions, and references to non-literary traditions, are weak intertexts that must clearly be interpreted with caution but that, just as clearly, should not be ignored.

In terms of origin, the authorities invoked by Andreas may be classified in two broad categories: clerical and courtly. This is not particularly surprising, for one of the few things that we know about the man whom several of the manuscripts call "chaplain of the King of France" *(capellanus regius Francorum)* is that he was both a cleric and a courtier. Indeed, it is the intersection between the clerical and courtly traditions in the *De amore* that constitutes the work's originality and provides much of its interest, as well as its difficulty.

Written in Latin, the clerical sources are the standard sources of medieval authority. They may be further divided into two sub-traditions: the pagan authors of classical antiquity and Christian writers, from the Bible and the Fathers to contemporary scholastics. The pagan classical authors are sometimes invoked for questions of method, as with the "rule of the logicians" previously mentioned or a passage on memory from the *Rhetorica ad Herennium,* which Andreas erroneously attributes to Cicero (*DA* 1.6.409 [160]). But most of the classical quotations deal with matters of substance.

The most frequently quoted classical author is Ovid, who is named only once (*DA* 1.6.8 [42]), but who provides fifteen verbatim or nearly verbatim quotations (in four cases the same passage is quoted twice).[12] Parry identifies five possible allusions to Ovid's poetry, to which Walsh adds another thirty, and several others have been suggested recently by Francis Cairns. The *Ars amatoria* and *Remedia amoris* will also figure prominently in the discussion of Andreas's models. Cicero is named four times in support of authoritative opinions, including the references to the *Ad Herennium* and the *De amicitia*. Parry and Walsh cite eleven other possible allusions to Cicero's writings, some doubtless classical commonplaces. There are no direct quotations from Cicero, only reminiscences of his works, perhaps because he is a prose writer. The only other classical authors named are Martianus Capella, to whom a passage from Virgil is wrongly attributed, and Donatus, for whom the reference has not been identified. Generic terms designating classical authors include *sapiens* referring to Ovid (twice) or to Cicero. In addition to Paris, two other classical figures are named as exemplary figures: Cato and Epicurus, exemplifying experience and gluttony.

After Ovid, the classical author most frequently quoted is Horace: four verbatim quotations from his poetry have been identified, along with two possible allusions. Three others, Claudian, Lucan, and Virgil, provide one verbatim quotation each. Except for the "rule of the logicians," all verbatim quotations are in verse. With three exceptions, the verse quotations can be found in Hans Walther, *Lateinische Sprichwörter und Sentenzen des Mittelalters,* so Andreas may be quoting from *florilegia.*[13] Parry and Walsh suggest another forty-five possible allusions to another dozen classical authors, those most frequently mentioned being Aristotle, Juvenal, and Seneca. Many passages for which more than one author can be cited are probably classical commonplaces.

The most important Christian source in the *De amore* is the Bible. Parry and Walsh have identified more than seventy biblical quotations or allusions, making the Bible by far Andreas's most important single

---

12. *DA* 1.2.7 (36), 3.19 (292) [*RA* 749]; 1.6.7 (42), 3.89 (314) [*Amores* 3.4.17]; 1.6.8 (42) [*Heroides* 4.75–76]; 1.6.34 (48), 3.25 (294) [*Metamorphoses* 2.846]; 1.6.100 (68) [*RA* 422]; 1.6.247 (110) [*Heroides* 4.11]; 1.8.4 (212) [*Heroides* 4.154]; 2.3.1 (230), 3.12 (290) [*Tristia* 1.9.5–6]; 3.14 (290) [*Heroides* 1.12]; 3.74 (308) [*AA* 1.349–50]; 3.94 (314) [*Fasti* 1.419].

13. Three of these quotations are introduced by the words *proverbium antiquum,* "an ancient proverb," and two are also quoted by Walter of Châtillon, both of which point to the same conclusion.

source from any tradition. More than one-half of the biblical passages are identified as such through the use of proper names or generic terms. In addition to five references to the biblical authors James, Paul, or Solomon, seven biblical passages are attributed to "God," "the Lord," or the "Author of truth." In ten passages exemplary figures from the Bible are mentioned by name: in addition to David and Solomon, Eve (three times), the Good Samaritan, and Samson. Another seventeen biblical passages are introduced by generic references to Scripture.[14]

For the patristic and medieval period, only one clerical source is mentioned by name: "Iohannicius," that is, Honeïn-ben-Ishaq, a ninth-century Arabic physician, to whom a medical opinion is wrongly attributed. Three generic expressions are used to identify clerical sources from the same period: *apostolica lex,* "apostolic law," and *sanctorum patrum regulæ,* "the rules of the holy fathers," introduce Christian commonplaces, and *physicalis auctoritas,* "the physicians," introduces an unidentified medical opinion. The *Facetus* ("Moribus et vita") attributed to Aurigena is the only medieval Latin work providing a verbatim quotation; that part of the *Facetus* also circulated as a pseudo-Ovidian *Remedia amoris,* but the verse in question is found among Walther's *Sprichwörter,* so Andreas's immediate source may be a *florilegium.* Parry and Walsh identify some fifty possible allusions to about two dozen different patristic and medieval philosophers, theologians, and poets. Those most frequently cited are Alan of Lille, St. Augustine, St. Jerome, and John of Salisbury. Walsh points to several reminiscences of the liturgy, as well as a number of possible references to canon law, to which the many examples catalogued by Rüdiger Schnell must be added. Many of the passages in question are doubtless medieval commonplaces. Medieval clerical culture also provided some important models for the *De amore,* beginning with its basic form as a scholastic treatise.

14. *Divina auctoritas/. . . mandatum/. . . scriptura; evangelica auctoritas/. . . lex/. . . scriptura/. . . sermo/. . . veritas* (3 times); *sacræ scriptæ; scriptura* (4 times); *sacra . . ./theologica scriptura.* Of the 74 biblical quotations or allusions identified, 41 (55%) come from the New Testament. As with Ovid, several biblical passages are cited more than once. In terms of distribution, 45 biblical passages, about three-fifths of the total, are found in Book One, with all the others in Book Three. Those introduced by proper or generic names are evenly distributed, with 20 in Book One, 19 in Book Three. No biblical allusion has been identified for Book Two.

In addition to these traditional, clerical sources of authority, Andreas invokes other sources that we may call courtly. Like the clerical tradition, the courtly tradition may be divided into two sub-traditions: that of vernacular love poetry and that of contemporary feudal society. The inclusion of such sources alongside Ovid or the Bible would appear to be a bold innovation on the part of Andreas, yet it may also be seen as a simple extension of the flexible, open-ended canon of medieval authorities. At the same time, Andreas's practice attests to the increased prestige in the late-twelfth century of the courtly milieu and its vernacular literature.

Andreas's treatment of his courtly sources is quite different from that of his clerical sources, if only for linguistic reasons. Like the clerical sources, the treatise was written in Latin, whereas the courtly sources were presumably in the vernacular. Here we have no trace of the bilingual technique later to be used by Gérard of Liège.[15] Andreas's method is that which will be adopted by Jean de Meun, but in reverse: just as Jean de Meun translates many Latin authors into French, so Andreas Latinizes his vernacular sources.[16] Consequently, we have no direct quotations from these sources, only allusions and commonplaces.

Andreas names no vernacular poets, but we must remember that many vernacular works are anonymous and that many others are best known by the names of their principal characters. Andreas does cite four characters from vernacular poetry as exemplary figures. Hugo of Auvergne, hero of a lost romance of the same name, is cited as an example of a man loved by a woman he has not wooed (*DA* 1.6.517 [194]). Exemplifying virgins who nevertheless loved, Iseult and Blanchefleur are named, along with a third figure who, depending on the manuscript, is either Anfelis from the romanticized epic *Folque de Candie* or else Fenice from Chrétien de Troyes's *Cligès* (*DA* 1.6.468 [178]).

Several narrative passages with strong links to vernacular poetry function as *exempla* in support of various arguments. The allegorical episode in the Fifth Dialogue known as the "Purgatory of Cruel Beauties," showing the fate awaiting women who reject love, is very close in

15. Carlson.
16. Regalado.

content to the contemporary Old French poem *Lai du Trot.*[17] The Arthurian adventures of the anonymous Briton knight that close Book Two, illustrating the winning of love through the accomplishment of deeds of prowess, contain narrative material with parallels in several Old French romances, including two of those by Chrétien de Troyes.[18] Both these passages fulfill a dual function in the *De amore,* not only serving as *exempla,* but also providing a basis of authority for the two lists of precepts or rules that they introduce, an authority emanating directly from the vernacular poetry. Finally, we should mention the anecdote in Book Two, introduced by the word *legitur,* "we read," illustrating the disobedience of women (*DA* 3.90–91 [314]); Per Nykrog has found several analogues for it among the *fabliaux.*[19]

In addition to these fairly explicit references to the courtly poetic tradition, the argumentation of the treatise is interspersed throughout with thematic material drawn from the vernacular poetry. In some cases we can perhaps suspect allusions to particular poets, as with the theme of far-away love made famous by Jaufre Rudel, but, by and large, we are dealing with commonplaces attributable to the entire courtly tradition.[20] For some of the courtly themes, such as the five stages of love, antecedents and parallels can also be found in classical and medieval Latin literature.

Among the courtly themes repeatedly developed by Andreas we find: the ennobling power of love, the necessity for fidelity and for concealment, the haughtiness of the lady, the danger of slanderers, the importance of sight and beauty in the generation of love, the passion of the lover, the beloved as object of dreams and meditation, and love as a cause of suffering and death. Likewise, many of the anti-feminist arguments developed in Book Three can be traced to the *fabliaux* tradition, although here we are perhaps dealing with two independent developments of a long anti-feminist tradition in Christian clerical writings.

17. O'Hara-Tobin, pp. 335–47. Cf. Grimes; Neilson.

18. Nitze, pp. 450–51.

19. Nykrog, p. 202.

20. Walsh cites some twenty parallels in vernacular poets such as Bernart de Ventadorn, Cercamon, Marcabru, Peire Vidal, Chrétien de Troyes, Gautier d'Arras, and Marie de France. Most of the themes could also be illustrated by other poets.

Several of the poetic genres cultivated in the vernacular literature provided important models for different parts of the *De amore*.

The last sub-tradition that constitutes a source of authority in the *De amore* is that comprising the attitudes and practices of contemporary feudal society, specifically that of the court. This aspect involves us in Julia Kristeva's broad definition of intertextuality, which includes transpositions between any two systems of signs, be they literary, oral, symbolic, social, or unconscious.[21] Andreas certainly does appear to practice this type of non-literary intertextual reference, although documents that would allow us to monitor the process are by definition lacking. This further extension of the notion of authority can be justified in terms of a common medieval metaphor that sees the world or nature as a book.[22]

The most obvious appeal to a social intertext is the use of prominent ladies of the court to decide disputed questions in three of the dialogues of Book One and in the Love Cases of Book Two. Playing on the ambiguity of the term *sententia*, which is used several times in this connection, the pronouncements of the ladies are both juridical "judgments" and authoritative "quotations," as is clear from the fact that some are cited elsewhere in the treatise.

The man of the Fifth Dialogue cites the authority of Eleanor of Aquitaine concerning the relative weight of nobility and worth of character (*DA* 1.6.185 [92]). The same queen is called upon to decide at least three of the Love Cases of Book Two, Chapter Seven (II, VI, and VII); three other decisions (Cases XVII, XIX, and XX,) are rendered by a person designated as "the queen," probably Eleanor, though some have argued that Adèle, queen of France, is intended. At the end of the Seventh Dialogue the question of the compatibility of love and marriage is adjudicated by the Countess of Champagne, presumably Eleanor's daughter Marie, whose decision is subsequently cited as authoritative by the man of the Eighth Dialogue (*DA* 1.6.444 [170]) and by the queen in Love Case XVII. Another opinion of the countess concerning the fidelity of prostitutes is cited by the Chaplain himself (*DA* 2.6.36 [248]), and seven of the Love Cases are entrusted to her arbitration.[23]

---

21. Jenny, pp. 38–40.   22. Curtius, pp. 319–26.
23. Cases I, III, IV, V, XIV, XVI, and XXI.

Two other noble ladies, Ermengarde, Viscountess of Narbonne, and Isabelle, Countess of Flanders, render another seven decisions between them.[24] Love Case XVIII is decided by the ladies of a court assembled in Gascony, and sixty other ladies are associated with the judgment rendered by the Countess of Champagne in Case XVI. Andreas himself cites "the decision of the ladies" (*DA* 2.6.31 [246]), for a matter not discussed in any of the Love Cases. He also discusses the procedure for submitting cases to ladies (*DA* 2.6.33 [248]), as does one of the decisions of the Countess of Champagne (Case XXI).

The practice of submitting disputed questions concerning love to the arbitration of ladies of the court was probably suggested by the dilemmatic debate poems of the vernacular literature, known as *partimen* or *joc partit,* where noble ladies are called upon to perform a similar function. Of course, it is impossible for us to know whether these ladies ever expressed such opinions or whether they even held them. Yet it is clear that Andreas attributes to them an authority not unlike that of the curriculum authors, and that this authority is based not on their literary activity, but on the prestige of their social standing. The appeal is to a social authority, though supported by a literary model.

The king of Hungary, outstanding for the contrast between his bad looks and his good character, evoked in the Third Dialogue (*DA* 1.6.143 [80]), is an exemplary figure, not unlike Paris or David in function, but drawn from contemporary society. The same is true of the handsome but debased Italian count with whom the Hungarian king is contrasted (*DA* 1.6.142 [78]), except that he is a negative example. The "very noble Robert" mentioned in the Fifth Dialogue (*DA* 1.6.229 [104]) could perhaps be considered in this light, though his function is primarily to reinforce the authority of the *exemplum* that follows.

The genuine proverbs quoted should doubtless also be included as social intertexts, but their identification is no simple matter. The word *proverbium* occurs fourteen times in the treatise, generally with reference to authoritative opinions.[25] In two cases the expression is *vulgare proverbium* (*DA* 1.6.29 [48], 507 [190]), apparently ascribing a popular

---

24. Ermengarde: Cases VIII, IX, X, XI, XV; Isabelle: Cases XII, XIII.

25. *DA* 1.6.29–30 (48), 425–26, 431 (166), 432 (168) [twice], 500 (188), 507 (190), 515 (192), 546 (204); 3.12 (290), 74 (308), 85 (312).

origin to the saying. In three cases, however, the expression *proverbium antiquum* designates quotations from Ovid and Lucan. In three other cases, including one in which the *proverbium* is described as *vulgare,* the passage in question comes from the biblical book of Proverbs (*DA* 1.6.29 [48], 425–26 [166]). Of the twenty-nine passages from the *De amore* to be found among Walther's *Sprichwörter,* twenty-two are, in fact, quotations from the classical poets (Ovid, Horace, Lucan, Claudian) or from the *Facetus,* and three others are from the Bible (Proverbs, Ecclesiastes). The remaining five may be genuine popular sayings, for they are of unknown origin, though one of them is quoted by John of Salisbury (*DA* 1.6.220 [102]); the Old French equivalent of another can be found in the collection *Li Proverbe au vilain* (*DA* 1.6.523 [196]). The treatise also contains several other unidentified quotations that are introduced either as proverbs (*DA* 1.6.515 [192]), or recognizably in verse (*DA* 1.6.15 [44]), or both (*DA* 1.6.507 [190], 546 [204]).

Finally, Andreas calls upon a certain number of social commonplaces, often identified by an appeal to public opinion. In his introduction to the Third Dialogue (*DA* 1.6.118–19 [72–74]), for example, he invokes the class consciousness of the feudal courts, which he sets dialectically against the poetic commonplace of "nobility of character," while appealing explicitly to "what people will think." We know from other sources that this class consciousness was stronger in northern France than in the south and that it had gained momentum in the course of the twelfth century.[26] Thus we can be reasonably sure that Andreas's argument is based on the authority of a certain social reality.

A special problem is presented by the characters' references to Andreas's own work in certain of the dialogues or Love Cases. In the Seventh Dialogue the man of the higher nobility, referring apparently to Book One, Chapter Five, of the treatise, invokes the authority of "the teaching of Andreas the Lover, chaplain of the royal court" (*DA* 1.6.385 [152]). In deciding Love Case XII in Book Two, the Countess of Flanders also cites "the teaching of the Chaplain" (*DA* 2.7.26 [260]), referring again to the same chapter. And in communicating his Twelve Precepts at the end of the Fifth Dialogue, the God of Love advises the

26. M. Bloch, 2:320–44; Frappier, "Vues," pp. 145–56.

nobleman to seek further clarification "in the book written to Walter" (*DA* 1.6.269 [116]), another obvious reference to the *De amore*.

Not only do the fictional characters cite Andreas and his treatise, they also quote each other. The man of the Eighth Dialogue refers explicitly (*DA* 1.6.438 [170]) to the discussion in the First Dialogue on the four stages of love (*DA* 1.6.64 [56]). Later in the same dialogue (*DA* 1.6.444 [170]) he invokes the authority of the Countess of Champagne on the subject of love and marriage, referring to the decision at the end of the Seventh Dialogue, also cited by the queen in deciding Love Case XVII. In addition, the dialogues contain more than forty references to the "rules," "precepts," "mandates," or "doctrine" of Love, most of which refer to one of the two codifications attributed to the King of Love.

The treatise thus presents a kind of circular *mise en abyme* in which we can distinguish as many as four separate levels of discourse.[27] In the Fifth Dialogue, for example, Andreas's discourse contains the discourse of the nobleman, which contains the discourse of the King of Love, which refers back to Andreas's discourse. What are we to make of this technique of "intratextuality"? It has been interpreted humorously by one critic, who sees it as proof that the entire work is an elaborate joke.[28] But it is equally possible that Andreas merely wished to underline the authoritative nature of his own work by adding it to the open-ended canon of classical and medieval authorities on the subject. In fact, these references do not appear to differ significantly in function from several internal cross-references made by Andreas himself in passages of direct authorial commentary, for example, when he refers to the Seventh Dialogue for a discussion of jealousy (*DA* 2.2.2 [228]). However we may interpret them, these references underline Andreas's concern for *auctoritas,* which is closely related to their significance.

Having thus identified Andreas's major sources of authority, what can we say about the uses to which he puts them, and what help can all this be to us in interpreting his work? First of all, the abundance and the heterogeneity of the authorities cited by Andreas appear significant,

27. On *mise en abyme,* see Dällenbach.
28. Weigand, p. 24.

in that they argue against any attempt to reduce the work to a single, homogeneous point of view. One of the things Andreas seems to be doing in the *De amore* is assembling all the pertinent opinions on any given question. His work may thus be viewed as a kind of *summa* on love, in the tradition of Abelard's *Sic et non* or Peter Lombard's *Sentences.*

The authorities cited are generally divorced from the source from which they emanate and quoted out of context. This is particularly evident in the case of the direct quotations, some of which are repeated in the course of the treatise, in different contexts and in support of different conclusions. But it is also true of the commonplaces, a fact that argues against any unconsidered use of the *De amore* as a key to the vernacular poetry.

Thus isolated from their sources, Andreas's authorities are reintegrated into a complex dialectic that forms the substance of his own discourse. This dialectal interweaving of authorities from different traditions can be seen with particular clarity in the dialogues. For example, the First Dialogue (*DA* 1.6.26–39 [46–50]), between a man and a woman both from the middle class, begins with an expression of hyperbolic praise, a poetic commonplace: "When the Divine Being made you there was nothing He left undone," to which the woman demurs, evoking with commonsense realism what "ought not to be required" of a woman of her class. In reply the man quotes "a common proverb," in fact a maxim from the biblical book of Proverbs, to the effect that self-praise is distasteful. The woman then cites a verse from Ovid to support the idea that if she is so noble, she should have nothing to do with a commoner like him. To this, the man replies by applying to himself the poetic commonplace of "nobility of character" that he has previously applied to the woman, and so on.

This dialectal interweaving of diverse authorities so characteristic of the dialogues is by no means limited to them. It is equally present in the passages of authorial commentary, such as the introduction to the Third Dialogue mentioned earlier. Indeed, it supplies the basic texture for the entire treatise. Most evident at the "micro" level of opinion and argumentation, it extends equally to the "macro" level of overall structures and models, a subject to which we can now turn.

Andreas and his models

The curriculum authors were not only sources of authority, they were also models for speaking and writing, in accordance with the medieval rhetorical principle of imitation. It is therefore not surprising that several of the authors quoted by Andreas in the *De amore* also played an important role in shaping the treatise. As with the authorities cited, the number and diversity of the models used in structuring the work is striking. Indeed, the heterogeneity of the types of discourse to be found in the *De amore* has always posed a problem for its interpretation. It is quite untenable to reduce the treatise to a single model, as has sometimes been attempted (e.g., Ovid misunderstood). Rather, the structure of the work reflects a kind of dialectical interplay between a number of models of diverse provenance, not unlike that which obtains for the citation of authorities.

The question of models is closely related to the problem of genre discussed above in Chapter 1, as well as to the interplay between rhetoric and dialectic that occupied Chapter 2. The most visible tension in the *De amore* is that which opposes the practical, Ovidian model of *ars* and the speculative, scholastic model of *scientia,* but that opposition is far from exhausting the subject. In addition to these more obvious clerical models of discourse, Andreas also makes a somewhat subtler use of a number of models from the vernacular literature, as we shall see. In some cases Latin and vernacular models converge.

The first, most obvious model for the structure of the *De amore* is that of the erotico-didactic poetry of Ovid, long recognized by the critics, and reemphasized recently by scholars such as Francis Cairn and Peter Allen.[29] The first two books of Andreas's work correspond roughly to the first two books of the *Ars amatoria,* and a similar relationship can be seen between Andreas's third book and the *Remedia amoris.* This association is reinforced by passages in which the Chaplain refers to his own doctrine as *ars amatoria* (*DA* 3.117 [322]) or even as *amoris ars et*

29. Cairns; Allen, pp. 59–78. Cairns's article was reprinted with incorrect attribution, presumably by mistake, among Karnein's posthumous papers (Karnein, *Amor est passio,* pp. 23–40).

... *amoris remedia* (*DA* 1.8.5 [212]), and it is reflected in many of the manuscript rubrics, as we saw in Chapter 1. We have also seen that Ovid is by far the classical source most frequently quoted in the treatise, and second only to the Bible among all Andreas's sources, which lends further support to the Ovidian hypothesis.

The *De amore* does not simply reproduce the structure of Ovid's love poetry, it modifies and adapts that structure in a variety of ways. This is most evident in the substitution of a *remedia*-type discourse for Book Three of the *Ars amatoria,* but there are also a number of less obvious modifications in the Ovidian schema that claim our attention. Starting from the reasonable hypothesis that Ovid provided the overall framework for the treatise, we shall try to discover where Andreas departs from the Ovidian plan and, if possible, why.

The *Ars amatoria* opens with an introductory passage (*AA* 1.1–34), which functions very much like the *Præfatio* in the *De amore,* explaining the reasons for writing (v. 4) and establishing Ovid's authority in the matter, based like that of Andreas on experience (*AA* 1.29; cf. *DA* 0.3 [30]). This is immediately followed by a passage in which Ovid expounds the plan that he will follow in the rest of the work:

Principio quod amare velis, reperire labora,
    Qui nova nunc primum miles in arma venis.
Proximus huic labor est placitam exorare puellam:
    Tertius, ut longo tempore duret amor.
Hic modus, hæc nostro signabitur area curru:
    Hæc erit admissa meta premenda rota. (*AA* 1.35–40)[30]

This brief outline corresponds closely to the material that will be treated in the first two books of the *Ars amatoria,* but there is no mention of the third book; nor is there any reference to the *Remedia amoris,* which is, of course, a separate work. Ovid's outline may well have inspired Andreas's *Accessus,* which combines it, however, with a scholastic model, that of the *accessus ad auctores.* In particular, the Ovidian passage may

30. Cf. trans. Mozley, p. 15: "First, strive to find an object for your love, you who now for the first time come to fight in warfare new. The next task is, to win the girl that takes your fancy; the third, to make love long endure. This is my limit, this the field whose bound my chariot shall mark, this the goal my flying wheel shall graze."

explain the fact that there is no reference in the *Accessus* to Book Three of the *De amore,* although the conjunction *igitur* points back to the *Præfatio,* where there is such a reference (see above, Chapter 1).

Andreas's first major modification of Ovid's plan is an absence, that of any discussion of how to find someone to love. This, the first of all tasks (v. 35), will occupy more than two hundred verses of the *Ars amatoria* (1.41–262), in which the poet enumerates at length the appropriate places for this type of "hunting": temples, the forum, the theater, the circus, public processions, banquets, and so on. The same subject is treated, albeit more succinctly, in the twelfth-century *Facetus* (vv. 131–60), in a part of that work that also circulated separately as a pseudo-Ovidian *Ars amatoria.* Even in the *Pamphilus,* whose eponymous hero is already in love from the very first verse, Venus advises the lover to seek out the places frequented by the beloved (v. 99), advice that has no equivalent in the *De amore,* although there is the briefest of allusions to the subject in the psychological description of the development of love: "[the lover] begins to look for a place and time opportune for conversing [with the beloved]" (*DA* 1.1.12 [34]). It is also curious to note that the *accessus* to the *Pamphilus,* somewhat overstating the case, sees in the work a manual on how to find girls: *Utilitas est ut hoc libro perlecto unusquisque sciat sibi pulcras invenire puellas* ("The usefulness is that, having read this book through, any man will know how to find himself pretty girls").[31]

What accounts for the absence of this important Ovidian theme from Andreas's discussion? Of course, the Roman institutions that Ovid designated as places to hunt had long since disappeared in the Chaplain's day, but one might have expected at least a briefer, medieval treatment of the subject like that found in the *Facetus* or the *Pamphilus.* The explanation lies perhaps in the influence of courtly vernacular literature on the *De amore.* There is never any question in the poetry of the troubadours and trouvères of looking for someone to love; indeed, the idealism of this literature excludes such a notion. In the courtly love song and the dawn song, the love relationship is already established, and no explanation is offered as to how it came into being. In

---

31. Huygens, p. 53; my translation.

the lyrico-narrative *pastourelle* and in the narrative lays and romances, love relationships usually develop *par aventure,* as a result of chance encounters. For the courtly vernacular literature, as in Andreas's definition *(Amor est passio . . .),* love is something that happens to you, not something for which you go looking. By contrast with the Ovidian cynicism evident in the *Facetus* and the *Pamphilus* on the subject of finding girls, the omission of this subject from the *De amore* may well have been inspired by the idealism of the courtly vernacular literature.

The material omitted leaves a gap in the *De amore* with respect to its Ovidian model, a gap that will be filled by the scholastic material contained in the first five chapters of the treatise. In fact, these chapters occupy the exact same position in Andreas's work as did the omitted material in Ovid's: immediately after the *Præfatio* and the *Accessus,* which together correspond to *AA* 1.1–40, and just before the advice on winning love. Moreover, the role accorded to vision in Andreas's definition of love echoes Ovid's emphasis on *looking* for girls (e.g., *AA* 1.44: *Quærenda est oculis apta puella tuis*).

In structuring the material of the first five chapters, Andreas calls on two medieval, scholastic models: that of the academic prologues *(accessus ad auctores)* and that of the twelfth-century treatises on friendship in the tradition of Cicero's *De amicitia.* The academic prologues, especially those to which Richard Hunt refers as "type-D" prologues, probably inspired Andreas's Chapter One, *Quid sit amor,* as well as his Chapter Three, *Unde dicatur amor.* Other early chapters are reminiscent of matters treated, for example, in Aelred of Rievaulx's *De spirituali amicitia:* Chapter Four, *Quis sit effectus amoris,* recalls Aelred's Book Two, *De fructu amicitæ et excellentia ejus,* while Aelred's Book Three, *Quomodo et inter quos possit amicitia indirupta servari,* is reflected in Chapter Two, *Inter quos possit esse amor,* and also in Chapter Five, *Quæ personæ sint aptæ ad amorem.* It should be added that Andreas's Chapter One covers some of the same material as Aelred's Book One, *De ortu amicitæ,* including the fact that their respective definitions of love share certain common features (see below, Chapter 5).

Chapter Six, *Qualiter amor acquiratur et quot modis,* brings us back to the Ovidian model. As the chapter title already suggests, the discussion on winning love is more systematic than Ovid's, calling upon the scholastic technique of *partitio* to divide the subject into its constituent parts. With its various ramifications, this subject will occupy not only Chapter Six but indeed all the rest of Book One.

Among the five means of acquiring love enumerated by Andreas, one receives an extraordinarily extended treatment: eloquence *(sermonis facundia)*, which is illustrated by the eight dialogues, comprising more than one-half of the entire treatise. This development constitutes a second major departure from the Ovidian plan. The *Ars amatoria* contains nothing resembling Andreas's model discourses. Although Ovid promises to explain how to "entreat" or "persuade" (*exorare, AA* 1.37) the beloved, the subject of eloquence is subsequently discussed rather briefly, primarily in connection with letter writing (*AA* 1.437–86, 607–30); all together it occupies less than one-tenth of Book One. It is unlikely that such brief remarks could be solely responsible for the considerable extension accorded this subject in the dialogues.

One possible model for the dialogues of the *De amore* is furnished by the *Facetus*. The pseudo-Ovidian *Ars amatoria* that occupies vv. 131–320 of that poem contains a sample conversation of fifty verses between lover and beloved (vv. 205–54). Much less extensive than Andreas's dialogues, it nevertheless constitutes more than one-fourth of the positive advice on love contained in the *Facetus*. Several features distinguish this dialogue from the dialogues of Andreas, however. First of all, it relates a single encounter, unlike the multiple conversations recorded by the Chaplain. More importantly, the girl avows her love already in her second speech (vv. 253–54), after only four verses of resistance (vv. 245–48), an outcome already predicted in the narrative introduction to her first speech (v. 244). Finally, at the end of the dialogue the hypothetical narration resumes, leading rather quickly to the inevitable *factum* (vv. 255–302). Like the *Pamphilus* on which it is loosely based, the *Facetus* presents, albeit in the imperative mode, the single, linear account of a successful seduction, in contrast to the multiple, open-ended dialogues of the *De amore*. It is therefore unlikely that the *Facetus* could be solely responsible for Andreas's dialogues, although it may have contributed, for the structural configuration of an illustrative dialogue between lovers within the framework of a didactic work on love remains striking.

Another, perhaps more promising explanation is provided by the existence in the vernacular literature of an immensely popular poetic genre devoted entirely to the winning of love through eloquence: the courtly love song *(canso/chanson)* of the troubadours and the trouvères. Like Andreas's dialogues, the love songs are many, and more or less interchangeable. Also like the dialogues, they present an essentially static situation, with no appreciable progression in the love relationship and no resolution at the end. Their treatment of the subject of love is characterized by a high degree of abstraction and idealization: although some of the early troubadours, such as William of Poitiers and Marcabru, use some fairly explicit sexual imagery, this had essentially disappeared by the "classical" period of troubadour poetry and was never fashionable among the trouvères. This contrasts with the sometimes graphic descriptions of the *Facetus* and the *Pamphilus* and corresponds to the relatively chaste language of Andreas, who seldom discusses physical lovemaking, and then only in vague, general terms, with expressions such as *amplexus* or *contactus*. The *cansos* of the troubadours not infrequently contain allusions to a disparity in social status between lover and beloved, a factor that may have contributed to Andreas's decision to organize the dialogues in accordance with the social class of the participants. Equating the excellence of the song with the sincerity of the lover's emotions, the love songs also posit between the rhetorical and the moral the same close relationship enunciated by the Chaplain in introducing the dialogues at the beginning of Chapter Six (*DA* 1.6.16 [44]).

The courtly love songs share certain rhetorical structures with Andreas's dialogues. The *canso* not only embodies the oral discourse of song, it is also a kind of letter, "sent" to the beloved through the agency of a jongleur, thus bridging the physical separation and distance that constitute one of the obstacles to the lovers' union. Expressed most explicitly in the *tornada* or *envoi* with which the poem ends, this aspect is developed systematically in the related genre known as the *saluts d'amour*, producing veritable love letters in verse. In accordance with its epistolary character, the love song adopts the petitionary structure of the *ars dictaminis*, the medieval rhetorical art of letter writing: a *salutatio*, usually the appellative *domna/dame*, and *captatio benevolentiæ*, consisting in praise of the beloved, are followed by a *narratio,* relating the lover's passion and suffering, ending in a *petitio,* or plea for "mercy." As we saw in the last chapter, this same rhetorical model usually informs the beginning speech of the male participants in the dialogues. Moreover, these beginning speeches are typically filled with metaphorical imagery, which could be borrowed from the vernacular lyric, such as the lover's description of his own plight in terms of shipwreck (*DA* 1.6.127 [74–76]). Following this beginning the dialogues usually revert to a forensic model of oral pleading, a model whose influence is equally perceptible in the love song. Many of the themes of the *chanson* are also developed in the later part of the dialogues.

The courtly love song presents not a dialogue, of course, but a monologue: the "continuous discourse" of rhetoric, to use Boethius's terminology. Nevertheless, the situation that it embodies is potentially "dialogic," a fact already recognized and exploited in the vernacular literature. The notion of a possible response by the lady is more or less implied in the structure of the poem, which is presented as a message to be sent to her in the hope of softening her rigor, presumably by eliciting a positive response. Certain of the troubadours expressly mention this possibility. Gaucelm Faidit complains that his lady has not answered his entreaties, while Raimbaut d'Aurenga and Arnaut de Mareuil both ask their respective ladies to answer their *saluts d'amour.*[32] A few texts go even further, presenting a veritable conversation between the troubadour and his lady. This may take the form of a rapid exchange of words within each verse, as is apparently the case in a poem by Peire Rogier,[33] or that of an exchange of one or more verses within each stanza, as in Aimeric de Peguilhan's *tenso* (debate poem) with an anonymous lady

32. Gaucelm Faidit, *S'om pogues partir son voler* (P.-C. 167, 56), v. 59; Arnaut de Mareuil, *Dona, gensor qe no sai dir,* v. 205; Raimbaut d'Aurenga, *Donna, cel qe us es bos amics,* vv. 7–8.

33. Especially *Ges non puesc en bon vers fallir* (P.-C. 356, 4), in which the identity of the poet's interlocutor is ambiguous, however: it could be a dialogue of the poet with himself, with a friend, or with the beloved. This poem was imitated in *Ailas, com mor!—quez as, amis?* (P.-C. 242, 3) by Giraut de Bornelh, where the interlocutor is clearly a friend, and in the romance *Flamenca,* where it forms the basis for a long conversation carried on between the lovers in the church, at the rate of one word each Sunday or feast day. Cf. ed. Appel, pp. 13–16; ed. Nicholson, pp. 21–26.

(P.-C. 10, 23) or in a similar poem sometimes attributed to Albert Marques de Malaspina (P.-C. 296, 1ᵃ). It may involve an exchange of whole stanzas, as in the bilingual *tenso* between Raimbaut de Vaqueiras and a Genoese lady,[34] or even that of a long refutation speech, like those that follow two anonymous Old French *saluts d'amour*.[35] In all these cases the lady questions, contradicts, and ridicules the lover's assertions and declarations of passion, much as in Andreas's dialogues.

The avowed purpose of the dialogues was to illustrate the winning of love through eloquence. According to Boethius's distinction, this should imply continuous discourse, like that of the love song. What we have, however, is the constant interchange of dialogue and debate. In terms of method we saw in this discrepancy a reflection of the subordination of rhetoric to dialectic in twelfth-century culture. At the level of models we can perhaps interpret the dialogues as an extrapolation from the love song, not unlike that of the *tensos* between the poet-lover and his lady. Whether or not Andreas was aware of these somewhat marginal lyric antecedents, his dialogues can be seen as a parallel development of a potential inherent in the *canso*. Of course, this vernacular model of debate on the specific subject of love is combined with the more general, scholastic model of the *disputatio,* whose influence is so evident in the dialogues.

Other types of poetic debate, vernacular and Latin, appear to have furnished models for the structuring of various parts of the *De amore,* including certain passages in the dialogues. The most important of these are the *pastourelles,* the debates between knights and clerics, and the dilemmatic debate poems *(partimens)*.

The *pastourelle* (Oc. *pastorela*) relates an encounter and conversation of a knight with a comely shepherdess in which he tries to seduce her. It is essentially a vernacular form, cultivated in both Old French and Old Occitan, but there are also a few Latin examples, including two by Walter of Châtillon. Much of the piquancy of this genre stems from the fact that it reverses the usual social relationship of the love song, which typically presents a poet-lover of modest origin wooing a highborn lady. In

---

34. *Domna, tan vos ai preiada* (P.-C. 392, 7). Cf. Gaunt, "Sexual Difference."
35. Meyer, pp. 147–49; ed. Schultz-Gora.

the earliest examples, such as Marcabru's *L'autrier jost'una sebissa* (P.-C. 293, 30), the shepherdess puts up a witty and spirited resistance, turning all the knight's efforts to ridicule. The subsequent evolution of the genre introduced a number of variants, including shepherdesses who are less recalcitrant or, especially in the northern French *pastourelles,* who are won over by the promise of gifts or the use of force.

The most obvious influence of the *pastourelles* on the *De amore* can be found in Book One, Chapter Eleven, *De amore rusticorum.* The advice that Andreas gives there, to use force if necessary to overcome the resistance of peasant women, may well reflect the prominence of this motif in the Old French *pastourelles.* A more subtle but perhaps more interesting use of this model can be seen in certain of the dialogues, particularly those involving a woman of the middle class *(plebeia).* In Dialogues Four and Six such a woman is addressed, respectively, by a nobleman *(nobilis)* and a man of the higher nobility *(nobilior),* so the social situation corresponds roughly to that of the *pastourelles.* This is reflected in the content of these dialogues, which turns around the question of social class, as in Marcabru's *pastorela.* Many of the arguments are, in fact, the same: the man seeks to flatter the woman by praising her "nobility," but she stresses the propriety of loving within one's rank, while also expressing concern for her own reputation. More widespread than the *tensos* between poet-lover and noble lady, the *pastourelles* may, in fact, have contributed to the whole idea of giving the women a chance to reply to the rhetoric of the would-be lovers.

The debates between knights and clerics were cultivated in both medieval Latin and Old French. The earliest representatives of the genre are the Latin poems known respectively as *Altercatio Phyllidis et Floræ* and the *Love-Council of Remiremont,* both probably from the first half of the twelfth century. In the former, the two maidens of the title debate the relative merits of loving a knight or a cleric, finally taking their dispute before the God of Love, whose court finds in favor of clerics. In the latter, the same question is debated satirically and parodically in a fictitious council among the nuns of a real convent, with the same outcome. The earliest Old French poem, *Blancheflor et Florence* or *Le Jugement d'Amours,* generally dated from the late-twelfth or early-thirteenth century, probably derives, like the other vernacular versions (two in Anglo-Norman and one in Franco-Venetian), from *Phyllis et Flora*. The Latin poems, especially *Phyllis et Flora*, appear most likely to have influenced Andreas.

Like the *pastourelles*, the debates between knights and clerics are reflected in a later chapter of Book One—in this case Chapter Seven, *De amore clericorum*—and also in the debate of the dialogues, namely the discussion on the love of clerics in the Eighth Dialogue (*DA* 1.6.478–499 [182–88]). Unlike the debate poems, these passages do not formally compare knights and clerics, but the comparison is implicit throughout. Most of the topics discussed are also found in the debated poems: the relative "honor" or nobility of the two classes; their relative generosity; the clerics' obligation to serve God; their greater knowledge and discretion; their propensity to gluttony and sloth; their inelegant dress; the prohibition against their engaging in battle. The extensive imagery of the *Altercatio* and the poems derived from it does not appear to have influenced Andreas's depiction in the Fifth Dialogue of the God of Love and his court, which is much more sober in tone, with a strong Christian, apocalyptic coloration.[36] However, the decision of Phyllis and Flora to submit the matter to the arbitration of the God of Love, including the bucolic setting (cf. *DA* 1.6.392 [154]), may have served as model for the end of the Seventh Dialogue, where the question of love and marriage is submitted to the Countess of Champagne.

The dilemmatic debate poems (Oc. *partimen/joc partit;* O.Fr. *jeu parti*) are an exclusively vernacular genre, cultivated in both southern and northern France. In these poems one poet invites another to choose either side of a dilemma, proposing to defend the proposition rejected by his opponent, after which the subject is debated in verse, with the opponents composing, on the same rhythm, melody, and rhyme scheme, alternating stanzas in defense of their respective positions. Many of the *partimens* of the troubadours end with the naming of judges, in most cases prominent ladies of the court, to decide the question debated, although the judgment itself is rarely included in the poem. Among the subjects debated, love in all its various aspects is by far the most frequent.

36. Ruhe, *Le Dieu d'amour,* pp. 84–91.

The influence of the *partimens* is visible in both the form and content of many passages of Andreas's dialogues, as well as in the Love Cases of Book Two. A rudimentary application of the scholastic techniques of *disputatio* to the subject of love, they anticipate the Chaplain's more systematic use of these same techniques. Like the *quæstiones disputatæ* of the scholastics, the subjects debated must be true dilemmas, with arguments that can be adduced on either side, in order for the poem to function properly. The practice of the disputants of the dialogues of inviting each other to choose a proposition to defend is clearly modeled on that of the vernacular debate poems. The same is true of the appeal to highborn ladies of the court to decide the Love Cases. Many of the actual dilemmas debated, in the dialogues and in the Love Cases, are also common to the *partimens*.[37]

The last six chapters in Book One serve either to complete the sociological schema of the dialogues or to address the other means of acquiring love enumerated at the beginning of Chapter Six (see above, Chapter 1). Their existence is thus related to the apparent intention of imposing on the Ovidian material a systematic, scholastic treatment. In addition to this internal motivation, several of these chapters deal with matters also discussed by Ovid or others, who can be seen as providing very general models for them.

Chapters Seven and Eleven, on the love of clerics and peasants, respectively, are both formally presented as a complement to the sociological framework of the dialogues, while taking much of their material from established poetic genres, as we have seen. Chapter Nine, "On Love Acquired by Money," recalls the passages in which Ovid warns against the giving of gifts (*AA* 1.399–436, 2.262–86). Chapter Twelve, "On the Love of Prostitutes," is a natural extension of that subject, but it also echoes the advice of the *Facetus* (vv. 137–40) against loving prostitutes. The *Facetus* (vv. 133–34) advises as well against the love of nuns, as does Chapter Eight, "The Love of Nuns," but the latter can also be seen as a natural extension of the preceding chapter on the love of clerics.

Book Two, "How Love Is Retained," comes back once again to the Ovidian plan, following up the advice on the winning of love with rec-

---

37. Liebertz-Grün, *Zur Soziologie*, p. 40; Neumeister, pp. 102–11.

ommendations on how to keep it, as does Book Two of the *Ars amatoria*. Not all the material contained in this part corresponds to the subject announced in the title, however. In addition to chapters on how love is maintained and increased, others discuss how it diminishes and ends.

Walsh (p. 13) sees in Chapters Three and Four a reflection of the *Remedia amoris*. The material in these chapters is not presented as positive advice on ceasing to love, however, but rather as a list of things to avoid if love is to be maintained. In fact, the word *remedium* is used at the end of Chapter Three (*DA* 2.3.8 [232]), referring to a remedy not for love but for love's decrease. The function of this material is very similar to that of the Ovid's advice to avoid quarrels (*AA* 2.145–76) or prolonged absences (*AA* 2.357–72). The principal difference is Andreas's systematic, scholastic treatment of the subject, visible not only in the separation of positive and negative advice, but also in the careful balance between proximate and remote effects: *conservari/augmentari; miniatur/finiatur*. Indeed, the Chaplain calls attention to his own careful "ordering" of this material at the beginning of Chapter Five: *His ita dispositis . . .* (*DA* 2.5.1 [234]).

If we wish to look for a model for Chapters Three and Four, beyond the internal, methodological explanation, we can perhaps find one in the twelfth-century literature on friendship. *De amicitia christiana* by Peter of Blois, for example, contains the following chapters:

XII. *De dilectione amici, et quæ eam impediunt;*
XIII. *Exempla eorum quæ amicitiam impediunt;*
XXIV. *Qualiter amicitia dissolvenda sit, et quam modeste;*
XXV. *Ex quibus causis amicitia dissolvatur potius quam rumpatur.*[38]

In addition to the general similarity in scope between these chapters and those of Andreas, there is also some common material. This could be due to an influence of Peter's chapters on the *De amore,* or it could merely reflect the inherent nature of the two closely related subjects.

38. "XII. On love of a friend, and what things are an obstacle to it; XIII. Examples of the things that are an obstacle to friendship; XXIV. How friendship is dissolved, and with what discretion; XXV. For what reasons friendship is dissolved rather than broken off" (my translation).

As a further application of scholastic procedures, Andreas singles out for separate treatment two other aspects of acquired love: Chapter Five, "On Recognizing Reciprocal Love," deals with verification of a continuing positive relationship (at least in theory, although many of the signs enumerated are negative); Chapter Six, "If One of the Lovers Breaks Faith with the Other," with the consequences of negative developments. Nearly as long as the first five chapters together, Chapter Six is not unrelated to the circumstances addressed in the *Remedia amoris,* but the treatment is very different. Far from dispensing advice on how to stop loving, the Chaplain refuses such advice to any man who would stoop to taking back an unfaithful lover (*DA* 2.6.18–19 [242–44]). The approach adopted in this chapter to the question of infidelity is juridical and casuistic, thus anticipating the Love Cases of Chapter Seven. Also evident here, as well as in the last two chapters of Book Two, is an effort to summarize and synthesize previous discussions.

We have already mentioned the role of the *partimens* in the elaboration of the Love Cases of Chapter Seven, for which they provided not only many of the dilemmas debated but also the idea of appealing to noble ladies of the court for a decision. To this model must be added that of canon law, whose influence is evident throughout the treatise, but especially in this most juridical of chapters. As Rüdiger Schnell has demonstrated, the canon law on marriage is directly responsible for a number of the cases and decisions discussed, in addition to its influence on the general form of the discussion. Moreover, the method of reconciling conflicting authorities known as the *sic et non* method, whose influence is so evident in the *De amore,* may have had its origin in the practice of the canonists; in any case, it found one of its best expressions in the *Decretum* of Gratian. The quasi-juridical character of the *partimens* must have facilitated the combination of this vernacular poetic form with the properly juridical model of canon law.

Canon law also provided the model for the Rules of Love contained in Book Two, Chapter Eight. Many of the canonist collections, imitating Justinian's *Digest,* are followed by a code entitled *regulæ juris.* According to the *Digest,* a *regula* is a brief summary of a case. This corresponds exactly to Andreas's practice, for many of the *Regulæ Amoris* are based on the Love Cases of Chapter Seven. Once again the Chaplain has combined this eminently scholastic model with a model from the vernacular literature, in this case Arthurian romance, which, beyond its exemplary value, provided a basis of authority, albeit fictional, for the rules. The same combination of models was already evident in the Purgatory of Cruel Beauties episode of the Fifth Dialogue.

The next place in the Ovidian plan should be occupied by advice to women, as in Book Three of the *Ars amatoria,* but Andreas has substituted for this the *Remedia*-type discourse of his own third book. Concerning this substitution, Walsh (p. 13) suggests that advice to women was neglected, "as irrelevant to twelfth-century conventions of courtship." It is not obvious to what specifically medieval conventions this may refer, for Ovid makes clear that it was already the custom in his day for the men to do the asking (*AA* 1.277–78, 705–14). A better explanation can perhaps be found in the clerical misogyny so evident in Book Three (*DA* 3.65–112 [306–20]). Ovid derived mildly misogynistic humor from relating the accusation that he is giving arms to the enemy (*AA* 3.7–8), before springing to women's defense, but it is hard to imagine that Andreas could offer advice and encouragement to those agents of the devil whom he will so virulently attack and whose wiles require no instruction.

Andreas's substitution preserves intact Ovid's general structural configuration of two books giving continuous advice to men followed by a third composed of contrasting material. Cairns points out that the close association of the *Remedia amoris* with the *Ars amatoria,* visible in the manuscripts as well as in the *accessus,* created a two-tiered opposition (between the first two and the third books within the *Ars,* and between all three and the *Remedia*), with respect to which Andreas's practice can be seen as a simplifying reduction. It may be that in twelfth-century clerical circles the *Remedia* was regarded as a kind of alternative ending, with the advantage of being more congenial to the clerical point of view. In any case, a contemporary model for Andreas's substitution can be seen in the *Facetus* (vv. 321–84), where a *Remedia amoris,* much more Ovidian in tone than the third book of the *De amore,* follows directly the advice to men on winning and keeping love, with no corresponding advice to women.

Despite its evacuation, Book Three of the *Ars amatoria* may have left its mark on the *De amore* at the level of content. The light-hearted misogyny evident throughout Ovid's love writings is most pronounced in his advice to women. Many of the tricks that the master teaches can easily be seen as ironic descriptions of what women already do: making lovers wait or fear a rival (*AA* 3.577–610), deceiving husbands and guardians (*AA* 3.611–98), feigning love (*AA* 3.667–82), and so on. This may have been the point of departure for the much more heavy-handed attack on women in Book Three of the *De amore.* Of course, Ovid has been supplemented by the standard sources of medieval clerical misogyny, such as Juvenal and Jerome, who provide the principal models for this part of the treatise.

The relationship of Andreas's Book Three to the *Remedia amoris* is scarcely less problematic than its relationship to the rest of the *De amore.* The two questions are closely connected. Ovid explains at length that he wishes to make no general attack on love, that his remedies are intended only for unsuccessful lovers (*RA* 1–78). This is precisely the kind of advice requested in the *Præfatio* by Walter, who wanted to know, among other things, "how those who are not loved can deflect the darts of Venus stuck in their hearts" (*DA* 0.1 [30]). This is not what the Chaplain provides, however, for Book Three is just the kind of all-out attack on love that Ovid disclaims. As the title carried in most of the manuscripts indicates, the treatise ends with a total "condemnation" or "rejection" *(reprobatio)* of love. It is curious to note, moreover, that the term *remedium* occurs sixteen times in the *De amore,* but not once in the third book.

Several scholars have pointed recently to the medieval *accessus* tradition on Ovid as providing a possible explanation of the relationship of the third book to the *Remedia amoris* as well as to the rest of the *De amore.* In this tradition the *Remedia amoris* is often viewed as a retraction designed to make amends for the fact that Ovid's earlier instruction had sometimes been abused by its recipients, thus giving the poet a bad reputation. If we suppose, with A. J. Minnis, that it is this medieval concept of Ovid that Andreas is imitating, the character of Book Three becomes more comprehensible.[39] Such an interpretation is not incom-

---

39. Minnis, *Medieval Theory,* p. xiv; idem, *Magister amoris,* p. 295.

patible with the conclusion that we reached concerning the Chaplain's method: just as Ovid realized (in the medieval view) that his earlier teachings were liable to be abused, so Andreas recognizes in his *Reprobatio* that the secular love ethic of Ovid and the troubadours is ultimately irreconcilable with Christian morality.

It is in the *accessus* tradition that John Baldwin places a previously unpublished *quæstio* of the school of Peter the Chanter in which it is debated whether the *Ars amatoria* should be taught in the schools.[40] The conclusion reached, that it should be taught, "not for use but as a warning" *(non ad usum, sed ad cautelam),* may also apply to the *De amore,* according to Baldwin. This idea is echoed in two strategic places in the treatise: in the *Præfatio* Andreas tells Walter that, once instructed, he will proceed more cautiously in love (*DA* 0.4 [30]), and at the beginning of Book Three he claims to have instructed his pupil not so that he may use this knowledge but so that he may refrain from using it, thus earning an eternal reward (*DA* 3.2 [286]). This interesting parallel may point at least to a part of Andreas's motivation. Unfortunately, the *quæstio* is scarcely less ambiguous in intention than the *De amore,* for it may represent a self-justificatory pretext for reading Ovid, couched hypocritically in the language of the ambient culture, rather than the expression of a sincere belief that the reading of the *Ars amatoria* can serve to strengthen Christian morality. Whatever the degree of sincerity we may ascribe to such declarations, they are not capable alone of accounting for all the material found in the first two books of the treatise. Even if cautionary instruction was Andreas's *principalis intentio* (*accessus,* p. 25), certain *secundariæ intentiones* are manifest, including the systematization of Ovid and the synthesizing of love-lore from various traditions.

Walsh again raises the perennial question whether Book Three may not have been added as an afterthought to a treatise originally composed of two books.[41] The absence of any reference to the third book in Andreas's *Accessus* seems to point in that direction, although this may be the result of an imitation of *Ars amatoria* 1.35–40, as we have seen. On the other hand, the clear allusions to the *Remedia* contained in the *Præ-*

---

40. Baldwin, "L'*Ars amatoria.*"; idem, *Language,* pp. 24–25.
41. Walsh, pp. 13–15; p. 33, n. 7; p. 244, n. 1; p. 286, n. 1.

fatio point in the other direction. Nor is there much support for this hypothesis in the manuscript tradition: Book Three sometimes circulated separately, but nowhere have the first two books been preserved in the absence of the third. And if we take Ovid to be Andreas's primary model, it is difficult to see how a composition consisting of only two books could have ever been envisaged as a satisfactory final form for the work. Of course, Ovid himself did add the *Remedia amoris* as an afterthought to the *Ars amatoria*—indeed, in the view of the medieval *accessus*, as a corrective—as Andreas must have been well aware even before beginning work on the *De amore*. In view of this precedent, perhaps we can see in Andreas's third book a pre-planned afterthought, as it were, which might help to explain its rather awkward relationship to the rest of the treatise.

An examination of the models upon which Andreas structured the *De amore* leads us to conclusions similar to those that we reached concerning his use of authority. As with the authors cited, the most striking features of the Chaplain's recourse to models are the heterogeneity of his sources and the constancy and intricacy of the processes employed to interweave materials from diverse provenances and traditions. Once again the results of our inquiry underscore the complexity of the work's inspiration.

Andreas's point of departure appears quite clearly to be the love writings of Ovid. The undisputed master for all matters relating to sexual love, Ovid is, after the Bible, the authority most frequently cited in the *De amore*. His influence is manifest in the tripartite structure of the work, and it is reflected in book and chapter titles and in the rubrics of many of the manuscripts. Encompassing the form as well as the content, the Ovidian inspiration remains a constant throughout the treatise.

The *De amore* is not simply an imitation of Ovid, with or without a misunderstanding of that author's intentions. It appears rather to be a deliberate and conscious reworking and adaptation of the Ovidian material in term of specifically medieval modes of thought and expression. As such it calls on several medieval models of discourse, Latin and vernacular, clerical and courtly, in reinterpreting the Ovidian love lore for twelfth-century audiences. Like the authoritative opinions cited, these diverse models of discourse enter into an intricate dialectic with the Ovidian framework and with each other, thus forming the complex structure of the entire work.

Throughout the treatise the interaction of scholastic and courtly models is striking. It may be the idealism of the vernacular poetry, for example, that inspired the omission of the Ovidian material on places to look for girls, but this gap is filled with a decidedly scholastic discourse, including a definition of love and the subsequent glossing of that definition, in which the clerical models of academic prologues and friendship literature both play a role. Likewise, the dialogues may have had as their point of departure the courtly love song, the most prominent example in medieval culture of an attempt to win love through eloquence, as well as the poetic debates between lover and lady that grew out of that genre, and yet the dialogues are organized according to the learned rhetorical principle of the levels of style and conducted with all the dialectical techniques of the *disputatio.* The final chapters of Book One complete the systematic, scholastic treatment of matters previously discussed while calling upon the poetic models of the *pastourelle* and the debates between knights and clerics for part of their material. The Love Cases of Book Two combine the vernacular poetic model of the *jeu parti* with learned juridical models from canon law, and the final chapter of Book Two uses an Arthurian tale to justify the appending of a code, in imitation of the canonists.

Book Three, "The Rejection of Love," should probably also be understood first of all as a medieval adaptation of Ovid. Here the courtly vernacular models are conspicuous by their absence, however, and scholasticism triumphs, in a systematic refutation of the courtly material of the previous two books. Conflating Ovid's two endings, Andreas converts the subtle anti-feminist irony of the *Ars amatoria,* Book Three, into the blatant clerical misogyny of his central diatribe against women. Especially, Ovid's remedies are transformed into a retraction, in accordance with the medieval Ovid of the *accessus* tradition, thus completing not only the Ovidian model, but also the Chaplain's dialectical, antithetic, scholastic description of that most complex phenomenon that is love.

From the above discussion the highly intertextual nature of the *De amore* emerges as one of its most striking features. Andreas's manifest concern for authority, his frequent recourse to earlier models of discourse, and the innovative uses that he makes of both authorities and models go far, I think, toward explaining the difficulty and ambiguity of his treatise, as well as its appeal. The *De amore* is not only a speculative treatise on love, a practical manual on the art of loving, or a religious homily on the dangers of concupiscence. It is all these and more. Through a bewildering combination of dialogues and letters, cases and codes, tales and allegories, quotations and allusions, descriptions and prescriptions, it appears, above all, as a discourse on the discourse of love.

Love, for Andreas, is not only an emotion or an activity, a way of feeling or of doing: it is especially a discourse, a way of speaking. Rather, it is many discourses, written and oral, ancient and contemporary, Christian and pagan, poetic and prosaic, all converging on this most fundamental phenomenon of the human experience. Hence the extreme complexity of Andreas's own discourse: very much in the spirit of the times in which it was written, it is a multiple, dialectical, "dialogic" discourse interweaving all the medieval varieties of the discourse on love.

4 ✤

THE PROBLEM OF IRONY

Andreas and the Critics

An *important aspect* of the form of the *De amore* remains to be discussed: the question of Andreas's alleged use of irony. This question does not arise from the language of the treatise itself, for neither the Greek borrowing *ironia* nor its Latin calque *dissimulatio* appears there. Nor is irony a major component of the scholastic method, with respect to which it occupies a rather marginal place, as one of the numerous figures of speech that may be used to embellish a discourse. Rather, it is the modern scholarly tradition that has brought the subject of irony to the fore, making of it a central, unavoidable question in Capellanus studies. Nevertheless, we shall see that a consideration of the Chaplain's scholastic method can provide new insights regarding this perennial problem.[1]

Among the various controversies surrounding the treatise on love attributed to Andreas Capellanus, none is more vexed than the question of the work's tone. Is the *De amore* to be taken as a serious, straightforward treatment of its subject, or should it be interpreted, in whole or in part, as humorous or ironic? This question is clearly of crucial importance to our understanding of the work and of its place in medieval literature, hence the considerable interest and passion that it has aroused.

A generation ago most scholars were in agreement in taking the work seriously and in viewing it as the earliest and best codification of

---

1. For an earlier version of this chapter, see Monson, "Andreas Capellanus and the Problem."

the love themes of the vernacular poetry. Over the last fifty years, however, ironic interpretations of the treatise have steadily gained ground, though not without resistance and opposition. Those of us who continue to use the *De amore* as a ready reference guide to courtly love do so, I suspect, with ever increasing uneasiness, and there must be many others who are simply perplexed.

The situation is further complicated by the fact that there is not just one ironic interpretation about, but several, including some that do not formally invoke the name of irony. And although the various ironic interpretations sometimes call on each other for corroboration and support, there are in some cases substantial grounds for doubt as to their mutual compatibility. Moreover, much of what has been written about Andreas and irony dispenses with any discussion of the theory of irony, ancient or modern, or of the relationship of the phenomenon to other, related but distinct, phenomena, such as humor, satire, or parody.

It therefore seems worthwhile to look at the problem as a whole, in an attempt to get an overview of it. That is what I should like to do in the following remarks. I shall begin with a few words on the theory of irony. Then I shall summarize and criticize the major ironic interpretations of the *De amore* that have been put forward to date, concentrating particularly on two of them. Finally, I should like to add a few observations of my own. Without harboring any illusion of being able to resolve the matter to everyone's satisfaction, I hope thus to provide a new and perhaps useful perspective on it.

Theory of irony

The theory of irony and related topics comprise a vast subject to which many books and articles have been devoted. I can reproduce here only the barest of outlines and such particulars as seem to me to be especially useful for the matter at hand.

In the wake of Roman rhetoric, the Middle Ages defined irony very narrowly, as a rhetorical device. It was generally viewed as a subcategory of allegory, which term was taken in the general, etymological sense of saying one thing and meaning another. Irony was specifically the case where one said one thing and meant the opposite. It was frequently viewed as a kind of deception and, in addition to the Greek term *ironia,* the Latin word *dissimulatio* was sometimes applied to it. Its most characteristic application was in epideictic rhetoric, where it was used to praise while appearing to blame or (more often) to blame through a pretense of praise. It was seen not only as a localized figure of speech, but also as a figure of thought that could be maintained throughout an entire discourse.[2]

Some early writers also discuss the indications by which ironic utterances can be identified. Quintilian (8.6.54) distinguishes three such clues: tone of voice (*pronuntiatio,* referring to oral delivery), the character of the speaker *(persona),* and the nature of the subject *(rei natura),* any one of which may betray irony if it is out of keeping with what is said. For the thirteenth-century rhetorician Boncompagno da Signa, gestures may be a clue to irony, if the speaker can be seen; otherwise, "manifest crime and impure conscience accuse the recipient."[3]

One of the major thrusts of the modern critical theory of irony, beginning toward the end of the eighteenth century, has been to expand immeasurably the scope of the phenomenon. Even verbal irony, the exclusive concern of early rhetorical theory, is no longer limited to saying one thing and meaning the opposite, for most critics would also include cases where the intended meaning is merely different from the apparent meaning, provided there is also an element of incongruity or incompatibility between the two meanings.[4] Beyond that, irony has been extended to include not only a way of speaking, but also a way of looking at

2. On the classical and medieval theory of irony see Campbell; Haidu, *Aesthetic Distance,* pp. 14–23; Lausberg, §§ 582–85 and 902–4; Sedgewick, pp. 3–27.

3. Excerpt from Boncompagno da Signa, *Rhetorica antiqua* (ed. Benton, "Clio and Venus," p. 37): *Verumtamen si videretur ille qui proponit yroniam, per gestus comprehendi posset voluntas loquentis. In absentia nempe manifestum delictum et immunda conscientia recipientem accusant* ("However, if the one proposing irony can be seen, the intention of the speaker can be understood from his gestures. In his absence, of course, manifest crime and impure conscience accuse the recipient" [my translation]). Benton's rather misleading translation (pp. 28–29), "manifest evil and impure belief indict the subject," appears intended to extend the scope of Boncompagno's pronouncement to cover works of literature, such as the *De amore* or the *Chevalier de la Charrete,* but it is clear from the context that *recipiens* refers to an individual who is the target or "victim" of the irony.

4. Cf. the definition of Green, p. 9: "the real or intended meaning . . . *diverges from, and is incongruous with,* the apparent or pretended meaning" (my emphasis).

situations, events, and even life in general. The justification for this extension is usually seen in the fact that situations or events often produce a semantic configuration similar to that which is characteristic of verbal irony.[5]

The extension of the term "irony" has given rise to a cottage industry in taxonomy, although no two critics seem to be in agreement about their systems of classification. The varieties of irony that have been identified or suggested include: verbal irony, Socratic irony, dramatic irony, satiric irony, comic irony, tragic irony, paradoxical irony, nihilistic irony, cosmic irony, romantic irony, and the irony of fate, of situation, or of events, to name only a few.[6]

One widely recognized distinction is that which separates, in the words of Douglas C. Muecke, "intentional irony" from "observable irony."[7] The most common form of intentional irony is verbal irony, in which a speaker (or writer) uses words to express his ironic intention. It is by no means limited to this, however, for ironic intention can also be expressed in various nonverbal ways, including gestures, actions, images, objects, music, and inarticulate sounds. Nor is verbal irony always intentional, for a given utterance may appear ironic to observers, without the speaker having so intended it. Observable irony also includes the irony of situation, or events, or fate, for, here again, no ironic intention is involved, although irony may be perceived by observers.

The dynamics of irony can be analyzed in terms of the tension between the two meanings that it brings into play. An obvious meaning is put forward in such a way as to make it unreceivable, thus forcing the audience to go beyond this unsatisfactory meaning to find another meaning that contradicts it. A superficial appearance is corrected and supplanted by an underlying reality. Thus irony has at its very foundation a dialectical impulse growing out of a confrontation of opposites. It is probably not by chance that the two phenomena irony and dialectic first made their appearance in Western culture together, in the dialogues of Plato.[8]

5. Knox, "Irony"; Muecke, *Compass,* pp. 119–247; idem, *Irony,* pp. 18–32.

6. Knox, "Irony"; idem, "On the Classification"; Muecke, *Compass,* pp. 40–63; idem, *Irony,* pp. 7–13.

7. Muecke, *Compass,* pp. 42–52; idem, *Irony,* p. 51.

8. Schaerer, pp. 185–86, has analyzed the dialectical mechanism of verbal irony in

Irony can be analyzed in the terminology of modern linguistics as the generation of two contradictory "signifieds" from a single "signifier."[9] Its communication is sometimes described in terms of a dramatic structure involving two audiences, one for each meaning. Whereas the naive, uninitiated audience will take at face value the obvious meaning of the ironic statement, the sophisticated, initiated audience will go beyond the superficial message to the underlying, fundamental message.[10] In practice the two audiences may include the same individuals, separated only by the split-second required to realize that they are in the presence of irony, or brought more gradually from error to enlightenment, as in the Socratic dialogues. Historically speaking, however, the use of irony to address simultaneously two completely different audiences has often been exploited to great effect, for example to express unconventional, unpopular ideas to an elite audience of like-minded people without detection or interference from official censorship.

Despite this subversive use, verbal irony differs from lying in that its primary purpose is not to deceive, but to be found out. An effective lie is one that everyone believes, but if no one perceives the second meaning of an ironically intended statement, then no irony will have been communicated. Verbal irony does intentionally violate some of the implied conventions of communication, described variously as the "sincerity code" or the "cooperative principle,"[11] but this violation is announced in some way, rather than concealed. Furthermore, this type of violation of the code is itself codified, canonized, institutionalized, so that it represents one of the possibilities available to any audience for the interpretation of a given utterance. This is one of the major features that irony shares with the other tropes, those figures of speech involving a transfer of meaning, for all are based on some sort of intentional, institutionalized transgression of linguistic norms.[12]

the following terms: the ironic speaker abandons his own opinion on a given subject and pretends to adopt the opinion of his adversary, but in a way or under conditions that prevent the latter from being deceived; this psychological "doubling" tends to provoke an inverse doubling in the adversary, who abandons his own opinion and adopts the speaker's. This view may be compared with a more recent analysis that sees in the ironic statement an implied quotation; see Sperber and Wilson.

9. Kerbrat-Orecchioni, pp. 110–11.   10. Muecke, *Irony,* pp. 39–44.
11. Kerbrat-Orecchioni, p. 116; Grice.   12. Kerbrat-Orecchioni, pp. 110–11.

The two-audience model for the communication of irony means that in any potentially ironic situation, any one of four types of transactions may take place, two of which are properly communicative and two of which are imperfectly so: (1) an ironically intended utterance may be interpreted ironically; (2) an utterance straightforward in intention may be taken at face value; (3) an ironically intended utterance may be taken at face value; (4) an utterance straightforward in intention may be taken ironically.[13] Only in the first two cases, where irony was both intended and perceived or neither intended nor perceived, has proper communication taken place. In the two latter cases, where irony is intended but not perceived or perceived but not intended, the communication process has aborted. Each type of interpretation, the straightforward and the ironic, has its own natural advantages, which may lead to its being extended beyond what was originally intended. Straightforward interpretations are more obvious and make far fewer demands on the perspicacity and interpretive skill of the audience. Ironic interpretations, on the other hand, enjoy the prestige of association with an interpretive elite, those clever enough to see the real meaning behind the obvious one. The twin dangers of underinterpretation and overinterpretation thus form the Scylla and Charybdis of irony.

It is at least in part because of this, that so much attention has been devoted to the mechanisms by which intentional irony is communicated.[14] How is it that an ironic speaker or writer makes his obvious meaning unacceptable to his audience, simultaneously reorienting their interpretation toward a contrary meaning? In the absence of any clue, the intended irony would probably go undetected by the audience, for whom the real meaning would thus be lost, or worse, replaced by its opposite. On the other hand, what Muecke calls "the principle of economy" means that irony is most effective, indeed most ironic, when the clues are reduced to a minimum.[15]

Many attempts have been made to draw up lists of the various de-

13. Schaerer, pp. 183–84.
14. Muecke, "On the Communication"; Booth, esp. pp. 47–86.
15. Muecke, *Irony,* pp. 52–53.

vices or indices, such as hyperbole, understatement, paradox, punning, and the like, that can be used to signal to an audience the presence of irony. Once again, I know of no two such lists that agree completely. Without going into the details, I believe that it is safe to say that the communication of intentional, and particularly verbal, irony always depends on the perception of some discrepancy, or inconsistency, or incongruity associated with the ironic utterance. This discrepancy can sometimes be found within the utterance itself, but perhaps more often it resides in the relationship between the utterance and its context.

The context of a given utterance, ironic or otherwise, can be broken down roughly into two major components: the textual or verbal context, which is the utterance's place in the broader verbal discourse of which it is a part, and the extra-verbal or extra-linguistic context, which is the situation in the real world in which the utterance is proffered. Each of these contexts has its own complexities, ambiguities, and difficulties in relation to the process of interpretation. Furthermore, the modern theory of intertextuality reveals another aspect of the context that participates to some extent in both the verbal and the extra-verbal components, for though it is linguistic and textual in nature, it is situated outside the immediate discourse, whose interpretation it nevertheless informs.

The extra-linguistic context includes, first of all, the immediate situation of enunciation with its principal components: the speaker (or writer), the immediate audience, and the subject. It also includes what speaker and audience know or believe about each other and about the subject, particularly what each knows or believes the other to know or believe about the subject. It includes the linguistic competence of the participants, with its grammatical, semantic, and stylistic components, as well as the assumptions of each about the other's competence. Finally, it includes the time, place, and immediate circumstances of enunciation, as they impinge on the subject and on the participants' attitudes toward the subject. Major discrepancies between an utterance and any aspect of the complex situation that generated it may serve as a signal to irony. But in many cases the pertinent features of the immediate situation are extremely topical in nature, and thus very vulnerable to being lost with the passage of time, which may make the intended ironies of a

passage or text indecipherable for wider audiences and future generations.[16]

The immediate situation is inscribed within a broader social and
cultural context, which is usually more accessible, though not without
its own problems. This broader context includes the knowledge, beliefs,
values, and practices of the society to which the participants belong,
particularly as they relate to the subject at hand. It also includes other
texts that are part of the culture of the society in question, that convey
its beliefs and values concerning the subject, and that have formed the
generic expectancies and competencies of members of the society. The
broad social and cultural context of a given time and place is seldom
homogeneous and usually includes a number of conflicting and competing tendencies. In many cases the crucial question for the assessment
of a potentially ironic passage will be what part or parts of its cultural
environment are pertinent to its interpretation.

Because of the ambiguities associated with the extra-linguistic context, ironic speakers or writers often include discrepancies within their
own text to serve as signals for the presence of irony. This is particularly
true of writers, since they can expect to reach an audience that may not
be familiar with the circumstances of enunciation. In the case of local
ironies, these discrepancies are often fairly easy to identify and interpret. They include devices such as those enumerated above. But when a
kind of global irony is suspected of extending over an entire text, the
process may become much more difficult. In such cases, a few scattered
discrepancies will usually not suffice to communicate a global ironic intention, for the audience may well fail to perceive them or, perceiving
them, may attribute them to the clumsiness or inattention of the author. For a global ironic intention to have a reasonable chance of being
perceived and communicated, the discrepancies must be sufficiently
abundant and form a sufficiently recognizable pattern to create an impression of purpose, rather than random chance.

The relationship of irony to humor, satire, and parody, as well as the
relation of the three last-mentioned to each other, is a very large subject
indeed. For our purposes it suffices to point out that, although all these

16. A similar observation with respect to satire is made by Highet, pp. 16–17.

notions overlap somewhat, they are far from coinciding perfectly, and it is certainly not helpful to use the terms interchangeably, as if they were more or less synonymous. The attempts to view irony as a subcategory of humor or humor as a subcategory of irony show quite clearly, I believe, that neither can be fully subsumed under the other.[17] Norman Knox distinguishes what he calls "comic irony" from "satirical irony" and both from several varieties of decidedly serious irony: "tragic irony," "nihilistic irony," and so on. Satire often makes use of irony, but it can also be expressed directly, through the use of invective.[18] Parody has something ironic at its base, since the imitation of other authors, works, or styles implies at a surface level a certain approval or admiration, which is undercut, however, at a deeper level through caricature; but, as Linda Hutcheon (pp. 145–49) has shown, the pragmatic force of parody may vary over a wide range, from the respectfully playful to the violently satirical. It is important to keep in mind the distinctions between these four notions, in order to avoid further confusing the already complex issue of irony.

Christian irony

Although irony has come to the forefront of Capellanus studies only in the last fifty years, I believe that it can be argued that ironic interpretations of the *De amore* go back much farther. The early ironic interpretations, which never invoke the name of irony, are all directed at Book Three, *De reprobatione amoris,* in which Andreas seems to retract much

17. Freud, p. 174: "*irony,* which comes very close to joking . . . and is counted among the subspecies of the comic." Knox's "comic irony," which "reveals the triumph of a sympathetic victim," is "comic" both in the happy-ending sense and in the ordinary sense (Knox, "Irony," p. 627; cf. Muecke, *Irony,* p. 51). According to Bergson, p. 127: "Sometimes we state what ought to be done, and pretend to believe that this is just what is actually being done, then we have *irony.* Sometimes, on the contrary, we describe with scrupulous minuteness what is being done, and pretend to believe that this is just what ought to be done; such is often the method of humour." This analysis is perhaps a bit too neat to be fully convincing.

18. Worcester, pp. 49 and 75, sees irony as a "type of satire," along with invective and burlesque, but it is probably more accurate to view satire and burlesque (or parody) as *genres* and irony as a *mode of expression* that often informs those genres but that can also exist quite independently of them. Cf. Hutcheon, pp. 140–45.

of what he said in the first two books. When John J. Parry (p. 19) wrote in 1941 that Andreas was "a none too sincere cleric" and that with the third book "doubtless he was attempting to appease his ecclesiastical superiors, who may well have been offended by the tone of the first two books," he is suggesting the existence of two different publics for the third book: on the one hand, the ecclesiastical superiors who supposedly were appeased by it; on the other hand, Marie de Champagne and her court, who presumably recognized, like Parry, the insincerity of the Chaplain's moralizing and did not allow it to interfere with their enjoyment of the first two books.

This interpretation, couched in the moral terms of "sincerity" rather than the esthetic language of "irony," goes back at least to an article published by Pio Rajna in 1891. Rajna (pp. 256–57) characterizes the third book as "not at all sincere" and suggests that it may have been written as an "anticipated defense" against the scandal that the first two books would provoke in ecclesiastical circles, or indeed that it may have been added after the outbreak of such a scandal.

This position is no longer much in favor, at least in published scholarship, but it is certainly not dead. Witness the recent studies by Ursula Liebertz-Grün in which the anti-feminine, anti-sexual doctrine of certain theologians is seen as a subject of satire in the third book and in certain passages of the first two books. Although the term "irony" is again absent, an ironic second level of meaning in the ostensibly conservative parts of the treatise is clearly implied. In fact, this interpretation goes well beyond the earlier view that the third book was defensive and hypocritical, viewing it as a kind of "quotation," designed to be seen through, so as to "expose" or "unmask" the opinions it purports to profess.[19]

It is especially with the name of D. W. Robertson Jr., however, that the ironic interpretation of the *De amore* is associated. His well-known views, part of a general attack on the notion of "courtly love," were expressed in three separate studies going back to the early 1950s.[20]

19. Liebertz-Grün, Review, pp. 310–12; idem, "Satire und Utopie." Cf. idem, *Zur Soziologie,* p. 58: "Das dritte Buch hat die Funktion eines demaskierenden 'Zitats.'"

20. Robertson, "Doctrine," pp. 36–39; idem, "Subject"; idem, *Preface,* pp. 84–85 and 393–448.

In "The Doctrine of Charity in Medieval Literary Gardens," Robertson argued that, based on a tradition of allegorical gardens in Christian writing going all the way back to Eden, the allegory of the God of Love and his court contained in Andreas's Fifth Dialogue should be interpreted ironically, as an implicit condemnation of *cupiditas.* He also suggests that such an ironic interpretation can be extended generally to the first two books of the treatise. In "The Subject of the *De amore* of Andreas Capellanus," he sought to show, through an examination of the beginning and the end of the treatise in the light of various classical and Christian authors, that Andreas's subject was concupiscence rather than courtly love, that his attitude toward that subject was one of uncompromising condemnation, and that he had treated his subject ironically in the first two books, which thus confirmed, rather than conflicted with, the straightforward condemnation of Book Three. Finally, in *A Preface to Chaucer,* Robertson devotes some sixty pages to an analysis of the treatise as a whole, concentrating particularly on the eight dialogues in Book One. Here he tries to show that the lovers' arguments are often self-contradictory, as well as conflicting with precepts of Christian doctrine well-known to any medieval audience, and that the total effect is ludicrous, leading once again to an ironic condemnation of the lovers and their position.

Despite criticism from several sources, Robertson has been followed in his interpretation of the *De amore* by a number of scholars, including R. J. Schoeck, John F. Benton, Christopher Kertesz, Barbara Marie Gaffney, Paolo Cherchi, Doris Ruhe, and Charles Dahlberg.[21] But it is especially a book by Alfred Karnein that gives the Robertsonian approach its current burning interest.[22]

Karnein follows Robertson fairly closely in his interpretation of the work itself and does not add much of substance at that level. His main

---

21. Schoeck; Benton, "Court"; idem, "Clio and Venus"; Kertesz; Gaffney; Cherchi, "Andreas' *De amore*"; idem, "New Uses"; idem, *Andreas and the Ambiguity,* esp. pp. 128–41; Ruhe, "Intertextuelle Spiele"; Dahlberg. Without invoking Robertson, other scholars have expressed views of the *De amore* close to his: Demats; Frappier, "Sur un procès," pp. 171–79; Tobin; Benoit.

22. Karnein, *"De amore."* Cf. idem, *"Amor est passio";* idem, "Andreas, Boncompagno"; idem, "Auf der Suche"; idem, "La Réception."

contributions to the subject concern two aspects of the *De amore*'s historical context: (1) the identification of the author and (2) the reception of the work in the Middle Ages, particularly in the thirteenth century.

Against the long-standing, widely held theory that the *De amore* was written at the court of Marie of Champagne, perhaps at the instigation of the countess herself, Karnein argues that the work originated in the 1180s in the chancellery of the king of France, Philip II Augustus. This hypothesis is supported by four pieces of evidence: (1) the fact that three of the manuscripts designate the author as "Andrew, chaplain of the King of France"; (2) the existence in the royal chancellery during this period of a young official, Gautier le Jeune, in whom Karnein sees the Gualterius to whom the *De amore* is dedicated; (3) the existence of several royal charters from 1190 to 1191 citing as witness a certain *Andreas cambellanus,* or "Andrew the Chamberlain," who could have written the treatise several years before, at an earlier stage of his career, when he was only a chaplain and not yet a chamberlain (Gautier le Jeune followed just such a career pattern, according to Karnein, though John Baldwin disputes this);[23] (4) the mention of the *De amore* in two mid-fourteenth-century inventories of royal charters, where it is found among the documents dating from before the time of Saint Louis, and where Karnein suggests that it may have been put by "Walter" himself. From this hypothesis Karnein draws the conclusion that the *De amore* cannot be interpreted as though it were a product of the courtly circles at the court of Champagne, that it should be seen as a clerical reaction to and condemnation of contemporary secular love literature, rather than as an attempt to promote that literature.

In his discussion of the *De amore*'s reception, Karnein tries to document a major change in attitude toward the work occurring in the vernacular literatures near the end of the thirteenth century. In the Latin tradition, the *De amore* appears primarily as a source of quotations in works of a pious, Christian nature. In particular, Albertanus da Brescia (1238), the first author to refer to Andreas, uses the definition of love found in the *De amore* to define what he calls *cupiditas.* The vernacular poetry is at first silent about Andreas, according to Karnein;

23. Baldwin, *Language,* p. 275, n. 52.

then late in the thirteenth century we observe a "change of paradigm" in his reception, as the treatise begins to be viewed as a positive *summa* on sexual love. Expressed in part in the *Livre d'Enanchet* and especially in the translation of the *De amore* by Drouart la Vache (1290), this new mode of reception would go on to become completely predominant in the fourteenth and fifteenth centuries. Thus Andreas's contemporaries, Karnein concludes, saw in the *De amore* a treatise against love, whereas the modern tendency to interpret it as a handbook on courtly love can be traced to the secularizing trends of the late Middle Ages.

In assessing the Robertsonian approach to the *De amore,* we must keep in mind the theoretical context in which this interpretation was first formulated. Robertson starts out from the position that medieval writers were Christians and therefore can be assumed to hold and express orthodox Christian ideas, even when that intention is not obvious. The key to understanding this is seen in the medieval habit of allegorical interpretation, applied particularly but not exclusively to Holy Scripture, which distinguishes the literal meanings from the (generally more acceptable) allegorical meaning. Thus apparently unorthodox writers must have intended and expected their writings to be interpreted allegorically.

In an early essay, "Historical Criticism," Robertson stated his position in the following terms:

> Medieval Christian poetry, and by Christian poetry I mean all serious poetry written by Christian authors, even that usually called "secular," is always allegorical when the message of charity or some corollary of it is not evident on the surface.[24]

He subsequently devoted a great deal of energy to applying this theory not only to Andreas Capellanus, but to a wide variety of medieval authors and works, including the troubadours, Chrétien de Troyes, Marie de France, the *Carmina Burana,* the *Romance of the Rose,* and Chaucer, denying in particular that any of them could have promoted anything like the modern notion of "courtly love," in which they would have

---

24. Robertson, "Historical Criticism," p. 14; repr. in idem, *Essays,* p. 10.

seen only the Christian sin of concupiscence.[25] In confronting this theory with the vast body of medieval love literature, one cannot help but wonder why the orthodox doctrine of Christian charity was expressed so systematically in such an indirect and obscure fashion, and also why medieval writers devoted so much energy to ironizing about a secular view of love in which no one apparently believed.[26]

Robertson's theory is based on a radical reduction of the cultural context brought to bear for the interpretation of medieval texts: only the Christian component of that context is deemed pertinent. But medieval culture was clearly much richer and more complex than this view would suggest. Medieval Christianity was certainly a dominant force in the culture, but it was itself riddled with internal conflicts, and it found itself in constant confrontation with such competing forces as the political and social reality of feudal society and, at least from the Twelfth-Century Renaissance onward, a strong secular current in the intellectual sphere.

Robertson's general theory is largely forgotten by recent scholars who follow his approach to Andreas Capellanus, and I suspect that many of them would find such a monolithic view of the Middle Ages unacceptable.[27] Yet Robertson's theory is, I believe, crucial to his interpretation of the *De amore.*

A large number of the discrepancies in which Robertson sees signals to irony are not discrepancies within the text, but rather discrepancies with respect to the presumed cultural context, namely Christianity. Thus the famous definition of love with which the treatise begins has nothing intrinsically ironic about it; the irony that Robertson attributes to it can be seen only as an outgrowth of the juxtaposition of this passage with the biblical and theological texts in the light of which Robertson claims it must be interpreted.[28] Likewise, the irony of the men in the dialogues advancing their own *probitas morum* as an argument for "committing fornication" assumes that *probitas* can have only its classi-

---

25. Many of these studies are reprinted in Robertson, *Essays.*
26. Similar objections are voiced by Kaske, pp. 189–90.
27. E.g., Cherchi, "Andreas' *De amore*"; Frappier, "Sur un procès."
28. Robertson, "Subject," pp. 150–55; idem, *Preface,* pp. 84–85.

cal and (especially) Christian resonances, that it is not possible to redefine it, as Andreas seems to do, in terms of certain courtly and feudal values, such as valor and courtesy. Of course, the substitution of the highly charged Christian term "fornication" for Andreas's vaguer, more neutral *amor* is also intended to heighten the discrepancy and thus the irony, but it rests on the assumption that Andreas's audience would have automatically made such a substitution, indeed that Andreas was counting on them to do so.[29] In this way, a network of interpretations is built up that becomes the "context" for interpreting all the other passages of the treatise, so that the entire edifice depends on the exclusively Christian cultural context that was assumed at the outset.

Like the earlier ironic reading of Book Three, the Robertsonian interpretation of the treatise is only partially ironic. Robertson does not even consider the possibility of reading Book Three ironically, yet, as several scholars have pointed out, the denunciation of love and of women is so exaggerated that it is hard to take it seriously, and it is punctuated by the repeated assertion that its extreme pronouncements admit of no exception, which could easily be taken as a signal for irony.[30] Moreover, if readers have been put into an ironic frame of mind in the course of reading the first two books, it is difficult to see how they could avoid carrying some of the same expectation over into the third book as well.

In fact, the case is even more complex than that, for despite his globally ironic interpretation of the first two books in terms of their general thrust, those books contain many pious and moralizing statements that Robertson takes quite literally. Thus readers are required constantly to shift gears back and forth between literal and ironic interpretations. How do they know when and how to do this? The answer is, of course, through the presumed Christian cultural context.

---

29. Robertson, *Preface,* pp. 402–3. Cf. ibid., pp. 442–43: "The humor of the dialogues is not modern humor; it depends for its effectiveness on an assumed scale of values which is not at all like the assumed scale of values which modern readers bring to texts and situations. The values involved are theological values derived from the Scriptures and moral values derived from classical literature. . . . These ideas are not in themselves humorous."

30. Kaske, p. 191 and n. 21; Donaldson, p. 161.

One of the weakest links in this interpretation is its inability to account for Book Two, "How Love May Be Retained." Robertson resumes it hastily, asserting that it "contains little that is not obvious in the light of the dialogues."[31] Karnein concludes that Book Two's tone is "factual and neutral" and that it "strongly supports the encyclopedic character of the work."[32] This description seems reasonable enough, but it is hard to see how it can be reconciled with Karnein's assertions elsewhere that the *De amore* is not a *summa* on love and was not so interpreted by Andreas's contemporaries.[33] If the second book is "neutral," if it does not contribute positively to the ironic interpretation of the *De amore* as a "treatise against love," then it inevitably weakens that interpretation by diluting it and blurring its focus.

Although Karnein follows Robertson in his interpretation of the *De amore,* he does not accept Robertson's monolithic view of medieval culture. Hence the importance that he attaches to the identification of Andreas and his milieu, as well as to the early reception of his work. These two parts of his study can be seen as an attempt to establish an immediate situation of enunciation capable of providing interpretive orientation within the complexities of the broad cultural context.

The evidence that Karnein adduces concerning Andreas's identity is impressive, and his hypothesis is perhaps the strongest yet put forward on this subject. The matter is far from resolved, however, for the identification of Andreas as "chaplain of the King of France" rests on only three manuscripts out of forty-one. Some scholars have seen these rubrics as a late amplification of a passage within the treatise where Andreas refers to himself as "chaplain of the King," with the passage in question referring to the King of Love whose court is described in the Fifth Dialogue.[34] If this hypothesis is correct, Karnein's case for identi-

31. Robertson, *Preface,* p. 444.

32. Karnein, *"De amore,"* p. 55: "Die Tonlage dieser Kapitel des 2. Buchs wird man noch am ehesten als sachlich-neutral empfinden. Die Mischung aus *courtoisie*-Regeln, ovidianischen Reminizenzen und Vorschriften aus der *amicitia*-Literatur des 12. Jahrhunderts stützt stark den enzyklopädischen Charakter des Werks." Cf. ibid., pp. 59 and 265, where the treatise as a whole is interpreted as an "Enzyklopädie der Sexualität."

33. Karnein, *"Amor est passio,"* p. 215; idem, *"De amore,"* pp. 13–14; cf. idem, "La Réception," p. 326.

34. H. A. Kelly, pp. 36; Liebertz-Grün, Review, p. 309. Cf. *DA* 1.6.385 (152): *Andreæ*

fying Andreas, deprived of the support of the manuscripts, becomes extremely circumstantial.[35]

Even if we accept the hypothesis that the *De amore* was written at the court of Philip Augustus, I do not believe that we can deduce from that all that Karnein would like to. We really do not know much about the mentality at the French court, except by way of an argument from silence, the fact that it seems not to have produced courtly romances, unlike the contemporary courts of Champagne and England. We do not know, for example, to what extent such romances may have been consumed there. If the *De amore* was written in Paris, then it is one of the best documents that we have on the mentality of the French court, and there is no reason to assume on the part of the society that produced and consumed it any less cultural complexity than that which is evident in the work itself. Presumably, Andreas's audience, like the Chaplain himself, were both clerics and courtiers; that is, they were familiar with and participated in both of the two main cultural currents that can be seen to inform the treatise. In fact, even twelfth-century clerical culture was not lacking in complexity where love was concerned, as is illustrated, for example, by the reception of Ovid in the *Facetus* and the *Pamphilus* or by the erotic Latin poems of the Ripoll manuscript.[36] Karnein's assertion that Andreas was "perplexed" by the vernacular love poetry, because the clerical world had "only unequivocally negative categories at its disposal" for dealing with love, seems to me without foundation.[37]

---

aulæ regiæ capellani; Karnein, *"De amore,"* p. 271. I have discovered a somewhat similar confusion in the Old Provençal manuscript tradition. See Monson, *Les "Ensenhamens,"* pp. 99–100.

35. In addition to Liebertz-Grün, skepticism concerning Karnein's hypothesis has been expressed by Ruffini, pp. x–xvi, by Baldwin, *Language,* pp. 16–17 and p. 275, nn. 51–52, and by Dronke, "Andreas Capellanus" (who assigns the work to the thirteenth century). It does not follow that the work's origin can with any real confidence be situated at the court of Champagne, as some have argued, for that hypothesis is also very conjectural. See Benton, "Clio and Venus"; idem, " Evidence." Cairns, p. 101 and p. 115, n. 4, cites the place of composition of the treatise among the "controversial questions" that "remain unanswered."

36. Goddard, *"Facetus";* "Pamphilus," ed. Pittaluga; Latzke, "Die Carmina erotica."

37. Karnein, *"De amore,"* p. 18: "Was Andreas verblüffte, war die Art und Weise,

The heart of Karnein's contribution is doubtless his work on Andreas's reception; but this study is based on several equivocacies that tend to obscure the question, rather than to elucidate it, and much of the evidence is obviously distorted by being forced into the Robertsonian mold.

The first such equivocacy is the use of the term "contemporaries" *(Zeitgenossen)* to designate the authors in the Latin tradition.[38] The earliest reaction to Andreas, that of Albertanus da Brescia, comes from a bourgeois milieu in northern Italy and dates from 1238, more than fifty years after the date when most scholars, including Karnein, presume the *De amore* to have been written. The intervening half-century had seen the rise of the Franciscan and Dominican movements, the Crusade against the Albigensians, and the establishment of the great medieval Inquisition, which was particularly active in southern France and northern Italy, the seats of Catharist and Waldensian heresy. Albertanus's world was immeasurably more pious and less secular than that of the northern French courts at the end of the Twelfth-Century Renaissance. If, as Karnein argues, Andreas's *Sitz im Leben* is crucial to understanding his reception of the vernacular love literature,[39] then Albertanus's *Sitz im Leben* must surely be just as important in assessing his reception of the *De amore.*

As for Andreas's other major "contemporary," Geremia da Montagnone, like Albertanus a northern Italian and a man of the law, there is some doubt as to whether his reaction to Andreas should even be included in the thirteenth century. The work that contains that reaction cannot have been written before 1295, and it may have been written as late as 1321, the last date for which Geremia's activity as a judge in his native Padua is attested.

The works of Albertanus and Geremia are clearly very pious in intention, but their inclusion of several quotations from Andreas Capel-

mit der volkssprachliche Literatur so ganz anderen, souveränen Gebrauch von einer Sache macht, für die in der Welt der Studierten nur eindeutig negative Kategorien zur Verfügung standen."

38. Karnein, *"De amore,"* pp. 17–19; cf. ibid., p. 265: "zu seiner Zeit"; idem, "Andreas, Boncompagno," p. 32; idem, "La Réception," p. 326: "contemporains."

39. Karnein, *"De amore,"* pp. 14–16 and 39; idem, "Andreas, Boncompagno," p. 31.

lanus does not prove that he shared their intention, nor even that they believed that he did. Geremia was quoting Andreas from a florilegium, as Karnein has shown. That fact precludes Geremia's having any opinion about the intention of the *De amore* as a whole, which he quite possibly never even saw. The same is probably also true of Albertanus's quotation of the definition of love and of several of the Rules of Love, two parts of the *De amore* that seem to have been anthologized very early. Karnein sees the use of Andreas's definition of love to define *cupiditas,* particularly the introduction of this definition with the words *de quo Gualterus tractavit*—"which (cupidity) Walter treated" or "on which Walter wrote a treatise"—as implying that Albertanus thought that "Walter" (i.e., Andreas) agreed with him as to the real subject of the treatise and as to the attitude that one should adopt toward it, but nothing could be less certain. Concerning the Rules of Love that Albertanus quotes in the same treatise, Karnein has shown that they are treated as positive rules of friendship, devoid of any sexual connotations. There is no reason to doubt that a similar appropriation and redeployment took place with respect to the definition of love as well. It thus seems doubtful whether Albertanus had any opinion about or concern for Andreas's intention. After all, the main function of a florilegium is to facilitate the quotation of authorities out of context.

Turning to the reception of the *De amore* in the vernacular literature, we find the same equivocacy on dating, particularly with respect to the *Livre d'Enanchet,* which Karnein assigns "probably" to "the second half of the thirteenth century."[40] Now this could be true—barely— since the *terminus ante quem* for this work is 1252, the date of one of the two manuscripts that preserve it.[41] Of course, it is rather more likely that the *Enanchet* dates from the first half of the century. Pio Rajna (p. 207), who knew only the other manuscript, dated 1287, said of this text that it "can not be much later than the writings of Albertanus."

Concerning three late-thirteenth-century poems in which he finds

---

40. Karnein, *"De amore,"* p. 179: "Das wohl der zweiten Jahrhunderthälfte angehörende . . . *Livre d'Enanchet*"; idem, "La Réception," p. 515: "Le *Livre d'Enanchet* date sans doute de la seconde moitié du XIIIe siècle."

41. Putanec; *GRLMA,* p. 134, § 2680.

no influence of Andreas, the arts of love by Jacques d'Amiens and by Guiart and the anonymous *Clef d'amors,* Karnein says only that they are from the thirteenth century. This is undoubtedly true, but the fact that these texts are discussed some fifty pages before *Enanchet* could easily give the impression that they are earlier than that work. In fact, *Enanchet* must be earlier by at least two or three decades.[42]

Doubtless the most curious aspect of Karnein's *Rezeptionsgeschichte* is his treatment of the condemnation of the *De amore* by the bishop of Paris, Etienne Tempier, in 1277. For Karnein this Latin *decretum* concerning Latin books and propositions banned from use at the University of Paris is part of the *vernacular* reception of the *De amore.* He explains that this is because the condemnation, coming some ninety years after Andreas wrote his treatise (but twenty to forty years *before* Andreas's "contemporary," Geremia da Montagnone, it should be noted), was provoked not so much by the *De amore* itself as by the "change of paradigm" in reception observable in the vernacular literature in Bishop Tempier's own time. One cannot help wondering to which of the vernacular works the bishop was reacting: to *Enanchet,* written at least twenty-five years before, which incorporated a partial adaptation of Andreas along with a good deal of other material, and which concludes with a suggestion for an allegorical interpretation, thus creating an ambiguity in intention similar to that of the *De amore?* To Tempier's close contemporary, also associated with the University of Paris, Jean de Meun, whose only echo of the *De amore,* according to Karnein's analysis, is the ten-line translation of Andreas's definition of love, in a speech by Reason against love, in a poem of twenty thousand lines? To Drouart la Vache's translation, undertaken thirteen years *after* the condemnation? For Karnein has shown at great length that these are the *only* vernacular reactions to the *De amore* for the entire thirteenth century. And one may further wonder, if it was these vernacular misinterpretations of Andreas that provoked the bishop's wrath, why there is no trace of a reference to any of them in the condemnation?

42. Karnein, *"De amore,"* pp. 131–34; idem, "La Réception," pp. 511–12. Cf. *GRLMA* 6/2, p. 162, § 3156 (*Clef* = ca. 1280); p. 165, § 3200 (Guiart = end of 13th century); p. 165, § 3208 (Jacques d'Amiens = last third, 13th century).

A more plausible explanation for the arbitrary assignment of the condemnation to the vernacular literature is the obvious difficulty of reconciling it in any other way with Karnein's general thesis. The condemnation is the earliest unambiguous reaction to the *De amore* that we have, and it suggests that the bishop found the treatise dangerous to faith and morals. Writing in Paris, the supposed place of origin of the treatise, and being a fellow cleric, Bishop Tempier was presumably an ideal audience for Andreas's irony. If he missed the irony, then many others must have missed it as well, all of which casts doubt on the effectiveness with which Andreas communicated it in the first place, if indeed that was his intention.

A more convincing interpretation of Karnein's evidence for the thirteenth-century reception of the *De amore* would distinguish two tendencies, both affecting Latin as well as vernacular literature, and both stretching right across the century. On the one hand, those who quoted Andreas from the florilegia, from Albertanus da Brescia to Jean de Meun to Geremia da Montagnone, adapted the quotations, as was customary, to their own contexts (which were generally conservative, in the spirit of the times), without necessarily knowing or caring what the original context may have been. On the other hand, those who seem to have been reacting to the *De amore* as a whole, or at least to some substantial part of it, from *Enanchet* to Bishop Tempier to Drouart la Vache, saw in the treatise a secular *summa* on sexual love and indeed, from the bishop's point of view, a dangerous one.

From the above discussion I draw three conclusions. First, whatever its intrinsic interest, the thirteenth-century evidence on the reception of the *De amore* can tell us little or nothing about how the treatise was read in the late twelfth century. Second, unfortunately but, it seems to me, inescapably, Karnein's considerable contribution to the reception of the *De amore* must be used throughout with extreme caution. Finally, to paraphrase Robertson's famous pronouncement on courtly love, the Robertsonian method can clearly be an impediment to understanding medieval texts.[43]

---

43. Cf. Robertson, "Concept."

Crypto-erotic irony

Robertson devotes a fair amount of discussion to passages in the *De amore* that he considers humorous, amalgamating the notions of "humor" and "irony" as if they were more or less synonymous. Yet, with its constant emphasis on Christian faith and morality, I think we must say that Robertson's is on the whole a seriously ironic interpretation. There are others, however, who see in the *De amore* a more jocular type of humor.

To my knowledge, the first suggestion that humor might be an important aspect of the treatise was made by Sidney Painter in 1940. Painter was also the first person I know of to apply the term "irony" to Andreas, although he did so only in passing and certainly did not mean to imply anything like the Robertsonian interpretation.[44] Such occasional references to "irony" are not infrequent in later humorous interpretations as well.

From the 1950s onward, perhaps in part in the wake of Robertson, such humorous interpretations of the *De amore* have become more widespread. Those who have espoused this view include: Hermann J. Weigand, W. T. H. Jackson, Robert E. Kaske, Norbert de Paepe, Donald R. Howard, John C. Moore, Joan M. Ferrante, George D. Economou, Douglas R. Buttruff, Michael D. Cherniss, Henry A. Kelly, Tony Hunt, Jean Leclercq, Rüdiger Schnell, and Neil Cartlidge.[45]

These humorous interpretations often approach the *De amore* from widely divergent viewpoints. For example, Jackson, Howard, and Buttruff see the treatise as a comedy of social manners reflecting the love games practiced at court. Michael Cherniss, on the other hand, views the work as a "literary comedy" burlesquing previous texts.

44. Painter, pp. 17–19 and 164–65. Even earlier West, p. 4, wrote of the *De amore:* "its tone, especially in the third part, . . . is often more in keeping with the cynicism of Ovid than with the seriousness of courtly love."

45. Weigand, pp. 18–25; esp. p. 24; Jackson; Kaske, pp. 191–92; De Paepe; Howard, pp. 95–97; Moore, "Love," p. 437 and n. 47; idem, *Love,* pp. 122–29; Ferrante and Economou, pp. 3 and 5–6; Buttruff; Cherniss; H. A. Kelly, pp. 24–25, 73, and 256; T. Hunt, pp. 125–28; Leclercq, pp. 71 and 116–17; Schnell, *Andreas Capellanus,* pp. 26–27, 31–35, 126, 132, 137, 144–48, 152, and 165–71; Cartlidge, pp. 25–27.

One of the earliest and most interesting of these interpretations is that of Hermann J. Weigand. Commenting on Andreas's practice of letting his characters cite as an authority the treatise of which they are a part, Weigand suggests that the entire work was written "tongue in cheek," and indeed that Andreas may have been practicing Romantic irony *avant la lettre,* as did Cervantes and Sterne. By the latter comment, I understand Weigand to mean that the Chaplain's discourse is one that intentionally undercuts itself at every turn. More recently Tony Hunt has reached somewhat similar conclusions based on an analysis of Andreas's use of dialectic.

The most recent humorous interpretation of Andreas's work is also the most extreme. This is the view that the *De amore* is a kind of elaborate dirty joke, composed of a series of obscene images and puns, thinly veiled beneath the surface of the text.

This interpretation was launched in 1979 by Betsy Bowden in an article entitled "The Art of Courtly Copulation." It has since been greeted enthusiastically by Hubert Silvestre and Bruno Roy, who have added further examples and extended the method's claims. Meanwhile, Beate Schmolke-Hasselmann has applied a somewhat similar approach, independently, it would seem, in her analysis of the Arthurian episode that closes Book Two.[46]

Although the "dirty-joke" school do not use the word "irony" in connection with their own approach—indeed Bowden (p. 68) speaks rather disparagingly of Robertson's "dredgings for irony"—I think it can be shown that theirs, too, is an ironic interpretation. Their analysis seeks to uncover a second level of meaning beneath the surface meaning. In a sense, this second meaning reinforces the secularizing tendencies in the first two books, rather than conflicting with them, yet it also

---

46. Bowden; Silvestre; Roy, "André le Chapelain"; Schmolke-Hasselmann. Jacquart and Thomasset, pp. 96–110, also espouse Bowden's method in an attempt to show that "the practice of *coitus interruptus* . . . does seem to be the main lesson taught by the [*De amore*]" (p. 104). It is further suggested that this method of contraception, here associated with Catharism, was an essential feature of "courtly love." The demonstration is not convincing, especially since most of the examples are taken from Andreas's translator, Drouart la Vache (see below, n. 70), with the dubious inference that the latter's alleged sexual puns in Old French were somehow implicit in the Latin original.

clearly undercuts any attempt to idealize love in those same books. If the analysis is extended to the third book, as Silvestre in particular suggests, then the overt and covert meanings are diametrically opposed to each other. Bruno Roy also brings the two-audience model into his discussion of latent erotic metaphors, "which can be spotted by those who want to see them, while remaining invisible to others."[47]

Betsy Bowden's essay centers upon an analysis of Andreas's Fifth Dialogue, which develops an allegorical description of the Palace of Love, as well as the apocalyptic vision of the "Purgatory of Cruel Beauties," here interpreted as a "wet dream." In the first part of the dialogue, Bowden sees a tissue of obscene wordplay. This includes puns on words whose sexual meaning is attested, though they also have non-sexual meanings: *radius* ("ray/rod") for the male member; *via* ("way"), *semita* ("path"), *porta, ianua, ostium* ("door/gate") for the female pudendum; *cognoscere* ("know"), *pulsare* ("beat/knock"), *peragere* ("traverse/transpierce/carry out or through") referring to sexual intercourse, and so on. It also includes several approximate puns on words for which no sexual meaning is attested, but which bear some resemblance to known sexual terms: for example, *pœna* ("punishment/pain") for *penis,* and *cunctus* ("all") for *cunnus* ("vagina"). In the last part of the dialogue, there is a shift, according to Bowden, to a series of Freudian images: "tree" or "rod" for the male member, "fountain" for the female pudendum, and "couch" for sexual intercourse. In conclusion Bowden (p. 81) calls for more work to determine whether the Fifth Dialogue is "a particularly obscene chapter, or one typical of the whole work."

This interpretation was greeted with great enthusiasm by Hubert Silvestre, who declared the matter "henceforth resolved."[48] Silvestre also proposes several new words for discussion, for example the adverb *penitus* ("completely"), which occurs over one hundred times in the treatise and which he sees as another reference to *penis,* or perhaps as a past participle meaning "provided with a penis." The obscene puns are found

---

47. Roy, "André le Chapelain," p. 67: "Pour qu'une métaphore latente dans un texte devienne repérable à ceux qui veulent l'y voir, tout en demeurant invisible aux autres, il faut qu'elle obéisse à certaines conditions littéraires précises."

48. Silvestre, p. 99: "La question me paraît désormais résolue grâce à une érudite américaine."

more or less uniformly throughout the three books, according to Silvestre, so that the pious appearance of the third book masks impious and sacrilegious derision and satire. Andreas was thus the earliest manifestation of the subversive current that would lead to the Libertines of the seventeenth and eighteenth centuries.

Bruno Roy proposes to formulate Bowden's hypothesis differently, by redistributing into new categories the facts discovered by her analysis. Roy distinguishes three types of phenomena: (1) the equivocal use of Latin sexual vocabulary, for which the recent book by James N. Adams is a particularly good source; (2) the sexualization of everyday Latin vocabulary, which may arise from ambiguities within Latin, but with respect to which the bilingualism of medieval clerics is attributed a dominant role; and (3) erotic metaphors. Like Silvestre, Roy adds a certain number of examples and corrections for each of his various categories. He concludes his remarks with a complex analysis of a passage in which he sees all three techniques at work: the discussion of the *lacertiva avis* in the Second Dialogue.

Beate Schmolke-Hasselmann's apparently independent "allegorical" interpretation of the Arthurian episode of Book Two centers on the two objects of the Breton knight's quest: the *accipiter* ("hawk"), which he must produce to win the love of his lady, and the *chirotheca* ("glove/gauntlet"), which he must produce to get the hawk. The former she sees as a metaphor for the lover and particularly for the male member, citing the common association of "bird" and "penis" in folklore, as well as the frequent presence of birds in the medieval iconography of love scenes.[49] In the latter she sees a metaphor for the female pudendum, admitting that this association is less common, but arguing that the frequent presence of gloves in amorous contexts in courtly romances is sufficient to lend credibility to her hypothesis. This leads to a reexamination of the curiously unmotivated intervention of the fairy helper, which, it is suggested, can be interpreted in terms of sexual initiation. The castle that

---

49. Schmolke-Hasselmann's iconographic evidence is far from constituting incontrovertible proof of her hypothesis: the presence of hunting birds perched on the wrists of male lovers is rather to be taken as a conventional symbol of their nobility, since hunting was restricted to the noble class. The mention of gloves in amorous contexts in the romances is doubtless susceptible of similar explanations.

must be stormed to get the hawk is viewed as a symbol of feminine resistance, making of Andreas's tale a forerunner of the *Romance of the Rose.* A political dimension is achieved through the implicit association of King Arthur with Henry II Plantagenet, whose interest in vernacular love literature is satirized. Thus an apparently banal story takes on new meaning at the level of *sensus allegoricus.*

What are we to make of the "dirty-joke" hypothesis? It is, of course, intriguing to think of ribald puns underlying some of the Chaplain's more solemn pronouncements, and the comic appeal of at least some of the proposed interpretations is obvious. Starting, for example, from the known fact that *pulsare,* "knock," is sometimes used as a rude metaphor for sexual intercourse, it is amusing to think that the description of the reluctant ladies in the Palace of Love as *illæ feminæ quæ nemini pulsanti aperiunt* (*DA* 1.6.226 [104])—"the women who open to no man's knock"—may perhaps be interpreted simultaneously on two complementary levels. If we also assume behind this passage the biblical intertext *Pulsate et aperietur vobis*—"knock, and it shall be opened unto you" (Matt. 7:7)—the piquancy is further heightened, not to mention the irony.[50] A significant number of such readings would doubtless go a long way toward enlivening what some have seen as an otherwise dull text.

Is that how medieval audiences read the treatise, and was that Andreas's intention? I believe that a close look at some of the readings proposed will reveal serious problems that cast real doubt as to whether a medieval audience *could* have read in that way.

The most vulnerable of these readings are doubtless the approximate puns on words for which no sexual connotation is attested. Betsy Bowden (p. 67) admits that "few of Andreas's double entendres form perfect puns," and Bruno Roy goes on to say:

> The principal problem that we encounter, in the analysis of puns, is the dilemma exactness/approximation. In practice approximation proves funnier than exact verbal calque, so criticism (especially for early texts) becomes nearly impossible.[51]

50. Bowden, p. 85, n. 36; Roy, "André le Chapelain," p. 61 and n. 7.
51. Roy, "André le Chapelain," p. 66, n. 24: "Le problème principal auquel on se

If criticism is impossible, how will we know when the interpretive process has got out of hand, the approximation being so remote that it is perceptible only to the most ardent of pun-hunters?

A case in point is the word *probitas,* in which Bowden (pp. 75–76) sees an "implied physicality" suggestive of a male erection. Of course, such physicality is not at all implied in *probitas,* only in its English gloss, "uprightness," and it is inconceivable that medieval French clerics could have found their way through English to make that association.

Sensing the difficulty, Hubert Silvestre (pp. 102–3) hastens to suggest that *probitas* may be a bilingual pun on the French *bite,* a slang word for the male member, but this interpretation has difficulties of its own. In the passage in question, the discussion concerned whether the man could *probitatem retinere* (*DA* .1.6.225 [104]), that is "keep an erection," according to Bowden. If we adopt Silvestre's suggestion, is it now a question of whether the man can hang on to his penis? Moreover, there are several passages earlier in the same dialogue in which the woman's *probitas* is discussed. What are we to make of that, with either of these hypotheses? Finally, the word *bite* is first attested in this sense at the end of the sixteenth century, some four hundred years after Andreas, which makes it highly unlikely that he could have made a pun on it.[52]

I cannot help but wonder whether the English "four-letter word" *cunt* may have also played a role in the association of *cunctus* with *cunnus. Cunctus* ("all") is an extremely common word, found throughout the treatise, being particularly suited to dialectical argumentation be-

---

heurte, dans l'analyse des jeux de mots, est le dilemme exactitude/approximation. L'approximation se révélant à la pratique plus comique que le calque verbal exact, la critique (surtout des textes anciens) devient presque impossible."

52. This use first appears in Bouchet, 1:105. Wartburg, *FEW* 15:384, gives "1394," but this is clearly a printing error, for Wartburg's source is Bouchet. Cf. *FEW* 1:384; *Trésor de la langue française* 4:547. Wartburg derives this use from a cross between two Old French verbs, *abiter,* "to approach, to touch," and *habiter,* "to have carnal relations," attested in the eleventh and thirteenth centuries, respectively, and Silvestre argues from this derivation that *bite* could have existed in Andreas's time. But Wartburg's etymology has been contested by Sjögren, pp. 386–87, who suggests a rather more plausible derivation from Middle French *bitte,* "mooring post, bollard," a nautical term of Norse origin first attested in 1382. This suggestion is accepted by Gamillscheg, p. 116, and by *Grand Robert,* 2:10, the latter analyzing this use as a "metaphor of form."

cause of its important logical implications. Interpreting it each time as a rude pun would not only do considerable violence to the text, it would also require a fair amount of verbal gymnastics. When it is used in the feminine or the neuter plural, *cunctus* takes on endings, such as *-a* or *-as,* that are impossible with *cunnus* and that further separate the form of these two words. When *cunctus* is used as an adjective, there is the problem, in reinterpreting it as a noun, of what to do with the noun that it otherwise would have modified. The fragility of this interpretation is underlined by the reservations of Bruno Roy, who, feeling that Betsy Bowden may be mistaken on this point, suggests that medieval people saw in *cunctus* the verb *coeo* and that *coitum* "isn't all that far a-way."[53] Roy's proposal seems to me even less convincing than the one it would replace, and it certainly would wreak havoc with several of the readings that Betsy Bowden has so carefully constructed.

This last example touches on one of the real weaknesses of this interpretation: its relative insensitivity to case endings. In the assimilation of *pœna* to *penis,* the reduction of the diphthong in the radical poses no problem (many if not most of Trojel's classical diphthongs must surely represent normalizations of the manuscript readings), but the case endings are another matter. For example, in the first occurrence of this word in the dialogue (*DA* 1.6.198 [96]), *pœnas* must be interpreted not as *penas,* or even as *penis,* but as *penem,* in order to get the sense which Betsy Bowden (p. 72) sees in the passage. Likewise, in the third speech of the woman, if we want to see a joke in *amantium me pœnis subiicere* (*DA* 1.6.209 [100]) or in *tot enim pœnis . . . [amantes] exponuntur* (*DA* 1.6. 210 [100]), we must read *penibus* for *pœnis* (see Bowden, p. 74). Karnein has pointed out a pun on *pœna* and *penis* by Boncompagno a generation after Andreas:

> Notula iocosa et vera. Nota quod ab initio et ante secula non fuit inauditum, quod aliqua mulier maximum penem reputaret ad penam, quare de magnitudine dissuadere nemo potest alicui muliere [sc. mulier*i*].[54]

---

53. Roy, "André le Chapelain," p. 66: "il se pourrait qu'elle se trompe; mais un médiéval lisait dans *cunctus* le verbe *coeo:* le *coitum* n'était pas si loin."

54. Karnein, "Andreas, Boncompagno," p. 35, n. 6, quoting Boncompagno, *Rhetorica antiqua,* ed. Purkart. "A little note, amusing and true. Note that from the beginning

This example is particularly instructive, as it shows that it is the explicit alternation of case endings, *penem/penam,* highlighted by the close similarity of form as well as by the syntax, that makes the pun possible.

Case endings are the foundation of Latin grammar, for without them no syntax is possible. If the case endings are destroyed through the process of punning, it is tempting to fall back on something like the analytic syntax of modern French or English to construct meaningful utterances. But can we feel reasonably certain that medieval clerics might have done the same?

The contortions to Latin syntax that this method sometimes imposes can be illustrated by the sentence *Credo . . . quod tam nobilis tantæque femina probitatis non diu permittet, me pœnis subiacere tam gravibus, sed a cunctis me relevabit angustiis (DA* 1.6.203 [98]), which Betsy Bowden (p. 73) interprets as meaning "[I believe] . . . that such an upright woman would not long permit [my] penis to be subjected to such burdens, but would with her narrow *cunnus* raise [me] up and relieve [me]." If we accept the puns on *relevare* ("raise up/relieve"), *pœna,* and *cunctus,* plus the fact that *probitas* is apparently to be taken literally here, without any pun intended, we still must make the following four adjustments to arrive at that sense: (1) for *me pœnis* we must read *meum penem* (by way of Old French *mon penis,* according to Bowden, but *pénis* is not attested in French until the seventeenth century);[55] (2) the adjective *gravibus,* which normally modifies *pœnis,* must be taken as a noun meaning "burdens," a use that is unattested; (3) the preposition *a* (*ab,* expressing separation) must be understood as the Old French *a,* in the instrumental use; (4) *cunctis . . . angustiis* must be interpreted as *cunno angusto* (unless we wish to attribute two or more *cunni* to the lady).

Similar problems attend the "literal translation" of the passage near the end of the dialogue on which the claim of "wet dream" is largely

---

and for centuries earlier, it was not unheard of that some woman considered a very large penis to be a punishment, for no one is able to dissuade any woman from [a penis of] great size" (my translation). I cannot agree with Karnein that this example "confirms" Bowden's theory.

55. In 1618, according to *FEW* 8:189, and *Grand Robert* 7:239. Even the status of *penis* in later Latin is open to question; cf. Adams, p. 36.

based: *circa fluenta sum deductus aquarum. Ibi crystallina virga dimissa illæsus ad propria remeavi* (*DA* 1.6.273 [118]), which is rendered "I was drawn out, surrounded by a flowing of waters. There, the crystal rod having been given up, I returned to myself unhurt." "Surrounded by a flowing of waters" is grammatically quite unacceptable for *circa fluenta . . . aquarum,* "drawn out" for *deductus* is highly unlikely, and "to myself/to oneself" for *ad propria* is unattested.[56]

Turning to the cases where a sexual meaning is previously attested, we can consider wordplay and metaphors together, for the known sexual words in Latin are nearly all transparent metaphors that have entered the lexicon. Here the "dirty-joke" interpretation would be irresistible, were it not for two factors: (1) all these words and images also have a nonsexual meaning; (2) all are imbedded in contexts that are either not sexual or only mildly so. Bruno Roy's explanation for the fact that the Freudian images in the Fifth Dialogue had previously escaped all modern readers can be applied to the examples of wordplay as well. According to Roy, "the attention of readers was constantly drawn by the author back to the global meaning of his allegory, rather than to the elements of its contents. . . . It was necessary that a reader [i.e., Betsy Bowden] free herself from this super-coherent literary framework for the sexual elements to become visible."[57]

What might have suggested to a medieval clerical audience that they should break out of the structure imposed by the syntax of the sentence or by the demonstrative or narrative logic of the text to go in search of obscene images and puns? Betsy Bowden stresses various difficulties or discrepancies in the surface meaning of the text, which could be viewed as signals for an underlying irony, and which her method claims to re-

56. Bowden, pp. 79–80. Lewis and Short, p. 526, gloss *deducere* with "to draw out" only in two very special contexts: (1) "to *draw out* a ship from the docks"; (2) "to *draw out, spin out* the thread, yarn." In our passage, the common meaning "to lead away" appears much more suitable. Niermeyer, p. 864, gives "home" as the gloss for the plural *propria* (from *proprium,* "landed property, demesne"), and that is surely the sense here.

57. Roy, "André le Chapelain," p. 67: "l'attention du lecteur était constamment ramenée par l'auteur sur le sens global de son allégorie plutôt que sur les éléments de son contenu. . . . Il aura fallu qu'une lectrice s'affranchisse de ce cadre super-cohérent littérairement, pour que les éléments sexuels deviennent visibles."

solve; but she rather tends to exaggerate difficulties that are often susceptible of solution at the surface level.

For example, Bowden (p. 75; cf. ibid., p. 67) takes Parry to task for his "bowdlerized" translation in the singular of the plural *ianuis* ("door, gates") in the description of Love's Palace (*DA* 1.6.223, 225 [102–4], 244 [108]). She sees in the fact that Andreas uses the plural, whereas the palace had previously been described as having only one door or gate on each side, as suggesting that it is the sexual parts of the women associated with this or that gate that are "open" or "closed," as the case may be. But Andreas's expression *ianuis portæ*, which is parallel to his use of *limine portæ* ("the threshold of the door or gate"), shows that *porta* (or *ostium*) describes the overall structure, whereas *ianua* is only a part of that structure, namely the movable part. Andreas clearly envisages a *double* door or gate *(porta)*, both sides *(ianuæ)* of which are either open or closed. That is also how the passage is understood by Claude Buridant (p. 83), who translates *ianuæ* with the French "battants."

Similarly, to reinforce her own proposal for a pun, Bowden (p. 72) claims that "Parry's rendering of *pœna* throughout as 'pain' is common in neither classical Latin nor medieval." This assertion is belied by the evidence of all the Romance languages, not to mention the fact that English "pain" goes back through Old French to Latin *pœna*. Lewis and Short, whose dictionary Bowden used, gloss *pœna* with "hardship, torment, suffering, pain," giving a number of examples, some as early as Seneca and Pliny the Elder.[58]

A very high density of potentially sexual terms could perhaps also be

58. Lewis and Short, p. 1390. Cf. Niermeyer, p. 783: "suffering, pain, misfortune, affliction." Old Provençal *pena* and Old French *paine* are used regularly in the poetry of the troubadours and trouvères to express the suffering of love. See Bec, pp. 550–51; Cropp, *Le Vocabulaire*, p. 285; Lavis, pp. 276–90. One possible explanation for Andreas's preference of *pœna* to Classical Latin *dolor* (aside from the latter's rather unfortunate resemblance to *dolus,* "deceit, guile, fraud," a resemblance that he would doubtless have exploited, had satirical punning been a major factor in his treatise) is the well attested medieval use of *pœna* to designate feudal levies on land. Cf. Niermeyer, p. 783: "cens, fermage—rental"; Du Cange, 6:382: *tributum, onus agris vel personis impositum.* This association reinforces the standard courtly metaphor comparing love service to feudal service. Latham, p. 339, and Souter, p. 308, both gloss *pœnalis* as "painful." Cf. Bowden, p. 72, for whom "its only recorded use" is "of punishment, penal."

taken as a signal for a second reading on a sexual level. That is, I believe, the main burden of Betsy Bowden's argument concerning the Fifth Dialogue. If we have to disallow a fair number of the approximate sexual puns, however, or even to reinterpret them along the lines suggested by Silvestre and Roy, this will also weaken considerably the contextual support for a sexual interpretation of ambiguous terms with known sexual uses. For example, in the "wet-dream" passage cited above, the term *virga* ("rod, wand/penis"), without the doubtful readings with which Bowden has surrounded it, loses most of its punch.

In some cases Bowden is content to point out possible puns on known sexual terms without bothering to integrate them into their contexts. In others she achieves a kind of integration only at the cost of rather questionable readings. *Cognoscere* can undoubtedly have the meaning "to know" sexually, but when the direct object of *cognoscere* is a noun clause expressing an indirect question, *quot ... subiaceant amantes angustiis* (*DA* 1.6.210 [100]; see Bowden, p. 74), for example, what can the sexual interpretation of the verb possibly mean? *Peragere* is also known in the sense "to exhaust sexually," but by glossing *ad omnia peragenda bona viam* (*DA* 1.6.208 [98–100]) as the "road to all good *peragenda*," Bowden (p. 73) makes of the gerundive a totally unattested noun whose precise meaning is not specified. Of course, the alternative would have been to read "the road to sexually exhausting all good things," which does not seem too satisfactory.[59]

It must be added that Bowden's article gives the impression of a

59. Other questionable readings and assertions in Bowden's article include: (1) the gloss (p. 72) "his lady's/her treasure" for *illum thesaurum* (*DA* 1.6.198 [96]; the lady herself is the treasure in question); (2) the characterization (p. 72) of *adferre* as "typically physical" (Lewis and Short, p. 66, devote about one-sixth of the space to literal uses), its glossing with "bring forward" (rather than the normal "bring"; Lewis and Short, ibid., gloss with "bring forward" only in the sense "bring forward, allege, assert, adduce"), and the suggestion that *ferre* (usually "bear, carry") would have been more appropriate here; (3) the characterization (p. 74) of *exponere* as "primarily physical" (Lewis and Short, p. 697, devote about equal space to literal and figurative uses); (4) the summary (p. 74) "trying *his* fortunes in the narrow pathways of love" [my emphasis] for a passage (*DA* 1.6.212 [100]) that clearly concerns the lady, not the man; (5) the suggestion (p. 79) that *avaritia* may refer to sexual incontinence, based on the fact that *castitas* is attested in the sense "*purity* with regard to gain, *disinterestedness* (opp. avaritia)" (Lewis and Short, p. 298).

much more systematic pattern than is actually the case, for her analysis leaves many passages virtually untouched, including some very considerable ones, amounting all together to something between one-half and two-thirds of the dialogue. Some of these passages do include attestations of words such as *pœna, cunctus,* and *probitas,* whose sexual meaning we are now doubtless expected to assume, but the syntactic and semantic integration of these "sexual" terms into their respective contexts is left to the ingenuity of the reader.

Extending the analysis to the entire work increases immeasurably the problem of perceptibility. If, on the one hand, the Fifth Dialogue is a "particularly obscene chapter," as Bowden (p. 81) suggests it might be, how did the medieval clerical audience know that it was time to shift into the "rude-joke" mode? Would they have spotted the imperfect pun on *pœnas* that forms the kernel of the first alleged joke, having already encountered the word *pœna* several times, presumably in more innocuous contexts? How would they have read the first eighty pages of the treatise, and how would that have conditioned their expectations for the Fifth Dialogue?

If, on the other hand, the entire treatise is to be interpreted erotically, as Silvestre and Roy seem to think, how would the medieval audience have known that? Would the fact that the *De amore* presents a secularizing account of sexual love have been a sufficient clue to set off the search for obscene puns? Some one hundred attestations of *penitus* are not very impressive in a corpus of nearly fifty thousand words. Even if they had succeeded in spotting all these attestations, would they have found the joke as funny the one-hundredth time as they did the first time? And what would they have been thinking, through all those interminable pages, as they waited for the next *penitus* to turn up?

Silvestre's suggestion that longer words, such as *probitas, penitus,* and *pœnitudo,* be broken up into syllables for the purpose of bilingual punning raises still further problems of perceptibility—and of method. As Bruno Roy has so aptly put it, the difficulty is "knowing where to stop."[60] Roy himself has trouble knowing where to stop, suggesting

---

60. Roy, "André le Chapelain," p. 73: "Ce qui rend difficile pour nous l'étude des jeux de mots des époques passées, c'est de savoir où s'arrêter."

(p. 66) that we investigate the presence of French "three-letter words" such as *vit, con,* and *cul* imbedded in longer Latin words. He even gives some examples for *vit* ("penis"): *vitare, evitare, invitare, vitium, divitie,* and the like. Whereas Bowden wisely confined herself for the most part to proposing alternative readings (however contorted), Silvestre and Roy abandon themselves to the hunt for dirty words, not to say dirty syllables. What these scholars are, in fact, proposing, without actually saying so, is a kind of "deconstruction" of the text that would make it unreadable at any level.

Perceptibility is not only in the text, it is also a matter of context, for it depends on the expectation that readers bring to the text, and that expectation is conditioned by the context of the ambient culture. As Bruno Roy has pointed out, those who see obscene images and puns in the *De amore* are those who want to see them. What reasons have we to think that obscene punning was a major expectation on the part of Andreas's public, an expectation sufficiently strong for Andreas to have supposed that he could succeed in communicating an obscene intention without making it any more explicit?

Betsy Bowden (p. 80) relates a suggestion of Peter Dronke that Andreas's work be interpreted in terms of the genre in which he wrote. Then, begging the complex and crucial question of genre, she goes on to suggest (pp. 81–82) that "this one harshly erotic dialogue stands solidly inside concentric circles of obscene contexts—within this treatise, within a neglected genre of Ovidian imitations, within a seldom-studied tradition of clerical games and incidental obscenity." Emphasizing the bilingual status of medieval clerics, Bruno Roy (pp. 63–64) calls attention to the bilingual punning of modern schoolboys, and he also cites a number of analogous medieval examples.

The existence of an important and neglected medieval clerical tradition of humorous, satirical, parodic, and erotic literature, including a fair amount of punning and wordplay, is undeniable. But as Jean-Charles Payen (pp. 50–52) has pointed out, the jokes and puns that we encounter in the poetry of the Goliards, the most visible strand of this tradition, are usually much more obvious and accessible than most of what Bowden and her followers see in Andreas. With the Goliards you do not have to look for double entendres, for, indeed, you cannot avoid them. Their very transparency can also be seen as an indication that the Middle Ages had a much greater tolerance of verbal nonconformism than we might be inclined to think today, with the attendant consequence that the motives for concealment often alleged may have been much less powerful than is now generally imagined.

Contrary to what we observe with the Goliards, the reading of the *De amore* proposed here is hermetic and subterranean. Hubert Silvestre sees evidence in the treatise of an "underground movement" practicing "occult subversion," and he tries to make of the very ambiguity of the text a positive proof of its subversiveness.[61] Referring apparently to the need to avoid detection and repression, Bruno Roy writes, "if the game of concealment practiced by the author had not been adroitly carried out, he would never have had an audience in the Middle Ages, especially not among monks."[62]

One important result of this hermeticism is that the theory can never be proved right or wrong, but must be accepted more or less on faith. Bruno Roy recognizes this fact and does not appear uncomfortable with it, except for what he calls the "constant threat of being challenged," the fact that a "literalist" reader can always deny the existence of a second meaning.[63] He seems to have forgotten that other danger which lies in wait for us all but which the challenges of others may help us to avoid: the constant threat of getting it wrong.

Doubtless Bowden, Silvestre, and Roy see obscenity in the *De amore* in large measure because they want to see it there. In this connection,

---

61. Silvestre, p. 103: "Il s'agit en fait de la manifestation d'un courant subversif . . ."; p. 104: "un mouvement 'underground' réellement antichrétien—pas seulement anti-clérical!—a bel et bien existé dès le haut moyen âge en Occident. . . . Ces manifestations peuvent prendre l'allure de la subversion occulte, comme c'est le cas ici"; p. 105: ". . . une des deux constantes des écrits pornographiques . . . étant leur ambiguïté délibérée."

62. Roy, "André le Chapelain," p. 60: "En effet, si le jeu d'occultation pratiqué par l'auteur n'avait pas été bien conduit, cette œuvre n'aurait jamais eu aucune audience au Moyen Age, et surtout pas chez les moines."

63. Ibid., p. 59: "Pour n'importe lequel passage du texte, si un lecteur 'dépravé' y perçoit un second sens, rien n'empêche un lecteur 'littéraliste' de nier qu'un tel sens existe. C'est cette menace constante de récusation qui rend difficile l'établissement d'une quelconque preuve en cette matière."

Silvestre's and Roy's efforts to salvage Bowden's doubtful puns on *probitas* and *cunctus* are particularly eloquent. Would that such enthusiasm were devoted to devising counter-tests capable of giving the theory some sort of scientific validation. It might be very instructive, for example, to compile statistics on the relative frequency of words such as *penitus* in the *De amore* as compared with other texts of the period. In the absence of such tests, how can we ever be sure that our theories tell us something worth knowing about the text and about the culture that underlies it, rather than being simply a reflection of our own preoccupations?

Beate Schmolke-Hasselmann's essay raises the question of the compatibility of the "dirty-joke" hypothesis with the Robertsonian brand of irony, for, although Bruno Roy (p. 59, n. 2) hails Schmolke-Hasselmann as a kindred spirit, and not without justification, much of her study is based on the work of Robertson and of Karnein. This is particularly true of the political dimension that she gives to her "allegorical" interpretation of the hawk episode, for it is a development of a suggestion by the Robertsonian John F. Benton that both Robertson and Karnein have also incorporated into their own interpretations.[64]

On the whole, I must agree with Hubert Silvestre's perception that Betsy Bowden's interpretation and his own undermine not only "court-

---

64. Betsy Bowden (p. 68) leaves no doubt about her disdain for Robertson, and Hubert Silvestre (p. 100, n. 3) is even more categorical concerning the Robertsonian interpretation of Paolo Cherchi, which Silvestre finds "henceforth inadmissible" (*désormais irrecevable*). At the Würzburg Conference of 1984, Cherchi avenged himself at the expense of Bruno Roy by facetiously suggesting that the latter's paper was also pornographic, since it contained the word *analyse,* which sounds a bit like *anulus* (Roy, p. 73), but in his own paper at the same conference, he suggested that the earlier studies of Bowden and Silvestre lend "some support" to his own approach (Cherchi, "New Uses," pp. 23–24). Karnein was remarkably discreet about the "dirty-joke" school: of Schmolke-Hasselmann he wrote only that she "interprets the hawk and the glove as sexual symbols," without in any way reacting to that suggestion (Karnein, *"De amore,"* p. 92, n. 44a); Bowden and Silvestre he consigned without comment to the bibliography (ibid., pp. 311 and 326). His later footnote on Boncompagno's punning (see above, n. 54) seems to express at least limited approval. The favorable reaction to my earlier criticism of this school expressed in Karnein, *Amor est passio,* p. 23, n. 3, is incorrectly attribute to Karnein (see above, Chapter 3, n. 29).

ly love" but also any pretension of piety. With all due allowance for the complexity of medieval clerical culture, I find it hard to see how Andreas and his contemporaries could have thought they were promoting Christian charity by exchanging ribald puns.

Yet, despite the obvious divergence on the ideological level, it seems to me that the schools of Robertson and Bowden have much in common. The two views of medieval culture underlying their respective interpretations of the *De amore* are poles apart, but they share a narrowness of focus crucial in both cases in orienting the expectation that readers are asked to bring to the text. Beyond that, I think that it can be argued that they operate with similar methodologies, each based on a hypothesis deemed so probable that it requires little or no testing, so that the assembling of a certain number of apparently corroborating examples is considered sufficient to validate it completely.[65]

That two such completely different theories could be seriously advanced and supported by scholars of unimpeachable credentials is itself eloquent testimony to the complexity of the *De amore* and of the medieval cultural context surrounding it, a complexity that belies the reductive tendency of both these theories.

Intentional versus observable irony

Having observed the problems and weaknesses inherent in the major ironic interpretations of the *De amore,* we still have to face an important question: how can we account for the persistence with which humorous and ironic interpretations are applied to this text? One hypothesis that we might wish to entertain is that the irony is in the eye of the beholder. Do modern and especially contemporary critics see irony in Andreas because they want to see it there?

There is no doubt that irony presently enjoys a certain fashion. It has been fashionable in modern literature and literary studies more or less continuously since the Romantics "reinvented" it some two hundred years ago, and in the last forty years it has become fashionable in

---

65. Crane's criticism of Robertson's "privileged hypothesis" can be applied to both schools.

medieval studies as well.[66] The fact that the general intellectual climate is favorable to ironic interpretations is doubtless a factor in their proliferation.

Nevertheless, certain texts obviously lend themselves much more than others to ironic interpretations. The frequency with which the *De amore* is interpreted ironically would lead us to believe that it is the text itself that invites such interpretations. It is the source of this relative susceptibility of the *De amore* to ironic interpretation that we must try to discover. What is there specifically in this text that frequently leads contemporary critics to interpret it ironically?

One of the fundamental problems in Capellanus studies has always been the apparent contradiction between the intention of the first two books, on the one hand, and that of the third book, on the other. This problem has always played a significant role in the formulation of the various ironic interpretations of the treatise. We have seen that the earliest ironic hypothesis interpreted the third book ironically, without actually saying so, in an attempt to solve this very problem. Likewise, one of the main points of Robertson's theory was that "there is no doctrinal inconsistency in the *De amore* as a whole," since the first two books are saying ironically what the third book says straightforwardly.[67] And of Betsy Bowden's hypothesis Bruno Roy writes: "It allows us to overcome the fundamental contradiction" of the *De amore*.[68]

Despite the ambition of resolving the contradiction, none of these hypotheses can really account for all the material in the *De amore*. Those who interpret the third book ironically tend not to take into account the many conservative statements in the first two books. We have seen that Karnein's admission that much of Book Two is ideologically neutral significantly weakens the Robertsonian hypothesis as an overall explanation of the treatise. Even Hubert Silvestre, who shows perhaps the greatest tendency of any of these scholars to generalize from a few examples, admits that "certain passages are almost totally lacking in

---

66. E.g., Haidu, *Aesthetic Distance;* idem, "Au Début"; Mickel; Rossman; Green; Gaunt, *Troubadours*.

67. Robertson, " Subject," p. 161.

68. Roy, "André le Chapelain," p. 72: "la lecture du *De amore* que propose B. Bowden . . . permet d'en surmonter la contradiction fondamentale."

puns and scabrous wordplay."[69] However sweeping the theoretical claims they sometimes make, none of these theories has succeeded in practice in establishing anything like the "continuous level of meaning beyond the literal" for which Robert Kaske (p. 192) has called.

Although they set out to resolve the fundamental contradiction in the *De amore,* humorous and ironic interpretations of the work tend to be caught up themselves in that same contradiction. The more candid critics recognize the difficulty of showing a sustained comic or ironic intention throughout the treatise. At the beginning of her essay, Betsy Bowden (p. 67) resumes the problem thus: "No one feels comfortable around Andreas Capellanus. His treatise on 'courtly love' seems too serious to be funny, too funny to be moral, and at the end too moral to be serious." In a somewhat similar vein, E. Talbot Donaldson wrote: "I think Andreas meant to be funny: my sense of humour is insufficiently robust for me to agree with Robertson and Drouart that he succeeded."[70] Even such a confirmed Robertsonian as John F. Benton recog-

---

69. Silvestre, p. 103, n. 9: "Certains passages sont presque dépourvus de calembours et de jeux de mots scabreux, notamment ceux qui renferment les historiettes contées par André."

70. Donaldson, p. 160. This is a reference to the late-thirteenth-century translation/adaptation of the *De amore* into Old French verse by Drouart la Vache (see ed. Bossuat), whose author reports having "laughed" on first reading Andreas's treatise: "Quant je l'oi veü/Et il en ot .i. poi leü,/La matere trop durement/Me plot, sachiez, certainement,/Tant, que j'en commençai a rire" (vv. 47–51). Robertson ("Doctrine," p. 37; "Subject," p. 145 and n. 4; pp. 153–54; *Preface,* p. 400) makes much of this passage as lending medieval support to his ironic interpretation, but Sargent has argued persuasively that Drouart's reaction is one of enjoyment, rather than amusement, and that several other statements by Drouart are incompatible with the Robertsonian thesis. A view of the "laughter" passage similar to Sargent's had previously been expressed by D. Kelly, "Courtly Love," p. 123. Karnein (*"De amore,"* p. 184; "La Réception," p. 523) appears to accept this view, hence his interpretation of Drouart as representing a turning-point in the reception of the *De amore.* Betsy Bowden, who appears not to know the article by Sargent, also cites this passage from Drouart in support of her own interpretation: "Why is this man laughing?" (p. 69). She then goes on (p. 70) to interpret Drouart's excision of the dream allegory in the Fifth Dialogue, on which her theory is largely based, as an attempt to avoid censorship in the wake of the condemnation of 1277. I find it difficult to understand why Drouart would have undertaken the arduous task of such a translation, only to leave out the parts that were the source of his amusement, or how he could have hoped thereby to amuse his fellow clerics, as his closing lines would suggest (vv. 7547–57; cf. Bowden, p. 69).

nizes a discrepancy between what he takes as Andreas's intention and what was actually achieved:

> If Andreas was doctrinally correct but psychologically ambivalent, he would not have been the last Christian moralist to find his irony had become inverted and confusing, justifying Bishop Tempier's condemnation not on grounds of his conscious intention but of his failure to control the feeling he brought to the task.[71]

And this is echoed by Karnein: "The fact that he wrote the treatise in this way was, finally, a victory for lay emancipation, even though the author himself was of the opinion that he had written an anti-feminist, anti-courtly treatise."[72]

Of course, any intention other than that which Andreas succeeded in actually carrying out can only be a matter of conjecture. But as long as we are speculating, I think that we could just as well entertain the contrary hypothesis: that Andreas has to a certain extent succeeded in being funny, at least to us, without necessarily having intended to do so. To put it another way, I think that there may well be a certain amount of observable irony in the treatise that may or may not have been intentional.

Besides the fundamental contradiction between the first two books and the third, there are in the *De amore* a great many smaller, more local discrepancies and inconsistencies. Critics such as Robertson and Bowden have pointed out a certain number of these discrepancies in support of their respective ironic interpretations of the work, but their remarks are far from exhausting the subject. Without apparently forming any recognizable pattern, these discrepancies and inconsistencies tend to undercut the discourse at every turn, creating a certain objective, observable irony. Hence the perspicacity of Hermann Weigand's suggestion that there may be a kind of romantic irony at work here. But was it, in fact, Andreas's intention to create irony in this way? A few examples may serve to illustrate the difficulty of assigning an obvious and

71. Benton, "Collaborative Approaches," p. 47.
72. Karnein, *"De amore,"* p. 107: "Indem er diesen Traktat so schreibt, gewinnt somit letztlich die Laienemanzipation eine Schlacht, auch wenn der Verfasser selbst der Meinung ist, er habe einen frauenfeindlichen, antihöfischen Traktat geschrieben."

stable ironic intention to discrepancies that are often susceptible of a more immediate explanation.

If Andreas had kept to his original definition, "Amor est passio . . ." (*DA* 1.1.1 [32]), he would not have had to ask how love may be acquired (Book One, Chapter Six), for he had already explained that it comes "from the sight of and excessive meditation upon the beauty of the opposite sex." What he is now talking about acquiring is not *amor,* the "suffering" that is love, as he has defined it, but rather what he calls elsewhere "the solaces of love" *(solatia amoris),* that is, the assuagement of that suffering through "carrying out all of Love's precepts in the other's embrace." Far from being an obvious signal for irony, this lax use of technical terms has so far apparently escaped the attention of all the critics, even those who favor an ironic interpretation. It is much more plausibly ascribed to the ambiguity of the word *amor,* as well as to a certain lack of linguistic and philosophical sophistication on the part of Andreas, a trait that he shares with many other writers of the early scholastic period.

In the same chapter Andreas advances a number of arguments to show the inferiority of "beauty" *(formæ venustas)* to "excellence of character" *(morum probitas)* as a means of "acquiring" love (i.e., producing it in someone else). This position again puts him in conflict with his definition of love, in which "beauty" *(forma)* was identified as the ultimate cause of the phenomenon. The point is not, however, that beauty is not effective in this connection, only that it ought not be resorted to. Andreas has shifted ground from a position of speculation to one of moralization, but we have no reason to doubt either the validity of his original observation nor the sincerity of the moral preference that he now expresses.

As a final example, Andreas's organization of the dialogues in terms of the social class of the participants presents a certain discrepancy with respect to the rhetorical frame of the *De amore,* in which the treatise is presented as a response to a request for advice on the part of one Gualterius. Whoever he may be, Gualterius presumably belonged to only one social class and therefore needed only three dialogues to complete his education, one for each of the three classes of women whom he might wish to address. This apparent lapse can hardly be seen as intended to cast either Gualterius or the characters in the dialogues in an ironic light. It is rather to be interpreted as arising from the application of divergent rhetorical principles: in the dialogues, the doctrine of the three levels of style, which medieval writers associated with differences of social class, in combination with the notion that persuasion arises from the personal qualities of the speaker, as well as from the emotions of the audience; in the preface and frame, the justification of the discourse in terms of the "affected-modesty" topos, of which one variant consists in attributing the work's origin to the request of a patron or a friend.

If we take the treatise as a whole at face value, there is a certain incongruity, indeed, a certain irony, inherent in Andreas's ostensible project: on the one hand, to systematize the thematic material of the vernacular love poetry and, on the other hand, to reconcile the poetic themes with Christianity and with Ovid. In the first place, the poetic themes are full of inconsistencies and thus ultimately unsystematizable, for the simple reason that they are not philosophy but poetry. For example, alongside the very common theme that emphasizes the role of sight in the generation of love, a less widespread but nevertheless significant variant has love arising, sight unseen, from the reputation of the beloved. Both these themes are reflected in the *De amore,* without the conflict between them ever being resolved: sight is such an integral part of the definition of love that the blind are excluded from participation (*DA* 1.5.1, 6 [38–40]), yet the man of the Seventh Dialogue claims to have fallen in love with a lady on whom he has never laid eyes (*DA* 1.6.322–23 [132]), and she appears to accept that claim without contradiction. Moreover, the doctrine of the troubadours, insofar as we can speak of them as having a doctrine, is probably not reconcilable ultimately with either Ovid or Christianity, let alone with both of them. With few exceptions, the troubadours manage to steer a middle course between the urbane cynicism of the *Ars amatoria* and the austere asceticism of the Fathers, producing a kind of idealized sensuality that has proved troublesome not only for Andreas but also for modern critics.

The basic incongruity of the project is further exacerbated by Andreas's method, for he proceeds by dialectic, constantly setting each opinion against its contrary, as Tony Hunt has argued. Just as there is a certain dialectic inherent in irony, so, too, there is a certain irony inherent in dialectic, as each statement tends to undercut the opposite view to which it is juxtaposed, and vice versa.

Andreas uses the tools of dialectic to reduce functional poetic ambiguities to unambiguous, didactic statements, making explicit ideas that were merely implicit in the poetry. Taken out of their poetic setting and confronted with ideas from other traditions in a much more complex context that, for want of a better word, we may call "life," the poetic commonplaces naturally tend to appear in a somewhat ironic light, which is primarily a reflection of their poetic character.

Dialectic also tends to polarize the discussion, pushing positions to extremes, as with the exclusion of the blind cited above. Likewise, the common poetic theme of adultery becomes "love can exert no power between husband and wife" (DA 2.7.42 [266]). The result is a further exaggeration of thematic material that is already very hyperbolic. As Quintilian (8.6.74) has observed, "hyperbole will often cause a laugh"; but Quintilian goes on to point out the ambiguity of that laughter, depending on the author's intention: "If that was what the orator desired, we may give him credit for wit; otherwise we can only call him a fool."

If we entertain my hypothesis that at least part of the irony observable in the De amore may be unintentional, are we therefore obliged to conclude that Andreas is a fool?[73] Do we not run the risk of patronizing our author, if we make him responsible for our inability to come to grips with his text? As Stanley Fish (p. 351) has pointed out, there is an unwritten convention in our profession that good criticism is that which makes the author and the work look good, so we shall not want to violate that convention without having a sound reason to do so.

There is, it seems to me, a certain justification in the idea that my hypothesis is not terribly flattering to Andreas. But he does not come off much better with the contrary hypothesis, for if he was trying to be funny or ironic, he went about it so clumsily that a great many people, from Bishop Tempier to Donaldson, have not got the joke.

From a scientific point of view, my hypothesis has the advantage of simplicity. If we posit an ironic intention to account for apparent flaws

73. Cf. Muscatine, p. 39, who calls Andreas "either an ironist or a nasty fool."

in the surface meaning of the text, we then have to admit flaws in the way in which the ironic intention was carried out, so maintaining the surface flaws saves one step. It also accounts better for the apparent random nature of the inconsistencies and discrepancies, which do not seem to conform to any easily recognizable pattern.

The convention that academic critics should try to make their authors look good assumes that the authors we study are, in fact, good authors. In most cases this assumption is no doubt justified, but no one would claim, I think, that less proficient authors do not exist, or even that those authors who make their way into our curriculum are always equally proficient in every aspect of their trade. There are sometimes other reasons, besides overall excellence, for the interest that we accord certain authors.

In the case of Andreas, it seems to me that much of our interest in his work derives from the inherent interest of his ostensible project, as I have described it above. Moreover, Andreas has succeeded to a remarkable degree in carrying out this project, for his is not only the earliest work of its kind, it is also in many ways the most thorough and systematic. This is why Gaston Paris and several generations of scholars after him thought that Andreas had already done most of the work for them, and that one had only to consult the *De amore* to find out what one needed to know about "courtly love." That this view has not withstood the close scrutiny of recent scholarship is not, I think, a particularly serious indictment of Andreas. If he left a fair number of loose ends and failed to carry his project all the way through, this is in large part, I would argue, because what he set out to do was to a certain extent unrealizable, because there was a certain measure of failure inherent in the project.

The problems that we see in the *De amore* are also to a great extent the result of the modern criteria that we tend to apply to the work. As Stanley Fish has further remarked, the qualities that we try to demonstrate in the works we study include complexity and unity.[74] No one can accuse the *De amore* of lacking in complexity, but its unity is much

---

74. Ibid. The other quality mentioned by Fish, "universality," is clearly no problem for a treatise on sexual love.

more problematic. This is why so much scholarly effort, including the ironic interpretations, has been devoted to trying to show the work's basic unity, generally at the expense of a radical reduction in its complexity. I am not at all sure, however, that Andreas and his contemporaries shared our modern concern for unity.

Concerning the medieval tolerance for inconsistency at the level of stylistic tone, Ernst Curtius wrote:

> The testimony already discussed permits the assumption that the mixture of jest and earnest was among the stylistic norms which were known and practiced by the medieval poet, even if he perhaps nowhere found them expressly formulated. We may, then, view the phenomenon as a fresh substantiation of the view that the Middle Ages loved all kinds of crossings and mixtures of stylistic genres. And in fact we find in the Middle Ages ludicra within domains and genres which, to our modern taste, schooled by classical aesthetics, absolutely exclude any such mixtures.[75]

Doubtless the same tolerance for inconsistency also extends to point of view, for it is a fundamental axiom of the dialectical method that all questions can be seen from more than one angle.

It is the search for unity that has led modern scholars to seize upon certain aspects of the *De amore* and to generalize from them, denying in the process the existence of other important aspects. Irony has become one of the major mechanisms of that denial. There is no doubt that Christian moralization exists in the *De amore,* and not only in the third book; playful and provocative eroticism in the Ovidian tradition is certainly also present, and there may well be a fair amount of wordplay, humor, and irony, intentional as well as observable, scattered throughout the treatise. But no one has yet demonstrated convincingly the presence of any of these running systematically throughout the work.

Having come to realize that Andreas has not done our work for us, we experience a strong temptation to finish his work for him by discovering a pattern that will tie up all the loose ends and fit everything neatly into place. But if Andreas is to teach us something about medieval culture—and I believe that he still has a lot to teach us—then we must resist that temptation.

75. Curtius, p. 424.

PART II

PROBLEMS OF MEANING

Andreas and the Courtly Themes

5 ❦

LOVE AND THE ONTOLOGICAL ORDER

Andreas's Scholastic Definition

In *the preceding chapters* we have seen that the *De amore* is a complex didactic enterprise interweaving the separate generic vectors that we have called *ars, scientia,* and *sapientia,* and that it is organized according to principles derived from the arts of the trivium, rhetoric and dialectic, especially the latter. We have also seen that, in accordance with its scholastic organization, it is concerned with assembling all pertinent opinions on the subject of love, and that it thus establishes an intricate dialectic between four main medieval traditions. The learned, Latin, clerical tradition includes a secular strand inherited from classical antiquity, especially the love writings of Ovid, as well as the dictates of Christian theology and canon law. Along with these standard sources of authority, Andreas also invokes contemporary, vernacular, courtly sources, that of the courtly vernacular love poetry and the "non-literary intertext" comprising the attitudes and prejudices of courtly feudal society. It is time to apply these findings to an analysis of the Chaplain's doctrine, including its psychological, social, and ethical components. We shall begin with the cornerstone on which the entire edifice is constructed, Andreas's definition of love.[1]

No aspect of the *De amore* has received more attention than the def-

1. For an earlier version of this chapter, see Monson, "Andreas Capellanus's Scholastic Definition."

inition of love with which it begins. Already in the Middle Ages this was among the best-known parts of the treatise: apparently anthologized very early in medieval florilegia, it is quoted, among others, by Albertanus da Brescia (1238), the earliest of medieval authors to react to Andreas, and by Jean de Meun, who translated it into Old French in the *Romance of the Rose*.[2] In modern times it has become the center of a lively controversy intimately connected with that which surrounds the meaning of the treatise as a whole.

Current discussion of Andreas's definition centers on the question whether it should be seen as an ironic allusion to Scripture in the Patristic tradition (D. W. Robertson, Alfred Karnein) or as a physiological description in the medical tradition (Paolo Cherchi, Rüdiger Schnell).[3] I shall argue that it is neither, that it is, within certain limits, a properly philosophical definition, firmly rooted in the tradition of early medieval philosophy, although it is not devoid of literary influences. Since the same philosophical tradition also provided the intellectual foundation of medieval medicine and theology, it is not unreasonable to assume that any similarity between Andreas's definition and contemporary medical or moral pronouncements is due to this common heritage.[4]

Andreas's first chapter, *Quid sit amor,* calls for a definition. As one of the "predicables" *(prædicabilia),* or basic notions by means of which anything may be predicated of anything else, *definitio* played a key role in dialectical argumentation.[5] Aristotle's *Topics* 6 and 7.1–3 are devoted

2. Karnein, *"De amore,"* pp. 61–62.

3. Resumed in ibid., pp. 59–71. Cf. Karnein, *"Amor est passio";* Robertson, " Subject"; idem, *Preface,* pp. 84–85; Cherchi, "Andreas' *De Amore,*" pp. 88–91; Schnell, *Andreas Capellanus,* pp. 159–65. Wack, "Imagination," argues for an influence of the Salernitan medical school on the treatise as a whole, including the definition. Nevertheless, she disputes (p. 108, n. 26) the influence of Arabic medical works alleged by Cherchi and Schnell, pointing out that *amor hereos* is a thirteenth-century concept.

4. The most prominent representatives, respectively, of the moral and medical traditions, those most frequently mentioned in connection with the *De amore,* are also major philosophers: St. Augustine and Avicenna.

5. According to Aristotle, *Topics* 1.4–5 (101b11–102b26), the four essential notions later designated as "predicables" were definition, property, genus, and accident. Medieval philosophers generally followed Porphyry's *Isagoge* in substituting species and differentia for definition, bringing the number of predicables to five. See Boethius (trans. Stump, pp. 237–61). For Aristotle definition also played an important role in demonstrative reasoning; see *Posterior Analytics* 2.10 (93b29–94a19).

to definition. It is also discussed at length in Cicero's *Topica* and in Boethius's commentary on that treatise.[6] Marius Victorinus (fourth century) wrote a treatise on definition, sometimes erroneously attributed to Boethius, which influenced encyclopedists such as Cassiodorus and Isidore of Seville, and, through them, the Middle Ages.[7] For thirteenth-century philosophers such as Alexander of Hales, definition *(modus definitivus)* was distinguished as one of the three main "modes" of human science *(modus tractandi),* along with division *(modus divisivus)* and ratiocination *(modus collectivus).*[8]

Definition is of species, or specific class. It proceeds by joining *genus,* or general class, to *differentiæ,* that is, the characteristics that distinguish the species being defined from other species of the same genus. Through definition one arrives at the "quiddity" *(quidditas)* of the thing defined, that is, its essence.[9]

The first chapter of the *De amore* begins with the following definition of love:

> Amor est passio quædam innata procedens ex visione et immoderata cogitatione formæ alterius sexus, ob quam aliquis super omnia cupit alterius potiri amplexibus et omnia de utriusque voluntate in ipsius amplexu amoris præcepta compleri.[10]

---

6. Cicero, *Topica* 5.26–6.29; Boethius, *In Topica Ciceronis,* 3 (PL 64:1090–1108).

7. [Marius Victorinus], *De diffinitione* (PL 64:891–910); Cassiodorus, *Institutiones* 2.3.14; Isidore, *Etymologiæ* 2.29. Cf. Chadwick, pp. 115–17; Wagner, p. 125.

8. Minnis, *Medieval Theory,* pp. 122–23. Alexander thus formalizes a distinction already discernable in Boethius's *Commentary on the Isagoge of Porphyry,* 2nd redaction, 1.7–9. Boethius's authentic logical works include a treatise on division and three on syllogistic reasoning.

9. For Aristotle, *Topics* 1.5 (101b39), a definition is a phrase indicating the essence of something. See also Boethius, *In Isagogen Porphyrii,* 1.7 (ed. Brandt, p. 153): *Definitio namque substantia monstrat, genus differentiis iungit et ea quæ per se sunt communia atque multorum in unum redigens uni speciei quam definit reddit æqualia.* Cf. McKeon, *Selections,* 1:86: "For the definition reveals substance, joins genus to differences, and, reducing to one species which it defines those things which are *per se* common and of many, it makes them equal."

10. *DA* 1.1.1 (32). Cf. Walsh, p. 33: "Love is an inborn suffering which results from the sight of, and uncontrolled thinking about, the beauty of the other sex. This feeling makes a man desire before all else the embraces of the other sex, and to achieve the utter fulfillment of the commands of love in the other's embrace by their common desire."

This definition is followed by a discussion of it, which occupies the rest of the chapter. Based on the eminently scholastic technique of *glossatio,* or glossing of terms, Andreas's discussion of his own definition provides a valuable source of information as to what he meant by it.

Passio

We may begin our analysis of Andreas's definition with the word *passio,* which forms its kernel. This term can be properly understood only by reference to the *Categories* of Aristotle. Called "predicaments" (*prædicamenta*) in the Middle Ages, the categories indicate the most universal classes to which all things can be reduced, and thus include all the attributes that can be predicated properly of any subject. They are ten in number: (1) substance, (2) quantity, (3) quality, (4) relation, (5) place, (6) time, (7) position, (8) state, (9) action, (10) passion. The categories are *summa genera,* for they have no genus themselves, though they constitute the genera for everything else.

The word *passio* is used in two distinct but related senses with respect to the categories. In the first place it refers to the tenth category, also designated by the infinitive *pati.*[11] In this sense *passio* is the correlative of the ninth category, *actio* (also *agere* or *facere*), and means simply the undergoing or receiving of an action.[12] In addition, *passio* is included among the four genera distinguished within the third category, quality: the third such genus is called "passive qualities and passions" (*passibiles qualitates et passiones*). This genus comprises the qualities introduced into a substance by a *passio* in the categorical sense, hence the common designation. Within this genus a further distinction is made based on the duration of the phenomenon: passive qualities are long-lasting and thus truly qualify the substance in which they inhere, whereas *passiones* are of relatively short duration and thus just barely distinguishable from the receptions of action that give rise to them.[13]

---

11. Aristotle is consistent in using the infinitive πάσχειν to refer to the tenth category, the noun πάθος in connection with the third genus of quality, although his use of the latter term is somewhat ambiguous (see below, n. 13). Medieval philosophers use *passio* and *pati* indifferently in referring to the tenth category.

12. Aristotle, *Categories* 4 (1b25–27, 2a3–4); 9 (11b1–7).

13. Aristotle, *Categories* 8 (9a28–10a10). Cf. Joachim, pp. 80–85. The distinction be-

In Andreas's definition, *passio* provides the ultimate genus (though not the proximate genus, as we shall see) for the species under consideration, *amor*. The other elements of the definition, *innatus, procedens ex visione . . .* , and *ob quam aliquis super omnia cupit . . .* , are the *differentiæ* separating this particular species from other species of the same genus. *Amor* is a *passio* in both of the senses described above, depending on the point of view adopted: in terms of its origin it is a *passio* in the categorical sense; subsequently it inheres in the individual as a quality.[14] For, as Boethius writes in discussing the third genus of quality, "Nothing prevents us from assigning one and the same thing with respect to its species, for different reasons, to more than one genus."[15] Because of

---

tween a "passive quality" (ποιότης παθητική) and a "passion" (πάθος) mirrors that which is made within the first genus of quality between a long-lasting "habit" (ἕξις, *habitus*) and a short-lived "disposition" (διάθεσις, *dispositio*). Aristotle's language is not unambiguous, however. Of short-lived "passions" such as fits of anger he says (9b32–33, 10a9–10) that they are "passions and not qualities" (πάθη μὲν . . . ποιότητες δὲ οὔ). This may mean that they are not "passive qualities" as previously described, for which "qualities" here would be an abbreviation, or else that they don't really belong at all to the third category, under which they are now being discussed, but rather to the tenth, because they don't last long enough really to qualify a substance. In his translation Boethius resolves the ambiguity by rendering οὔ, "not," as *minime*, "barely": *quare passiones huiusmodi dicuntur, qualitates vero minime* (AL 1/1–5:26–27). Cf. Translatio Guillelmi de Mœrbeka (ibid. 1/1–5:104): *passiones dicuntur, qualitates autem non*. To complicate matters further, Aristotle also uses "passive qualities" to designate those qualities that *produce* passions, such as the sweetness of honey or the whiteness of white objects.

14. This difference in point of view corresponds to the distinction that Aquinas makes between considering something in the process of becoming or as having become *(considerare ut in fieri/. . . ut in facto esse)*. See *ST* 3a 78.2, contra (ed. Blackfriars, 58:170–71). The distinction between love as being and as becoming is reproduced implicitly in Andreas's definition, in the distinction between internal and external causes (see below).

15. My translation. Cf. Boethius, *In Categorias Aristotelis* 3 (PL 64:250): *Nihil impedit, secundum aliam scilicet atque aliam causam, unam eamdemque rem gemino generi speciei suæ supponere*. Boethius's discussion concerns how a given quality can be both a "state" *(habitus)* and a *passio*, but the same argument can also be applied to the ambiguity of *passio*. Boethius's example is Socrates, who as a father falls under the category "relation," but as a man, under "substance." Thus by "thing" *(res)* he seems to mean the particular, but definition is of species, not of the particular. And since definition is indicative of essence, each species can have only one true definition, and so can fall under only one category. In fact, *amor*, like *passio*, is used equivocally to designate two different but related species, a kind of reception and a kind of quality introduced by that

its complexity, we shall examine the term *passio* in some detail before proceeding to a discussion of the *differentiæ*.

That love is a *passio* as described above is a classical and medieval commonplace. It appears to have its origin in the *Ethics* of Aristotle. Thomas Aquinas discusses the question *utrum amor sit passio,* quoting Aristotle's positive opinion, which he also adopts. Aristotle seems to have the quality in mind, for he opposes love the *passio* to friendship the "habit" *(habitus),* an apparent reference to the first genus of quality.[16] Aquinas, on the other hand, appears to use *passio* more in the categorical sense, defining it as denoting "the effect produced in a thing when it is acted upon by some agent."[17] Of course, love is a *passio* in both senses, as we have seen.

As a quality *passio* often takes on the more restricted meaning of "suffering" or "illness."[18] According to Aquinas this is the meaning of *passio* in its most proper sense.[19] Elsewhere he explains the basis for this restriction: the reception of an action tends to force out a natural quality and replace it with an alien quality, thus altering the substance.[20] In

---

reception. On the definition of equivocal terms see Aristotle, *Categories* 1 (1a1–6); Abelard, *Dialectica,* pp. 592–93.

16. Aristotle, *Nicomachean Ethics* 8.5 (1157b28–29): ἔοικε δὴ μὲν φίλησις πάθει, ἡ δὲ φιλία ἕξει. Cf. Translatio Grosseteste (AL 26/1–3:305, 527): *Assimilatur autem amacio quidem passioni, amicicia autem habitui.* Although this interpretation is not incontrovertible, for *habitus/habere* (ἔχειν), "state, condition, habit, having," is also the eighth category, it is reinforced by the fact that it is under the third genus of quality that Aristotle discusses the emotions (see below).

17. *ST* 1a2æ 26.2: *SED CONTRA est quod Philosophus dicit, quod amor est passio. RESPONSIO: Dicendum quod passio est effectus agentis in patiente.* Cf. Walsh, pp. 15–16, who also cites Quintilian, *Institutio oratoria* 6.2.12 *(amor* πάθος).

18. On *passio* as "suffering" and its evolution toward the modern association with sentiment, see Lerch; Auerbach, "Remarques"; idem, "Passio"; idem, *Literary Language,* pp. 67–81.

19. *ST* 1a2æ 22.1, contra (ed. Blackfriars 19:5, 19:5–7): "The Latin verb *pati, to suffer* or *undergo* or *be acted upon,* is used in three ways. First, in a perfectly general sense, it is used whenever any quality is received. . . . Sometimes the quality lost is one whose presence was inappropriate in the subject: for example, when an animal is healed, it may be said to 'undergo' healing, for it recovers its health by shedding its illness. At other times, the opposite happens: for example, a sick man is called a 'patient' because he contracts some illness by losing his health. It is this last kind of case which is called *passio* in the most correct sense. . . . Thus sorrow is more naturally called a passion than is joy."

20. Thomas Aquinas, *In quattuor libros Sententiarum* 3.15.2, ar. 1a, co (trans.

the context of a discussion of human sexual love, it is not surprising that this third, more restricted meaning should also come into play, drawing on a long classical and medieval tradition concerning the pain and suffering of love. In fact, Andreas's subsequent discussion of his own definition seems to waver between the categorical meaning of *passio* and its more restricted sense as a negative quality.

In discussing the word *passio* itself, Andreas appears to equate it with *angustia* ("anguish, torment"), thus associating it with the notion of "suffering": *Quod amor sit passio, facile est videre. Nam, antequam amor sit ex utraque parte libratus, nulla est* angustia *maior.*[21] The ensuing passage goes on to elaborate on this torment, relating it primarily to "fear" *(timor)* but also to the frustration of "hope" *(spes).* According to a tradition both literary and philosophical going back to classical antiquity, fear and hope are counted among the four principal emotions, along with joy and sorrow.[22] In the *Metalogicon* John of Salisbury presents these four principal emotions as arising from the physical senses: "joy" *(gaudium)* and "pain" *(dolor)* result directly from pleasant or unpleasant sensations in the present, whereas *timor* and *spes* constitute the dual outcome of the imagination's acting upon the data of sense perceptions with regard to the future.[23] It is somewhat paradoxical that Andreas

---

McKeon, *Selections,* 2:477–78): "It is required by the nature of passion that the quality introduced be extraneous and the quality forced out be connatural, and this is so because passion imports a certain victory of the agent over the patient; but all that which is conquered is as it were drawn beyond its proper bounds to alien bounds; and therefore alterations which occur beyond the nature of the thing altered are most properly called passions, as sicknesses more properly than states of health."

21. *DA* 1.1.2 (32) [my emphasis]. Cf. Walsh, p. 33: "It is easy to see that love is a suffering, for until it is equally balanced on both sides there is no greater discomfort."

22. Following Virgil (*Æneid* 6.733), St. Augustine (*De civitate Dei* 14.3, 6–8) gives fear, *desire (cupiditas),* sorrow, and joy as the principal emotions, but Aquinas (*ST* 1a2æ 25.4) follows Boethius (*De consolatione philosophiæ* 1.7, vv. 25–28) in substituting "hope" for "desire." So also John of Salisbury. Aquinas goes on to order the emotions of love, desire, and hope as a progressive movement toward the good, coming to rest in joy; likewise, hate, aversion, and fear form a progressive movement toward the bad, coming to rest in sorrow.

23. *Metalogicon* 4.10.15–16 (trans. McGarry, p. 219): "If it visualizes our future state as dire, fear arises; but if it paints a bright picture of a future brimful with profit and pleasure, hope springs in the breast"; cf. ibid., p. 217. John of Salisbury also associates desire with this process: *Hinc nascitur et cupiditas . . .* (*Metalogicon* 4.10.17). Chalcidius,

should associate *amor,* a form of attraction, with *timor,* a form of repulsion. It is not the object of his desires, however, that the lover fears, but rather "anything which might be harmful" (*omne quod aliquo posset modo nocere; DA* 1.1.3 [32]) to their realization. Thus the Chaplain explains and justifies the negative connotation often associated with *passio.*

In his commentary on *innatus,* on the other hand, Andreas opposes *passio* to *actio* in a way that recalls its status as the tenth category:

> Quod autem illa passio sit innata, manifesta tibi ratione ostendo, quia passio illa ex nulla oritur *actione* subtiliter veritate inspecta; sed ex sola cogitatione, quam concipit animus ex eo, quod vidit, passio illa procedit.[24]

A key to understanding this difficult passage is the phrase *subtiliter veritate inspecta,* "if the truth be carefully examined," for it indicates that the preceding assertion, *passio illa ex nulla oritur actione,* is a paradox not easily grasped by the intellect. How, indeed, can a passion not be the result of an action? For, as we read in Abelard's *Dialectica,* "All passions are necessarily produced by actions, nor can there be any passion which has not been generated by a corresponding action."[25]

Nor is that the end of the difficulty, for *cogitatio* is also an *actio* in a more narrow sense. Although *agere/actio* and *facere/factio* are both used in a general sense to designate the ninth category, they also serve as the basis for a generic distinction within that category. For thirteenth-

---

whom John is following in this passage, is much closer to Andreas, for he appears to identify love with desire, and he sees it as giving rise to hope and pleasure or to sadness and pain, depending on its outcome: *Omnis porro talis cupiditas mixta est cum uoluptatis et doloris affectu consequenterque amor huius modi rerum inter dolorem uoluptatemque positus inuenitur; spes quippe fruendi uoluptatem creat, dilatio tristitiam et dolorem* ("Besides, all such desire is mixed with a feeling of pleasure and pain, and consequently love of this kind of things is found to be situated between pain and pleasure: indeed, hope of enjoyment creates pleasure, delay, sadness and pain"; Chalcidius, *In Timæum,* § 194 [Plato Latinus 4:216]; my translation).

24. *DA* 1.1.8 (34) [my emphasis]. Cf. Walsh, p. 35: "I can demonstrate by a clear argument that the feeling of love is inborn. A careful scrutiny of the truth shows that it arises not from any action, but solely from the thought formed by the mind as a result of the thing seen."

25. My translation. Cf. Abelard, *Dialectica,* p. 108: *Omnes autem passiones ex actionibus necesse est inferri nec potest esse passio quam non sua generet actio.*

century scholastics such as Aquinas, that action which goes forward from the agent into another matter, such as heating or drying, is called *factio;* for that action which remains in the agent, such as acts of the intellect, the term *actio* in its most proper sense is reserved.[26] Properly speaking, *cogitatio,* which Andreas opposes to *actio,* is in fact an *actio,* in both the general and the restricted senses. The *passio* that is love is thus the result of an *actio* in both senses of the term, but not, at least not directly, of a *factio.*

By substituting *actio* for the more proper *factio* Andreas has created a paradox to which his somewhat apologetic accompanying remark calls attention. This apparently infelicitous use of terms is perhaps not attributable solely to Andreas's inadequacy as a philosopher, for he was writing in the early scholastic period, when the terminology on this point appears not to have been fully settled. In his *De anima* Isaac de Stella (d. ca. 1169) uses a phrase very similar to Andreas's to describe the process by which the *ratio* abstracts forms from bodies: *Abstrahit enim a corpore quæ fundantur in corpore;* non actione sed consideratione.[27] It seems apparent that both Andreas and Isaac use *actio* to refer to external, physical acts, those that will later be designated by the term *factio.*

In the passage immediately following, Andreas twice uses the term *actus,* cognate and synonym of *actio,* in ways that again recall the latter term's relation to *passio* in the categorical sense. In the first case *actus,* in the plural, describes the movements of the limbs of the beloved as reproduced in the imagination of the lover: *Postmodum mulieris incipit cogitare facturas, et eius distinguere membra suosque* actus *imaginari.*[28]

---

26. *ST* 1a2æ 57.4, contra (ed. Blackfriars 19:51): "Producing [*facere*] and doing [*agere*] differ, as stated in the *Metaphysics,* in that producing is an action passing into external matter, thus to build, to saw, and the like; whereas doing is an activity abiding in the agent, thus to see, to will and the like." Cf. Aristotle, *Metaphysics* 9.8 (1050a30–1050b1); *ST* 2a2æ 134.2, contra (ed. Blackfriars 42:172–73).

27. Isaac de Stella, *De anima* (PL 194:1884; my emphasis). For Isaac the faculty that he calls *ratio* is situated between the *imaginatio* and the *intellectus.* It thus corresponds approximately to the *vis cogitativa,* which has as one function to abstract forms from bodies, and which Aquinas also calls *ratio particularis* (*ST* 1a.79.4). William of Conches, *In Timæum,* § 34 (ed. Jeanneau, pp. 100–102), presents a distinction of faculties similar to Isaac's.

28. *DA* 1.1.10 (34) [my emphasis]. "After that he starts to think about the way the woman is fashioned, to distinguish her parts, and to imagine their activities" (my

These particular "acts," with their physical and psychological components and ramifications, epitomize the general "action" of which loving constitutes the passive reception. In the second case *procedit ad actum* designates the "reaction" to the impulse received from the initial action: *Postquam vero ad hanc cogitationem plenariam devenerit, sua frena nescit continere amor, sed statim procedit ad* actum.[29] The reaction to love has been described at length by Aquinas:

> The effect produced in the orexis [*appetitus,* the appetitive faculty of the soul] by a desirable object is a sense of affinity with it, a feeling of its attractiveness; then this gives rise to a movement of the orexis towards the object. For there is a certain circularity in the orectic process, as Aristotle remarks; first the object works on the orexis, imprinting itself there, as one might say; then the orexis moves towards the object, with the purpose of actually possessing it; so the process ends where it began. The first effect produced in the orexis by the object is called *love,* which is simply a feeling of the object's attractiveness; this feeling gives rise to an orectic movement towards the object, viz. *desire;* and finally this comes to rest in *joy.*[30]

This description of the lover's reaction mirrors Aquinas's doctrine, which sees the positive emotions as constituting a progressive movement toward the good, passing from love by way of desire to joy.[31]

---

translation). Both Parry and Walsh mistranslate this passage, mistaking the reference of *suos.* Parry (p. 29) renders *suosque actus imaginari* as "to think about what she does," but Andreas clearly distinguishes between *eius,* which refers to the beloved, and *suos,* which does not. Walsh's rendering, "he begins to picture the role he can play" (p. 35), is more grammatical, but it complicates unnecessarily the visual image of the beloved by including the lover himself. Only the reading that sees in *membra* the antecedent of *suos* is fully satisfactory on both the grammatical and semantic levels. It also better accounts for the use of the enclitic *-que* with its usual implication of a particularly close relationship between the items joined.

29. *DA* 1.1.11 (34) [my emphasis]. Cf. Walsh, p. 35: "Now when he attains this stage of detailed reflexion, his love cannot keep control over its reins, but at once advances to action."

30. *ST* 1a2æ 26.2, contra (ed. Blackfriars, 19:67).

31. See above, n. 22. The fact that "hope" is not included here is perhaps due to the fact that it is associated with the "irascible" faculty of the soul *(vis irascibilis),* along with courage, fear, despair, and anger, whereas love, hate, desire, aversion, joy, and sorrow all depend on the "concupiscible" faculty *(vis concupiscibilis),* and thus belong to a different subgenus of the emotions.

Andreas's phrase *procedit ad actum* recognizes what Aquinas will later call the "circularity" of the psychological process of love. Like Aquinas, the Chaplain assigns a prominent role in this process to desire. Already in the definition desire is intimately associated with the movement toward the love object: the lover "desires above all else the embraces of the other" (*super omnia cupit alterius potiri amplexibus; DA* 1.1.1 [32]). The following discussion stresses repeatedly the role of desire in the lover's reaction. Upon seeing the beloved, the lover "immediately begins to lust after her in his heart" (*statim eam incipit concupiscere corde; DA* 1.1.9 [34]). After reflecting on her anatomy he "desires to put each part to its fullest use" (*cuiusque membri officio desiderat perpotiri; DA* 1.1.10 [34])—a phrase which recalls the words of the definition— and "satisfaction cannot come quickly enough to [his] desiring mind" (*cupienti animo nil satis posset festinanter impleri; DA* 1.1.12 [34]). Conventional literary metaphors in the Ovidian tradition are also used to evoke the lover's desire: he "burns with love" (*ardescit amore; DA* 1.1.9 [34]), and his "love cannot keep hold of the reins" (*sua frena nescit continere amor; DA* 1.1.11 [34]).[32] It is this movement of desire that pushes the lover to "act," thus completing the circle that goes from "action" to "passion" to "reaction."[33]

As we have seen, Andreas's identification of love as a *passio* draws on a long philosophical tradition, whose complexity is reflected in the definition and its subsequent discussion. With his emphasis on the process by which love is generated, he often appears to take *passio* in its categorical sense, but elsewhere he views love as a quality, stressing the negative connotations often associated with the third genus of that category.

---

32. Despite the biblical resonances of *concupiscere corde* (cf. Matt. 5:28), this language of desire is not an automatic signal of ecclesiastical condemnation, for Augustine acknowledges that all the emotions, including desire, can be good or bad, depending on their object (*De civitate Dei* 14.8–9). So also Aquinas, *ST* 1a2æ 24.

33. In the medieval commonplace of the "five stages of love," *actus* sometimes replaces *factum* as the final stage; e.g., *Carmina Burana* 154, v. 10: *In lecto tacite Venus exprimit* actum (my emphasis). It is not impossible to take Andreas's phrase *procedit ad actum* in that sense, but that is not the most obvious interpretation.

Innatus

The other really difficult term in Andreas's definition is *innatus*. Its usual meaning is "innate," that is, "existing in the subject from birth," and more particularly (to distinguish it from "congenital," which may mean "present *accidentally* from birth") "inherent, natural." That is how the term is interpreted in Andreas's definition by Robertson and Karnein, who see in it a reference to the Christian doctrine of original sin. But such a reading would enmesh Andreas in logical contradiction.

Love itself cannot possibly be "innate" in the sense described above, for as a *passio,* in whatever sense of the word, it must be the result of an *actio.* What could be "innate" in this sense could only be a certain capacity or "power" *(potentia)* for loving, a subspecies of the scholastics' "power of being affected" *(potentia passionis/. . . patiendi/. . . passiva).*[34] Such an innate capacity would be subsumed under the second genus of quality, "natural capacity or incapacity" *(potentia naturalis vel impotentia).*[35] According to Andreas's own definition, however, love is a *passio,* not a *potentia.* By associating with it *innata* in this sense, the Chaplain would be guilty of a mistake of genus.

Furthermore, in terms of the manner of predication, love as Andreas has defined it can be predicated of the subject only *per accidens,* as an "accident," whereas such an innate quality would be predicated *per se,* inhering in the subject as a "property."[36] As we read in Dante, "Amore non è per sé sì come sustanzia, ma è uno accidente in sustanzia."[37] The "accidental" status of love is underlined by Andreas's repeated insistence

34. Aristotle, *Metaphysics* 9.1 (1046a11–13).

35. Aristotle, *Categories* 8 (9a14–27).

36. According to Aristotle, *Topics* 1.5 (102a18–30, 102b4–26), a "property" *(proprium)* is a characteristic that does not belong to the essence of a thing but that nevertheless belongs necessarily to the thing and to it alone, and so is predicated convertibly of it, whereas an "accident" *(accidens)* is a characteristic that may or may not belong to the thing.

37. Dante Alighieri, *Vita nuova* § 25 ("Love is not itself a kind of substance, but it is an accident in a substance" [my translation]). Cf. Guido Cavalcanti, *Donna mi prega,* vv. 2–3: *un accidente . . . ch'è chiamato amore* ("an accident . . . which is called love" [my translation]) ; *ST* 1a2æ 22.2, contra, ad 3: *hujusmodi passio animæ convenire non potest nisi per accidens* ("This sort of emotion cannot occur except as an accident" [my translation]).

on the particular circumstances that give rise to it, if and when they occur: *visio* and *cogitatio*.

The only way to make sense of *innatus* in this context appears to be to take it literally and etymologically: *in-natus*, "born within." This I understand to mean not that love is present at the birth of the subject, but rather that love itself is born or generated *within* the subject. So understood, *passio innata* refers to a standard scholastic distinction between *passiones exteriores*, or . . . *exterius illatæ*, or . . . *ab extrinseco illatæ* ("exterior/external/extrinsic passions"), that is, sense perceptions, and *passiones interiores*, or . . . *intrinsecæ*, or . . . *ab intrinseco causatæ* ("interior/internal/intrinsic passions"), that is, emotions. The classic formulation of this distinction opposes *passiones corporis* ("passions of the body") and *passiones animæ* or *animi* ("passions of the soul" or "mind").[38] The expression *animi passio* is used by Andreas in the Seventh Dialogue (*DA* 1.6.378 [148]), referring to jealousy.

In the *Categories* (9b33–10a10) Aristotle discusses "passions" and "passive qualities" in relation to the soul, with anger and irascibility, respectively, as examples, although the expression *passio animæ* as such does not occur there.[39] Elsewhere he uses *passio* without qualification to

---

38. Deferrari and Barry, pp. 802 and 804. The expression *a passionibus extrinsecus sibi allatis* is used by Andreas's contemporary, William of Conches, in a philosophical discussion of the physical senses: *In Timæum* 34 (ed. Jeanneau, p. 101). The distinction was also current from late antiquity in both the moral and (especially) the medical traditions, as is clear from the attestations recorded in the *Thesaurus linguæ latinæ*, 5/2 (1931–1953), col. 1992, ll. 10–12: *exterioribus passionibus* (St. Ambrose, *Sermon on Psalm 118*); ibid. 5/2, col. 2021, ll. 72–73: *in externis passionibus* (Cælius Aurelianus, fifth-century physician); ibid. 7/1 (1934–1964), col. 2236, ll. 29–33: *de internis passionibus* and *interiorum passionum* (Cælius Aurelianus); ibid., 7/2 (1956–1979), col. 53, ll. 49–50: *ad omnes intrinsecas passiones* (Alexander Trallianus, sixth-century physician).

39. Medieval philosophers generally follow Aristotle in considering the *passiones animæ*, or emotions, under the third genus of quality. Aquinas's discussion of love is somewhat exceptional in this regard. See, for example, Philip the Chancellor, *Summa de bono* (ca. 1225–1228), 2:810: *Dicitur etiam passio qualitas quæ est in vi motiva, scilicet irascibili* ("Also said to be a passion is the quality which is in the motivating faculty, namely the irascible [faculty]" [my translation]). The *vis irascibilis* is the faculty of the soul responsible for the emotion under discussion, courage. Philip's contemporary, William of Auvergne, gives a much fuller discussion in his *De virtutibus* (*Opera omnia*, 1:119): *Si quis autem dixerit quod Aristoteles non intellexit in passionibus, nisi malas dispositiones animarum nostrarum, et eas vocavit passiones, pro eo, quod læsiones ipsarum sunt, non vide-*

describe emotions such as anger, pity, and fear (e.g., *Rhetoric* 2.1 [1378a20–30]). In the Latin tradition the *locus classicus* is provided by St. Augustine, *De civitate Dei* 9.4–6 and 14.3, 6–10. Citing Cicero (*De finibus* 3.20; *Tusculan Disputations* 3.4), Augustine discusses the controversy opposing the Stoics to the Platonists and Peripatetics as to whether the wise man is subject to emotions. He concludes that the emotions may be either good or bad, depending on the end toward which they are directed by the will. In addition to *passio animi* he uses a variety of other expressions to refer to the emotions: *perturbatio (animi)*, "perturbation, disturbance," a term borrowed from Cicero, which underlines the negative connotation often associated with *passio; affectus* or *affectio*, "affect," that is, the fact of being affected by something (thus a close synonym of *passio*); and *motus*, "motion," that is, the fact of being "moved" (hence the etymology of the modern word "emotion"), for action and passion are inseparably connected with movement.[40] Included is a discussion of love (14.7), as well as of the four principal emotions (14.3, 6–8) to which we have already referred. The *passiones animæ* also furnish the context for Thomas Aquinas's discussion of the four principal emotions and of love.[41]

That this is indeed what Andreas had in mind is made clear from

---

tur Aristotelem intellexisse. Passiones enim apud ipsum sunt dispositiones non permanentes, sed statim transeuntes, quemadmodum in libro Prædicamentorum *manifestum est . . . non enim intelligenda passio, effectus illatioque actionis, sicut in libro* Sex principiorum, *sed dispositio solummodo non permanens* ("If anyone should say that Aristotle understood by passions only bad disposition of the soul, and that he called them 'passions' because they are wounds of the soul, it would seem that he does not understand Aristotle. For passions are non-permanent dispositions, immediately passing away, as is clear from the *Categories*. . . . Passions should not be understood as the effect and result of an action, as in the *Book of Six Principles*, but only as non-permanent dispositions" [my translation]). William's discussion centers on the question, also discussed by St. Augustine, whether the emotions should be considered as bad per se; like Augustine, William answers in the negative. His argument, however, that emotions are qualities rather than inflicted "wounds" (*læsiones*), appears to ignore the fact that, even as a quality, a *passio* always has its origin in the reception of an action.

40. According to Aristotle, *Physics* 3.3 (202a13–202b29), motion is the actualization of a potential for activity or passivity. Cf. *ST* 1a2æ 22.1, ad 2: *passio est motus, ut dicitur in* Phys. See also *Liber sex principiorum* 2.20, 23 (AL 1/6–7:39–40).

41. *ST* 1a2æ 22–48; esp. q. 25, a. 4; q. 26–28.

his discussion of *innata*. Here the proximate, psychic cause of love *(cogitatio)* is stressed, almost to the complete exclusion of its remote, physical cause *(visio):* ex sola cogitatione, *quam concipit* animus *ex eo, quod* vidit, *passio illa procedit* (my emphasis). This is also how the passage was understood by most of its early translators: "maladie de pensee" (Jean de Meun); "passions ou maladie dedans nee" (Drouart la Vache); "una passione dentro nata" (Riccardiana version); "una passione nata dentro dell'anima" (Antonio Pucci), "une passion ou affection de l'ame" (*Echecs amoureux* commenatary, BN fr. 9197); "una interior passione et desiderio ò vogliamo dire affettione d'animo" (Angelo Ambrosini).[42]

The kernel of Andreas's definition, *passio innata,* identifies love not only as an "affect" *(passio)* but also as belonging to a standard subgenus of that category, that of the "internal affects," or emotions. It is not any emotion, but "a certain" *(quædam)* emotion. The rest of the definition can be seen as a gloss of *quædam,* having as its function to indicate the *differentiæ* distinguishing this particular emotion from all others.

Aristotelian causality

Before examining the other *differentiæ,* we must pause to note that the definition as a whole is formulated in terms of Aristotle's theory of causality. Andreas makes explicit reference elsewhere in his treatise to this theory, which was just coming into fashion in his time, thanks to recent translations of the *Physics* and the *Metaphysics*. Aristotle's theory distinguishes four "causes" of a given phenomenon: the "formal cause"

---

42. Guillaume de Lorris and Jean de Meun, *Roman de la Rose,* v. 4348 (ed. Lecoy, 1:134); Drouart, v. 138–39 (ed. Bossuat, p. 4); Riccardiana version (ed. Battaglia, p. 5); Pucci, § 38.17 (ed. Varvaro, p. 275); Karnein, *"De Amore,"* p. 212 (*Echecs* commentary), 237 (Ambrosini). Cf. Monson, "Andreas Capellanus and His Medieval Translators." Karnein's assertions that "keiner der Übersetzer behält jedoch *innata* bei, ohne neu zu deuten" (ibid., p. 61) and that with Jean de Meun "*innata* bleibt unübersetzt" (ibid., p. 192) are false. The translations of Antonio Pucci, the *Echecs amoureux* commentary, and Angelo Ambrosini show with particular clarity the scholastic sense of *innata:* "nata dentro dell'animo"; "de l'ame"; "interiore . . . d'animo." Only three early translators understood it in the common sense of "innate": *una passione naturale* (Barberiniana version; ed. Ruffini, p. 7); *una passione innata* (Florentine gloss on Ovid; Karnein, "De Amore," p. 231); *ain angeboren leiden* (Johann Hartlieb, p. 67).

(causa formalis), the "material cause" *(causa materialis),* the "efficient cause" *(causa efficiens),* and the "final cause" *(causa finalis).*[43]

In Andreas's definition, *passio* evokes the formal cause, or form-giving principle, usually associated with species or, as here, with genus.[44] *Innata* refers to the material cause in terms of the "substance" *(substantia)* affected, in this case "non-physical" substance *(substantia incorporea* or *incorporealis),* namely the mind or soul.[45] The phrase *procedens ex visione et immoderata cogitatione formæ alterius sexus* designates the efficient cause, or factor effecting the change (the only factor retained in the modern notion of causality). And the remainder of the definition, *ob quam aliquis super omnia cupit alterius potiri amplexibus et omnia de utriusque voluntate in ipsius amplexu amoris præcepta compleri,* indicates the final cause, that is, the end or purpose of love.

As a further refinement, Andreas has carefully grouped these four causes according to a classic scholastic distinction between "intrinsic" and "extrinsic" causes *(causæ intrinsecæl. . . extrinsecæ):* the intrinsic causes are the formal and material causes, which are mentioned first and together, followed by the extrinsic causes, that is, the efficient and final causes.[46] Moreover, the two extrinsic causes are broken down with

43. Aristotle, *Physics* 2.3 (194b16–195b30); *Metaphysics* 5.2 (1013a24–1014a25). Cf. d'Alverny, pp. 435–37, 460.

44. Aristotle, *Physics* 2.3 (194b26–27) and *Metaphysics* 5.2 (1013a26–28), associates the formal cause not only with species but also with genus. Cf. *ST* 1a2æ 18.7, ad 3/3 (ed. Blackfriars, 18:31, 33): "though in another sense a genus can also be considered as being fuller of form than a species in that it is more unqualified and less restricted."

45. [Helwicus Theutonicus], *De dilectione Dei et proximi,* in St. Thomas Aquinas, *Opera omnia,* vol. 15 (Parma, 1864), p. 276: *Dilectio cum sit accidens, non habet materiam ex qua, sed in qua; et in quantum est accidens vel forma accidentalis, sic subjectum in quo est et quod informat, est ejus materia* ("Since love is an accident, it does not have matter *from* which it is made but *in* which it is made; and insofar as it is an accident or an accidental form, the subject in which it resides and which it informs is its matter" [my translation]).

46. Aristotle, *Metaphysics* 12.4 (1070b22–25). Cf. the prologue to Peter of Tarantasia, commentary on II Thessalonians, 2nd redaction: *In quolibet opere concurrunt quatuor causæ: duæ extrinsecæ que sunt de fieri, scilicet efficiens et finis; due intrinsecæ quæ sunt de esse, scilicet materia et forma. In fieri rei, efficiens inchoat et finis consummat; in esse rei, materia inchoat et forma consummat.* ("In any created thing, four causes come together: two extrinsic [causes], which concern becoming, namely the efficient and final [causes]; [and] two intrinsic [causes], which concern being, namely matter and form. In

striking symmetry according to another scholastic distinction between "immediate" and "remote" causes *(causæ propinquæ seu proximæl. . . remotæ)*, separated in each case by the conjunction *et.*[47] *Ex visione . . .* indicates the remote efficient cause, [*ex*] *immoderata cogitatione . . .* , the proximate efficient cause. Likewise, *alterius potiri amplexibus* designates the immediate final cause, *omnia . . . præcepta amoris compleri*, the remote final cause.

That Andreas was familiar with Aristotle's theory of causality is clear from a passage in the Eighth Dialogue, where the efficient and final causes are mentioned, with specific reference to love. In debating whether the solaces of the upper half or the lower half of the body are to be preferred, the woman argues that in impotent men the efficient cause of love is lacking (*DA* 1.6.540 [200]). In naming virility as the efficient cause of love, the woman is playing on the ambiguity of the word *amor*. Here the term designates not the suffering that is love, according to the definition, but rather the act of making love. This shift in meaning parallels that made by Andreas at the beginning of Chapter Six, when he inquires "how love is won." In his reply the man refers, more properly, to the "solaces of the lower part" as the *final* cause of love (*DA* 1.6.544 [202]). It should be noted that the woman eventually accedes to the man's position concerning the relative value of the upper and lower parts. It may be that she has intentionally advanced a specious argument to test the alertness of her opponent.[48] In any case, the latter's designation of the "solaces of the lower part" as the final cause of love seems to confirm our interpretation of the equivalent expression in the definition.

Although Andreas's use of Aristotelian causality remains implicit in

---

the becoming of a thing, the efficient [cause] begins it, and the final [cause] completes it; in the being of a thing, the matter begins its, and the form completes it" [quoted by Minnis, *Medieval Theory,* p. 249, n. 17; my translation]). See also Deferrari and Barry, p. 138.

47. Minnis, *Medieval Theory,* p. 77; Deferrari and Barry, p. 141.

48. Walsh, p. 200, n. 196, suggests that "there is perhaps a hint of scholastic joking" in the woman's discussion of the efficient cause. In any case, *amor* is used equivocally, with a shift in category from a *pati* to a *facere*. Cf. *ST* 1a2æ 26.2, contra, ad 2: *Amor non est ipsa relatio unionis, sed unio est consequens amorem* ("Love therefore is not the union itself; union is the result of love" [ed. Blackfriars, 19: 67]).

the definition, it forms a pattern too striking to be ignored. It embodies the principle, enunciated in the *Posterior Analytics,* that to know the causes of a thing is the same as to know its essence.[49] This implicit use of Aristotle's theory anticipates by several decades its formal application to love in the thirteenth century, for example in the treatise *De dilectione Dei et proximi* attributed to Helwicus Theutonicus.[50]

The two internal causes, the formal cause *passio* and the material cause *innata,* define love generically as an emotion, as we have seen. It remains for the two external causes, the efficient and the final, to define it specifically within that genus. We must now take a closer look at those two external causes.

The efficient cause

According to Andreas's definition, love is the result of two successive *passiones,* an external *passio corporis,* or sense perception, followed by an internal *passio animæ,* or emotion. That is the basis of the Chaplain's distinction between the remote and proximate efficient causes: *ex visione et . . . cogitatione.*[51] A very similar psychological process is described by Andreas's contemporary, John of Salisbury, in the passage of the *Metalogicon* previously mentioned: *Est autem sensus ut Calcidio placet passio corporis. . . . Et in hunc modum ex sensu proueniunt cetera per imaginationis opem, ut amor.*[52] This passage shares with Andreas's

49. *Posterior Analytics* 2.2 (90a14–15, 31–32); 2.8 (93a3–4). Cf. Fortenbaugh, pp. 12–16.

50. *De dilectione Dei et proximi* 3.7, *De causis et effectibus dilectionis* (pp. 276–79). Cf. Chydenius, pp. 24–27. For a modern application of Aristotelian causality to medieval love see Schnell, *Causa amoris,* esp. ch. 2 (pp. 53–76).

51. According to Aristotle, *De anima* 1.5 (410a25–26), thinking, like sense perception, is a kind of passion; that is, in perceiving or thinking the soul both acts and is acted upon. Cf. *ST* 1a2æ 22.1, contra: *sentire et intelligere est quoddam pati* ("Perceiving and understanding are a kind of suffering" [my translation]).

52. *Metalogicon* 4.9.14–15; 4.10.27–28 (ed. Hall, pp. 148–49). Cf. *Metalogicon* (trans. McGarry, pp. 217, 220): "According to Chalcidius, sensation is 'a bodily state of being affected by action'. . . . In like manner [our] other emotions all proceed from sensation, through the activity of the imagination. Which also holds true of love"; Chalcidius, *In Timæum* § 194 (Plato Latinus 4:216). Although these two passages are separated by fifty lines of text, they are part of a continuous discussion on the role of the physical senses

definition the view that love is derived from a complex "affect" *(passio),* including an external sense perception and a further psychic manipulation of that perception. Because he is discussing human psychology in general, John speaks of *sensus* rather than *visio,* but, thanks to a long tradition, there can be no doubt that vision is the particular type of sensation to be associated with his example, *amor.*[53]

Otherwise the main difference between John's language and Andreas's is John's use of *imaginatio* rather than *cogitatio* to describe the intervening psychic operation. According to a fairly standard scholastic psychology going back to Avicenna's *De anima,* translated in the mid-twelfth century,[54] the terms *imaginatio* and *cogitatio* designate distinct but closely related phenomena. The *vis cogitativa* and *vis imaginativa* (or *imaginatio*) are both among the "internal senses" and thus a part of the "sensitive," rather than the "rational," soul. Both are involved with the reproduction and manipulation of the data of sense perception, *imaginatio* on an immediate level and *cogitatio* on a somewhat higher level of abstraction, so that together they form a kind of progressive bridge between the senses and the reasoning intellect.[55] It is tempting to see *imaginatio* and *cogitatio* as more or less equivalent in this context. Indeed, Bruno Nardi glosses *cogitatio* in Andreas's definition with the Italian *immaginazione.*[56]

In the discussion following his definition, Andreas uses both the verbs *cogitare* and *imaginari* to describe the psychological process of falling in love: *Post modum mulieris incipit* cogitare *facturas, et eius distinguere membra suosque actus* imaginari.[57] This use of these verbs corre-

---

in cognition. Most of the intervening material concerns the function of the imagination, a subject also discussed by Andreas in the commentary following his definition.

53. See Cline.

54. D'Alverny, pp. 444–45. The roots of the doctrine go back to Aristotle and Galen (see Wolfson).

55. Bundy, esp. ch. 9 (pp. 177–98); Wolfson; Harvey.

56. Nardi, p. 6: "Ho reso la parola *cogitatio* . . . colla parola *immaginazione* . . . giacchè il cogitare di cui intende il Capellano, come risulta della definitione dell' amore, non è funzione dell' intelletto, ma di quella che i medievali chiamarono la *vis cogitativa* che è, al pari della fantasia, uno dei sensi interiori." Wack, "Imagination," p. 101, also argues that for Andreas *cogitatio* and *imaginatio* are synonymous.

57. *DA* 1.1.10 (34) [my emphasis]. See above, n. 28.

sponds closely to the usual distinction of faculties in medieval psychology. The *vis imaginativa* not only retains the images of sense perception *(imaginatio retentiva)*, it also combines them, producing in the mind new images that have never actually been perceived by the senses *(imaginatio formativa)*. It is this latter type of imagining or fantasizing that Andreas evokes with the expression *suosque actus imaginari*. The *vis cogitativa*, on the other hand, has as its first function to distinguish one from another the impressions collected by the imagination. It is thus that Andreas uses in close parallel construction the two more or less synonymous expressions *cogitare facturas* and *distinguere membra*. In addition, *cogitatio* is often associated with estimation or opinion *(æstimatio/exæstimatio/vis [ex]æstimativa/opinio)*, which functions in brute animals as well as in humans to distinguish between the useful and the harmful, the pleasant and the unpleasant. This accounts for Andreas's repeated use of *cogitatio* and *cogitare* to describe the perception of the attractiveness of the love object, giving rise to a movement of desire:

> Postea vero, quotiens de ipsa *cogitat,* totiens eius magis ardescit amore, quousque ad *cogitationem* devenerit pleniorem. . . . Postquam vero ad hanc *cogitationem* plenariam devenerit, sua frena nescit continere amor, sed statim procedit ad actum.[58]

It should be added that, as the highest faculty of the sensitive soul, the *vis cogitativa* directs all the others. This perhaps explains the fact that the entire psychological process described by means of the verbs *cogitare, distinguere, imaginari,* and *rimari* appears to be subsumed under the general rubric *cogitatio plenior* (or . . . *plenaria*). Without exaggerating the precision or technicality of Andreas's use of these terms, we can see that, for the specific emotion under consideration, his description of psychological processes compares very favorably in terms of refinement and comprehensiveness to that of John of Salisbury.

Andreas's definition specifies that the *cogitatio* which produces love is *immoderata*.[59] This expression, which also occurs three times later in

---

58. *DA* 1.1.9, 11 (34). Cf. Walsh, p. 35: "Whenever subsequently he thinks about her, he burns with love for her more each time, until he reaches the stage of more detailed reflexion. . . . Now when he attains this stage of detailed reflexion, his love cannot keep control over its reins, but at once advances to action."

59. For a fuller discussion of this word, see Monson, *"Immoderatus."*

the treatise, is problematic. Glossing *immoderata* with its modern derivative "immoderate," some have seen in it an implied condemnation of
excess. For those who view the *De amore* as an ironic condemnation of
cupidity, this notion is related to the *vehemens amator,* the "too-ardent
lover" denounced by theologians in the tradition of Saint Jerome. For
those who place the definition in the medical tradition, it evokes rather
the physicians' pathological *amor hereos* or *heroicus,* the melancholic
"loveres maladye of hereos"—a somewhat anachronistic association,
however, for as Mary Wack has shown, *amor hereos* was unknown in the
West until the thirteenth century.[60] Most recently, John Baldwin stresses the importance of *immoderatus* in the definition and invokes both
traditions in interpreting it.[61]

Although "immoderate" is the most obvious translation for *immoderatus,* it is not the only possibility. The word is formed from the negative prefix *in-* and *moderatus,* the perfect passive participle of *moderare*
or deponent *moderari,* both derived from *modus,* "measure, standard,"
and both meaning "to measure, to limit, to restrict, to regulate." Thus
the first meaning of *immoderatus* is "without measure, unlimited,
boundless," the equivalent of *immensus,* "immense," which is similarly
derived from *mensus,* the past participle of *metiri,* "to measure." In this
morally neutral, strictly quantitative sense *immoderatus* is used especially to describe natural phenomena, as when Cicero writes of *immoderatus æther,* "the boundless ether," or when Lucretius applies the term to
"matter" *(corpus)* and the "void" *(inane).* More to the point for our purpose, Ovid, whom Andreas knew and imitated, writes of his "boundless
desire" to return from exile: *res inmoderata cupido est.* When used in reference to human behavior, *immoderatus* takes on the secondary meaning "unrestrained, excessive, intemperate, immoderate," which soon
came to predominate.[62]

A close examination of Andreas's own discussion of *immoderatus* in
Chapter One of his treatise seems to suggest that the term is used there
with its neutral, quantitative meaning:

60. Wack, "Imagination," p. 108, n. 26. Cf. idem, *Lovesickness,* 182–85.
61. Baldwin, "Five Discourses," p. 808; idem, *Language,* pp. 141–42.
62. *Thesaurus linguæ latinæ,* 7:483–484; 8:1212–1220; *Oxford Latin Dictionary,* pp.
837, 1122. Cf. Cicero, *De natura deorum* 2.25.65; Lucretius, *De rerum natura* 1.1013;
Ovid, *Epistulæ ex Ponto,* 4.15.31.

> Non quælibet cogitatio suffit ad amoris originem, sed immoderata exigitur; nam cogitatio moderata non solet ad mentem redire, et ideo ex ea non potest amor oriri.[63]

What is required for love to occur is a thought that will "recur to the mind" *(ad mentem redire)*. This recalls fairly explicitly the progressive intensification and reciprocal reinforcement of meditation and desire described earlier in the same chapter.[64] For this process to take place, the initial reflection on the beloved must already be of a certain intensity, must have a certain obsessive quality *(ad mentem redire)*, to which the term *immoderata* apparently refers, rather than to any reprehensible notion of excess.

So understood, the expression *immoderata cogitatio* describing the efficient cause of love is closely related to the expression *super omnia cupit*, "desires above all else," used in the same definition in relation to love's final cause. A person who is truly in love is occupied exclusively with thoughts of and desire for the beloved. This principle is stated explicitly near the beginning of Chapter Two: *Ad hoc totus tendit conatus amantis, et de hoc illius assidua est* cogitatio, *ut eius quam amat fruatur amplecti.*[65] Similar ideas are expressed in the *Præfatio (DA* 0.3 [30]) and in the Rules of Love: *XXIV. Quilibet amantis actus in coamantis* cogitatione *finitur.*[66] In Chapter Four this exclusive preoccupation with the beloved will give rise to the principle of chaste fidelity to one woman *(castitas)*.

The neutral use of *immoderatus,* in the sense "intense" or "exclusive" suggested in Chapter One, also finds confirmation later in the treatise. For two of the three later occurrences of our expression, the word *assiduus,* "continuous, constant," is added, so that it is now *assidua et im-*

---

63. *DA* 1.1.13 (34). Cf. Walsh, p. 35: "Any casual meditation is not enough to cause love; the thoughts must be out of control, for a controlled thought does not usually recur to the mind, and so love cannot arise from it."

64. *DA* 1.1.9–11 (34). Cf. note 58, above.

65. *DA* 1.2.2 (34) [my emphasis]. Cf. Walsh, p. 35: "Besides, the whole impetus of the lover is towards enjoying the embraces of the beloved, and this is what he thinks of continually."

68. *DA* 2.8.47 (282) [my emphasis]. Cf. Walsh, p. 283: "Every act of a lover is bounded by thoughts of his beloved."

moderata cogitatio that is required to produce love (*DA* 1.6.559 [206]; 2.6.1 [238]). *Assiduus* has a quantitative meaning far removed from any suggestion of medical pathology or moral condemnation. It is used several times alone to describe *cogitatio,* including the passage from Chapter Two quoted above.[67] Its coupling in two cases with *immoderatus* underlines the quantitative nature of the entire expression while giving it two distinct dimensions: *assidua* indicates the extension of the meditation in time, whereas *immoderata* refers apparently to its intensity.

In several later passages *immoderatus* or adverb *immoderate* describes love itself, rather than the meditation giving rise to it, with what again appears to be a neutral, quantitative meaning. The first of the Love Cases of Book Two, Chapter Seven, presents a man who was bound "exclusively" to a lady by love: *immoderate ligaretur amore* (*DA* 2.7.1 [250]), which P. G. Walsh (p. 251) translates as "head over heels in love." Likewise, the man of the fifth love case loved his lady "without reservation": *immoderate amabat* (*DA* 2.7.14 [254]), or "unstintingly," according to Walsh (p. 255). In both these cases the Countess of Champagne found in favor of the man whose love was so described, and in the first it is stipulated that the lover has "committed no sin": *Nec enim in aliquo prædictus peccavit amator* (*DA* 2.7.5 [250]). In the Seventh Dialogue the marital affection between a husband and his wife is described, again with no apparent nuance of condemnation, as *nimia et immoderata affectio,* which Walsh renders as "great and boundless affection."[68] These examples bolster Andreas's contention in Chapter One that, with regard to love, a meditation or affection short of "immoderate" is insufficient.

Further confirmation comes from several of the medieval translations/adaptations of the *De amore.* The majority opt for the most obvious translation of *immoderata* in the definition, rendering it with words or expressions indicative of excess, but three of them adopt language denoting meditation of great intensity: "grandissimo pensiero," 'very

---

67. *DA* 1.2.2 (34); 1.6.280 (120); 1.6.181 (120). Cf. *assidua contemplatio* (*DA* 1.6.326 [134]), *assidua imaginatio* (*DA* 2.8.48 [284], Rule XXX). *Immoderata cogitatio* occurs without *assidua* at *DA* 1.5.6 (40).

68. *DA* 1.6.368 (146); cf. Walsh, p. 147. It is thus not entirely true, as Baldwin, *Language,* p. 141, contends, that Andreas opposes "the affection of love" that "is excessive and immoderate" to "marital affection, which is comfortably complacent."

great thought' (Barberiniana version), "par penser aprés profondement et continuelment," 'thinking afterwards deeply and continuously' (*Echecs amoureux* commentary, BN fr. 24295), "consideration . . . si fort fichee et imprimee en son cuer et en sa pensee," 'consideration . . . so strongly stuck and imprinted in his heart and thoughts' (*Echecs amoureux* commentary, BN fr. 9197).[69] The definition is missing from the fragmentary Catalan translation, but subsequently *immoderata cogitatio* is translated as "bon pensament," 'good (i.e., 'abundant'?) thought,' and *nimia et immoderata affectio* is rendered "gran desig," 'great desire.'[70] Drouart la Vache follows Jean de Meun's tendentious translation of *immoderata* as "desordenee" in the definition, but for two later passages he prefers neutral expressions, rendering *nimia et immoderata affectio* as "afection grant," 'great affection' and *immoderate amabat* as "mout durement amer soloit," 'used to be very seriously in love.'[71] In line with its rendering of *immoderata* in the definition, the Barberiniana version later translates *immoderata cogitatio* as "grande pensiero," 'great thought' and *assidua et immoderata cogitatio* as "molto pensare e continuo" or "continuo molto pensiero," 'much continuous thought.'[72] All these *interpretationes difficiliores* show an awareness on the part of several medieval translators of the ambiguity of *immoderata* and the appropriateness of its less common meaning in certain contexts.[73] They thus join the later occurrences of *immoderatus* in lending support to an conclusion that could already be deduced from Andreas's discussion of the term in Chapter One.

69. Ed. Ruffini, § 3.1 (p. 7); Badel, p. 307; Karnein, *"De Amore,"* p. 212. Cf. Monson, "Andreas Capellanus and His Medieval Translators."

70. Ed. Pagès, pp. III, LX. Cf. *DA* 1.5.6 (40); 1.6.368 (146). See also "fort ligat d'amor" (p. CI) for *immoderate ligatur amore* (*DA* 2.7.1 [250]); "amaua fortment" (p. CIV) for *immoderate amabat* (*DA* 2.7.14 [254]).

71. Drouart, vv. 140, 3449–50, 5732–33 (pp. 4, 100, 164). Cf. *DA* 1.1.1 (32); 1.6.368 (146); 2.7.14 (254). Jean de Meun's paraphrase of Andreas's definition is colored by the fact that it is part of a speech by Reason against love.

72. Ed. Ruffini, §§ 9.7, 18.299, 30.2 (pp. 15, 195, 233). Cf. *DA* 1.5.6 (40); 1.6.559 (206); 2.6.1 (238).

73. Both Ovid (*Amores* 1.6.59; *AA* 2.20) and Thomas Aquinas (*ST* 1a 98.2, ad 3; 2a2æ 153.2, ad 2) express doubts about the possibility of controlling sexual love, and although the troubadours vaunt the virtue of moderation *(mezura)*, there are many passage in which they claim to love immoderately. For a fuller discussion, see Monson, *"Immoderatus."*

The final cause

In defining sexual union as the final cause of love, Andreas presumably sees in it not only the "goal" of the lover, but also the natural conclusion toward which the emotion of love itself is directed. The view that union is the ultimate end of love also has a long tradition, as is clear from the following passage from Aquinas:

> There is this much of 'union' about love that, as a result of the pleasure felt in the orexis at the thought of the object, a person feels towards that object as if it were himself, or a part of himself. Love therefore is not the union itself; union is a result of love. Hence Dionysius calls love *a force that leads to union,* and Aristotle says that union is an effect of love.[74]

Sexual union is that which follows naturally from love, making it whole or complete. In scholastic terms, it is love's "perfection" *(perfectio)*. In his commentary on the definition Andreas refers to unconsummated love as an "imperfect thing" *(res imperfecta; DA* 1.1.3 [32]) and to mutual love as the case where "the love of each is perfected, carried out, brought to completion" *(amor utriusque perficitur; DA* 1.1.6 [32]). According to Peter of Tarantasia, "In the becoming of a thing, the efficient cause sets it in motion, and the end completes or perfects it."[75]

The fact that Andreas breaks the final cause down into immediate and remote causes probably reflects not only the philosophical tradition but also the literary tradition, for it may well be a reference to the classical and medieval commonplace known as the "five stages of love" *(gradus . . ./quinque lineæ amoris).*[76] This theme is invoked by Andreas in his First and Eighth Dialogues, and it also plays an important role in his distinction between "pure" and "mixed" love.[77] In the classical formulation, the five stages of love are *(visus), alloquium, contactus, oscula,* and *factum,* the first being sometimes omitted. According to the varia-

74. *ST* 1a2æ 26.2, contra, ad 2 (ed. Blackfriars, 19:67).

75. My translation. Cf. Peter of Tarantasia, commentary on II Thessalonians, 2nd redaction: "In fieri rei, efficiens incohat et finis consummat" (quoted by Minnis, *Medieval Theory,* p. 249, n. 17). See above, n. 46.

76. Friedman; Curtius, pp. 512–14; Dronke, *Medieval Latin,* 2:488–89; Akehurst, "Les étapes"; idem, "Words and Acts."

77. *DA* 1.6.59–64 (56), 438 (170), 470–75 (180). See below, Chapter 8.

tion developed in Andreas's dialogues, *amplexus,* "embracing," replacing *contactus,* "physical contact," represents the second (*DA* 1.6.471 [180]) or third (*DA* 1.6.60 [56], 438 [170]) of four stages.[78] It is this same term, *amplexus,* that designates the proximate final cause in the definition: *alterius potiri amplexibus.* In the dialogues the ultimate goal is described as *totius personæ concessio* ("the yielding of the whole person"; *DA* 1.6.60 [56]), *extremum solatium* ("the ultimate solace"; *DA* 1.6.471 [180]), or *extremum Veneris opus* ("the ultimate work of Venus"; *DA* 1.6.473 [180]). This last image is particularly close to the expression used in the definition to describe euphemistically the same phenomenon: *omnia . . . præcepta amoris compleri* ("to carry out all of Love's precepts"). The fact that the first stage, *visus/visio,* figures so prominently in Andreas's definition also reinforces the likelihood that the *quinque lineæ* influenced his "final cause." Incidentally, there is an apparent reference to the second stage, *alloquium,* "conversation," in the lover's reaction to his "suffering" as described in the discussion of the definition: *Incipit etiam quærere locum et tempus cum opportunitate* loquendi.[79] Thus the definition and subsequent discussion contain references to four of the five stages of love, with only *oscula,* "kissing," omitted.

In fact, the entire definition elaborates a process very similar to that described by the topic of the five stages of love. It is a complex process involving several steps: (1) sight *(visio);* (2) meditation *(cogitatio);* (3) desire *(concupiscere);* (4) heightened meditation *(cogitatio plenior);* (5) unbridled desire *(frena nescit continere);* (6) action *(procedit ad actum).* This progressive process parallels that of the traditional topic, whose be-

---

78. Andreas's four stages are, according to the First Dialogue, *spei datatio* ("the giving of hope"), *osculi exhibitio* ("the granting of a kiss"), *amplexus fruitio* ("the enjoyment of an embrace"), and *totius personæ concessio* ("the yielding of the whole person"). This schema is repeated at the beginning of the Eighth Dialogue but later modified in the discussion of "pure" and "mixed" love: *oris osculum* ("kissing on the mouth"), *lacerti amplexus* ("embracing with the arms"), *verecundus amantis nudæ contactus* ("modest contact with the nude lover"), and *extremum solatium* ("the ultimate solace")/*extremum Veneris opus* ("the ultimate work of Venus"). The fact that both *amplexus* and *contactus* appear in this last formula is due to the rhetorical strategy of the lover, who maintains the same number of steps but advances the whole process in the direction of the goal.

79. *DA* 1.1.12 (34) [my emphasis]. Cf. Walsh, p. 35: "He begins . . . to contrive a place and time affording opportunity to converse."

ginning and ending points are the same, but there is one important difference: whereas the *quinque lineæ* remain entirely external and physical, the process described by Andreas is, except for its first and last steps, internal and psychological. It is a process that originates in the external, physical world, then proceeds by means of the sense organs to the mind, where it is further elaborated, then redirected outward toward action in the external world, coming to rest ideally in the object that gave rise to it in the first place.

We can now draw some conclusions. We have seen that Andreas defines love as an "affect" *(passio),* particularly as an "internal affect," or emotion. Specifically, it is that emotion whose efficient cause is the effect on the senses of the beauty of the opposite sex and whose final cause is the act of sexual union. This is, of course, a considerable restriction with respect to St. Augustine or St. Thomas, who see *amor* as a synonym of *dilectio* and as having a variety of possible objects.[80] Such a restriction is perhaps a reflection of the prominence accorded to love between the sexes in the imaginative literature of the period. In any case, for Andreas *amor* is nothing more nor less than sexual love.

From the above discussion it is clear that Andreas's definition of love is thoughtful, well balanced, and carefully constructed. It is, in fact, the aspect of the treatise that most rigorously reflects the generic vector that we have called *scientia.* According to the standards of the time in which it was written, it is a properly scientific definition drawing on a long philosophical tradition. It is presumably this common tradition that accounts for its similarity not only to certain passages from John of Salisbury and Aquinas but also to various moral and medical writings of the patristic and medieval periods.

A comparison with the definition of love proposed by Andreas's contemporary Aelred of Rievaulx reveals, despite certain differences, the clear presence of a common tradition behind the two formulations. In the first book of his *De spirituali amicitia,* Aelred describes friendship as a subspecies of love, then goes on to define the latter in the following terms:

80. *De civitate Dei* 14.7; *ST* 1a2æ 26.3.

Est autem amor quidam animæ rationalis affectus per quem ipsa aliquid cum desiderio quærit et appetit ad fruendum; per quem et fruitur eo cum quadam interiori suauitate, amplecitur et consuerat adeptum.[81]

At the center of Aelred's definition is the expression *animæ . . . affectus,* corresponding to the Chaplain's synonymous formula, *passio . . . innata.* Aelred then goes on to delimit the phenomenon specifically within the genus of "emotions" by describing its final cause in terms of "desire for enjoyment" *(cum desiderio quærit et appetit ad fruendum),* corresponding to Andreas's *super omnia cupit . . . potiri.* There is no mention of the efficient cause, however, and so the careful balance of the Chaplain's formulation is absent. Like St. Augustine and St. Thomas, Aelred has a much more general conception of love, with many possible love objects *(aliquid),* and the qualification of the soul as "rational" *(rationalis)* gives the definition an intellectual cast that is lacking in Andreas. Nevertheless, some of the sensuality of the *De amore* is present in the metaphorical use of *amplector,* corresponding to the Chaplain's *amplexus.*

In ideological terms Andreas's definition appears to be neutral. It is neither a programmatic manifesto promoting the fashion of courtly love, nor the ironically critical ecclesiastical condemnation of such a program. Nor is it a clinical description of the symptoms of a disease. In discussing the negative connotation of *passio,* Andreas enumerates the fears and torments of the lover, but on the following page he describes in great detail, with no apparent disapproval, the psychological development of the lover's desire. The definition draws on both the philosophical and the literary traditions of the Middle Ages, but it brings to its subject the objective detachment of science.

This is not to say that Andreas is a systematic thinker of the first order. We have seen that his definition and his subsequent discussion of it

---

81. Aelred, *De spiritali amicitia,* 1:19 (ed. Hoste and Talbot, p. 292). Cf. trans. Williams, p. 32: "However, love is an affection of the rational mind through which the mind seeks something for itself with desire and strives to enjoy the object of its desire. Love also enables the mind to enjoy the object of its desire with a certain internal pleasure, and once it has attained the object of its desire it embraces it and preserves it." For further discussion of Andreas's relationship to Aelred, see Jaeger, *Ennobling Love,* pp. 114–16.

exhibit difficulties with respect to the use of key terms such as *passio* ("passivity"/"suffering"), *innata/interior,* and *actio/factio,* although these problems are perhaps ascribable to fluctuations in terminology in the early scholastic period. Moreover, the rest of the treatise is not always as rigorous as the definition, as is clear from the reference to Aristotelian causality in the Eighth Dialogue.[82] Clearly conversant with the language and methods of medieval philosophy, Andreas adapts this knowledge freely to the complex requirements of his hybrid enterprise.

Despite these qualifications, however, the definition of love that Andreas proposes is artfully crafted and philosophically sound, and it is not at all surprising that it should have enjoyed such great popularity throughout the later Middle Ages. Without exaggerating the philosophical rigor of a work in which literary influences certainly play an important role, we can perhaps derive from this conclusion concerning the definition an invitation to take a little more seriously than many of us do at present the speculative intentions of the treatise as a whole.

82. Another example of philosophical laxity is provided by the long exchange in the Seventh Dialogue devoted primarily to the definitions of love and jealousy (*DA* 1.6.367–85 [146–52]). Although the authority of Andreas is invoked near the end of the passage (§ 385), the definitions discussed offer only a pale reflection of the rigorous definition of Chapter One, not to mention the fact that several different definitions are proposed for the same phenomenon, theoretically an impossibility. See above, Chapter 2.

6 ❋

LOVE AND
THE NATURAL ORDER

Psychology and Physiology

Chapter One of the *De amore* offers an essentially psychological
definition of love, as we have seen. It identifies the phenomenon under discussion as an "internal affect" *(passio innata),* that is, an
emotion, then it goes on to describe its specific character in terms of the
("efficient") causes, physical and psychological, that give rise to it *(visio,
cogitatio)* and the goals, psychological and especially physical, to which
it is directed *(amplexus, amoris præcepta compleri).* In commenting on
this definition, the rest of Chapter One fills out the psychological
processes involved in love's origin, development, and progress toward its
goal *(cogitatio plenior, concupiscere, actum).* The Chaplain thus elaborates a complex process involving several steps, an essentially internal,
psychological process that parallels the external, physical process described by the traditional topic of the *quinque lineæ amoris.*

Beyond this most scientific of chapters, many other passages in the
De amore raise questions or carry implications concerning the psychology and physiology of love. These discussions are most concentrated in
the theoretical, scholastic chapters that open Book One, but far from
being limited to those chapters, they are also found dispersed throughout the entire treatise. The present chapter will unite such passages and
examine them in light of each other and of Andreas's definition. From
this examination an idea will emerge as to how the Chaplain viewed
love as a natural phenomenon.

Andreas's discussion of love psychology and physiology draws on a variety of sources and traditions. It makes use of a number of basic notions from scholastic philosophy and psychology, as we have seen with respect to the definition, and also from medieval medicine. Equally important, however, are the literary sources, including the love writings of Ovid as well as the lyric poetry and romances of the troubadours and trouvères. The problems raised explicitly or implicitly by the treatise concerning the nature of love are the result of conflicts between these traditions or, in some cases, of unresolved conflicts within a given tradition.

For the sake of clarity, our discussion of love psychology and physiology in the *De amore* will be organized around a certain number of basic concepts, many of which appear already in Andreas's definition. Of course, such a separation is artificial, for these concepts constantly interact with each other throughout the treatise. Nor is it easy to separate the psychological and physiological aspects of love from the social and moral questions with which they are inextricably intertwined. Nevertheless, the latter concerns will be reserved for the last two chapters of our study.

Sight and beauty

According to Andreas's definition, the ultimate efficient cause of love is sight *(visio),* namely that of the beauty of the opposite sex *(formæ alterius sexus).* This association of love with sight has behind it a long tradition. The *Ars amatoria* begins with advice on "looking" for girls, and the classical and medieval commonplace of the five stages of love usually begins with *visus.* The lyric poetry of the troubadours as well as the medieval vernacular romances often identify the first sight of the beloved as the crucial moment in the generation of love, sometimes describing it allegorically in terms of Love's arrow entering the eye and striking the heart. The same image recurs in Petrarch and his Renaissance imitators under the label *innamoramento pergli occhi.* The association of sight with falling in love is also important in the medieval medical tradition, for example in the *Prose Salernitan Questions.*[1]

---

1. *The Prose Salernitan Questions,* B16 (ed. Lawn, p. 10). Cf. Baldwin, *Language,* p. 140.

Among the later references to sight in the treatise, the first and most striking occurs in Chapter Five, "What Persons Are Suited for Love." Here the blind are excluded from loving because they cannot see an object on which to reflect immoderately (*DA* 1.5.6 [40]). To my knowledge, no external source has been identified for this restriction. It is probably just a logical deduction from the prominent role assigned to sight in Andreas's definition, to which the final clause, "as was shown fully above," alludes explicitly. It underlines forcefully the importance ascribed to sight in the generation of love.

The exclusion of the blind, Andreas continues, applies only to falling in love, and so does not prevent someone in love who later goes blind from continuing to love (ibid.). This remark should be seen in the light of Andreas's discussion of *cogitatio* in Chapter One. Once the sense organs have implanted images on the mind, according to the standard medieval psychology that Andreas appears to follow, the "inner senses" of imagination, cogitation, and memory can analyze them, store them, and reproduce them, indeed recombine them in configurations not included in the original sense perceptions. Thus the blind man's "inner eye," as it were, can continue to furnish images of the beloved for his meditation even after his physical sense organs have ceased to function.

Alongside the poetic commonplace emphasizing the role of sight in the generation of love, a less widespread but nevertheless significant theme has love arising, sight unseen, from the reputation of the beloved. This paradoxical variant on the traditional theme, sometimes referred to as *amor ex auditu* ("love from hearing"), was made famous by Jaufre Rudel in his poems celebrating a "far-away love" *(amor de lonh)*. It is also represented in the romances, especially *Partonopeus de Blois* for the twelfth century, followed by such thirteenth-century examples as Jean Renart's *Guillaume de Dole* and the anonymous *Flamenca*. It is also reflected in the *De amore*, particularly in the dialogues.

At the beginning of the Fifth Dialogue the man laments the fact that he rarely has the opportunity to enjoy the physical presence of the lady (*DA* 1.6.198 [96]). This absence is compensated, the passage explains, by the lover's meditation *(cogitatio)* on the beloved, which allows him to see her with "the eyes of the heart" *(cordis oculi)*. The situation described is that of a lover who rarely sees the beloved, not of one who has never seen her. In terms of the role of sight in the generation of love, it is similar to that of the man who has become blind after falling in love.

The same theme of *amor de lonh* returns in the Seventh Dialogue, but in terms much closer to those of Jaufre Rudel. The man thanks God, he says, that he is now able to see in the flesh that which his soul desired to see above all else (*DA* 1.6.322–23 [132]). As in Jaufre's *Lanquan li jorn,* the sight of the beloved is the object of intense longing, and it is associated with the notion of divine intervention. Moreover, it is the reputation of the beloved that has furnished the mechanism by which the lover has become enamored, and it is only now, upon seeing her, that he can verify the truth of that reputation (ibid., §§ 323–24). The woman accepts the lover's claim without contradiction (*DA* 1.6.327 [134]), although it is difficult to reconcile it with Andreas's reasons for excluding the blind from loving.[2]

The role sight plays in the further development of a love already initiated is discussed in several passages of the treatise. In the passage from the Fifth Dialogue cited above, the meditation on the beloved in the absence of the sight produces in the lover both pain *(pœnas)* and consolation *(solatia).* When he sees her, consolation predominates; otherwise he is subject to great pain (*DA* 1.6.198, 200–201 [96–98]). The woman immediately grants the man the right to see her (*DA* 1.6.205 [98], 209 [100]), but this fails to mollify him: sight being only the first of the five traditional stages of love, he naturally continues to press for further concessions. In a later passage of the Seventh Dialogue the woman cites her physical separation from the man as an argument against accepting his love (*DA* 1.6.359 [142–44]). The woman maintains that daily sight of the beloved increases love, referring to a "rule of Love" not found in the list of Book Two, Chapter Eight (*DA* 1.6.360 [144]).[3] The man replies

---

2. It is therefore all the more curious that, near the end of the same dialogue, the man should accuse the woman, on grounds that are not clear, of promulgating a definition of love that includes the blind, contrary to the teachings of the Chaplain (*DA* 1.6 385 [152]). See above, Chapter 2.

3. Rules XV and XVI (*DA* 2.8.46 [282]) relate the physical effects on the lover of seeing the beloved and being seen by her, namely pallor and a faster heartbeat, which could well be interpreted as signs of at least a temporary increase in emotion.

that the difficulties of separation give love all that much more value, increasing the pleasure of the lovers when they are able to be together (*DA* 1.6.361–64 [144]). The woman finally concedes that physical separation is not a valid criterion for choosing or not choosing a lover (*DA* 1.6.365 [144]).

This subject is taken up again in the beginning chapters of Book Two, in a discussion that generally supports the position of the man in the Seventh Dialogue, but not without contradiction. In Chapter One Andreas advises the lover who would maintain love to frequent only rarely the places where the beloved is (*DA* 2.1.5 [224]), presumably for reasons of discretion. In Chapter Two the Chaplain reports the opinion that love can be increased by making it difficult for the lovers to see each other (*DA* 2.2.1 [228]), arguing subsequently that going away will increase love (*DA* 2.2.4 [228]). In Chapter Three he goes so far as to claim that love is diminished by too many opportunities to see the beloved (*DA* 2.3.1 [230]). The opinion cited at the beginning of Chapter Two is probably that of Ovid, who advises absence as a means to inflame the beloved (*AA* 2.349–56).

In contrast to this advice, Book Two, Chapter Two names the sight of the beloved as a way to increase love (*DA* 2.2.5 [228]). Contradiction with the advice previously cited is avoided through the stipulation that sight should be apprehensive and secretive for the desired effect to take place. This restriction is perhaps an echo of *AA* 3.579, where Ovid advises women not to leave their men too secure in the enjoyment of their favors. Ovid's advice on the role of sight in maintaining love is complex, not to say contradictory: just before advising men to take trips, Ovid counsels them to let themselves be seen often, at least in the beginning (*AA* 2.345–48), and of the trips he warns that they should not be too long (*AA* 2.357–72). The element of contradiction on this subject evident in Book Two of the *De amore* is probably a reflection of Ovid.

Before leaving the subject of sight, we must say a few words about the related theme of beauty. The sight that gives rise to love, according to the definition, is that of beauty *(forma)*, namely the beauty of the opposite sex. This theme recurs in many passages scattered throughout the treatise, expressed by various terms, especially *forma/formosus* and *pulcher/pulchritudo,* but also *venustas/venustus* and *species.* Many of these passages discuss beauty in relation to social or moral questions to which we shall return in Chapters 7 and 8, but some also have interesting psychological implications.

The most extensive discussion of beauty is found near the beginning of Book One, Chapter Six, where this quality is listed among the five ways of acquiring love. Most of this passage is devoted to demonstrating the superiority of character to beauty in this connection. Of course, Andreas begrudgingly admits (*DA* 1.6.3 [42]) the efficacy of beauty in acquiring love, an efficacy that cannot be denied, for indeed beauty was named in the definition as the ultimate efficient cause of the phenomenon. The objections to beauty expressed here are essentially moral rather than psychological.

The Chaplain's reservations about beauty involve two complementary aspects. On the one hand, Walter is warned to avoid being ensnared by the beauty of women (*DA* 1.6.9–10 [42–44]). This warning will be repeated in the chapter on nuns (*DA* 1.8.4–6 [212]). At the same time he is advised not to place too much reliance on his own physical beauty, which would be unlikely to secure him a discerning lover (*DA* 1.6.8–9 [42]), and Ovid's advice to use moderation in the care of the body (*AA* 1.505–24, *Heroides* 4.75–76) is cited. This recommendation is again advanced in the woman's "sermon" on courtly values in the Third Dialogue (*DA* 1.6.156 [84]), and also in Book Two (*DA* 2.1.6 [226]). The anti-feminist diatribe of Book Three mentions beauty primarily as an object of envy on the part of other women (*DA* 3.73–74 [308], 94 [314]). In all these passages, psychological observations are intimately connected with moral considerations; it is precisely the undeniable psychological power of physical beauty that requires its subordination to moral concerns.

Physical beauty is discussed throughout the dialogues. Usually the man begins by praising the woman's beauty, to which she objects, after which the subject becomes a general topic of discussion. The debate is most developed in the First and Fourth Dialogues, in which the female protagonists are women of the middle class. At the beginning of the Second Dialogue Andreas counsels against praising the beauty of noblewomen, who are less susceptible to flattery (*DA* 1.6.69 [58]). In the First Dialogue the man tells the woman who rejects his praise that if she is not really as beautiful as he says, this only proves that he really loves her, since he sees her as beautiful (*DA* 1.6.31 [48]). The same argument is advanced by the man of the Fourth Dialogue (*DA* 1.6.181–82 [90]). It is possible, of course, to see these men simply as flatterers preying on the credulity of women of the middle class, but if we take their contention seriously, it points to an interesting conclusion: the essentially subjective nature of the perception that give rise to love. The same conclusion emerges from a pronouncement of Andreas himself in Book One, Chapter Four: when all the lover's thoughts are on the beloved, any other woman seems rough and inelegant to him (*DA* 1.4.2 [38]). As this last passage underlines, the crucial role in the generation of love belongs not to sight but to thought *(cogitatio),* which is capable even of influencing what the lover sees. In the words of the proverb, beauty is in the eye of the beholder.

Andreas's view of the relationship of sight to love is paradoxical, even contradictory. In discussing the genesis of love he lays great stress on the importance of sight as the remote efficient cause, but it is apparently not an absolute requirement, as can be seen from the *amor ex auditu* of the Seventh Dialogue. Once love is established, sight seems to be more of a handicap than an advantage, although it can serve to increase love under specific circumstances. The object of the sight that gives rise to love is the beauty of the opposite sex, but beauty is itself subjective, depending for its perception on the thought that it subsequently generates. These paradoxes reflect not only the complexity of the subject but also an imperfect synthesis of the diverse sources on which the Chaplain draws.

Meditation, desire, and will

Meditation *(cogitatio)* plays a central role in the psychological process of loving described in the *De amore.* Andreas emphasizes its importance already in the somewhat exaggerated commentary that accompanies his definition: *ex sola cogitatione . . . passio illa procedit* (*DA* 1.1.8 [34]). Its significance is also underlined by the repeated use of the noun *cogitatio* and the corresponding verb *cogitare:* they occur ten times in the first chapter alone and another sixty-four times in passages scattered throughout the treatise, usually with the beloved as the object of reflection. Sometime these terms appear to have a fairly precise meaning close to that which they had in medieval psychology (e.g., *DA* 1.1.10 [34]); elsewhere they can be understood in the more general, nontechnical sense of "thinking, thought."

We saw in the last chapter the important place occupied by *cogitatio* in medieval psychology, which saw in it the highest of the "inner senses." *Cogitatio* is completely predominant among the "inner senses" in the psychological discussions of the *De amore*. The imagination is mentioned in only three passages of the treatise. In Chapter One and in the Eighth Dialogue (*DA* 1.1.10 [34]; 1.6.558–59 [206]) *imaginari* and *imaginatio* refer to fantasizing about the amorous "acts" *(actus, gestus)* of the beloved. In both these passages the imagination is cited along with *cogitatio,* but the function it performs is apparently distinct, corresponding to that of the *imaginatio formativa* of medieval psychology. In the Rules of Love, on the other hand, *imaginatio* fulfills the function of the philosophers' *imaginatio retentiva*, retaining and reproducing an image of the beloved: "XXX. The true lover is preoccupied by a constant and unbroken picture *(imaginatio)* of his beloved" (*DA* 2.8.48 [284]). The term *memoria* occurs in eight passages of the *De amore*, of which half refer, if only tangentially, to the lover's memory of the beloved.[4]

Thought and love are closely associated in several medieval traditions. For the physicians *cogitatio* is an integral part of the particular type of melancholy known as love. In the poetry of the troubadours and trouvères, meditation on the beloved is a common theme, conveyed typically through terms such as *penser* and *cossirier.* In the romances it is often represented allegorically through the technique of psychomachia.[5] Andreas's emphasis on meditation synthesizes these various traditions.

The pivotal role of *cogitatio* in the psychological process of loving stems from the fact that it is a part of both the *passio* that is love and the reaction to that passion. As a passion *cogitatio* is the final destination of

---

4. These passages concern, respectively, mourning for a deceased lover (*DA* 1.6.435 [168]), discretion in public recollection of the beloved (*DA* 2.1.5 [224]), forgetting as a remedy for love (*DA* 2.6.6 [240]), and mementos of the beloved (*DA* 2.7.49 [268]).

5. Sutherland.

the impulse received from the vision of the beloved, but it is also at the origin of the reciprocal impulse of attraction that draws the lover toward the love object. According to Aristotle, thinking, like sense perception, is a kind of passion; that is, in perceiving or thinking the soul both acts and is acted upon.[6] This dual status of thought is closely connected with the intimate relationship that Andreas establishes between thinking and loving.

We have already seen the importance of thinking as a relay of the impulse received from the sight of the beloved. Although sight is generally necessary to set the process in motion (aside from the *amor ex auditu* of the Seventh Dialogue), *cogitatio* takes up and prolongs this initial impulse, to such an extent that further sight is unnecessary for the preservation and development of the emotion. This is particularly clear in the case of the man who has become blind after falling in love, but it also applies to the man of the Fifth Dialogue who is generally deprived of the sight of the beloved. Such passages lend some justification to the exaggerated language of the first chapter: *ex sola cogitatione . . .*

The crucial role of thought in the generation of desire is clear from the discussion of the definition in Chapter One: *Nam quum aliquid videt aliquam aptam amori et suo formata arbitrio, statim eam incipit concupiscere corde.*[7] The expressions *aptam amari* and especially *suo formata arbitrio* indicate a "judgment" *(arbitrium)* with respect to the object of sight carried out by the cogitative faculty or, more particularly, the estimative faculty (also called *arbitrium*) that is closely associated with it. This judgment gives rise "immediately" *(statim)* to a movement of desire *(concupiscere)* in the appetitive faculty, so that these two successive movements of the soul are just barely distinguishable.

From this point on, meditation and desire develop together and exercise a reciprocal influence upon each other, still according to the same passage: *postea vero quotiens de ipsa cogitat, totiens eius magis ardescit amore, quousque ad cogitationem devenerit pleniorem.*[8] The result of this

---

6. *De anima* 1.5 (410a25–26). Cf. *ST* 1a2æ 22.1: *sentire et intelligere est quoddam pati* ("Perceiving and understanding are a kind of suffering" [my translation]).

7. *DA* 1.1.9 (34). Cf. Walsh, p. 35: "When a man sees a girl ripe for love and fashioned to his liking, he begins at once to desire her inwardly."

8. *DA* 1.1.9 (34). Cf. Walsh, p. 35: "and whenever he subsequently thinks about her,

process of reciprocal stimulation, "fuller meditation" *(cogitatio plenior),* is analyzed in terms of its constituent parts: *cogitare, distinguere, imaginari,* and *rimari.* It gives rise in turn to "unbridled" desire *(sua frena nescit contenere),* pushing the lover to "go into action" *(procedere ad actum)* to obtain the object of his love.

This close association between meditation and desire is confirmed by the passage from the Seventh Dialogue devoted to the definition of love: *Quid enim aliud est amor nisi immoderata et furtivi et latentis amplexus concupiscibiliter percipiendi ambitio?*[9] This less rigorous, abbreviated definition nevertheless has certain features in common with Andreas's own definition of Chapter One. Neglecting the efficient cause of love, it concentrates on the final cause: the impulse of "desire" *(ambitio)* toward the "embrace" *(amplexus)* of the beloved. It is interesting to note the word *immoderata* modifying *ambitio;* it is the same word that modifies *cogitatio* in Andreas's original definition, thus establishing a kind of equivalency between the two concepts.

Of the various constituents of love, desire is the one most consistently emphasized by all medieval traditions. Desire figures prominently in the definitions of love proposed by physicians as well as philosophers. Aquinas defines love as "a feeling of the object's attractiveness [or desirability]" *(complacentia appetibilis).*[10] In Ovid, the personification of desire, Cupido, is identified with the God of Love, Amor, a practice Andreas imitates (*DA* 1.6.459–60 [176]; 1.9.3 [212]). Expressions of desire constitute an important element of the love poetry of the troubadours and trouvères. In view of this multiple tradition, it is no surprise that desire also plays an important role in the *De amore.*

Desire is mentioned more frequently by Andreas than is meditation. It is generally expressed by the verbs *cupere, desiderare,* or *appetere* or their derivatives, which are attested all together more than one hundred times in the treatise. In the dialogues desire is evoked twice as often by

---

he burns with love for her more each time, until he reaches the stage of more detailed reflexion."

9. *DA* 1.6.368 (146). Cf. Walsh, p. 147: "Love is nothing other than an uncontrolled desire to obtain the sensual gratification of a stealthy and secret embrace"; *DA* 1.6.376 (148).

10. *ST* 1a2æ 26.2, contra (ed. Blackfriars, 19:66–67).

the men as by the women, perhaps a reflection of the importance of this theme in the vernacular love song. Although one may desire many different things, the reference in more than two-thirds of the occurrences is to love. In many cases, the explicitly stated object of desire is sexual activity with the beloved, as already in the definition of love: *cupit alterius potiri amplexibus* . . . *(DA* 1.1.1 [32]).

Sexual activity, the object of the lover's desire, is mentioned frequently in the *De amore,* but usually only in vague and general terms. The word most often used in this connection is *amplexus,* "embracing," which occurs fifty-five times. Several chaste circumlocutions are also found: "the works of Venus/love/the flesh" *(opus . . ./opera Veneris/. . . amoris/. . . carnis);* "the deeds of Venus/love" *(actus Veneris/. . . amoris);* "the precepts/mandates of Love" *(præcepta . . ./mandata amoris),* and the like. *Commixtio* is found only twice in the medieval sense of "sexual intercourse" *(DA* 1.12.1 [222]; 2.3.2 [230]), the classical *coitus* not at all. Kissing *(osculum)* is mentioned only nine times; except for the kisses of encouragement and reward given by the Lady of the Woods to the British knight in the Arthurian tale of Book Two *(DA* 2.8.7 [272], 43 [280]), these passages all concern the commonplace of the stages of love.

Notably absent is the discussion, common in the medical manuals, of such physiological phenomena as erection or ejaculation. Even Ovid's gingerly discussion of arousal techniques and positions *(AA* 2.703–32; 3.769–808) finds no reflection in the *De amore.* For all such questions, Andreas refers his readers to the "manuals": *amoris mandata, id est ea quæ in amoris tractatibus reperiuntur inserta (DA* 1.2.2 [34]). The reproductive function of sexuality, which plays such an important role in the discussions of physicians, philosophers, and theologians, is mentioned only twice, both times in connection with marriage *(DA* 1.6.383 [150]; 3.46–47 [300]). On the whole, the discourse that Andreas's most resembles with its discrete references to physical love is that of the vernacular love poetry.

Andreas's definition of love specifies that "Love's commands" must be carried out "by common consent" *(de utriusque voluntate).* This stipulation raises the question of the role of the "will" *(voluntas)* in his psychology of love. The concept of the will most prevalent in the central Middle Ages is that of "rational appetite." Present in the West from the mid-twelfth century with the Latin translation of St. John Damascene's *De fide orthodoxa,* this view reached its fullest development in the writings of Aquinas. It sees will as a species of appetite, the latter a generic faculty or power to incline toward objects apprehended as good and away from objects perceived as not good. Psychic appetites are seen as either sensory or intellectual; the former, usually synonymous with desire, inclines toward or away from objects known through the sense perceptions, whereas the latter, also known as will, inclines toward or away from universal objects apprehended through the intellect or reason. The will is thus one of two faculties of the rational soul, along with cognition. The obligation to subordinate the lower sensory appetite to the higher intellectual appetite plays a central role in medieval ethics. Aquinas sees some acts of volition as free, others as determined, but the general tendency throughout the Middle Ages was to recognize a high degree of freedom of will in the choice between good and evil.[11]

The term *voluntas* occurs eighty times in the *De amore.* In many passages it appears to express an idea scarcely distinguishable from that of desire. In fact, it is with "desire" that both John J. Parry and P. G. Walsh translate this term in the definition. There are other passages, however, where Andreas appears to distinguish clearly between desire and will, and indeed to oppose the two concepts.

At the beginning of the Second Dialogue, the man of the middle class explains his temerity in wooing a noblewoman in terms of a conflict between his "heart" *(cor)* and his "will" *(voluntas).* If he could keep his heart within the bounds set by his will, he says, he would remain silent, but his heart spurs on his will to seek greater things than he is able to express (*DA* 1.6.70 [58–60]). In this description the "will" appears to represent a reasoned acceptance of social convention (loving within one's own class) which is overruled by amorous desire, represented by the "heart," conventional seat of the emotions. This conflict is reminiscent of the debate between Love and Reason (the latter associated, as here, with social convention) that Lancelot experiences in Chrétien de Troyes's *Chevalier de la charrete* (vv. 314–44) in deciding whether to get into the cart of infamy.

11. Bourke, pp. 9–11, 53–76; Kemp, pp. 82–88.

The opposition between "will" and "heart" recurs in the Sixth Dialogue in the form of a *quæstio disputata* posed by the woman. The man's
remarks are reasonable, she says, if only her heart would consent to her
will. Her will is to accept his proposal, but her heart absolutely opposes
what she desires with her whole will. So which should she favor, she
asks, her heart or her will? (*DA* 1.6.310 [128]).[12] The woman's will is apparently persuaded by the rational arguments *(ratio)* of the man; nevertheless she does not love him. In answer to her question the man opines
that she should choose the side of "truth and justice," thus bolstering
the position that he has previously advanced. The woman disagrees,
however, arguing that one cannot be "compelled" to love (i.e., by rational arguments), and she proposes a compromise: one should love
only that which is "desired by [both] heart and will" *(quod . . . corde ac
voluntate appetitur)*.

A somewhat different compromise is proposed by the man of the
Eighth Dialogue, again in response to a *quæstio disputata*. The question, really a case, concerns which of two lovers a woman should retain,
an earlier one who has returned after being presumed dead or a second
whom she has taken in the absence of the first (*DA* 1.6.551–60 [204–6]).
The solution to the dilemma depends primarily on the "will or desire"
(arbitrium vel voluntas) of the woman, according to the man. Even if
she feels no inclination toward the first lover, he explains, she should
forcibly compel her "desire" *(voluntas)* to seek that which she originally
approved with "her heart's desire" *(cordis desiderium)*. However, if she
sees that her "desire" *(voluntas)* does not respond, she can keep the second lover.

The opposition expressed here is similar to that previously observed,
although the use of terms is rather confused. The "reasonable" solution
of returning to the first lover, actually the application to love of a rule
from the canon law on marriage (see below, Chapter 8), should be imposed, if possible, by the "will" *(arbitrium)* on the woman's "desire"
(voluntas), but the latter still has the last word. The role of *voluntas* here

---

12. Unfortunately for the clarity of the passage the woman speaks of what she "desires with her whole will" *(plena voluntate desidero)*; later (*DA* 1.6.312 [128]) she will
speak of "the will of her heart" *(cordis voluntas)*.

is similar to that of *cor* in the earlier passages, hence the hesitation of Parry and Walsh, who translate the term first by "desire" and subsequently by "will." Despite this linguistic confusion, the woman approves the man's solution, asserting that it is supported by "all the wisdom of learning."

We might note in passing that the subordination of beauty to moral character recommended at the beginning of Book One, Chapter Six, supposes the possibility of controlling the impulses of desire through the exercise of the will. It is perhaps compatible, just barely, with the compromise suggested by the woman of the Sixth Dialogue, the ideal situation where the promptings of desire and will coincide. It is more difficult to reconcile it with the position agreed upon by the disputants of the Eighth Dialogue, that in cases of conflict desire should have the final word.

The "common consent" clause of the definition is taken up again in several later passages in the treatise, not without contradiction. In the second chapter, Andreas notes that a lover obtains from his beloved nothing that he can relish unless it come from her voluntarily (*DA* 1.2.8 [36]). In Book Two he declares that love is diminished if a woman sees her lover going too far in demands of love, giving no thought to his partner's modesty (*DA* 2.3.3 [230]). A faithful lover should endure any hardships rather than embarrass his beloved with excessive demands, the passage continues, and he who does not respect his partner's modesty should be called a traitor, not a lover. These observations are formalized in the Rules of Love: "V. What a lovers takes from the beloved against her will has no relish" (*DA* 2.8.44 [282]), and a Precept of the Fifth Dialogue draws their practical consequence: "XII. In practicing love's solaces do not exceed your lover's desires" (*DA* 1.6.269 [116]).

All this contrasts sharply, however, with the discussion of pure and mixed love in Book Two (*DA* 2.6.38–39 [248–50]). The question raised is whether one of two lovers practicing "pure" love (i.e., without coitus) can properly resist the request of the other to change to "mixed" love (including coitus). While expressing a personal preference for pure love, Andreas declares that, in the absence of a prior agreement requiring mutual consent, it is not permissible for one lover to resist the will of the other. Even if such an agreement exists, he adds, it is not right for a woman to refuse to comply with her partner's desires if he persists, for in practicing love's solaces, each lover is bound to accede to the other's desires (*DA* 2.6.39 [250]). The final, explanatory sentence in this passage recalls another of the Rules of Love: "XXVI. Love can deny nothing to love" (*DA* 2.8.48 [282]). Apparently this rule takes precedence over that of not exceeding one's partner's wishes. The questions are not raised whether the woman's love will be diminished by her partner's insistence, or whether the successful lover will "relish" the additional concessions so obtained. Nor is this last question raised in connection with the advice of Book One, Chapter Eleven, to use compulsion with peasant women (*DA* 1.11.3 [222]).

The many references to thought, desire, and will contained in the *De amore* reinforce the essentially psychological nature of the phenomenon proclaimed in the first chapter. Physical love is discussed only in general terms, as the "final cause" or goal of loving, or occasionally as a step on the way to that goal. The insights that the treatise provides into the psychological processes of love are neither very technical nor very profound; they probably owe more to literary sources than to philosophical or medical writings. The most controversial aspect of the discussion concerns the relationship between desire and will in the process of loving, a question combining the generic vectors that we have called *scientia* and *sapientia*. The intention is manifest to reconcile opposing positions, an enterprise that is only partially successful, with results that are somewhat contradictory.

Capacity to love

Book One, Chapter Five concerns what people are "suited" *(aptus)* for love, that is, capable of loving. This capacity, defined in terms of psychology and physiology, takes up again and expands on the definition of Chapter One, particularly those parts relating to the efficient and final causes of love. This most physiological of chapters applies to the subject of love insights from both medieval medicine and canon law. Its pronouncements are further elucidated in several passages later in the treatise.

Chapter Five first states two general requirements, one psychological, the other physiological: the potential lover must be "of sound mind" *(compos mentis)* and "capable of carrying out the works of Venus" *(aptus . . . ad Veneris opera peragenda).* Although neither stipulation is discussed further here, they are both very revealing of Andreas's conception of love, setting the tone for the entire chapter.

The requirement that the lover be of sound mind does not appear to reflect the definition of love given in the first chapter, except insofar as a minimum of sanity is doubtless necessary to carry on the meditation that gives rise to love. It is reflected briefly, however, in Book Two *(DA* 2.3.3–5 [230]) in the observation that love is diminished if the lover is found to be foolish or if he engages in the prolixity of a fool or a madman. Moreover, madness is named in the following chapter among the factors that bring love to an end *(DA* 2.4.5 [232]).

This requirement conflicts with a long tradition that sees love as a kind of madness. In fact, Andreas alludes to this tradition in Book Three *(DA* 3.60–61 [304]), claiming that the loss of sleep occasioned by love alters the brain and the mind, making one mad and deranged, and that the excessive meditation associated with this emotion leads to a deterioration of the brain. Subsequently he argues *(DA* 3.62 [304]) that the wise are made even more insane by love, citing Solomon and David as examples. If we confront these claims with the "sound mind" clause of Book One, Chapter Five, we might logically conclude that love begets madness, which in turn make love impossible. The madness of Solomon and David, however, did not keep them from loving; on the contrary, it prevented them from controlling their lust, according to Andreas's analysis *(DA* 3.64 [306]).

The unsatisfactory conclusion reached serves to orient our inquiry in another direction. We should probably see in Andreas's remark concerning the sound mind of the lover not a psychological observation but a legal requirement. The view of love presented is that of a contractual arrangement, modeled on the marriage contract. The "sound mind" clause simply specifies one of the conditions necessary for a binding contract. In canon law insanity was generally considered an impediment to marriage, since it prevented the required consent from occurring.[13]

13. Schnell, *Andreas Capellanus,* p. 96; Brundage, pp. 195, 201, 243, 288. Insanity

The second requirement refers explicitly to the final cause of love stated in the definition, the "carrying out of all of Love's precepts." If we take it at face value, it carries the doubtful implication that those who are physically incapable of lovemaking are, by that very fact, unable to experience the emotion of love, that is, unable to desire the activity of which they are incapable.

This subject is taken up again in the Eighth Dialogue, in the debate over the relative value of the consolations of the upper and lower halves of the body (*DA* 1.6.538–40 [200]). The woman, who defends the lower half, argues that a woman of outstanding beauty but incapable of carrying out "Venus' works" would be rejected by all as "unclean." Furthermore, a man who is frigid or impotent, she continues, has no desire for the pleasures of the flesh. Although placed in the mouth of a woman, this analysis represents a masculine point of view, regarding the case of the woman from the external, social angle of public opinion, that of the man from the internal, psychological optic of desire. In both cases, though for different reasons, the sexually incapacitated are barred from participating even in "pure" love.

Whatever the validity of this position, it seems probable that Andreas's pronouncement at the beginning of Chapter Five was influenced by another source. In canon law, the incapacity to "pay the marriage debt" is frequently cited as an impediment to marriage and also as grounds for divorce.[14] It is apparently this principle that Andreas is applying here to love. Impotence is cited in Book Two, along with madness, among the causes that may put an end to love (*DA* 2.4.5 [232]).

Beyond these general requirements, Andreas mentions three other restrictions to the capacity to love: one may be prevented from loving by age, blindness, or excessive lasciviousness. We have already discussed, in connection with the role of sight, the exclusion of the blind, a physiological limitation relating to the efficient cause of love. It remains to examine the other two.

The age limitations affect both the upper and lower ends of the

---

was grounds for divorce under Roman law and also frequently in the Middle Ages (ibid., pp. 39, 288), which may account for its association in the *De amore* with the ending of love relationships.

14. Schnell, *Andreas Capellanus,* pp. 96–97; Brundage, pp. 200–203, 290–92.

scale, with some variation in application according to sex: theoretically, men may love between the ages of fourteen and sixty, although Andreas recommends a minimum age of eighteen; for women the age limits are twelve and fifty. The ages of twelve for girls and fourteen for boys are those prescribed by canon law as the minimum ages for marriage.[15] The relevancy of this observation is reinforced by the influence of canon law on the requirements of sanity and potency. The explanations offered by Andreas, however, are psychological and physiological in nature, relating to the efficient and final causes of love.

The exclusion of older people is explained in terms of a loss of heat and an increase in humidity. This is a reference to the Galenic system of the four humors, in which the various humors are seen as correlated with relative degrees of heat and moisture.[16] Since heat is a necessary component of sexual activity, according to this system, a reduction of heat due to aging results in a corresponding reduction in sexual capacity. Older people are able to have sexual intercourse *(coire),* Andreas claims, but the pleasure *(voluptas)* derived from it is no longer sufficient to produce love. The problem is what would now be called a loss of libido, not unlike that which prevents the impotent from engaging in "pure" love.

No explanation in given in Chapter Five for the difference in upper age limit between men and women. In the Eighth Dialogue (*DA* 1.6.456 [174]) it is claimed that women are "sooner wasted by age"; why this should be is not explained, although it is correlated with an earlier starting age for sexual activity in women. It may be that Andreas's restriction is based on a masculine appraisal of the physical attractiveness of older women. When the woman of the Eighth Dialogue claims to be too old for love (shortly before claiming to be too young), the man replies by praising her beauty (*DA* 1.6.446 [172]).

Chapter Five also offers no explanation for the lower age limits of twelve and fourteen, although it justifies at length Andreas's preference for the somewhat higher limit of eighteen for boys. Two reasons are al-

15. Parry, p. 32, n. 8; Walsh, p. 40, n. 19; Schnell, *Andreas Capellanus,* pp. 86–92; Brundage, p. 357.

16. Jacquart and Thomasset, pp. 48–52; Cadden, pp. 183–88.

leged. The first impediment is the tendency of younger men to be over-come with embarrassment over minor matters, which may have either of two deleterious consequences. It may keep them from "perfecting love," that is, presumably it may affect their potency. We may note in passing that no mention is made of the well-known modesty of girls, perhaps because it presents no physical barrier to their "carrying out all of Love's precepts." If, on the other hand, younger men succeed in per-fecting their love, their embarrassment may extinguish it. The pseudo-Aristotelian *Problems* (4.9) raises the question why younger men hate their partners once sexual relations are over, attributing the phenome-non not to embarrassment but to "discomfort" over "violent change." Whatever the cause, this tendency is related to the second, "more im-portant" *(efficacior)* reason why younger men cannot love, namely their inconstancy.

The inconstancy of younger men is explained in terms of an inabili-ty on their part to "meditate" *(cogitare)* on "the mysteries of Love's realm." The "mysteries" in question may well refer to the "bodily se-crets" *(corporis secreta)* of the beloved, her body parts, their imagined ac-tions, and the like, which are the object of "fuller meditation" *(cogitatio plenior)* according to Chapter One. The argument appears to be that, whether from inexperience of these bodily secrets or embarrassment over them, the meditation of younger men on a potential love object cannot become sufficiently intense *(immoderata)* to prevent them from also considering other possible love objects. This juvenile inconstancy is not unrelated to the question of "excessive lasciviousness," the final ma-jor impediment to loving, to which we shall return.

When the matter is taken up again in the Eighth Dialogue (*DA* 1.6.453–57 [174]), the minimum age limits given are twelve for women and eighteen for men, the rationale for the difference being the relative capacity for constancy. It is difficult not to see a pun in the remark that prior to eighteen a man cannot be a "firm lover" *(firmus amator)*, espe-cially since the question of the potency of younger men has already been raised in Chapter Five. Rule VI of the Rules of Love (*DA* 2.8.44 [282]) states that males usually love only on reaching "full maturity" *(plena pubertas)*, with no such restriction for women.

Two somewhat contradictory reasons are given for the greater constancy of younger women as compared with younger men. The first concerns the Galenic system of humors, particularly the attribution in the Galenic tradition of a hot temperament to men and a cold temperament to women. The argument is that cold objects, such as metal, heat up more quickly than warm objects, such as wood, when additional heat is applied. In the case of younger men and women the heating agent is presumably the physiological change that taken place at puberty, making sexual activity possible.

The other explanation given for early female constancy is that women wear out earlier; it is therefore "not surprising" that they should also start earlier. The argument is not properly causal but rather analogical: it is not *because* they will wear out sooner that women start sooner, unless we are expected to see here a providential edict of Nature, who is invoked a little earlier in the same passage. Nor is it clear what an early start has to do with constancy, unlike the greater relative heat presumably necessary to produce the fuller meditation capable of attaching the lover to a single object. Perhaps there is a confusion here between capacity for sexual relations and capacity for faithfulness. Moreover, if the comparison with wood and metal objects were maintained, one might well conclude that hotter objects cool faster when heat is removed, and thus that men should "wear out" sooner than women.[17]

Although the canon law on marriage probably provided the point of departure for Andreas's age limitations, he took the liberty to modify its provisions with respect to younger men and to add upper limits for both sexes. He attempts to justify these restrictions in terms of human physiology, calling upon the Galenic system of humors, with the discussion of the Eighth Dialogue continuing that of Chapter Five, which promised further explanations later (*DA* 1.5.5 [40]). Nevertheless, the analysis is placed in the mouth of a male suitor, whose main purpose is to convince the woman that she is not too young to love, rather than to found a coherent physiology of love, which may account for the incon-

17. Love Case XX discusses age *preference* (rather than capacity) based on the physiology of "natural instinct." The queen proclaims that younger men usually prefer older women, older men prefer younger women, and women of all ages prefer younger men. The explanation would require a "medical investigation" (*DA* 2.7.47–48 [268]).

sistencies. It is also possible that, despite Andreas's efforts to provide a physiological explanation, his claim of greater constancy on the part of younger women is really based on a sociological observation, that of much greater sexual freedom accorded to young men in medieval society.[18]

The last major restriction regarding the capacity to love concerns what Andreas calls "excessive abundance of pleasure" *(nimia voluptatis abundantia).* From the subsequent discussion it is clear that what is designated by this expression is an excessive desire for, or addiction to, sexual pleasure (cf. *DA* 1.5.7 [40]: *voluptatis cupido).* The equivalent expression used in Book Three is "excessive lust" *(nimia luxuria).*[19] This condition is characterized by the fact that, having engaged in "ample reflection" *(multas cogitationes)* about one woman, or even having enjoyed her favors, upon seeing another woman the subject immediately desires the embraces of the latter, forgetting the favors of the first. Thus, like a shameless dog or a donkey, he desires to indulge his lust with every woman he sees, forsaking reason, which separates human beings from the animals (*DA* 1.5.7–8 [40]).

The psychological condition described constitutes an infraction of the "exclusivity" clause of the definition, according to which the lover "desires above all else" *(super omnia cupit)* the embraces of the beloved. This inconstancy has already been described as normal in young men under the age of eighteen, so what is under discussion here is the persistence of this syndrome into adulthood. In terms of the love psychology previously developed, the condition stems from a lack of concentration, an inability to develop a "fuller meditation" about one woman, capable of resisting the distractions provided by all the others.

The "excessive" *(nimius)* character of the phenomenon described must be carefully distinguished from the "immoderate" *(immoderatus)* nature of the reflection that gives rise to love. Indeed, they are more or less opposites, for it is the lack of an "immoderate" meditation on one

18. Brundage, p. 284.

19. The equivalency of these expressions is underlined by their use in parallel constructions, as the subject of the verb *vexare: nimia voluptatis abundantia* vexat (*DA* 2.8.48 [284], Rule XXIX); *nimia . . . luxuria* vexat (*DA* 3.106 [318]) [my emphasis]. Cf. *DA* 1.6.443 (170), 1.10.6 (220), 3.49–50 (302).

woman that leaves the man open to the excess of "thinking about" (and desiring) all of them. Thus, the meditation on the first, later abandoned, woman in the description of Chapter Five is extensive *(multas cogitationes),* but apparently not sufficiently intensive to be qualified as "immoderate."

As promised at the end of Chapter Five, this subject is taken up again in Book One, Chapter Ten, *De facili rei concessione petitæ.* Here Andreas explains that "the easy granting of the thing requested" is in women the equivalent of "excessive abundance of pleasure" in men (*DA* 1.10.5 [220]). In fact, the two Rules of Love devoted to this question appear to break down along gender lines: Rule XXIX is formulated in the masculine, excluding from loving "the man who" *(quem)* suffers from "excessive abundance of pleasure" (*DA* 2.8.48 [284]), whereas Rule XIV, stating that "an easy conquest makes love cheap" (*DA* 2.8.46 [282]), seems to be directed primarily toward women.[20]

There are indications in Chapter Ten, however, that the easy granting of a woman's favors should be seen as a symptom of the condition rather than an equivalent. When, in the absence of gifts, a woman surrenders herself easily to a suitor, "it is claimed" that she does so from an excess of carnal pleasure, which will also cause her to do the same later with respect to another suitor (*DA* 1.10.1 [218–20]). In other words, a woman's lack of adequate resistance creates a presumption of future infidelity on her part. This principle doubtless goes a long way toward explaining the long probationary period, including various "steps," imposed upon suitors by the women of the dialogues: it is not only the men's virtue that must be demonstrated by this process, but also the women's.

Nor is lack of resistance the only indication of excessive desire for pleasure in women. In the introduction to the Third Dialogue Andreas declares that a man of the middle class must exceed in worth of character all those who are above him in rank in order to gain the love of a woman of the higher nobility, for otherwise "it is assumed" that the noblewoman who accedes to such a suitor is motivated by an "excessive abundance of pleasure" (*DA* 1.6.119 [74]).

20. The latter rule echoes sentiments expressed by two different participants in the dialogues (*DA* 1.6.361 [144], 521 [194]).

For men the standard is notably slacker. In Book Two Andreas asserts that a man should not be considered unworthy of love for taking advantage of an occasion for a romp in the grass with an unknown woman, or someone's maid, or a prostitute—that is, unless he does it too often and with several women, in which case it "would be assumed" that he suffers from "excessive abundance of pleasure" (*DA* 2.6.10–11 [240]). It is not clear how this relative laxity for men can be reconciled with the claim, repeated in the Rules of Love (*DA* 2.8.45 [282], Rule XII), that "true love" so unites the hearts of two lovers that they cannot desire the embraces of someone else, but rather studiously avoid such solaces as odious (*DA* 1.10.5 [220]).

Excessive desire for pleasure is presented not as a behavior pattern, but rather as a psychological predisposition to a behavior pattern. That is why the detection of indicative signs plays such an important role. In its practical application, this psychological concept has strong social overtones in terms of social class and especially gender, providing a striking example of the masculine bias that informs the entire treatise. It also has strong moral implications relating to the claim that "true love" gives rise to the relative "chastity" of fidelity to one partner.

In addition to the major aspects of the question discussed in Book One, Chapter Five, two other subjects developed in the *De amore* are related to the capacity to love. One is raised in passing in the Eighth Dialogue; the other constitutes the principal subject of Book One, Chapter Two.

In debating the relative value of the solaces of the upper and lower parts of the body, the man of the Eighth Dialogue argues that the pleasure of the lower part "quickly disgusts" those who indulge in it (*DA* 1.6.537 [200]). He has previously claimed, in the related discussion concerning "pure" and "mixed" love, that the latter "quickly wanes and lasts [only] a short time" (*DA* 1.6.473 [180]). This is essentially the same claim that is made in Chapter Five concerning younger men, but now it is extended to include all ages. Carrying out all of Love's precepts has, according to this argument, the paradoxical effect of putting an end to love.

The effect on love of its consummation was apparently a current topic of interest in courtly circles in Andreas's time. The Old Provençal *partimen* between Peirol and the Dalfi d'Alvernha, *Dalfi, sabriatz me vos* (P.-C. 366, 10/119, 2) is devoted to the question whether love increases or decreases once it is consummated. The question remains unresolved, as is usual for the *partimens.* Since this poem is approximately contemporary with the *De amore,* it is impossible to know whether one of these works may have influenced the other, or whether they represent independent developments of a fashionable subject of discussion.

Some critics have seen in the passage from the Eighth Dialogue the physiological foundation for a Platonic theory of love. It should be remembered, however, that it is first and foremost an argument in a debate. There is, of course, on the physiological level, a cessation of desire immediately following orgasm, but it is only temporary. In her reply the woman underlines this principle metaphorically, expressing a preference for "healthy food" that satisfies and that, once digested, allows hunger to reassert itself (*DA* 1.6.542 [202]). Moreover, Andreas himself illustrates implicitly the fragility of the argument that consummation destroys love, by writing a second book to show how love, once "perfected" (i.e., consummated) can be maintained.

The main function of Chapter Two, *Inter quos possit esse amor,* is to limit love relationships to those between people of the opposite sex. It can be seen as a further elaboration of the expression "of the other sex" *(alterius sexus)* in the definition of Chapter One. This is a very different kind of restriction from those of Chapter Five, in that it excludes no one, theoretically, from loving, but it limits everyone in the choice of a partner. This difference presumably accounts for the separate treatment.

The principal explanation offered for this restriction is that people of the same sex cannot carry out love's "natural acts" together. In other words, the final cause of love, the "carrying out of all of Love's precepts," requires sexually differentiated anatomical parts. In the absence of these, certain acts can be carried out, of course, but they are presumably not "natural"; and "what nature denied, love blushes to embrace" (*DA* 1.2.1 [34]).

The importance of anatomical parts and physiological acts is reemphasized by the woman of the Eighth Dialogue in the course of the debate over the upper and lower parts (*DA* 1.6.539 [200]). If the solaces of love were limited to the upper part, she argues, nothing would prevent two men from giving each other said solaces, which would be "wicked *(nefandus)* to describe and sinful *(criminosus)* to carry out." The use of the adjectives *nefandus* and *criminosus* to qualify such practices illustrates the ethical nature of the objections raised, despite the appeal to nature.[21] Andreas's position and that of the woman of the Eighth Dialogue reflect not only the teachings of medieval medicine but also those of Christian theology and canon law, all of which concur in their general condemnation of homosexuality.

From the above discussion it appears that, with the possible exception of the requirement of mental sanity, all the restrictions applied by Andreas to the capacity to love are related either to the efficient cause or to the final cause of love as delineated in the definition of Chapter One. To the efficient cause can be assigned not only the exclusion of the blind, but also the excessive desire for pleasure, which stems from an inability to develop a sufficiently intense meditation on and desire for a particular partner. The ability to achieve sexual union is mentioned specifically as a requirement, and it is also invoked to explain the exclusion of homosexuality. The question of age is related to both the efficient and final causes, especially for men, since it has implications, at both ends of the scale, for potency, and also, with respect to younger men, for constancy.

For all these limitations, psychological and physiological factors are intertwined, but with differences in emphasis. The restrictions relating to the efficient cause are essentially psychological in nature, whereas those relating to the final cause are predominantly physiological. The exclusion of the blind—the exception that confirms the rule—is based on a physiological condition, but its ultimate justification is the role of sight in the development of meditation and desire. Conversely, the discussion of desire in connection with the potency of older men shows the impossibility of separating physiology from psychological factors.

In addition to the these "natural" factors, moral considerations are evident throughout the discussion, especially in the influence of canon

---

21. This conclusion is already implicit in Book One, Chapter Two (*DA* 1.2.1 [34]) in the reference to "blushing" *(erubescit),* a traditional metonymy for shame.

law, discernable at several points. Social considerations also come occasionally into play, including class sentiment and a pronounced gender bias. Despite the complexities of the discussion, it is possible to summarize the Chaplain's essential doctrine on this point with the observation that love as he conceives it presupposes the physiological capacity to engage in sexual union as well as the psychological capacity to limit oneself to a single partner.

The dynamics of love relationships

Although much of the *De amore* centers on the process by which love originates, in the individual and in the couple, the subsequent development and evolution of love relationships is also a significant subject of discussion. It is the major focus of Book Two, and certain aspects of it are raised already in the first book.

The first point that emerges in this connection is the difficulty of establishing a reciprocal love relationship. According to Andreas's definition, the lover desires above all else to carry out all of Love's precepts "by common consent" *(de utriusque voluntate).* By this phrase the Chaplain appears to indicate that consummation alone is not the lover's goal, but rather consummation achieved through a certain reciprocity of sentiment. That is why "love" (i.e., consummation) obtained either in exchange for monetary consideration or as a result of "favors too easily granted" (i.e., excessive desire for carnal pleasure on the part of one's partner) will subsequently be rejected as not representing "true love" (*DA* 1.6.2 [42]; Book One, Chapters Nine and Ten). Book Two describes the ideal relationship as "two persons joined together in mutual fidelity and harmonious in the identity of their wishes" (*DA* 2.4.4 [232]).

In the discussion following the definition in the first chapter, Andreas uses the expression "one-sided love" *(singularis amor)* to designate nonreciprocal love relationships (*DA* 1.1.5 [32]). In the same passage he distinguishes two aspects of this situation: the physical consummation of love (or lack thereof) is described in terms of love's "perfection" (*res imperfecta, perficitur; DA* 1.1.3, 6 [32]), whereas reciprocity of sentiment is evoked by the phrase "equally balanced love" (*amor ex utraque parte*

. . ./. . . ex altera parte libratus; DA 1.1.2, 5 [32]). The woman of the Eighth Dialogue makes the same distinction: *amor perfectus atque libratus* (*DA* 1.6.552 [204]). She has previously rebuffed the man by claiming to have already established a "reciprocal" *(libratus)* love relationship with another man (*DA* 1.6.532 [198]).

The *Accessus* introducing the *De amore* refers to "reciprocal love" *(amor mutuus),* promising to treat the question of how to recognize it (*DA* 1.0 [32]). This is, indeed, the subject of Book Two, Chapter Five, *De notitia mutui amoris.* Nothing is more necessary to lovers, Andreas declares, than certain knowledge of each other's feelings, for without it they can expect little honor, and may suffer great loss, from the relationship (*DA* 2.5.1 [234]). Case V of the Love Cases deals with the consequences of a relationship that is not reciprocal. The Countess of Champagne rules that a woman who does not reciprocate a man's love should not seek to retain him (*DA* 2.7.14–15 [254]).

Although Book Two, Chapter Five, is theoretically about reciprocal love, it is primarily devoted to the opposite, the lack of reciprocity or the waning of reciprocity. These can be detected by a number of signs: avoidance of one's partner, lack of ardor in lovemaking, increased fault-finding, avidity for material gain, and so on. It may be that an absence of these symptoms can be interpreted positively, but that is never stated and probably should not be assumed. Aside from pallor, the only positive indices cited are the jealousy or fear provoked, respectively, by feigned interest in someone else or by feigned anger toward the beloved. The proposal of such devices to test the constancy of a partner may itself be taken as indicating a fairly low level of confidence in the chances for reciprocity.

The major image used by Andreas in connection with the problem of reciprocity, that of "scales" *(libramen),* picks up again on the notion of "balance" developed in the first chapter, embodying it in a conventional emblem of justice. In Book One, Chapter Four, after praising the marvelous effects of love, the Chaplain nevertheless advises Walter against loving, citing the fact that Love is an "untrustworthy judge" who bears "unequal weights" in his hand (*DA* 1.4.3–5 [38]). This image is combined with that of the sailor whom Love does not guide to a safe haven but leaves to flounder on a stormy sea, thus indicating metaphorically that the "injustice" that one risks when embarking on the enterprise of love is that of not having one's feelings reciprocated. The end of the passage promises a fuller treatment of the subject elsewhere, but in place of that we have only a brief discussion in the dialogues.

In the Second Dialogue, between a man of the middle class and a noble woman, the subject of reciprocity, expressed in terms of equal or unequal weights, is intertwined with the question of equality or inequality of social class. In his first speech the man argues that Love makes no distinction based on inequality of birth but considers only whether a person is capable of "bearing Love's arms"; likewise, the woman should not consider the man's rank but only whether he is truly in love (*DA* 1.6.71–72 [60]). The woman accepts the man's first proposition but not the conclusion that he derives from it; for if the question whether the other is in love were the only pertinent factor of discrimination, she reasons, that would invalidate the saying that Love carries unequal weights in his hand. The woman goes on to refute the commonly held opinion that Love is an unjust judge. If he carries unequal weights in his hand, she asserts, this is for a most just reason: having observed the natural propensity of all men to sexual desire for anyone of the opposite sex, Love did not wish to compel women to love whoever solicits their favors, but left it rather to the discretion of each woman to decide whether or not to love a given suitor (*DA* 1.6.83–87 [62–64]). In other words, the problem of lack of reciprocity in love relationships is a direct consequence of the principle of a woman's freedom of choice.

In his reply the man amends his earlier statement, adding good character to the criteria that the woman should consider in making her choice; in this form, he claims, his proposition is not incompatible with the saying about Love's unequal weights. He also agrees that no injustice should be imputed to Love on account of the freedom accorded to women to accept or not the solicitations of a suitor. This freedom is granted, the man contends, so that women may have more merit by making the *right* choice, the one that corresponds to Love's wishes (i.e., that she accept this suitor)—just as the Heavenly King has given mankind free agency but would prefer that we use it to do good (*DA* 1.6.104–6 [68–70]). The woman never responds to this argument, but simply uses her freedom of choice to dismiss the man on the grounds of his inferior rank (*DA* 1.6.110–11 [70–72]).

In Book Three Andreas draws from the problem of reciprocity an argument against loving. Women are totally incapable of reciprocating a man's love, he argues, for they are wholly motivated by greed (*DA* 3.65 [306], 112 [320]). Moreover, Love is not a "just ruler," for he often carries unequal weights, forcing a man to love a woman who cannot be won with any amount of effort (*DA* 3.113–16 [320–22]). This position contrasts less than one might expect with the discussion of the first two books, for nowhere is much optimism expressed about the prospects for establishing reciprocal relationships. Even Book Two promises only to explain how to maintain love that has been "consummated" (*perfectus; DA* 2.2.1 [228]). It is probably not a distortion of Andreas's views to say that for him consummation is generally easier to achieve than true reciprocity of sentiment.

The other major aspect of the dynamics of love that emerges from the *De amore* is the relative instability of established love relationships. This principle is reflected in several of the Chaplain's pronouncements and in the Rules of Love. In Book One, Chapter Two, Andreas declares that love is always either increasing or decreasing; the same idea is repeated in Rule IV of the Rules of Love (*DA* 1.2.6 [36]; 2.8.44 [282]). Moreover, once love begins to decrease, it soon comes to an end (*DA* 2.3.8 [232]), and once it is ended, the chances of reviving it are poor (*DA* 2.4.6 [234], 2.6.5 [238]). These last two observations are combined in another Rule of Love, Rule XIX (*DA* 2.8.47 [282]).

The details of the processes thus delineated are the subject of the first four chapters of Book Two, on how love can be maintained, increased, decreased, and ended. If we take Rule IV seriously, however, Chapter One appears to be superfluous, except for reasons of symmetry, for love can presumably be maintained only by being increased. Otherwise, the remarks of these chapters are rather miscellaneous and random, sometimes even contradictory. They present a combination of psychological observations on the processes in question and practical advice on how to control these processes. Many moral judgments are also included. We shall have occasion to discuss most of these matters elsewhere in other contexts. Significantly, each of the four chapters ends

with a declaration to the effect that the list presented is only partial and
may be supplemented by the ingenuity of the reader.

One aspect of the decline of love relationships deserves our attention here: the abandonment of a partner in favor of another. This subject is examined in Book Two, Chapter Six, *Si unus amantium alteri fidem frangit amanti,* and it is also treated in several of the Love Cases
and in the Rules of Love. Much of this discussion is moral and juridical,
concerning the proper disposition of such cases, the imposition of punishments, and the like, but it also contains some interesting psychological implications.

According to Andreas, it is impossible to love more than one person
at the same time. This principle is embodied in Rule III of the Rules of
Love, which states that "no one can be bound by two loves" (*DA* 2.8.44
[282]). In truth, this statement is somewhat ambiguous: in view of the
legalistic approach to love frequently adopted in the *De amore,* the expression "be bound" *(ligari)* may well refer to a legally "binding" contractual arrangement, but it also appears to evoke the psychological
"bonds" of love. It is perhaps to a distinction between these two levels
of interpretation that Book Two, Chapter Six, alludes in attributing the
rule in question to "the natural and general tradition about love" (*DA*
2.6.2 [238]). In invoking the same rule in her judgment about love and
marriage at the end of the Seventh Dialogue, the Countess of Champagne emphasizes figuratively the psychological dimension, stating that
no on can "be wounded" *(sauciari)* by love for more than one person
(*DA* 1.6.399 [156]).

The impossibility of loving two persons at the same time can be
seen as a consequence of the definition of love proposed in the first
chapter of the treatise. It stems from the exclusivity of the lover's desire,
expressed in the definition by the phrase *super omnia cupit.* Moreover, it
is related to the notion of "immoderate meditation" *(immoderata cogitatio)* and to the impossibility of concentrating all of one's attention simultaneously on two different objects. The latter point is stressed in
two different passages of the treatise. In the Eighth Dialogue the man
argues that the only way one can fall in love with a new partner is
through engaging in "continuous and immoderate meditation" *(assidua
et immoderata cogitatio)* about the person (*DA* 1.6.558–59 [206]). Using

the same expression, Andreas claims in Book Two that it is impossible for "continuous and immoderate meditation" not to give rise to a new love, expelling the existing one (*DA* 2.6.1 [238]). Elsewhere the fact that one's partner frequently recalls the deeds of someone else or shows unusual interest in that person's activities and behavior is cited as a sign that a new love is being contemplated (*DA* 2.5.5 [236]).

The principle of loving only one person at a time is reemphasized by Andreas in the discussion on pure and mixed love. The question is whether someone can love one person with pure love and another with mixed love. The Chaplain answers that this is impossible, for although pure and mixed love appear very different, they are the same in substance and proceed from the same affection of the heart. They are two modes or aspects of the same substance, just as one can quench the same thirst *(appetitus)* by drinking wine or water or a mixture of the two (*DA* 2.6.23–25 [244–46]). This answer underlines once again the essentially psychological nature of love, the fact that it is an emotion, composed of meditation and especially desire, with respect to which physical considerations, the degree or manner of realization of that desire, are "accidental" or tangential.

The primary consequence of Rule III, on the impossibility of loving two persons, is contained in Rule XVII, which states that "a new love puts flight to an old one" (*DA* 2.8.47 [282]). These two clearly related ideas are, in fact, explicitly linked in two earlier passages of Book Two (*DA* 2.4.3 [232], 2.6.1–2 [238]).

The question arises as to how someone already in love can fall in love with someone else, given the fact that "true love" so unites the hearts of two lovers that they cannot desire the embraces of someone else, but rather studiously avoid such solaces as odious (*DA* 1.10.5 [220]; cf. 1.4.2 [38]; 2.8.45 [282], Rule XII). This question is, in fact, raised by the Chaplain in the course of his discussion of infidelity. Without wishing to express an opinion on whether such a change of heart is legitimate, Andreas attributes it to the compulsive attraction that one feels when struck by the shaft of a new love (*DA* 2.6.21 [244]). This rather tautological explanation echoes Rule IX of the Rules of Love, which states that "no one can love unless impelled by the persuasion of love" (*DA* 2.8.45 [282]; cf. 1.6.180 [90], 553 [204], 558 [206]).

Pursuing the matter further, the same passage declares that "a true lover can never desire an new love, unless he first knows for some definite and sufficient reason that the old one is dead." This account leaves intact the principle that one can love only one person at a time, since the first love must have ended for the second to occur. It also carries the additional implication that the exclusivity of the lover's desire is limited to the duration of his love, with no presumption that the latter will last forever.

The converse corollary of Rule III is found in Rule XXXI, which states that "nothing prevents one woman being loved by two men, or one man by two women" (*DA* 2.8.48 [284]). This rule is related to the freedom of choice claimed by the women in the dialogues and illustrated in certain of the Love Cases (e.g., Cases IV, XI). Since the person loved by two individuals can, at most, return the love of only one of them, this situation delivers yet another blow to the general prospects for reciprocity.

In summary, Andreas's analysis of the dynamics of love relationships leaves little room for optimism. Reciprocal relationships are difficult to achieve, and when they do occur, they tend to be unstable. They are threatened in particular by the possibility of being superseded by a new love. This precarious state of affairs can only contribute to the fears and suffering of the lover, to which we can now turn.

Fear and suffering

In defining love as a *passio* in Chapter One, Andreas did not neglect the secondary meaning customarily attached to this term, that of "suffering." The association of love with suffering has a long and complex history involving several traditions. Ovid develops frequently the conventional allegorical image of the lover who is "wounded" by the arrows of Cupid, and the advice of the *Remedia amoris* is presented as a cure for an illness. It is also as an illness, subsumed under the general category of melancholy, that love is viewed in the medical tradition. The pains and sufferings of the lover constitute a prominent theme in the lyric poetry of the troubadours and trouvères, as well as in the vernacular romances. All these various strands of the tradition associating love with suffering are exploited in diverse degrees in passages scattered throughout the *De amore*.

In Chapter One (*DA* 1.1.2–7 [32–34]) the suffering that is love is described in terms of "anguish" or "torment" (*angustiæ*) and especially of "fear" (*timor*). The passage goes on to enumerate various fears to which the lover is subject, either before or after the realization of his love. These fears are directly related to the dynamics of love relationships discussed above: before realization it is the problem of reciprocity that occasions the lover's fears; afterward it is the instability of love relationships. In both situations, Andreas affirms, the catalogue of the lover's fears is inexhaustible.

Beyond the first chapter, fear, usually the lover's fear, is mentioned another thirty-five times in the treatise, generally expressed by *timor/timere* or their derivatives. In Book Two Andreas declares that "a true lover is always fearful" (*DA* 2.5.8 [236]), and this same principle is recorded among the Rules of Love (*DA* 2.8.47 [282]): *XX. Amorosus semper est timorosus*. In Book Three (*DA* 3.14–16 [290]) the Chaplain uses the many fears of lovers as an argument against loving, citing a verse from Ovid (*Heroides* 1.12).

In the dialogues the lover's fear takes the form of a certain timidity with respect to the beloved, probably a reflection of the exploitation of this theme in the lyric poetry of the troubadours and the trouvères. Thus the lover must overcome the fear of approaching the beloved (*DA* 1.6.168 [86]), of addressing her (*DA* 1.6.197 [96]), and especially of contradicting her (*DA* 1.6.563 [208]). The lovers are not alone in expressing their fears, however: the women of the dialogues also have reason to fear deception (*DA* 1.6.475 [180]), especially by men of higher rank (*DA* 1.6.286 [122], 293 [124]), loss of virginity (*DA* 1.6.466 [178]), and gossip (*DA* 1.6.332 [136]).

More frequently than their fears, Andreas's lovers discuss the opposite of fear, that is, their "hope." Attested twice in the first chapter, *spes/sperare* occur another fifty-five times in the treatise, with nearly two-thirds of the attestations found in the dialogues. As the first of Andreas's four stages of love (*DA* 1.6.60–63 [56], 438 [170]; 2.6.34–35 [248]), the "granting of hope" is also the most frequent boon that the lovers request of the ladies. Thus the dialogues take on a rhetorical structure reminiscent of the vernacular love lyric, basing the lover's plea on the combined narration of present pains and hopes for the future.

Somewhat paradoxically, the lover's many fears concerning the outcome of his love are accompanied by a total lack of fear regarding other matters. In the second chapter Andreas notes that lovers can be seen "making light of death and fearing no threats" (*DA* 1.2.4 [36]). The lover's fearlessness applies especially to warfare, as we shall see; in Book Two Andreas declares that love is diminished by timidity in battle (*DA* 2.1.8 [226], 2.3.4 [230]). This paradoxical combination of fear and fearlessness can be seen as an extension of the *super omnia cupit* clause of the definition: the exclusivity of the lover's attachment to the love object accounts not only for his many fears concerning that object but also for his relative indifference with respect to everything else.

In Chapter Four, *Quis sit effectus amoris,* Andreas is concerned only with the moral effects of loving. This condition also carries with it certain physiological effects, however, which are mentioned elsewhere in the treatise, particularly in the Rules of Love. Rules XV, XVI, and XXII, respectively, list pallor, increased heartbeat, and loss of sleep and appetite among the symptoms of love (*DA* 2.8.46–47 [282]). In Book Two, Chapter Five, pallor is cited as a sure sign that one's partner is truly in love (*DA* 2.5.6 [236]). The primary source of these observations is Ovid, who advises wryly that lovers adopt a pale, thin look to illustrate their love and soften the hearts of their ladies (*AA* 1.723–38).

In Book Three Andreas draws from these physiological effects of love an argument against loving. Love weakens the body in three ways, he asserts: through the effects of sexual intercourse, through lack of nourishment, and through loss of sleep (*DA* 3.57–61 [304]). This passage combines the Ovidian image of the pale, thin lover with opinions from the medical tradition. In fact, Andreas call upon the "authority of the physicians" *(physicalis auctoritas)* in support of the deleterious effects of sexual intercourse, which he goes on to describe in some detail in terms of poor digestion, perturbation of humors, fever, and so on. This description does, indeed, reflect the medical tradition, but only part of it, on a delicate subject about which physicians were of two minds. For in addition to these adverse effects, they saw sexual intercourse as having several beneficial consequences, at least for certain persons, and especially as constituting the specific treatment for the illness that is love.[22]

The most frequent references to suffering in the *De amore* are the many descriptions of the lover's "pain." This notion is expressed sometimes by means of *angustia,* as in the first chapter, but more frequently by *dolor* and especially *pœna.* All together these terms occur nearly one hundred times in the treatise. More than two-thirds of these occurrences are found in the dialogues, where they constitute a major element of the lover's plea, as in the vernacular love lyric.

Not infrequently the description of the lover's pain is reinforced with conventional metaphors. The lover may describe himself as having been wounded by Love's arrow (e.g., *DA* 1.6.72–75 [60], 103–5 [68], 356 [142]). Or he may characterize his condition as an illness (*DA* 1.6.207 [98], 522 [194]) or compare it to a shipwreck (*DA* 1.4.3–4 [38]; 1.6.127 [76], 358 [142]; 2.6.22 [244]; cf. 1.6.115 [72]). All these images are common to the Ovidian tradition and to that of the vernacular literature.

The hyperbolic extension of the theme of the lover's pains is the image of dying of love. Frequent in the vernacular love lyric, it is no less so in the *De amore,* particularly in the dialogues, where it is often combined with the images mentioned above (*DA* 1.6.76–77 [60], 127 [76], 206–8 [98], 522 [194]).[23] The man of the Fourth Dialogue accuses the woman of homicide because of the risk to his life occasioned by her delay in granting him his wishes (*DA* 1.6.191–93 [94]). To forestall the same accusation, the woman of the Fifth Dialogue grants the man the right to see her, without which he claims he cannot live (*DA* 1.6.205 [98]). It is perhaps at least in part in reply to this theme that Andreas argues in Book Three that love leads to homicide, citing as an example the case of David and Uriah (*DA* 3.29 [294], 44 [300], 64 [306]).

Closely connected to the theme of suffering in many passages of the treatise is the notion of a remedy or cure. Sometimes the term employed is "medicine" *(medicina),* especially in passages that develop the image of love as an illness (*DA* 1.6.202 [98], 522 [194]). More frequently

---

22. Jacquart and Thomasset, pp. 83, 117–18; Wack, *Lovesickness,* pp. 66–70; Cadden, pp. 271–77.

23. See Toury; cf. Monson, "Andreas Capellanus and Reception, p. 4; pp. 10–11, n. 18."

it is *remedium,* with its obvious Ovidian resonances, that expresses this notion. Of the sixteen occurrences of this term, one-half are found in the dialogues and refer to relief of the lover's pain; elsewhere the sense is generally closer to that found in Ovid, for example, in the second sentence of the Preface or when Andreas describes himself as *amoris præ-doctus remedia* (*DA* 1.8.5 [212]). The most common term used in this connection is *solatium,* which occurs nearly eighty times, one-half of them in the dialogues, including eleven attestations of the expression *amoris solatia.* Although the phrase "solaces of love" functions as a conventional euphemism for sexual pleasure, the original meaning is that of soothing or assuaging the suffering that is love. On one point the physicians, the poets, and Andreas all agree: the ultimate remedy for the condition in question is the "carrying out of all of Love's precepts." In the dialogues, however, the lovers generally limit themselves to requesting the first step in that direction, the granting of hope (e.g., *DA* 1.6.127 [76], 191–92 [94], 207–8 [98], 283 [120])—a tactical concession that reflects the influence of the vernacular love lyric.

Although love's suffering is primarily an argument used by the lover to soften the heart of the beloved, occasionally this same argument is turned against him. After listening to the man's description of his own hardship, the woman of the Fifth Dialogue concludes that such a painful experience is utterly to be avoided (*DA* 1.6.209–10, 213 [100]). In reply to this crafty argument the man introduces the apocalyptic vision of the Purgatory of Cruel Beauties, recounting the "pains"/"punishments" *(pœnas)* that await in the next life all those who refuse to love in this (*DA* 1.6.219 [102]ff.). Likewise, the woman of the Eighth Dialogue advances the many pains of the lover as an argument against loving (*DA* 1.6.411–13 [160–62]). She also cites the "dangers of death" in this connection, reinterpreting the courtly image of dying of love in terms of the Christian concept of "spiritual death." All this anticipates the use of the same argument in Book Three. Love is to be avoided, Andreas asserts, because it is the source of boundless suffering in both this life and the next (*DA* 3.5 [286], 22 [292], 48 [300]).

Andreas's treatment of love's suffering owes much more to the poets—Ovid as well as the troubadours and trouvères—than to the physicians, although the latter are not totally neglected. Thus it wavers constantly between the psychological and the physiological, the literal and the metaphorical. Rather than attempting to analyze this suffering in any depth, the Chaplain surrounds it with a certain number of conventional poetic images: love as a wound, an illness, a shipwreck, a cause of death. Especially, he uses it as an argument to advance the cause of the lover, in imitation of the vernacular love lyric. Characteristically, he also draws a counterargument from the same material: a prudential rationale for the avoidance of love.

Jealousy

One aspect of the lover's suffering, jealousy, deserves separate treatment because of the importance that it assumes in the *De amore*. Since this subject is discussed primarily in the context of the debate on love and marriage, we shall return to it in Chapter 8. Nevertheless, it contains certain psychological implications that merit our attention here.

According to Andreas, jealousy is an inseparable concomitant of love. The man of the Seventh Dialogue calls jealousy "the very substance of love," asserting that true love cannot exist without it (*DA* 1.6.371, 377 [146–48]). This claim is ratified by the Countess of Champagne in her judgment at the end of the dialogue (*DA* 1.6.399 [156]), and it is included among the Rules of Love: II. *Qui non zelat amare non potest.*[24] The probable source of this doctrine is Ovid, who establishes a close link between love and jealousy in several of his love writings (*AA* 2.435–54, 2.539–54; *RA* 767–94; *Amores* 1.4, 2.5, 3.11a).

The close connection between love and jealousy is reemphasized in several passages in Book Two relating to the dynamics of love relationships. Chapter Two lists jealousy among the factors causing love to increase, calling it the "nurturer" *(nutrix)* of love (*DA* 2.2.2 [228]). This observation is reaffirmed in two of the Rules of Love, Rules XXI and XXII (*DA* 2.8.47 [282]). By virtue of this principle, a women abandoned by her lover is advised in Chapter Six to feign interest in another man, so as to rouse the lover's jealousy and win back his love (*DA* 2.6.6

---

24. *DA* 2.8.44 [282]. Cf. Walsh, p. 283: "The person who is not jealous cannot love."

[238]). A similar strategy is recommended in Chapter Five as a test of the love of one's partner (*DA* 2.5.6–7 [236]). Ovid, too, advises lovers to make the beloved fear a rival (*AA* 2.435–54; *Amores* 1.8.95–99; cf. *RA* 767–94).

These recommendations are tempered somewhat by other remarks in the same chapters. According to Chapter Three, an affair *(commixtio)* with another woman will cause love to diminish, even if love is not involved in the affair (*DA* 2.3.2 [230]). Among the factors bringing love to an end, Chapter Four includes "fraudulent and deceitful duplicity of heart" (*DA* 2.4.3 [232]), which presumably means the same thing. Clearly the lover must exercise caution in this delicate area, for if the suspicion of other interests can sometimes be helpful, definite knowledge of infidelity is generally harmful.

The man of the Seventh Dialogue proposes the following "description" of jealousy:

> Est igitur zelotypia vera animi passio, qua vehementer timemus propter amantis voluntatibus obsequendi defectum amoris attenuari substantiam, et inæqualitatis amoris trepidatio ac sine turpi cogitatione de amante concepta suspicio.[25]

Like love in Andreas's definition, jealousy is first designated generically as an "emotion" *(animi passio),* then specified through the adjunction of *differentiæ.* Here three in number, the *differentiæ* indicate the three different types of "fear" *(timere)* or "anxiety" *(trepidatio)* or "suspicion" *(suspicio)* that form the constituent parts of jealousy. Each of these three "aspects" *(species)* or "parts" *(partes)* of jealousy is related to one of the three protagonists of a conventional love triangle: the lover is concerned about his own possible inadequacy to fulfill his partner's wishes, about a possible lack of reciprocity on the part of his partner, and about the real or potential existence of a rival. Intimately related to the factors of instability and non-reciprocity that characterize the dynamics of love rela-

---

25. *DA* 1.6.378 [148–150]. Cf. Walsh, pp. 149–151: "Jealousy is a genuine mental emotion which provokes sharp fear in us that the substance of our love is being diminished through a failure to serve the wishes of the loved one. There is anxiety that love is not evenly poised, and suspicion against a lover is aroused, but this is unaccompanied by base thoughts."

tionships, these concerns echo the fears of the lover enumerated in the first chapter of the treatise.

One aspect of the man's definition appears to be extraneous: the stipulation that the suspicion about the existence of a rival should be "unaccompanied by base thoughts" *(sine turpi cogitatione)*. Unlike the other elements of the definition, this phrase embodies a moral judgment concerning the relative "turpitude" of infidelity on the part of a spouse or a lover. Its purpose is to set up an opposition between the "true jealousy" of the lover and the "base suspicion" of the husband, a distinction that will play a crucial role in the discussion on love and marriage. That this is not a psychological distinction, however, is clear from a passage of Book Two: referring the reader explicitly to the discussion of the Seventh Dialogue, Andreas asserts that not only true jealousy but also base suspicion has the effect of causing love to increase (*DA* 2.2.2 [228]). The fact that they function identically on the psychological level seems to indicate that the two entities distinguished are, in fact, essentially the same.

Despite the frequent intrusion of moral considerations, a fairly clear picture of jealousy as a psychological phenomenon emerges from the treatise. An outgrowth of the dynamics of love relationships and of the precariousness of the lover's situation, it is closely related to the fears that haunt every lover. It is thus an inseparable concomitant of love and can, if exercised with caution, play an important role in stimulating the latter emotion.

In light of the preceding remarks, it is clear that the status of love as a natural phenomenon is an important topic of discussion in the *De amore*. In the words of the man of the Second Dialogue, *res enim est amor quæ ipsam imitatur naturam.*[26] Particularly concentrated in the early chapters, the treatment of this subject is pursued in many other passages scattered throughout the treatise, including the Rules of Love, which are devoted in large measure to cataloguing the results. This focus coincides for the most part with the generic vector of the work that we have called *scientia*.

26. *DA* 1.6.72 [60]. Cf. Walsh, p. 61: "Love is a thing which imitates Nature herself."

Starting from an essentially psychological definition of the phenomenon, the discussion concentrates primarily on the psychology of love, not without certain incursions into the realm of physiology. The aspects of the subject treated include the role of sight and meditation in the generation of love, the function of desire and will in its subsequent development, the physical and mental aptitudes required for loving, the dynamics that the process generally assumes once it is set in motion, and the pain and suffering, fear and jealousy, that are the habitual result of those dynamics. Most of these topics are already contained in Andreas's definition of love, with respect to which the subsequent discussion can be seen as a further explication and elaboration.

With the exception of the first chapter, the Chaplain's discussion of love psychology does not constitute an in-depth, systematic treatment of the subject. Scattered throughout the treatise, it is fragmented and sometimes contradictory. It is also frequently mixed with considerations of another order, either social or, more often, moral.

Characteristically, Andreas's discussion brings to bear on the subject opinions from a wide variety of medieval traditions, including the love writings of Ovid, the vernacular love poetry of the troubadours and trouvères, early scholastic philosophy, medieval medicine, and canon law. Generally, it attempts, with more or less success, to mediate between these traditions and to synthesize their findings. Nevertheless, the literary sources remain by far the most important sources for the Chaplain's love psychology. This fact probably accounts in part for a certain superficiality and lack of originality observable in his treatment of the subject.

Despite these reservations, the *De amore* presents a fairly unified and consistent conception of love as a natural phenomenon, emphasizing throughout the central role of meditation and desire. It is also consistent in expressing pessimism concerning the possibility of establishing and maintaining reciprocal love relationships. Beyond their intrinsic interest, these conclusions in the domain of psychology carry important implications for both the social and, especially, the moral spheres.

LOVE AND THE SOCIAL ORDER

Courtly Values and Feudal Society

T*he complex of medieval love* conceptions commonly known as "courtly love" contains an important social component. The term that many modern scholars use to designate these ideas refers first of all to the social milieu in which they originated, the aristocratic circles of the feudal courts. Whether or not they reflect the social practices of the courts, they are embodied in a large corpus of vernacular love literature produced in that milieu, literature in which social considerations play an important role. By far the most pervasive image in the love lyrics of the troubadours and trouvères, for example, is the "feudal metaphor," which compares the relationship of the lover to his lady with that between a vassal and his lord. Not without reason, some scholars have seen in courtly love a "feudalization" of love.

The dialogues of the *De amore,* which constitute more than one-half of the treatise, are organized around the social class of the participants. Not surprisingly, social questions make up an important part of their contents. Particularly concentrated in the dialogues, social matters are also raised in many other passages scattered throughout the treatise. Nor are they limited to the question of class that provides their point of departure, for several other related matters also figure prominently in the discussion. The social implications and ramifications of love thus form one of the major centers of interest of the work.

The treatment of social questions in the *De amore,* unlike that of the other subjects discussed, relies primarily on contemporary, medieval sources. These comprise two main traditions: that of the vernacular love literature and that of the ideas and practices of feudal society. The first of these traditions is easily verifiable in the poetic texts; the latter, that of the non-literary and perhaps even non-verbal "social intertext," is more difficult to pin down, but no less real. Together they make up the non-clerical, vernacular sources that we have called "courtly." Certain of the social themes of vernacular poetry do have classical antecedents, and for some not specifically medieval social questions classical authors such as Ovid exercised a direct influence on the treatise. The social problems raised generally concern conflicts between these traditions or, in some cases, contradictions within one of them. As with other matters, Andreas usually seeks compromise and synthesis between conflicting authorities.

We have seen that Andreas's treatment of the psychology of love is sometimes difficult to separate from social considerations. Likewise, the distinction between the social and the moral is often far from clear. Questions such as love and marriage, for example, or love and the clergy have obvious and important implications both for social organization and for ethics. Here I shall limit the discussion to matters relating exclusively or primarily to medieval secular society, reserving for the last chapter the questions in which Christian morality constitutes an important factor. As in the preceding chapter, I shall, for the sake of clarity, organize my remarks around a limited number of concepts, keeping in mind that they are all interrelated.

Nobility

Social promotion through love is an important theme in the poetry of the troubadours. Although himself of the highest nobility, the first troubadour, William of Poitiers, proclaimed that love is capable of transforming a churl into a courtly man or a courtly man into a churl.[1] The troubadours frequently stress the nobility of the woman whose love they seek and their own temerity in placing their aim so high. At the same time, they claim that love, though unrequited, makes them

---

1. *Mout jauzens me prenc en amar* (P.-C. 183, 8), vv. 29–30.

better, inspiring in them an emulation of the beloved through which they hope to become worthy of the elevated love for which they long. Expressed fleetingly and sporadically in the poetry, this complex of ideas takes on a more substantial form in the thirteenth-century biographies of the troubadours known as the *vidas* and *razos*. The "life" of Bernart de Ventadorn, for example, asserts that he was born the son of a servant but that he later aspired to the love of Eleanor of Aquitaine, granddaughter of William of Poitiers and queen, successively, of both France and England.[2]

When the ideas of the troubadours were introduced into northern France in the mid-twelfth century, they encountered a much stronger class sentiment on the part of the northern aristocracy than that which prevailed in the South. Moreover, this sentiment increased in the course of the century, as the French nobility consolidated its position. In the courtly romances, which constitute the most important expression of courtly ideas in the North, all the protagonists are noble, and social mobility is hardly ever an issue. This thematic difference appears to reflect a difference in social climate underlying the literatures in Old French and Old Provençal.[3]

The conflict in values between the egalitarian tendencies of the troubadours and the strong class sentiment of the North is reflected in the *De amore,* generally taking the form of an opposition between "nobility of birth" *(sanguinis nobilitas)* and "nobility of character" *(morum nobilitas).* This question is confined essentially to the dialogues, where it represents the single most important topic of discussion. Drawing on the sociological organization of that part of the treatise, it is particularly developed in those dialogues in which one of the participants is a commoner. The Second Dialogue is devoted almost exclusively to this subject.[4]

2. Boutière and Schutz, § VI, A–B, pp. 20–28. Whether or not the *vida* is of historical value with regard to Bernart's biography, it is indicative of an early "reception" of troubadour poetry.

3. Frappier, "Vues," pp. 145–46; M. Bloch, 2:320–44.

4. The term most often used to designate social class, *ordo,* "order, class," occurs with this meaning 68 of 86 times. It is followed by *genus,* "birth, descent," so used 49 or 50 of 69 times. Other terms employed in this connection include: *sanguis,* "blood, linage" (17 of 28 occurrences); *origo,* "origin" (10 of 34 occurrences); *gradus,* "rank" (8 of 23

The introduction to Book One, Chapter Six, claims that human beings were all originally equal according to nature and that it was differences in "worth of character" *(morum probitas)* that caused the introduction of class distinctions (*DA* 1.6.14 [44]). Based on a classical commonplace,[5] this argument is repeated in substantially the same form by the men of the First and Second Dialogues (*DA* 1.6.33 [48], 91 [64]). The point is to establish nobility of character as the functional equivalent of nobility of birth for purposes of wooing. The man of the Third Dialogue carries the "origins" argument one step further, declaring that "from ancient times" class boundaries have applied only to those who were found unworthy of their rank or to those who remain within their rank because they were unworthy of a higher one (*DA* 1.6.135–36 [76–78]).

Closely related to the origins argument is the theme of ennoblement through virtue or through love. Book One, Chapter Four, states that love can endow a man of even the humblest birth with nobility of character (*DA* 1.4.1 [38]). The passage of Chapter Six cited above adds that many of those who trace their descent from the first nobles have degenerated into the opposite condition, and "the converse of this statement is likewise true" (*DA* 1.6.15 [44]), which presumably means that many whose ancestors were not noble are worthy of nobility. After praising the "nobility" of the woman of the middle class, the man of the First Dialogue, also a commoner, claims that worth of character lends nobility not only to women but also to men (*DA* 1.6.35 [48]). In the Second Dialogue the man of the middle class, while agreeing with the noblewoman that one should stay within the bounds of one's own class, argues that worth of character grants him a place in the ranks of the nobility (*DA* 1.6.97 [66]). The man of the Third Dialogue develops from this principle a compelling syllogism: "Character alone makes a man worthy of ennoblement, and since nobility alone deserves the love of a noblewoman, by rights good character alone deserves the crown of a noblewoman's love" (*DA* 1.6.141 [78]).

---

occurrences); and *stipes,* "stock" (6 times). These terms are often combined: *generis vel sanguinis . . . origo* (*DA* 1.6.32 [48]); *sanguinis ordinem sive gradum* (*DA* 1.7.4 [210]); etc. Cf. Baldwin, *Language,* p. 51; p. 284, n. 30.

5. Curtius, pp. 179–80.

A related argument frequently invoked by the men is that Love or Nature compels them to love, with no regard to social class. The man of the Second Dialogue argues that, just as Love, imitating Nature, makes no class distinctions but forces everyone to love, so also the woman should not consider the class of a suitor but only whether he has been wounded by Love (DA 1.6.71–72 [60]). In the Third Dialogue the man claims that it is Nature's impulse that pushes him to go beyond the bounds of his class, and he reproaches the woman for trying to impose limits not recognized by Nature (DA 1.6.134 [76]). The man of the Fourth Dialogue chides the woman for not knowing that it is Love alone that makes men love, with no consideration for nobility nor beauty (DA 1.6.180–82 [90–92]). According to the man of the Sixth Dialogue, it is Love's command that one should not make class distinctions in matters of love, for Love seeks to adorn his palace from all social ranks and to have all serve him on equal terms (DA 1.6.288–89 [122], 298 [124–26]).

The egalitarian arguments of the men are countered each in turn by the women of the dialogues. Presenting her own version of the origins argument, the woman of the Second Dialogue claims that it was not without cause that class distinctions were established among men, but rather with the idea that each should stay within the boundaries of his own class (DA 1.6.80 [62]). Later she argues that if worth of character were the only pertinent criterion, the ancient establishment of social classes would have to be considered superfluous, which is absurd (DA 1.6.107–8 [70]). In the Third Dialogue the woman underlines the figurative nature of "nobility" of character, pointing out that, whatever a man's merit, only the power of a prince can actually change his social rank (DA 1.6.138 [78]). Thus the women defend themselves against the solicitations of their suitors by upholding the established order.

The comparison that recurs most frequently in the dialogues in connection with social class is that of birds. This figure combines the Ovidian image of love as a kind of hunting (AA 1.45–50) with the medieval convention that makes of falconry a symbol of nobility, based on the fact that hunting was restricted to the noble classes. The woman of the Second Dialogue asks rhetorically whether a kestrel could overcome a partridge or a pheasant by its own strength, adding that such prey is more suitable for falcons or hawks (*DA* 1.6.82 [62]). The man replies that it is only for their courage that hawks and falcons are prized, and that sometimes we see noble falcons that fear common sparrows and are put to flight by kestrels, in which case the latter should be considered as falcons, whatever the status of their parents (*DA* 1.6.100–101 [68]). The woman answers that in such cases the falcon remains a falcon, although a poor one, and the kestrel remains a kestrel, however good (*DA* 1.6.110 [70]).

Out of the discussion of class distinctions arises the question whether worth of character is more to be valued in a person of nobility or in a commoner. The man of the First Dialogue asserts that the woman of the middle class is all the more to be praised since her "nobility" comes not from birth but only from her good character (*DA* 1.6.32 [48]). Later he applies the same argument to himself, claiming that a man who owes his goodness only to his own efforts has more merit than one who is aided by noble origins (*DA* 1.6.37–38 [50]). In the Fourth Dialogue the nobleman formulates the problem in terms of a "disputed question" for the woman of the middle class to resolve (*DA* 1.6.169 [86]). The woman replies that good character is more natural, and therefore more praiseworthy, in a person of nobility (*DA* 1.6.171–72 [88]), thus countering in advance the man's praise of her own nobility of character. The man upholds the opposite position, according to the rules of the *partimen,* invoking the same argument as the man of the First Dialogue (*DA* 1.6.173–75 [88]), along with the bird image (§ 174).

Underlying this discussion is an assumption shared by disputants on both sides of the question: that virtue is "natural" in a person of noble origin, exceptional in a commoner. The sentiment of the natural superiority of the aristocracy was widespread in medieval society, on both sides of the Loire, extending to all classes of society. It is encountered frequently in medieval literature, with respect not only to moral character but also to physical beauty. It is reflected in the modern languages in words such as Eng. "gentle" or Fr. *gentil* "kind," both derived from Med. Lat. *gentilis,* "noble."

Such class sentiments are expressed in many passages of the dialogues, interwoven with the egalitarian arguments about worth of character. In the Second Dialogue the noblewoman, indignant at being solicited by a commoner, is restrained from rebuking him with harsh language by the thought that this would be unbecoming to a woman of her class (*DA* 1.6.78 [62]). The man subsequently praises the gentility of her reply, which he finds in keeping with her noble status (*DA* 1.6.89 [64]). The woman of the Third Dialogue, of the higher nobility, upbraids the man for suggesting that she might promise him hope without intending to keep her promise, for nothing could be more shameful to a noblewoman than such behavior (*DA* 1.6.131 [76]). Later she encourages the man to bestow his generosity on those in need, especially if they are of good character or from the noble class, categories apparently seen as more or less equivalent (*DA* 1.6.149 [82]). The "noblesse oblige" motif is also invoked by the woman of the Seventh Dialogue, who reminds the man of the higher nobility that good character is only to be expected from men of his class (*DA* 1.6.330 [134]). He replies by expressing the hope that she will live up to her own noble status by accepting his suit, thus contributing to his moral improvement (*DA* 1.6.336 [136]).

The relationship of nobility to physical beauty is raised in the Third Dialogue, when the woman objects that the man of the middle class does not have the long, slender calves and moderately sized feet expected of knights (*DA* 1.6.140 [78]). He responds with two examples from recent history, that of an Italian count whose physical beauty was matched only by his lack of character, and that of a Hungarian king, renown for his moral qualities despite the mediocrity of his physical appearance (*DA* 1.6.142–44 [78–80]). In the First and Fourth Dialogues the men stress the power of Love to make even an ugly woman appear beautiful to the lover (*DA* 1.6.31 [48], 181–82 [90]), which may imply that the women, both commoners, are beautiful only in the eyes of their respective suitors.

The woman of the First Dialogue, a commoner, declares with characteristic modesty that the highest wisdom should not be expected of a woman of her class (*DA* 1.6.28 [48]). This opinion is apparently shared by Andreas: in the introduction to two of the dialogues he warns against excessive praise of noblewomen, less susceptible to flattery than women of the middle class (*DA* 1.6.25 [46], 68–69 [58], 322 [132]). It is belied, however, by the witty and spirited defense by the women of the middle class in the three dialogues in which they appear. None of them is taken in by flattery, particularly concerning their "nobility," and two of them cleverly turn this argument against the suitor.

In the First Dialogue the woman tells the man, also a commoner, that if she is as noble as he says, she should seek a nobleman's love rather than his (*DA* 1.6.34 [48]). Accepting the nobleman's contention that worth of character is more to be praised in a commoner, the woman of the Fourth Dialogue draws the conclusion that she should give her love to a worthy commoner rather than to him (*DA* 1.6.183 [92]). The woman of the Sixth Dialogue ironizes about the felicity of a common maid found worthy of the love of a count, before going on to describe the danger of being seduced and abandoned by such an illustrious suitor, with irreparable damage to her reputation (*DA* 1.6.285–87 [120–22]). Not only the tone but also many of the arguments recall *pastorelas* such as Marcabru's *L'autrier jost'una sebissa* (P.-C. 293, 30), which may have served as model for these dialogues.

Beyond its discussion by the disputants in the dialogues, Andreas himself addresses the subject of social class in one passage: the introduction to the Third Dialogue (*DA* 1.6.116–23 [72–74]). Opposing a man from the middle class and a woman from the higher nobility, this dialogue reproduces the classic social situation of the troubadour lyric reflected in the *vida* of Bernart de Ventadorn. From the point of view of the aristocratic males who dominated medieval society, it is the most transgressive of relationships, which may account for the Chaplain's personal intervention at this point.

Andreas's discussion of love in relation to social class shows a strong desire to reconcile two diametrically opposed positions: the principle announced at the beginning of Chapter Six that "only virtue is worthy of the crown of love" (*DA* 1.6.15 [44]) and the pronounced class sentiment of the northern aristocracy, who found socially transgressive relationships repugnant. A commoner who wishes to court a woman of the higher nobility must enjoy "great nobility" (§ 116), by which nobility of character is obviously understood; indeed, he should exceed in "great nobility" all men of the nobility and the higher nobility (§ 118). The justification offered for this requirement concerns the reputation of the lady, whom public opinion will otherwise suspect of an "excessive abundance of pleasure"; only the commoner's reputation for excellence of character can dispel such suspicion (§§ 117, 119).

Andreas's compromise has two important consequences for a woman of the higher nobility who finds herself courted by a commoner but who is concerned for her own reputation. The first is that she may accept the commoner's suit only if no one of equal worth can be found in one of the higher classes (§ 120). Questions such as the prior claim of an earlier suitor (see below, Chapter 8) are not considered, and the freedom of choice frequently proclaimed by the women of the dialogues is subordinated to the tyranny of public opinion. The other consequence is that she must test the constancy of the commoner by many trials before granting him the hope of her love (§§ 121–23). This stipulation is related to the question of love too easily granted as well as to that of service.

Acceding to the authority of the literary theme of nobility of merit, Andreas admits the possibility of love between a woman of the higher nobility and a commoner, but the many precautions with which he surrounds this highly transgressive relationship show how completely he shares the class sentiment of the northern aristocracy. Concerning public opinion and its impact on the woman's reputation, he invokes the "rule of the logicians" to show that if worth can not be found in the nobility, where one would expect it, it is not likely to be found in a commoner (§§ 117–18). Subsequently he justifies the need for much testing of an apparently worthy commoner on the grounds that qualities which go "beyond the nature" of the individual tend to be ephemeral, just as a kestrel born with sufficient fierceness to subdue a partridge loses this quality after a year because it is "beyond its nature" (§§ 121–22). Thus the Chaplain clearly shares with the disputants of the dialogues the assumption of the natural superiority of the aristocracy, separated from commoners by differences in behavior as instinctual as those that separate diverse animal species, with rare counterexamples constituting the exceptions that confirm the rule.

This conclusion is reinforced by the treatment of peasants *(rustici)* in the chapter devoted to them *(DA* 1.11 [222]). In contrast to his implicit approval of the literary peasants of the *pastourelles* reflected in the dialogues with women of the middle class, Andreas's approach to real peasants is harshly repressive. Although he distinguishes carefully between male and female peasants, with very different recommendations for the two sexes, his attitude toward both is one of utter contempt, presumably reflecting the point of view of the aristocratic males who dominated medieval society.

Of male peasants the Chaplain claims that they cannot serve in Love's court, because they are naturally driven to love, like horses or mules, as Nature's impulse urges them. Love for them is seen as an animal instinct, far removed from the refinements of an art. In place of *solatia amoris,* Andreas sardonically suggests for such persons the "solaces" of the ploughshare and the hoe. If it should occur, however rarely, that they are spurred to go beyond their nature, he continues, it is not expedient to instruct them in Love's teachings, lest they neglect the cultivation of the fields in favor of activities alien to their nature. In short, someone must produce the wealth to make possible the leisure necessary for pursuing the art of love.

Concerning peasant women the Chaplain does offer instruction, not for the women themselves, but for men such as Walter who might be attracted to their love. This advice contains essentially two points: the use of abundant praise to begin, and the use of violent force to "overcome their shyness" and thus to conclude. The first point recalls the susceptibility to flattery that peasant women share with women of the middle class, according to the introduction to the First Dialogue (*DA* 1.6.25 [46]). For the second, P. G. Walsh (p. 23) invokes the influence of the *pastourelles.* Violence is used, in fact, in a number of the northern *pastourelles,* unlike the troubadours' *pastorelas,* suggesting once again a difference in social attitudes, and perhaps in social practice, between the two regions.[6] This underlying social reality may be reflected directly in Andreas's advice or indirectly by way of the literary model of the northern *pastourelles*—or indeed through a convergence of these two factors.[7]

Andreas's advice on wooing peasant women is reminiscent of the

6. Gravdal, pp. 104–21. By Gravdal's count (p. 105), 38 of 160 Old French pastourelles, or "18%" (actually 24%), include rape scenes, whereas she finds only one such scene for 30 Old Occitan *pastorelas* (p. 166, n. 3; p. 169, n. 28).

7. Ovid has been invoked for both aspects of Andreas's advice on peasant women: Walsh (p. 47, n. 37) refers to the discussion of praise in *AA* 1.613–14, Cairns (p. 106) to

discussion in Book Two of men who seize a passing opportunity for a romp in the grass with an unknown woman, a practice to which the Chaplain does not object, as long as it does not occur too often. For such actions to be permissible, it is stipulated that the man should have no intention of starting a new love. If he goes to some pains to obtain the woman's favors, the assumption is that he is interested in her love, not just her body, especially if she is noble (*DA* 2.6.10–12 [240]). For men like Walter a lasting relationship with a peasant woman is un-thinkable, so the Chaplain's use of the word "love" here must be under-stood as referring to sexual intercourse, the "taking of one's pleasure" with the women in question.

The sexual appropriation of peasant women is the corollary of the exclusion of their men from loving. Peasants of both sexes are reduced to the status of domestic animals, entirely at the service of their aristo-cratic, male masters, albeit in different functions. Andreas adds that his remarks are intended not to persuade Walter to love peasant women, but only to teach him what to do, in case, through lack of foresight, he should find himself impelled to love them. Here the Chaplain appears to speak in an ecclesiastical capacity. Sympathetic to the nobility, he does not condemn their sexual exploitation of the peasantry, but as a cleric he cannot really advocate such behavior, hence his disclaimer.

The question of social class in relation to love is the most important social problem raised by the *De amore,* as well as the most controversial. This accounts for the considerable space devoted to this subject, espe-cially in the dialogues. The treatment of this topic provides a clear ex-ample of Andreas's method of systematic confrontation of opposing opinions with a view to reconciling them.[8]

The emphasis on the literary theme of nobility of merit is striking,

---

that of the use of force in *AA* 1.669–706. But Ovid offers advice on dealing with women in general, whereas Andreas is concerned specifically with behavior appropriate to women of the lowest social class. If there is an Ovidian influence here, it is a striking ex-ample of the "medievalization" of Ovid.

8. According to Baldwin, *Language,* p. 51, "As a cleric André was not ignorant of the trifunctional scheme, long established in ecclesiastical circles, that divided all society into three orders *(ordines)* according to distinctive functions: the *laborator,* the peasant who works; the *bellator,* the knight who fights; and the *orator,* the cleric who prays." Cf. ibid., p. 284, n. 31; Duby. It is true that Andreas's social classification includes represen-

but the context of assumptions surrounding the discussion of this theme reflects the conservative, aristocratic climate in which the treatise was produced. Maintaining that worth of character should be the ultimate criterion for choosing a love partner, Andreas nevertheless limits the impact of this principle by the many restrictions placed on socially transgressive love relationships. If a commoner wishes to court a noblewoman, it is not sufficient that he be worthy, he must be more worthy than all the nobles, and he must continue to prove this through a long period of testing. As for peasants, they are excluded from the art of love, not only by their nature, but also for economic reasons, although their women are fair game to satisfy the passing fancy of the nobles. What remains of the egalitarian tendencies of the troubadours could scarcely offend the social sensibilities of the northern aristocracy for whom the treatise was presumably written.

Deeds and service

The foundation of the feudal system, the bond between lord and vassal, was a reciprocal relationship with rights and obligations on both sides. The vassal owed his lord not only allegiance but also service, which usually meant military service. In return the lord promised his vassal protection as well as material remuneration, usually in the form of a fief, a piece of land that continued to belong to the lord but that the vassal had the exclusive right to exploit. Thus service and its reward were central features of the entire arrangement.[9]

---

tatives of each of the three *ordines,* and he may well have been aware of the tripartite distinction of functions, but he certainly does not give it much emphasis. In the *De amore,* the *bellatores* are divided into *nobiles* and *nobiliores,* the *laboratores* into *plebeii* and *rustici* (with access to love accorded only to the former), so that there are five social classes rather than three. The separate, superior status attributed to clerics at the beginning of Book One, Chapter Six (*DA* 1.6.20 [46]) is taken away in regard to love in the following chapter (*DA* 1.7.4 [210]), with the clergy reintegrated into the other social classes; this brings the number of classes with access to love back to three, but these are not the classical *ordines.* The terms *laborator* and *orator* do not occur in the treatise; *bellator* occurs only once in a passage of Book Two far removed from the discussions of class distinction (*DA* 2.1.8 [226]). And throughout the treatise, *ordo* appears to refer primarily to hierarchical distinctions of rank rather than to distinctions of function.

9. Ganshof, pp. 69–105, esp. pp. 81–93.

Comparing the love relationship to the vassalic bond, the "feudal metaphor" of vernacular love literature also gives a prominent place to reciprocity. The lover expresses his sentiments through "service" to his lady, through which he hopes to earn a "reward," namely the lady's love. In the lyric poetry of the troubadours this "service" consists of the sincerity of the poet-lover's emotions as well as the excellence of the song that constitutes their direct expression. In the northern romances the lovers are not poets but knights, and so their service takes the form of military exploits performed for the beloved or in her honor.[10]

The lover's service to the lady is also a frequent theme in the *De amore*, especially in the dialogues. The terms *servitium*, "service," and *servire*, "to serve," occur some forty times in the treatise. Even more often this idea is expressed by *obsequor* and *obsequium*, which are found more than sixty times in the medieval sense of "service." There are also twenty-six occurrences of *ministerium*, "service," and its derivatives *minister* and *ministrare*, in various usages, ten of which refer to the service either of ladies or of Love. The subject of service is often raised in connection with the discussion of nobility, for service to the lady is the principal way in which the lover can prove his worth of character.

The service of the lover usually takes the form of "deeds" *(facta)* performed by him, often "praiseworthy deeds" *(laudabilia facta)* and especially "good deeds" *(bona facta, benefacta, beneficia)*. The term *bona,* "good things," is also used frequently in this sense, generally introduced by verbs meaning "to do, to perform," such as *facere, perficere,* and *peragere.* In the Third Dialogue, for example, the woman accepts the man's arguments about the importance of worth of character over physical beauty or social class, but she objects that he has no "good deeds" *(benefacta)* to his credit *(DA* 1.6.145 [80]).

Although the nature of the "deeds" performed by the lover often remains vague, not infrequently it is specifically military service that is evoked, as in the courtly romances and in the feudal institutions on which they are modeled. In more than thirty passages, most of them in the dialogues, the terms *militia* and *militare* are used to signify, respec-

---

10. Wechssler, "Frauendienst"; idem, *Das Kulturproblem,* pp. 140–81; Pellegrini; Lejeune; Kasten; Jonin; Monson, "L'Antonomase."

tively, "service" and "to serve." Usually these terms occur in the allegorical figure of "serving in Love's army," which combines the Ovidian image of love as a kind of warfare (*AA* 2.233–36; *Amores* 1.9) with the literal military service of the medieval knight.

Other passages refer more explicitly to military service in the literal sense. In the lesson given by the woman of the Third Dialogue, the man is advised to be courageous in battle as well as hardy, wise, cautious, and clever in the face of enemies (*DA* 1.6.155 [82–84]). In the Eighth Dialogue the woman argues that, being a cleric, the man can not participate in battle as love requires (*DA* 1.6.490 [186]; cf. ibid., §§ 495–96). In Book Two Andreas advises the man who wishes to maintain his love to make sure that his courage in battle is clear to all (*DA* 2.1.8 [226]), for love is diminished if the woman realizes that her lover is timid in war (*DA* 2.3.4 [230]). The best illustration of military service in pursuit of love is the exemplary tale of the Briton knight that closes Book Two.

The question arises in the Eighth Dialogue whether the woman should prefer a suitor who lets his actions speak for themselves or one who presents his case verbally (*DA* 1.6.504–19 [190–94]). This opposition between service expressed in words and that expressed in deeds corresponds to a generic distinction between vernacular love lyric and courtly romance. Like the poet-lover of the love song, the man is attempting to win love through eloquence, and so he naturally supports verbal presentation, citing the biblical passage "Seek and you will obtain" (§ 508; cf. Matt. 7.7; Luke 11.9). Just as naturally the woman defends the opposite position, maintaining especially her own right to choose. A related problem is raised by the woman of the Seventh Dialogue, who accuses the man of reversing the proper order of courtship: first he should get some good deeds to his credit before making a verbal solicitation (*DA* 1.6.353–54 [142]). In the Fourth Dialogue the woman tells the man that if he will translate his fine words into deeds he cannot fail to win a suitable reward (*DA* 1.6.195 [94]).

As numerous passages in the treatise make clear, the lover's service should benefit not only the beloved, but everyone, especially all women. Book One, Chapter Four, lists among the effects of love the habit of performing gracefully many services for all (*DA* 1.4.1 [38]). In the Third Dialogue the man expresses the intention of serving everyone on behalf of the beloved (*DA* 1.6. 126 [74]), a promise repeated by the man of the Fourth Dialogue (*DA* 1.6.194 [94]). The woman of the Third Dialogue exhorts the man not to be a lover of many women, but rather a servant of all of them for the sake of one (*DA* 1.6.155 [84]). When the man of the Seventh Dialogue proposes to do just that, the woman objects that it would be an injustice to the other ladies to ascribe all the man's deeds to her alone (*DA* 1.6.342 [138]), to which the man replies that the other ladies should find other men willing so to honor them (*DA* 1.6. 346–47 [140]). Precept VII recommends obedience in all things to the commands of the ladies as well as zeal in joining in the service of Love (*DA* 1.6. 269 [116]). To maintain love, Book Two advises the lover to offer his obedience and services freely to all ladies (*DA* 2.1.9 [226]).

The obligation of service to all reflects a contemporary social phenomenon as well as a prominent feature of the courtly romances. Thirteenth-century treatises on chivalry such as the anonymous *Ordene de chevalerie* and the *Libre de cavayleria* of Ramon Lull express a growing social consciousness of the knightly class, with antecedents that doubtless went back to the twelfth century. Both discuss the knight's duty to protect the weak, such as widows and orphans, thus providing this professional category with a social justification in which the Christian notion of charity was an important ingredient.[11] In the courtly romances can be observed a process of transfer or sublimation by which the love of a lady is won through a series of adventures involving typically the rescue of damsels in distress. Often the rescued damsel offers to reward the hero's service directly with love or marriage, but this reward is rejected out of fidelity to the beloved, thus building up credit, as it were, on the good-deeds account of the hero, for which the recompense will be the winning of the beloved at the end of the romance.[12] It is especially this latter model that is reflected in the *De amore.*

Throughout the dialogues the notion of service is closely associated with that of reward. The term *præmium* occurs thirty-four times in the

---

11. Keen, pp. 6–11; Flori, pp. 204–33.
12. Monson, "L'Antonomase."

dialogues, usually in this sense. The reward due for services rendered is also discussed frequently in terms of "remuneration" *(munus, remunerari),* occasionally in terms of "retribution" *(retributio, retribuere).*

In the First Dialogue the man argues that it would be contrary to sound reason for good deeds to go unrewarded (*DA* 1.6.67 [58]). The man of the Third Dialogue promises unstinting service, firm in the hope that this will bear sweet fruit (*DA* 1.6.126 [74]). He ends with the prayer that God may ever increase his own desire to serve as well as the willingness of the woman to reward him according to his merit (*DA* 1.6.165 [86]). In the Fourth Dialogue the man prays that God may induce the woman to accept his service, so that he may ever increase in doing good and thus earn the reward for which he longs (*DA* 1.6.178 [90]). The man of the Fifth Dialogue expresses confidence in his own good deeds and in the woman's sense of justice, which will not leave his service unrewarded (*DA* 1.6.279 [120]).

In the Seventh Dialogue the combined notions of service and reward are developed with specific reference to feudalism. The man asks that the woman accept him as her "special man" *(specialis homo),* since he is devoted uniquely to her service, and that his deeds obtain from her the reward that he seeks (*DA* 1.6.338 [136]). The reference is to the feudal rite of "homage," by which one man becomes the "man" *(homo),* or vassal, of another.[13]

Whatever the term evoking the reward for service, it is invariably the woman's love, or at least the hope of it, that is so designated. This is made especially clear in the Seventh Dialogue when the woman feigns ignorance concerning the nature of the reward requested (*DA* 1.6.344 [138]). The man answers that the reward on which all his hopes are set is that which it would be an unbearable pain to forgo, that which would bestow an abundance of riches if possessed, namely the lady's love (*DA* 1.6.351 [140–42]). It is because of the nature of the reward that the service to many must be performed in honor of only one, the one from whom the reward is sought, in accordance with the principle of fidelity to a single love partner.

The men's offer of service puts the women of the dialogues in a

13. Ganshof, pp. 72–81.

difficult position. They can hardly fail to encourage such a noble enterprise as service to all, but the rules of disputation and concern for their own reputation require them to avoid making any concessions regarding the granting of their love, which is not only the principal object of contention in the debate, but also the reward due for service. Thus the women must find a way to accept the offer of service without committing themselves to reward it.

The woman of the Third Dialogue encourages the man in his noble intentions of service, but points out that the granting of her love is out of the question because of the wide disparity in social rank between them (*DA* 1.6.128–29 [76]). In the Fifth Dialogue the woman accepts the man's offer of service, granting in return the right to see her, but nothing more, for she is irrevocably opposed to subjecting herself to the servitude of love (*DA* 1.6.204–5 [98], 209–10 [100]). The woman of the Seventh Dialogue is pleased to be the inspiration for the man's good deeds, but she also warns him to curb his excessive praise of her, thus implicitly rebuffing his advances (*DA* 1.6.327–28 [134]).

Love is not only the reward for good deeds, it is also the principal factor that inspires them. According to the man of the First Dialogue, no man will be able to perform good deeds unless he is urged by the persuasion of Love (*DA* 1.6.50 [52]). At the beginning of the Eighth Dialogue the man states succinctly what he perceives as the dual obligation of women in response to men's service: they must help good men's hearts to remain devoted to good deeds, and they must honor each according to his deserts (*DA* 1.6.404 [158]). This double relationship gives rise to a controversy concerning the order in which service and love should succeed each other. In general, the men ask to be loved so that they can be inspired to do good deeds (e.g., *DA* 1.6.178 [90]), whereas the women insist that the men must perform good deeds before they can expect to be loved (e.g., *DA* 1.6.46–48 [52], 353–54 [142]).

This problem of timing is discussed at length in the First Dialogue, with particular reference to the age of the suitor (*DA* 1.6.40–67 [50–58]). In reply to the woman's expressed repugnance at accepting the love of an old man, the man argues that his age has allowed him to accumulate many praiseworthy deeds to his credit, and that he who has performed the greater service deserves the greater reward (§§ 42–43). This argument is repeated by the woman later in the dialogue, her opponent having now become a young man (§ 54). The young man replies that one should distinguish between a mature man who has done no good deeds and a youth who is not yet old enough to have done any; only the latter deserves encouragement (§§ 56–57). The woman who takes on such a youth and inspires him to do great deeds will have earned far greater honor than one who simply repays with her love services already rendered (§§ 52–53). As a further precaution, the woman should limit her favors initially to the first three stages of love, reserving the final consummation until the youth has proven his worth through his deeds (§§ 59–64). Apparently accepting the general thrust of the man's argument, the woman simply urges him to get on with his good deeds (§ 66).

The same problem is taken up again in two of the Love Cases of Book Two, with results less favorable to the inexperienced suitor. Case XIII tells of a woman who took on a worthless knight and who by her love and teaching made a worthy man of him. The knight later deserted her for another woman, but the Countess of Flanders rules that he must return to the woman who has devoted so much effort to his improvement (*DA* 2.7.28–30 [260–62]). Case VI concerns a conflict between a mature knight endowed with many virtues and a young man of no worth, both of whom sought the love of a certain woman. Although the youth argued that the woman would gain much praise for helping him to improve in worth, Queen Eleanor judges it imprudent to take on such a lover, especially when a fully deserving one is available (*DA* 2.7.16–17 [254–56]). Both these cases, and especially the queen's ruling, cast some doubt on the assurances of the man in the First Dialogue.

The tale of the Briton knight in Book Two (*DA* 2.8.1–50 [270–84]) provides an exemplum illustrating concretely the themes of service and reward discussed in abstract terms elsewhere in the treatise. The hero is embarked on a symbolic quest for a hawk, conventional emblem of nobility, in the course of which he will have occasion to test his strength and courage in single combat against several formidable adversaries. In short, he wishes to obtain "nobility" through military service.

The knight has undertaken this adventure at the bidding of a beautiful woman whose love he seeks (§ 3). The young woman whom he meets in the woods is first of all a helper, but also a surrogate of the beloved, an example of the many whom he must serve for the sake of one. This role of surrogate is made clear not only by the description of the young woman's great beauty (§ 2), but also by the "kiss of love" that she gives him before and after his adventure (§§ 7, 43). By their respective places in the story, these kisses symbolize the dual role of love with respect to deeds of prowess, that of inspiration and that of reward. The single kiss given for encouragement is followed by thirteen more once the adventure is successfully completed, demonstrating the principle that the woman should limit her favors until the man has proven his worth. Although restricted in scope to the requirements of the adventure, the young woman's instructions (§§ 4–8) to the knight, whose youth is repeatedly emphasized (§§ 14, 16, 22), illustrate the educative function of love, not unlike the woman's lesson in the Third Dialogue.

The clearest expression in this tale of the role of love in inspiring exploits of prowess is the claim that the knight must defend to obtain the hawk: that he loves a lady more beautiful than that of any knight in Arthur's court (§§ 4–5, 37). In the end, the knight's lady, acknowledging his intrepid efforts as proof of his utter faithfulness, rewards his labors with her love (§ 49). Thus the paradigm of inspiration, service, and reward is represented twice, in mirror images framed one within the other: that of the surrogate and that of the beloved.

Throughout most of the *De amore,* including the dialogues and the tale of the Briton knight, military service in pursuit of love is idealized, as in the courtly romances. In a few passages, however, especially later in the treatise, a more realistic approach is adopted. Case XV of the Love Cases concerns a knight who, having lost an eye or some other physical adornment in combat, is rejected by his lady as no longer attractive. Ermengarde of Narbonne finds against the woman, for disfigurement is the natural outcome of warfare, which is the usual way by which a man earns a lady's love (*DA* 2.7.35–36 [262–64]). As in the case of the woman abandoned by her lover after she had made a worthy man of him, the principle appears to be that of a fair return on an investment. What makes this case so interesting is the fact that serious injury is considered as a possible, even likely, outcome to combat, whereas this possibility is hardly ever envisaged in the romances.

In Book Three Andreas cites as an argument against love the fact that it often leads to deadly, inescapable warfare (*DA* 3.43 [300]). The woman of the Eighth Dialogue justifies her refusal of love on the grounds that it gives rise to the dangers of death for many, although in light of the context in which she is speaking, she may have in mind the biblical sense of "spiritual death" (*DA* 1.6.411 [160]). She also finds love particularly inappropriate for knights, who are exposed daily to death in battle and thus should avoid actions likely to offend the Heavenly King, whose judgment they will have to face (*DA* 1.6.412 [160–62]). All these comments underline the fact that, contrary to the idealized image of the romances, military service, whether or not it is carried out in pursuit of love, is not without risks.

The third book also argues that the service of love is really a harsh servitude (*DA* 3.14–17 [290]). This argument was already anticipated by Andreas in the early chapters of the treatise (*DA* 0.3 [30], 1.4.3 [38]) and by the woman of the Fifth Dialogue in her own rejection of love (*DA* 1.6.209 [100], 218 [102]). A later passage of the third book describes the rewards that the devil accords to the knights who serve him: pain and suffering, proportional to the service rendered (*DA* 3.39–41 [298]). Thus the feudal metaphor is "deconstructed," so to speak, and turned against itself.

The concept of service provides one of the key social themes of the *De amore*. It is discussed extensively throughout the dialogues, and it receives a striking illustration in Book Two, in the tale of the Briton knight. The theme of service is intimately connected with that of nobility, for it is primarily through the performance of good deeds that worth or nobility of character is established. Based on the feudal metaphor with its emphasis on the reciprocity of service and reward, the development accorded this subject is among the clearest examples of the influence exercised upon the treatise by the vernacular love literature. As in the romances, it is especially military service that is considered, although the verbal "service" of the love lyric also receives passing mention.

Hardly controversial, the theme of service lends itself less than others to the dialectical treatment typical of the *De amore*. Nevertheless, the dual relationship of love to service, that of inspiration and reward, does give rise to an important debate as to which should come first. The solution adopted, in the First Dialogue and in the tale of the Briton knight, appears to be one of gradualism in according the woman's favors, based on the notion of stages of love, with only minor concessions by way of encouragement, followed by more substantial ones once worth is demonstrated. This compromise is called into question, however, by the judgment of Queen Eleanor in Case VI, which comes down heavily in favor of love as reward.

Characteristically, Book Three turns the theme of service against itself, equating service with servitude and calling attention to the dangers of warfare. Both these arguments were fleetingly anticipated earlier in the treatise. Despite these objections, the notion of service to all for the love of one remains among the most important positive values conveyed by the *De amore*.

Courtesy

An important element of the advance in civilization known as the Twelfth-Century Renaissance was a new refinement of social manners, especially in the milieu of the feudal courts. This essentially social phenomenon was soon reflected in the literature emanating from the same milieu. The poetry of the troubadours frequently cites *cortezia* among the virtues of the poet-lover or of his lady. According to the context, the meaning of this term may vary between a vague, general notion comprising an entire constellation of virtues and a much more precise notion of social refinement. By its etymology it evokes the aristocratic milieu of the feudal "courts" where such virtues were presumably practiced.[14] In the northern romances, *courtoisie* was second only to military prowess among the qualities of the perfect knight. The paragon of "courtliness" in the Arthurian romances of Chrétien de Troyes is Gawain, the nephew of Arthur, who functions as a model for comparison against which all the protagonists are measured, in terms not only of bravery but also of social grace.[15]

14. Lazar, esp. pp. 21–46.
15. Monson, "La 'Surenchère,'" pp. 244–45.

Although much less developed than nobility or service, the theme of courtesy occupies a significant place in the *De amore*'s discussions. It is expressed most often by the adjective *curialis,* obviously calqued on the vernacular *cortes/courtois,* or by its derivatives *curialitas* and *curialiter.* All together they occur twenty-six times. The classical *urbanus/urbanitas* is found nine times with the same meaning. The opposite quality is generally represented by *inurbanus/inurbanitas,* once again with nine occurrences. In three cases the latter idea is conveyed by *rusticitas.* The subject is discussed primarily in the dialogues, and it is also illustrated in several of the Love Cases and in the tale of the Briton knight. There is no reference to it in the third book.[16]

Numerous passages in the treatise stress the importance of courteous behavior, often without ascribing any specific content to that notion. According to the woman of the Third Dialogue, a man who seeks the love of a woman of character, especially one of the higher nobility, should be adorned with every courtliness (*DA* 1.6.145 [80]). This same quality is again recommended several times in the lesson that follows (*DA* 1.6.150–51 [82], 159 [84]). Book Two states as a "general rule" that lovers should not omit, but rather execute with zeal, whatever courtesy demands or urges (*DA* 2.1.10 [226]). The Precepts of the Fifth Dialogue formalize the same principle: XI. "In all things show yourself to be polite [urbanum] and courteous [curialem]" (*DA* 1.6.269 [116]).

Courtesy is intimately connected with the other social values discussed above. It is frequently associated with an equally vague notion of "good deeds" (*DA* 1.6.42 [50], 49 [52], 147 [80], 305 [126]), recalling the knightly heros of the vernacular romances. As with deeds, it is love that is the source of all courtliness (*DA* 1.6.49 [52], 147 [80], 197 [96], 305 [126], 412 [160]). The duties of women include, according to the woman of the Eighth Dialogue, urging all men to perform courteous deeds and to reject acts of boorishness (*DA* 1.6.410 [160]). In the Second Dialogue the man argues that nobility originally arose from good character and human worth, "kindled by courtesy" (*DA* 1.6.91 [64]). Several other passages mention courtesy as an indispensable constituent of nobility (*DA* 1.6.36 [48], 78 [62], 89 [64], 94 [66], 330 [134]).

---

16. On the language of courtesy, see Jaeger, *Origins,* pp. 127–75.

A few passages give a more precise idea of what Andreas means by courtesy, especially those that describe it negatively in terms of behavior to be avoided. The lesson of the Third Dialogue equates courtesy with generosity in the giving of food to the poor (*DA* 1.6.150 [82]). A similar association is made by the man of the Second Dialogue and the woman of the Seventh Dialogue (*DA* 1.6.95 [66], 330 [134]). In the debate over the upper and lower halves of the body, the man of the Eighth Dialogue argues that the solaces of the upper half can be obtained in a more courtly fashion without violating the modesty of either partner (*DA* 1.6.545 [202]). Case XVI of the Love Cases qualifies as discourteous the behavior of a lady who accepts the love suit of a man originally engaged as go-between for another (*DA* 2.7.38 [264]). In the Arthurian tale the Briton knight tells the doorkeeper who has objected to his presence at the king's table that it would be discourteous to deny him hospitality, all the more so since he is a knight on a knight's business (*DA* 2.8.23 [276]). Once the knight has beaten the doorman in single combat, the latter pleads for his life, claiming that it would be discourteous to kill a conquered foe (*DA* 2.8.30 [278]). Although the list of actions described either as courteous or as discourteous is rather heterogeneous, they all have in common a concern for a certain delicacy in social relations.

The most frequent situation associated with courtesy concerns the use of language. The two disputants of the Second Dialogue agree that harsh and discourteous words are incompatible with nobility (*DA* 1.6.78 [60–62], 89 [64]). The lesson of the Third Dialogue declares that evil tongues cannot remain within courtesy's threshold (*DA* 1.6.151 [82]). According to the woman of the Eighth Dialogue, the encouragement to do good deeds and acts of courtesy that women should give to all men includes greeting them with courtesy and with a pleasant countenance (*DA* 1.6.410 [160]). This advice, which recalls that of the *Ensenhamen de la dompna* by Garin lo Brun,[17] is illustrated in the Arthurian tale by the Lady of the Woods, who greets the Briton knight with courtly words before sending him off in quest of the hawk (*DA* 2.8.2

---

17. Garin, *Ensenhamen*, vv. 257–466, 509–648, in Sansone, pp. 41–107, esp. pp. 61–68, 70–74; cf. Monson, *Les "Ensenhamens,"* p. 75.

[270]). The Briton knight apparently profits from this example, for he in turn greets with courteous words the knight guarding the bridge, in sharp contrast to the latter's surly reply (*DA* 2.8.11 [272]), and at the end of his adventure he courteously takes leave of Arthur's court before returning with the scroll containing the Rules of Love (*DA* 2.8.41 [280]).

Not surprisingly, courteous language is particularly appropriate to courtship, an association developed especially in the Eighth Dialogue. In the debate over service through deeds or through words, the man claims that a courteous request by a suitor is preferable to silence (*DA* 1.6.518 [194]). Subsequently the woman qualifies his insistence as discourteous, however, in particular his unwillingness to accept without proof her claim that she is already bound by another love (*DA* 1.6.530 [198]). The man replies that he is only defending his own interests and that there is nothing discourteous about that (*DA* 1.6.535 [200]). A woman who has no intention of loving a given suitor should reject him with courteous words, according to the woman of the same dialogue, rather than keep him dangling (*DA* 1.6.525 [196]), a recommendation again reminiscent of Garin lo Brun that will later be repeated by the man (*DA* 1.6.558 [206]). On the other hand, a woman can gracefully and courteously invite even a silent suitor to love her, according to the woman, without compromising her own modesty (*DA* 1.6.516 [194]). Thus the principle of the woman's freedom of choice remains intact, provided proper attention be given to the social graces.

Although general approval of courteous behavior is expressed throughout the *De amore,* one objection is raised concerning it near the beginning of the Eighth Dialogue: the possibility that it may be used to mask less favorable intentions. That man is no friend, the man argues, who greets another with a smiling face and pleasant words but who offers him no concrete help in his hour of need. Likewise, having greeted a suitor with a pleasant reception and courteous words, a woman should not hide behind a pretext of piety to avoid making any concrete commitment to him (*DA* 1.6.414, 417 [162]). The problem raised is that of the giving of false hope, to which courtesy itself may contribute, according to the man. This problem was raised already by the woman of the Third Dialogue, but with a different emphasis. In her lesson on the art of love, she equates with behavior "less than courteous" the giving of false promises, and at the end of the dialogue she invokes this principle of courtesy in refusing to grant hope to the suitor (*DA* 1.6.159 [84], 164 [86]).

The numerous references to courtesy in the *De amore* make of it a significant secondary theme reflecting contemporary society and the vernacular literature. It is an important complement to military prowess and service, as in the courtly romances, and thus an essential constituent of nobility. It is called for in a variety of social situations, especially those involving the use of language, of which courtship is a prominent example. Except for the minor objection raised by the man of the Eighth Dialogue, courtesy is viewed throughout the treatise as a beneficial, noncontroversial virtue, and thus as one of the most positive consequences of love.

Wealth and generosity

The relationship of wealth and generosity to love is one of the most complex themes of the *De amore*. Unlike the social themes examined above, the discussion of this subject is not limited to certain chapters of the treatise, but extends to almost every part of it. The treatment of this theme also differs in that it makes significant use of clerical sources, classical and Christian, in addition to the courtly sources. This multiplicity of sources doubtless contributes to the complexity of a subject with many ramifications.

In all of these traditions, generosity is praised and avarice condemned. The Aristotelian concept of the liberal man was developed by Roman writers such as Cicero and Seneca, who were available to Andreas. The Bible also recommends generosity, which the Christian tradition associates with Christian charity. On the other hand, both the classical and Christian traditions also warn against prodigality, of which excessive generosity may be an important aspect.

It is the vernacular literature that places the greatest emphasis on generosity, also establishing a positive link between this virtue and sexual love. The troubadours were for the most part mercenary poets, dependent for their livelihood on the beneficence of noble patrons, whom they naturally exhort to be generous and to avoid avarice.[18] Transferring metaphorically this economic concept to the realm of sentiment, they encourage their respective ladies to love them not only as a reward for service but also as an act of generosity. In the courtly romances this theme is exemplified by the renowned generosity of King Arthur, illustrated especially in the conventional motif of the "rash boon," the binding promise to fulfill a request whose precise nature and content are not yet known.[19] The related theme of hospitality is also developed in the romances, whose protagonists are knights errant and thus have frequent occasion to accept the hospitality of others.[20] Prodigality does not become an issue in the vernacular tradition until very late, long after the *De amore*.[21]

Because of its idealism, the courtly vernacular literature hardly ever confronts problems posed by limitations in material wealth, much less the question of venal love, but these are significant subjects in the classical and Christian traditions. Ovid makes a number of wry comments on the advantages of wealth and the handicap of poverty in pursuing love affairs (*AA* 2.161–68, 255–86; *RA* 741–50), and he also offers lovers advice on how to limit the financial damage (*AA* 1.399–436). Venal love is strongly condemned by both classical wisdom and Christian morality, and the venality of women is an important theme in classic and Christian misogyny.

The complexity of this multiple tradition is fully reflected in the *De amore*. Throughout the treatise, the relationship of generosity to love is emphasized in terms generally reminiscent of the courtly vernacular literature. Unlike the vernacular literature, however, Andreas also devotes considerable attention to the relationship of love to wealth and poverty and to the question of venal love, drawing primarily on classical and Christian sources. This unusual juxtaposition of matters normally treated separately gives rise to some interesting and unexpected problems.

Numerous passages in the treatise stress the importance of generosi-

18. Köhler, "Reichtum"; Cropp, "L'Expression."

19. Frappier, "Le Motif"; cf. Köhler, *L'aventure,* pp. 26–42; Baldwin, *Aristocratic Life,* pp. 98–104.

20. Bruckner; Baldwin, *Aristocratic Life,* pp. 109–13.

21. Monson, Les *"Ensenhamens,"* pp. 78–79; Cropp, "L'Expression."

ty in relation to love, describing it often in negative terms, as the avoid-ance of avarice. The very first effect of love listed in Book One, Chapter Four, is that the true lover cannot be degraded with any avarice (*DA* 1.4.1 [38]). The lesson on the art of love in the Third Dialogue also be-gins with this subject, doubly emphasized, advising the man not only to reject avarice but also to abound in generosity (*DA* 1.6. 149 [82]). The first of the Precepts in the Fifth Dialogue recommends avoiding avarice like a noxious plague and embracing its opposite (*DA* 1.6.268 [116]). Book Two states that abundant generosity is important for maintaining love, and that moral worth is destroyed and love diminished by miserli-ness (*DA* 2.1.7–8 [226], 2.3.2 [230]). Rule X of the Rules of Love de-clares that love is habitually banished from the home of avarice (*DA* 2.8.45 [282]). The same image is expressed in slightly different terms in Chapters Two and Nine of Book One, the latter passage invoking the rule in question (*DA* 1.2.8 [36], 1.9.13 [216]). Even Book Three advo-cates generosity, equating it with "works" in the biblical dictum "Faith without works is dead" (*DA* 3.55–56 [302–4]; cf. James 2.20, 2.26).

In the dialogues the obligation to display generosity plays a role in the discussion of several other important topics: nobility, outward ap-pearance, the love of the clergy. In the debate on nobility in the Second Dialogue, when the woman objects that the commoner's business activ-ities are incompatible with his ambition of loving, he replies that he en-gages in business not to amass wealth, but solely to acquire the means with which to exercise his generosity. Convinced only in part, his oppo-nent allows that a tradesman may be worthy to love a woman of the middle class, but not a noblewoman like herself (*DA* 1.6.79 [62], 92–96 [66], 109 [70]). The man of the Eighth Dialogue having described him-self as a "generous giver," the woman asks for proof of this alleged gen-erosity and, calling attention to the man's shabby clothes, asks why he has not yet donated them to those less fortunate. To this the man replies that he has intentionally worn old clothing to illustrate the distinction between outward appearances and inner worth, and that it is precisely in favor of generosity to others that he has neglected his own wardrobe (*DA* 1.6.422, 424 [164], 427–30 [166]). Later in the dialogue the woman argues that the man, now a cleric, cannot engage in the generosity re-quired for love unless he steals the wherewithal from others. The man answers that God has admonished all men, clerics and laymen alike, to be generous; moreover, the woman's objection applies only to those clerics who have wholly renounced the world and its possessions, and on closer examination not even to them (*DA* 1.6.490, 494–95 [186])— apparently a sly witticism concerning the seriousness with which the clergy observes its vows of poverty.

The related theme of hospitality is discussed only briefly in the *De amore,* in the lesson of the Third Dialogue, which recommends that the lover readily proffer hospitality to all (*DA* 1.6.160 [84]). This principle is reaffirmed, albeit for his own benefit, by the Briton knight, who defends his right to sit at the king's table, but the doorman's insistence that this privilege is reserved for the knights assigned to the palace can only be taken as a negative example of hospitality (*DA* 2.8.23–24 [276]).

In addition to the many references to generosity in the literal sense, this notion is also invoked metaphorically regarding the granting of love, as in the troubadours. The verb *largiari* and the noun *largitio* are used fifty-six times to describe the "bestowing" of a woman's love, or at least the hope of it; this represents nearly one-half of all the occurrences of *largus* and its derivatives. In the debate of the First Dialogue concerning whether love or service should come first, the man, young and inexperienced, argues that it would be more to the woman's credit to give him her love as an act of pure generosity rather than as payment for past deeds. The woman answers that if this principle were accepted, it would put those who do good deeds at a disadvantage, contrary to Love's teaching (*DA* 1.6.51 [52], 54 [54]). In the Eighth Dialogue it is the woman who claims the right to exercise her generosity by bestowing her love on a man who serves her only through his deeds. The man replies with an allusion to Seneca to the effect that he who must ask more than once for a favor has bought it dearly; from this he concludes that the woman's love is owed to him, not only because of his deeds but also because of the asking. The woman answers that love is not a matter for commerce but a gratuitous act of generosity, forcing the man to admit that his earlier discussion of love in terms of obligation was merely figurative (*DA* 1.6.505 [190], 509, 512–15 [192], 519 [194]).

It is perhaps because of the danger of prodigality that Andreas often discusses generosity in negative terms, as an avoidance of avarice. Already in the second chapter of the treatise he warns against the threat of prodigality. The wise lover does not throw away riches like a wasteful steward, he declares, adding, however, that this should not be taken as an inducement to avarice. Rather, one should avoid prodigality by every means, while embracing generosity with both arms (DA 1.2.5–8 [36]). Book Three also warns against the deadly sin of prodigality, but with a difference: it is now presented as an inevitable result of love (DA 3.19–21 [292]).

The ambiguous relationship of love to material wealth is illustrated in the very first chapter of the De amore in the description of the many fears of the lover: if he is poor, he fears that the beloved may scorn his poverty; if he is rich, he perhaps fears that previous parsimony may be an obstacle (DA 1.1.4 [32]). The idea that the excessive amassing of wealth may be taken as a prima facie indication of avarice is reaffirmed implicitly in Book Two, Chapter Three, where this activity, along with the propensity to bring frivolous law suits, is listed among the factors causing love to decrease (DA 2.3.7 [232]). The same chapter gives a more detailed description of the process by which poverty also brings about a decrease in love. Directly or indirectly, the love of both partners is affected: the lover preoccupied with financial worries cannot devote proper attention to the development of his love (perhaps a failure to maintain an immoderata cogitatio with respect to the love object?); moreover, his sleep suffers and his appearance is altered, with the effect that he is almost inevitably cheapened in the eyes of the beloved (DA 2.3.1–2 [230]). Book One, Chapter Two, analyzes the same process in somewhat different terms: poverty plunges the lover into melancholy, making him irascible and altering his behavior toward the beloved, so that he becomes an object of fear, thus causing love to diminish (DA 1.2.5–7 [36]).

The melancholy of the impecunious lover and his preoccupation with financial matters are difficult to reconcile with another observation that recurs in several passages: lovers' relative indifference to material wealth. According to the second chapter of the treatise, the true lover would rather be despoiled of all his riches, deprived of everything that the human mind can imagine as necessary for living, rather than forgo his love (DA 1.2.3–4 [34–36]). The man of the Sixth Dialogue declares that without the woman's love he would regard an abundance of worldly possessions as the direst poverty, but that with it he would consider himself rich indeed, however poor materially (*DA* 1.6.282–83 [120]). Likewise, the man of the Seventh Dialogue affirms that to possess the woman's love would be to abound in all riches (*DA* 1.6.351 [140–42]). Book One, Chapter Nine, describes the plight of a deceived lover, to whom his most valuable possessions in the world appear a small price to pay for the expensive honor of a deceitful nod from the beloved (*DA* 1.9.15 [216]). Lovers who find themselves in this situation derive more pleasure from that which they are known to have given away than from that which they have retained for their own use (*DA* 1.9.4 [214]). Book Three includes in its description of the servitude of love the fact that there are no riches that could make the lover as happy as the enjoyment of his love, for if he gained the whole world but suffered the loss of his love, he would consider it all as the direst poverty, but as long as his love goes according to his wishes, he believes that no penury can harm him (*DA* 3.15–16 [290]). The lover's indifference to material wealth is closely related to his propensity to prodigality.

Poverty is not only a barrier to love, it is also one of its consequences. Book One, Chapter Two, paints a picture of lovers, indifferent to material considerations, who scatter their wealth and are reduced to the depths of poverty (*DA* 1.2.4 [36]). Chapter Nine describes a lover, captivated by a woman's guile, who is forced to steer his boat to the shores of poverty (*DA* 1.9.15 [216]). Among the arguments against love, Book Three cites the fact that it gives rise to hateful indigence and paves the way to the prison of poverty, forcing the lover to inevitable prodigality, which no abundance of possessions can satisfy, so that he is plunged into the depths of poverty, and there is no crime that he shrinks from committing to gain the riches with which to feed his love (*DA* 3.19–21 [292]). By causing deadly warfare, a later passage adds, love transforms abundant riches into wretched indigence, but without the benefit of any generosity on the part of the possessor (*DA* 3.43 [300]). And in the final summation, love is charged with devouring all wealth with its voracity (*DA* 3.115 [320]). If we compare these passages with those that describe the role of poverty in diminishing love, we arrive at a paradoxical circularity in the chain of causality: love causes poverty, which destroys love.

At the beginning of Book One, Chapter Six, "an abundance of riches" is listed among the five ways of acquiring love. Immediately afterward, however, Andreas expresses the personal opinion that this particular means to the desired end should be banished forever from Love's court, and he vows to give a fuller explanation later (*DA* 1.6.1–2 [40–42]). The promised discussion is found especially in Book One, Chapter Nine, "On Love Acquired by Money," but it also extends to Chapter Twelve, "On the Love of Prostitutes," and to several passages of Book Two.

The main message of Chapter Nine is that true love cannot be won by money or other gifts: coming only from affection of the heart, it is granted gratuitously out of pure generosity, and so it cannot be valued at any price nor cheapened by financial considerations (*DA* 1.9.1 [212]). As proof of this, Andreas cites the Rule of Love (X) according to which love and avarice cannot dwell in the same abode, with "avarice" applying here not to any lack of generosity on the part of the lover, but rather to the greed of a venal beloved (*DA* 1.9.13 [216]). Several indices are listed for recognizing a woman who desires not to love but to extract money: the recounting of the good deeds of someone who has showered gifts on his beloved, the praise of another lady's adornments, the complaint that some of her own possessions have been pawned, requests for jewelry under some verbal pretext (*DA* 1.9.12 [216]). The true character of such women becomes apparent once the money runs out, for then the lover becomes an object of contempt and hatred (*DA* 1.9.5 [214]). In discussing the recognition of reciprocal love, Book Two reiterates the idea that a love partner preoccupied with extracting possessions from the other is far removed from the affection of a lover, intent not on loving but on taking advantage of another's wealth (*DA* 2.5.9 [236]).

A woman really in love, according to Book One, Chapter Nine, always rejects and hates gifts from her lover, wishing rather to increase his wealth so that he may always have resources sufficient to gain praise through his generosity. She considers whatever he gives to others for her sake or in order to win praise as increasing her own wealth (*DA* 1.9.7 [214]). Thus the principle of serving all for the sake of one is extended to the virtue of generosity.

The competing principles of the lover's generosity and the beloved's avoidance of greed give rise to a problem concerning the role that financial considerations should play within the relationship. Andreas's approach to this problem is one of moderated compromise, with careful consideration given to the circumstances. Even if she is in severe financial straits, Chapter Nine declares, the woman who is really in love considers it a very serious matter to diminish her lover's wealth. It is no discredit to a women, however, in a time of urgent need to accept gifts from a lover and to take advantage of his generosity. The lover, for his part, should not allow the beloved to suffer from material want, if he is able to offer her any assistance. It would be very shameful for a lover enjoying abundant possessions to allow his partner to be gripped by any need. If, on the other hand, the woman has abundant wealth, she should be satisfied if her lover makes seemly gifts to others for her sake (*DA* 1.9.8–9 [214]).

Book Two lists among the causes that bring love to a resentful and ignominious end the failure of a lover with abundant resources to come to the aid of a partner suffering great financial hardship (*DA* 2.4.2 [232]). Similarly, the warning that a partner eager to take advantage of the other's possessions is not really in love is tempered by the restriction: "unless driven to this by the greatest personal material necessity" (*DA* 2.5.9 [236]).

Such financial contingencies are the subject of Case III of the Love Cases, which considers them in relation to the choice of a love partner. The question raised concerns which of two men exactly equal in birth, lifestyle, and character, but with great disparity of material wealth, should be chosen as a lover. The Countess of Champagne renders a complex decision that goes beyond the present case, taking into account not only the men's merit but also the financial circumstances of the woman. The first principle established is that it would be an injustice to prefer vulgar wealth to noble and decorous poverty. Indeed, noble poverty is preferable to noble wealth, provided the woman is wealthy, for it is more to her credit to help a meritorious poor man with her abundance than to bind herself to someone rich. If the woman herself is poor, however, she would do well to seek a rich lover, for if both lovers are beset with poverty the chances are slim that their love can survive (*DA* 2.7.9–12 [252–54]).

Case XXI raises the delicate question of the types of gifts that a lover can legitimately accept from a partner. Citing a number of examples, the Countess of Champagne gives as a general guideline the following rule: any small gift may be accepted that can be used for care of the body or cultivation of appearance, or that can serve as a remembrance of the partner, provided no suspicion of avarice can arise from its acceptance (*DA* 2.7.49 [268]).

Much of Book One, Chapter Nine, is devoted to the denunciation of venal women, who are compared to prostitutes. Indeed, they are worse than prostitutes, for the latter ply their trade openly and deceive no one, whereas the former falsely pose as fine ladies to beguile men and rob them of their wealth (*DA* 1.9.2–3 [212]). If a man's lust drives him to commerce with venal women, he would do better to frequent brothels, where he can procure the same services at a better price (*DA* 1.9.10–11 [214–16]). Book Two likewise condemns, and assimilates to prostitutes, women who offer themselves to men in the expectation of a gift (*DA* 2.6.37 [248]).

One of the chief indications that a woman is after a man's money, according to a remark often repeated, is delay in the granting of her favors. Chapter Nine states that venal women force men to languish for love in order to extract gifts from them (*DA* 1.9.3 [212]). Book Three declares that by their very nature women seek to enrich themselves, not granting their partners the solaces they desire. Having traveled the world and made many inquiries, Andreas has never met a man who knew of a woman who does not delay her favors until she has received a gift (*DA* 3.65–66 [306]).[22] Even after consummation, women withhold their customary solaces once the gifts stop flowing (*DA* 3.112 [320]).

It is doubtless in light of the notion of venal delay that we should interpret Case XIX of the Love Cases. A knight, having unsuccessfully sought the love of a lady, sends her presents, which she accepts, but without softening her attitude toward him. He complains that by accepting the presents she has given him the hope of her love, which she

---

22. Book Three also asserts that "a woman is unable to refuse gold, silver, other gifts, or to deny the consolations of her person on request" (*DA* 3.110 [320]), a claim hard to reconcile with the idea that all women delay their favors in the hope of a gift.

is now frustrating. The queen's judgment declares that the woman should either refuse the presents or repay them with the gift of love; otherwise she should be classified among the prostitutes (*DA* 2.7.45–46 [266–68]). Curiously, "prostitution" consists not in exchanging one's favors for a gift, but in withholding them.

A somewhat similar problem is raised in Book Two, Chapter Six, but without the complication of gifts. The question is whether a woman who has granted a lover hope or some other of the first three stages of love has the right to withhold the final stage. The Chaplain declares that a respectable woman should not delay her promises without good cause, for such deceit is typical of prostitutes (*DA* 2.6.34–35 [248]). Already in the Third Dialogue the woman refuses to give the man false hope on the grounds that it would be behavior worthy of prostitutes (*DA* 1.6.131–32 [76]). In both passages, as in Case XIX, false hope is equated with delay in granting favors, with an attendant presumption of venality.

It is interesting to compare these remarks with those of Book One, Chapter Ten, on favors too easily granted, the other means of acquiring love that Andreas summarily rejects. From this confrontation emerges a picture of the very delicate position in which a woman finds herself, according to the *De amore,* upon being solicited by a suitor. If she gives in too easily, it will be assumed that she is motivated by excessive carnal desire, with the further assumption that she is likely to be unfaithful to her lover with whoever else solicits her love. If, on the other hand, she holds out too long, it will be assumed that she is interested only in stringing the man along to get his money. In short, she is either a slut or a prostitute. There is perhaps no other feature of the treatise, including the anti-feminist diatribe of Book Three, that better illustrates the depths of the Chaplain's misogyny.

Life is not long enough, according to Chapter Nine, to recount all the misdeeds of venal women (*DA* 1.9.18 [218]). Although gratuitous love can rarely be found, because many women are degraded by their ardor for money, lovers should nevertheless exert all possible effort in search of a partner whose loyalty will not be altered by the onset of poverty or adversity (*DA* 1.9. 14 [216]). This slight possibility of finding a disinterested partner becomes a complete impossibility in the third book. The anti-feminist diatribe of Book Three devotes more space to the avarice of women than to any other single subject (*DA* 3.65–74 [306–8], 78–79, 81 [310], 105 [318], 110–12 [320]). In fact, it begins and ends with the discussion of this trait, presented as the ultimate explanation and proof of the assertion that no woman is capable of really loving. The discussion refers explicitly throughout to "all women," and Andreas twice reiterates the claim that there is no exception to the rule (§§ 72, 79).

In light of the Chaplain's earlier denunciation of venality, one might easily conclude that in his opinion there are no women (or, according to Chapter Nine, very few women) who are not prostitutes, or worse. In the same Chapter Nine, however, Andreas laments the fact that the honorable name of ladies is debased by the acts of prostitutes, and he challenges all ladies of high character to rise up in arms and defend their rights against the usurpation of unworthy women (*DA* 1.9.11 [216]). The chapter ends with a disclaimer: the Chaplain's intention is not at all to denigrate honorable women, who are the source of all good in the world, but rather to denounce the lives of those greedy women who do not blush to dishonor with their deeds the company of respectable women and to profane their service under a pretext of love (*DA* 1.9.19–20 [218]).

Andreas's attitude toward avowed prostitutes is somewhat ambiguous. He expresses a certain grudging respect for their frankness, as we have seen, by contrast with the falseness of those venal women who claim respectability. In Book Two he relates, on the authority of the Countess of Champagne, the opinion that if by some miracle a prostitute should fall in love, she is incapable of being unfaithful to her lover (*DA* 2.6.36 [248]).[23] In the chapter devoted to prostitutes, however, the Chaplain declares that they should be utterly avoided, for several reasons: because with them one always commits the sin of lewdness, because they rarely give themselves to anyone without receiving a gift, and

23. Curiously, this pronouncement is attributed to the countess's desire to call attention to the baseness of men who chase after prostitutes and to punish their experience. It is not obvious how the mention of this positive trait could have the desired effect; indeed, it could conceivably have the opposite effect of encouraging men to frequent prostitutes.

because one's reputation is likely to suffer from their association. This scholastic enumeration scarcely goes beyond the obvious, that men go to prostitutes precisely to commit acts of lewdness in exchange for gifts. Nevertheless, it illustrates the convergence of three distinct approaches to the subject: the moral, the practical (or economic), and the social. Returning briefly to his rhetorical frame, Andreas concludes with the observation that the favors of prostitutes can usually be obtained without much coaxing, so no instruction on this point is necessary (*DA* 1.12.1–2 [222]).

The numerous references in the *De amore* to wealth and generosity make these themes and their relationship to love a major preoccupation of the treatise. A complex subject with many ramifications, it draws on all the traditions available to the Chaplain, and many of its implications extend beyond the social sphere to the areas of psychology and morals. From the entire discussion an important conclusion emerges: the impossibility of separating love from the material and financial contingencies that surround it.

The point of departure for this discussion is the praise of generosity, based especially on the celebration of this quality in the vernacular love literature. Unlike the troubadours, however, Andreas considers the possibility of excessive generosity leading to financial ruin, with disastrous results for the love relationship. Following Ovid, the Chaplain warns against the wiles of venal women, but he also attempts to reconcile the caution that must be exercised in this regard with the imperative of generosity, arriving at a moderate and circumstantial discussion of the role of financial considerations within the love relationship. Nevertheless, in certain passages, especially in Book Three, the mild, urbane misogyny of an Ovid gives way to the virulent anti-feminism of the clergy, resulting in a discourse of excess in which "woman" becomes more or less synonymous with "prostitute."

Reputation

As the external, public projection of inner worth, reputation plays an important role in the social dynamics of any culture, but in none more so than in the courtly culture of the Middle Ages reflected in the vernacular love literature. The "service" that the troubadours devote to their ladies includes singing the ladies' praises, thus making their worth known to all. Also concerned for their own reputation, the troubadours generally "signed" their love songs, unlike the usually anonymous epic poetry of the same period, so that their poems served as proof of their own moral, sentimental, and aesthetic excellence. The importance of this concept in troubadour culture is illustrated by the Old Provençal expression *pretz e valor,* in which *valor* signifies inner worth, *pretz* the public projection of that worth in terms of reputation.[24] This theme is also represented negatively in the troubadour lyric by the *lauzengiers,* the "flatterers" or "slanderers" whose rivalry with the poet threatens the reputation of the lovers, forcing them to use the utmost discretion to avoid the revelation of their love.[25] In the courtly romances, the reputation gained through deeds of chivalry represents public endorsement of the hero's merit and often provides the basis for winning or re-winning love. In the romances of Chrétien de Troyes such renown is associated with a new identity for the hero, that of the Knight with the Lion, for example, whose reputation for valor redeems the fault of Yvain, or that of the Knight of the Cart, whose single-minded pursuit of love ignores conventional notions of reputation, thus creating a new, higher standard of merit.

In the *De amore* the references to reputation abound, especially in the dialogues, but also throughout the treatise. The noun *fama,* "fame, reputation," and its contrary, *infamia,* occur altogether 44 times. The verb *reputare,* "to think, to consider," is attested 42 times, generally expressing a value judgment concerning a given mode of behavior. The theme of reputation is also conveyed by many of the references to "glory" *(gloria)* or to "honor" *(honor),* which, along with their derivatives, are found respectively 30 and 61 times. The term used most frequently to evoke this theme is *laus,* "praise," which, including its derivatives, occurs 135 times, often expressing a favorable opinion regarding particular behavior, as in the expression "praiseworthy deeds" *(facta laudabilia).*

The treatment in the *De amore* of the theme of reputation corre-

---

24. Schutz; Cropp, *Le Vocabulaire,* pp. 426–32.
25. Monson, "Les Lauzengiers."

sponds closely to that observed in the vernacular love literature. As in that literature, it is closely intertwined with all of the various other social themes discussed above, typically as the public projection of inner values. In a few passages, however, it relates rather to certain of the moral questions to be examined in the next chapter.

Reputation plays an important role, first of all, in the discussion of nobility. In the introduction to the Third Dialogue, in which Andreas intervenes personally to resolve the question of loving across class boundaries, reputation is the decisive factor in his opinion, impinging on the matter in two different ways. The Chaplain's primary concern is for the reputation of the woman of the higher nobility who loves a commoner: even among the common people this is considered lowering and demeaning, for she is presumed to suffer from an excessive abundance of pleasure. This suspicion can be dispelled, however, provided the commoner's reputation for worth is sufficiently established (*DA* 1.6.119 [74]). In the Sixth Dialogue the woman of the middle class expresses concern that her own reputation would suffer, if ever it came to the attention of the common folk that she had transgressed the natural limits of her class by accepting the suit of a man of the higher nobility (*DA* 1.6.292 [122–24]). The woman of the Seventh Dialogue also invokes this theme in reminding the man of the higher nobility of the special obligations incumbent on members of his class: their reputation is more harmed by boorishness or failure to perform good deeds, she claims, than is that of those less elevated (*DA* 1.6.330 [134]).

In the *De amore* as in the courtly romances, reputation is associated especially with good deeds, which enhance the fame of both the man who performs them and the woman who inspires them. Reputation provides the chief vehicle by which the suitor's service can become known to the beloved, and thus can be rewarded. The young man of the First Dialogue speaks of the great honor that will accrue to the woman for teaching him to be worthy of her love, but she rejects him in favor of one more experienced, on the grounds that he who does more good deeds should receive greater honor (*DA* 1.6.53–54 [54]). In the Third Dialogue the woman objects that she has not heard of any good deeds that redound to the man's glory, for, she reminds him, great fame is required of him who seeks the love of a noblewoman (*DA*

1.6.145 [80]). In the Fifth Dialogue the man offers himself as a servant to the woman's glory, and she acknowledges that his reputation is such that it would not be to her own honor to refuse his service (*DA* 1.6.199 [96], 204 [98]). The man of the Eighth Dialogue claims that all the words and deeds of good men are devoted entirely to the praise of women and that only by performing deeds in the service of women can the men themselves be accounted worthy of praise (*DA* 1.6.405 [158]). In Case XV of the Love Cases, Ermengarde of Narbonne declares that that woman is unworthy of any honor who abandons her lover after he has been injured in battle (*DA* 2.7.36 [264]).

Reputation is sometimes mentioned in connection with courtesy (*DA* 1.6.143 [80], 330 [134]), more often in relation to wealth and generosity. Women must encourage men, according to the woman of the Eighth Dialogue, to make sure that their own reputations are not blackened by parsimony (*DA* 1.6.410 [160]). Later in the same dialogue the man argues that the fame of those who neglect their own interests to care for the needs of others should be spread abroad through praise (*DA* 1.6.430 [166]). Chapter Nine states that a woman really in love wants her lover to increase his wealth so that he can gain fame through his generosity, and that greedy women are dishonored by their avarice (*DA* 1.9.7 [214], 14 [216]). Chapter Twelve lists loss of reputation among the arguments against frequenting prostitutes (*DA* 1.12.2 [222]).

Associated primarily with the social virtues, reputation is also invoked in connection with moral considerations. According to the woman of the Eighth Dialogue, a virgin soon loses her honor, and her reputation is ruined by a slight rumor; repudiation by a husband who discovers her loss of virginity may lead to total disgrace, making her an object of contempt for all (*DA* 1.6.452 [174], 467 [178]). Men, too, have reason to fear loss of reputation, not only from frequenting prostitutes, as we have seen, but also from loving nuns (*DA* 1.8.1 [210]). These arguments are taken up again and developed in Book Three: men and women (especially the latter), clerics and laymen, all risk the loss of their good name by engaging in love and forsaking chastity (*DA* 3.24–28 [294], 34–35 [296], 115 [320], 118 [322]).

Since love itself may be a cause for scandal, lovers cannot be content with advancing their reputation through positive actions such as service or generosity; they must also take care to avoid the revelation of their relationship. Discussed extensively by Ovid (*AA* 1.488–90; 2.389–96, 602–40; 3.483–98, 611–58) as well as by the troubadours, the discretion that lovers must employ to conceal their love also constitutes an important theme in the *De amore*. In certain passages this theme is related to the threat to the lovers' reputation posed by "slanderers" *(maledici)*, quite obviously calqued on the vernacular *lauzengiers*. In other passages it is associated with the Ovidian figures of the go-between or the confidant (cf. *AA* 1.351–74; 2.251–60; *Amores* 1.8, 11), developed especially in the *Pamphilus* and in the *Facetus* (vv. 168–204), but only occasionally in the vernacular love poetry.[26]

The importance of discretion in love affairs is stressed throughout the treatise. Near the beginning of Book One, Chapter Six, Andreas argues that wisdom is preferable to beauty in a love partner, since wise lovers are better able to keep their love a secret, without which it cannot long endure (*DA* 1.6.4–6 [42], 12 [44]). In Book Two the very first requirement listed for the preservation of love is the obligation to ensure that it is kept secret, and the publication of a love relationship is cited among the ways in which it generally comes to an end (*DA* 2.1.1–2 [224], 2.4.2 [232]).[27] This claim is consecrated by one of the Rules of Love: "XIII. Love divulged rarely endures" (*DA* 2.8.46 [282]). In Love Case XXI, the Countess of Champagne advises lovers who have received a ring from their partner to wear it with the stone on the inside of the hand, because all lovers are bound to keep their love a secret (*DA* 2.7.50 [268]). In Book Three the Chaplain asserts that women are totally unable to keep a secret (*DA* 3.70 [308], 102–3 [316–18]), which presumably means that a true and lasting love relationship with them is impossible.

26. Walsh (p. 35, n. 11) cites Cercamon, *Ab lo temps qe's fai refreschar* (P.-C. 112, 1b), vv. 43ff. *(messatges),* and Bernart de Ventadorn, *Can vei la flor, l'erba vert e la folha* (P.-C. 70, 42), vv. 50ff. *(mo messatger).* These are just two examples of jongleurs called upon in the *tornadas* of *cansos* to deliver the message to the lady by performing the song, thus assuming a de facto function of go-between. See Paden.

27. Book Two also claims, however, that love increases if, on being divulged, it happens to endure; normally it does not endure once it is made public, but disappears entirely (*DA* 2.2.3 [228]).

The principle of discretion in love affairs plays a role in several discussions in the dialogues. When the man of the Sixth Dialogue asks the woman whether her heart is set on another, she refuses to answer, citing the law of love and the custom of lovers (*DA* 1.6.302–3 [126]). In the Seventh Dialogue the man argues that it is preferable that lovers be separated by a great distance, for it is thus easier to keep their love a secret; she rejects this argument, however, affirming that the concealment of a love affair depends more on the wise and discreet behavior of the lovers than on the distance that separates them (*DA* 1.6.364–65 [144]). When the woman of the Eighth Dialogue cites as an argument against loving the danger that love poses for the reputation of virgins, the man replies that if she takes care to love prudently, choosing a prudent and discreet man as her lover, her secret will be preserved and her modesty will not suffer (*DA* 1.6.452–53 [174]). Later in the same dialogue the man argues that if the woman keeps him dangling too long, he will not be able to refrain from haunting the place where she is, with disastrous results for their reputation (*DA* 1.6.523–24 [196]). When the woman claims to be already bound by another love, the man tries to quibble about whether she is *suitably* bound by the other relationship, to which she replies that he must take her word for it, because Love's tradition teaches that no one should reveal the secret of his love (*DA* 1.6.526–30 [196–98]). At the end of the dialogue, the woman cites the danger of "evil suspicions," that is, concern for her reputation and that of her opponent, as a reason for bringing their discussion to a close (*DA* 1.6.560 [206]).

It is first of all with respect to the "common folk" *(vulgus)*, to "ordinary people" *(vulgares)*, that the lovers' discretion must be exercised to avoid "divulging" *(vulgare, divulgare)* their love. The *De amore* contains numerous references to public opinion and to the potential threat that it poses for the lovers' reputation. The fear of "common gossip" *(vulgi rumores)* is cited in the very first chapter of the treatise among the many fears of the lover (*DA* 1.1.3 [32]). In the Second Dialogue the man of the middle class invokes public opinion in defending his business activities, and he asks of the noblewoman only those favors that can be granted without arousing common gossip (*DA* 1.6.93–95 [66], 99 [68]). In the introduction to the Third Dialogue it is the opinion of the common folk that dictates that a woman of the higher nobility can give her love without reproach to a commoner only if he enjoys the highest reputation for good character (*DA* 1.6.119 [74]). The woman of the Sixth Dialogue, a commoner, voices the apprehension that her reputation might be damaged if the common folk learned that she had transgressed the boundaries of her class by loving a man of the higher nobility; the man responds by ridiculing the notion of a love consummated before the common folk (*DA* 1.6.292, 294 [122–24]). The man of the Eighth Dialogue, a cleric, argues that it is not in God's eyes, but only in the opinion of the common folk, that the clergy are considered disgraced by minor failings such as loving (*DA* 1.6.492 [186]). He later invokes the calumnies of the common folk in urging the woman not to delay too long the granting of her favors (*DA* 1.6.524 [196]).

Public opinion is not the only concern of discreet lovers: a more active threat to their reputation comes from "slanderers" *(maledici)*. This subject is developed especially in the Sixth and Seventh Dialogues, in terms reminiscent of the *lauzengiers* denounced by the troubadours. The man of the Sixth Dialogue answers the woman's concerns for her reputation with the argument that to refrain from loving because of the slander of the wicked is to give an easy victory to those whose purpose is to impede the actions of good men and to oppose the consolation of lovers. The woman acknowledges this threat, but reserves the right to exercise her freedom of choice, which the man in turn acknowledges, still insisting, however, that it is a grave injustice to cheat a worthy suitor of his just reward because of baseless suspicions and the actions of evil men. The faithful lover should not be rejected, he adds, on the pretext that some only pretend to love, for it is most unfair to charge one man with the sins of another (*DA* 1.6.294–95 [124], 299–301 [126]). In the Seventh Dialogue the woman responds to the man's initial praise with an admonition to avoid praising or blaming anyone excessively, thus giving rise to an extended discussion of praise and blame. The man will continue to sing the woman's praises so long as she deserves it, ceasing to do so only if her merit ceases, and even then he would refrain from blaming her. Nevertheless, she would still have to contend with the slanderers, who have no scruples about spreading bad reports and whose meat and drink it is to ruin other people's reputation. The woman replies that it is impossible to keep the slanderers from disseminating their evil stories; rather than attempting to correct them, one should spurn their company, relying on a clear conscience to preserve one's reputation. The man denies any wish to burden the woman with the correction of the slanderers, his only concern being that her deeds should continue to show her as she truly is, thus confounding the gossip-mongers (*DA* 1.6.328, 332–33 [134–36], 340–41, 345 [138–40]).

Not only must lovers defend their reputation against slanderers, they must be especially careful not to emulate them. The lesson on the art of love in the Third Dialogue includes the injunction never to utter a word of disparagement against anyone, for slanderers cannot remain within the threshold of courtesy (*DA* 1.6.151 [82]). Several of the Precepts of Love condemn the activities of the *lauzengiers*, especially Precept IX, *Maledicus esse non debes*, but also Precept III, which warns against attempting to subvert established love relationships, and Precept X, which counsels not to denounce lovers, and perhaps even Precept V, which prohibits lying (*DA* 1.6.268–69 [116]). The man of the Seventh Dialogue declares that one should disparage neither good nor bad men, for in the eyes of the prudent such behavior does not harm the reputation of the disparaged but only that of the disparager (*DA* 1.6.332 [134–36]). This principle is repeated in Book Three (*DA* 3.76 [310]). Book Three also insists at length that all women are slanderers (*DA* 3.70, 75–77 [308–10], 100–101 [316]), which points once again to the conclusion that they cannot be worthy lovers.

The obligation to employ discretion in love affairs gives rise to a potential conflict with respect to another principle enunciated in the *De amore,* the promotion of the beloved's reputation through service, in particular through the verbal service of praise. This conflict is examined in two passages of Book Two, with special attention given to the problem posed by the *lauzengiers.*

In the first chapter of the Second Book, praising one's partner is listed among the prescriptions for maintaining love, but with the provision that only moderate praise should be used, avoiding verbose and repeated recollections of her. The passage goes on to recommend other measures of discretion, including the admonition to haunt only rarely the place where the beloved is and to refrain from physical signs when encountering her in the company of others. Indeed, lovers should treat each other in public as strangers, lest someone spying on their love obtain material for malicious gossip, and they should exchange nods only if no one is watching (*DA* 2.1.5–6 [224]).

In the first of the Love Cases, a man who has been enjoined by his beloved to refrain from singing her praises in public subsequently defends her reputation against the malicious gossip of slanderers, whereupon she declares that he has lost her love forever by disobeying her command. The Countess of Champagne rules that the man has not acted improperly in refuting the gossipmongers, and that the woman's demands were excessive (*DA* 2.7.1–5 [250–52]). By contrast, the knight of Case XVIII, having revealed the secrets of his love with no attenuating circumstances, is barred forever from loving by the ladies of the court of Gascony, with the same punishment decreed for any woman who breaks the ban (*DA* 2.7.43–44 [266]).

The discretion of lovers does not exclude recourse to a "confidant" *(secretarius)* and "messenger" or "go-between" *(nuntius, internuntius),* but it does place certain restrictions on their use. The lover's first reaction to the suffering of love, according to the first chapter of the treatise, is to look for a "helper" *(iuvamen)* or a go-between (*DA* 1.1.11 [34]). Book Two cites among the indications that the love of one's partner is waning the fact that she avoids the lover's messenger, that she refrains from sending her own messenger to him, or that her messenger becomes lax about delivering her messages (*DA* 2.5.3 [234]). On the other hand, Precept VI states that one should not have many people privy *(secretarios)* to one's love affair (*DA* 1.6.268 [116]). This precept is quoted almost verbatim by the man of the Sixth Dialogue, and the woman of the Eighth Dialogue alludes to it (*DA* 1.6.294 [124], 530 [198]).

The conflict between the requirement of discretion and the use of helpers is adjudicated by Andreas himself in Book Two, Chapter Six. The question arises in relation to the submission of disputes between lovers to the judgment of the ladies, as in the Love Cases of the following chapter, a practice that apparently contravenes the principle of discretion. The Chaplain decrees that a given love affair can legitimately be revealed to three other persons: a confidant for each of the partners and a go-between on whom they mutually agree. In case of conflict between the lovers, these helpers should present the case anonymously to the ladies for judgment, thus preserving the secrecy of the relationship (*DA* 2.6.32–33 [246–48]). The Countess of Champagne reiterates in Case XXI the principle of submitting love disputes anonymously for judgment, for the sake of confidentiality (*DA* 2.7.51 [270]).

The use of confidants and go-betweens gives rise to certain problems that are discussed in the Love Cases. Case XIV concerns a woman whose lover stayed away for a long while on an expedition overseas, whereupon she, despairing of his return, took another lover. Chastised by the first lover's confidant, the woman defended her action, citing among other arguments the fact she had received neither letter nor messenger from the abandoned lover, although there was no lack of messengers. The Countess of Champagne rules against the woman on the grounds that the first lover's absence was motivated by a most praiseworthy reason (presumably military service, such as a crusade),[28] and that nothing should give a woman in love greater joy than to hear the praises of her lover resound from distant lands. Moreover, the lover acted with great prudence, the countess finds, in refraining from sending letters or messengers, given the requirement to keep the love secret and the danger that it might be divulged through the wickedness of the messenger or through his death (*DA* 2.7.31–34 [262]). In short, for reasons of confidentiality, the public message of the lover's reputation should be substituted for the much more compromising private exchange of letters between the love partners.

In Case XXI the Countess of Champagne again addresses the problem of confidentiality in correspondence, recommending that lovers refrain from signing their love letters and from stamping them with their seal, unless they have a secret seal known only to themselves and to their confidants (*DA* 2.7.51 [270]). This problem is also of concern both to Ovid and to the troubadours, although they propose other solutions. Ovid recommends that love letters be written by the hand of a slave, that lovers learn different styles of handwriting, that feminine grammatical forms be used for male correspondents, that messages be writ-

---

28. The expression *ultramarina expeditio* probably refers to the Crusades, since *Ultramare* was often used in the Middle Ages to designate the Holy Land. Walsh (p. 262, n. 41) associates this case with the Crusades, pointing out a mention in Ordericus Vitalis of the threat made by the wives of crusaders to remarry if their husbands did not hasten to return.

ten in the bath and hidden in a confidant's clothing or on her person, that milk be used to write invisible messages, to become visible upon the application of charcoal, and so on (*AA* 2.395–96; 3.483–98, 619–30). For the love songs of the troubadours, which function as a kind of love letter with the jongleur serving as go-between, confidentiality is assured, at least fictionally and symbolically, by the use of code names *(senhals)* to refer to the beloved.

Case XVI tells of a knight who, unable to converse freely with his beloved, engaged a confidant to act as a go-between and court the lady for him, by which means he hoped to ensure the secrecy of the relationship. The confidant, however, courted the lady for himself and succeeded in winning her love. The Countess of Champagne, with the aid of a court of sixty ladies, declares that the treacherous confidant and the woman who has basely accepted him deserve each other, but that both should be excluded forever from the love of anyone else and, indeed, from the company of knights and ladies (*DA* 2.7.37–40 [264]). This case illustrates especially well the ambiguous relationship of confidants and go-betweens to the problem of discretion: although such helpers can serve to safeguard the secrecy of a love affair, they can also imperil the confidentiality—and indeed the integrity—of a relationship.

From the preceding remarks the theme of reputation emerges as one of the most pervasive of the social themes treated in the *De amore*. In fact, it is intimately connected with all the other social themes, assuming the function of an external, public projection of inner worth. It is through the lover's reputation that his nobility of character, his deeds and service, his courtesy and generosity, can be recognized by his social milieu and, coming to the attention of his beloved, be suitably rewarded.

According to Andreas, reputation is a two-sided value: an attribute not only to be acquired through positive action but also to be safeguarded through defensive measures. Paradoxically, love, which is the source of all the social virtues, and thus ultimately of reputation, is also potentially a major cause of loss of reputation. Hence the importance accorded in the treatise to discretion and secrecy in the conducting of love affairs.

The confidentiality of a love relationship does not depend solely on the prudence of the lovers. By virtue of its eminently social character, the defense of the lovers' reputation involves them in interaction with two other types of personages with strong literary antecedents, in addition to a general, diffused notion of "public opinion": adversaries, in the form of slanderers, and helpers, namely confidants and go-betweens. From this interaction arise the only controversies associated with the generally noncontroversial subject of reputation: the conflict between defending the beloved's reputation against slanderers and maintaining the secrecy of the relationship, or the paradox of confiding one's love to helpers as a means of ensuring confidentiality. The subject of confidants and go-betweens also provides the only significant incursion of the Ovidian tradition into a discussion largely dominated by the influence of the vernacular love literature.

Less controversial than the moral questions to be examined in the next chapter, the social themes of the *De amore* have received much less attention from the critics. Nevertheless, they constitute one of the major focuses of the treatise, as the preceding discussion demonstrates. The treatment of social questions is especially concentrated in the dialogues, but it also extends well beyond them, involving every part of the work. The point of departure for Andreas's consideration of social issues is the question of nobility and social class, around which the dialogues are organized. From this initial focus, several other important subjects are drawn into the discussion: deeds and service, wealth and generosity, courtesy and reputation. These social values are all closely interrelated, for it is through service, courtesy, and generosity that one acquires nobility of character, of which reputation is the public expression.

Whereas the Chaplain's examination of love psychology and physiology is primarily descriptive in nature, and thus subsumed under the generic vector that we have called *scientia,* the treatment of social questions is essentially prescriptive. This does not exclude, of course, the existence of certain descriptive elements, such as the discussion of the effect of poverty in diminishing love, which also concerns the realm of psychology. In terms of the other generic vectors that we have distinguished, the prescriptive thrust of Andreas's treatment of social matters is somewhat ambiguous, relating especially to *ars,* but without excluding *sapientia.*

The five ways of acquiring love listed at the beginning of Chapter Six include worth of character, of which nobility of character is presented as a functional equivalent (*DA* 1.6.13–15 [44]). Since the other social virtues of service, courtesy, and generosity are all constituents of nobility, they too should be seen above all as a means to the desired end. As for reputation, its practical, instrumental role is clear from the fact that it provides the bridge between the social virtues and their reward.

At the same time, the Chaplain appears to be concerned with establishing this complex set of social values as an end in itself, as a self-contained, secular ethical system, based on the refinement and sublimation of the sexual love that inspires it, parallel and complementary to Christian morality. The effectiveness of the social virtues as a means of acquiring love depends on the degree to which the lovers, especially the women, recognize this system of values and apply it to the decisions of their love life. It is clear from the discussion that Andreas would like lovers to recognize and apply these values, thus justifying the marked preference that he himself expresses for this particular means to the desired end. In addition to this secular ethical thrust, social questions such as venal love and prostitution also have important implications for Christian morality.

The theme of nobility provides the most important controversy relating to social matters, the conflict between the egalitarian tendencies of the troubadours and the greater class consciousness of the northern French courts. Several controversies more limited in significance and scope are raised in connection with the other social themes: the question whether love or service should precede the other; the conflict between the lover's generosity and the beloved's avoidance of greed; that between preserving the secrecy of a relationship and defending the beloved against slanderers. For all these questions Andreas seeks the middle ground of a reasonable compromise, in which he is generally successful. This does not prevent him from adopting in Book Three an extreme position with respect to many social questions, arguing that love is a servitude, that it inevitably destroys wealth and reputation, and that no woman is able to love, since all are greedy, are slanderers, and are unable to keep a secret.

The relative lack of controversy surrounding the social issues raised in the *De amore* reflects the relative homogeneity of the sources used for this part of the discussion. Only the subject of wealth brings into play the full panoply of courtly and clerical authorities evident elsewhere in the treatise. Otherwise, except for the influence of the Ovidian tradition regarding the subject of confidants and go-betweens, the social debate is dominated by the contemporary, courtly sources, especially the vernacular love literature.

The social themes and their treatment provide what is probably the best evidence of the influence exercised by vernacular poetry in the creation of Andreas's Latin scholastic treatise. At the same time, the Chaplain's largely successful efforts to compile, elucidate, and systematize the diffuse and fleeting social references and evocations of vernacular poetry constitute one of the major achievements of the *De amore*.

8 ❀

LOVE AND THE MORAL ORDER

Courtly Values and Christian Ethics

In *any society,* love between the sexes has significant moral implications and raises important moral problems; in none more so than in the Christian society of the Middle Ages. Throughout the period, the clergy of the Christian Church struggled, more or less successfully depending on time and place, to impose on secular society the ideals of sexual austerity inherited from the Fathers. As a member of the clergy, Andreas Capellanus was not indifferent to the requirements of Christian morality regarding sexual love, despite the obvious influence on his treatise of the secular, courtly circles in which he also moved. The shock between these two distinct, often antagonistic cultures in which the Chaplain participated doubtless forms the most important single focus of interest in his work.

The moral problems that it poses constitute the aspect of the *De amore* that has received the most attention from the critics. This subject is generally addressed globally, in terms of whether Andreas was for or against sexual love: whether he really meant to promote it in the first two books, whether he was sincere in rejecting it in Book Three, how and to what degree these two apparently antithetical thrusts of his discourse can be reconciled. The matter is more complex, however, than a simple dichotomy between "for" and "against" would indicate. Long before his rejection of love in the third book, the Chaplain had undertaken in the first two books a systematic effort to accommodate the troubadours' secular love ethic to the standards of Christian morality.

This effort, which included several separate strands, deserves a more detailed examination.

As previously observed, the moral questions raised by love are often intertwined with psychological or social considerations. Certain of the psychological questions treated, such as that of "excessive abundance of pleasure," are really moral problems in disguise. We have also seen that Andreas's treatment of social themes gives rise to a self-contained secular ethic based on the social value of love. The focus of the present chapter will be morality in a narrower sense, limited essentially to Christian morality. Even within this narrow focus, the Chaplain's approach to love and morals involves several components other than the straightforward rejection of love. It includes the Christianization of the secular love ethic of the vernacular literature, as well as various attempts to limit sexual activity within love relationships between the sexes. Also included in our discussion will be social questions, such as love and marriage or love and the clergy, in which Christian morality plays a major role.

The Christian tradition obviously provides a major source for this part of the Chaplain's doctrine. This includes the Bible and the Fathers, contemporary canonists and theologians, and many Christian commonplaces. The other major source for this part of the work is the vernacular love poetry of the troubadours and trouvères, whose secular love ethic is systematically opposed to the teachings of Christian morality. The opposition is not total, however, for without abandoning the sensuality of physical love that provides their initial inspiration, the troubadours manage to incorporate into their love conceptions a high degree of sublimation and idealization, including many Christian elements. It is thus at least conceivable that, unlike the urbane, cynical hedonism of an Ovid, their secular love ethic could be reconciled with Christianity. This is apparently the challenge that Andreas takes up in the first two books of his treatise, before finally rejecting love in Book Three. This entire effort, including both of its antithetical components, must be viewed together as forming the major constituent of the generic vector that we have called *sapientia*.

Love and virtue

One of the most important and original aspects of the poetry of the troubadours is their tendency to idealize physical love between the sexes. Even such a critic of the notion of "courtly love" as E. Talbot Donaldson recognizes in their works a general propensity to what he calls "sublimation" of the sexual instinct.[1] The claim made by Bernart de Ventadorn that love, even (or perhaps especially) unrequited, makes him a better person (*Chantars no pot gaire valer* [P.-C. 70, 15], vv. 13–16) is repeated by many later colleagues. Recognizing the social and moral excellence of the beloved and their own temerity in placing their aim so high, the troubadours nevertheless maintain that love inspires in them an emulation through which they hope and expect to become worthy of their lady.

The troubadours usually develop in general terms the idea of moral amelioration through love, as in the passage cited above. Given the generally secular tone of most early troubadour poetry, this ambiguous theme can be most readily interpreted along the lines of a secular social ethic, like that which we saw in the last chapter. However, a Christian interpretation, based on the frequent use of religious imagery in the same poetry, is also possible.[2] In the more explicit northern French romances, the deeds of service performed by knightly protagonists in the pursuit of love often take on markedly Christian overtones. An early example is the *pitié* ("pity"/"piety") that inspires Yvain in many later episodes of Chrétien de Troyes's *Chevalier au lion,* already foreshadowed by the Christian symbolism of the lion and the serpent in the scene from which the romance takes its name. This literary trend, reflecting an important religious influence in the formation of the social consciousness of the knightly class, will be expressed directly in the treatises on chivalry of the thirteenth century.

The view of love as a source of moral improvement plays a significant role in the *De amore,* which develops it in terms reminiscent of the vernacular love literature. Indeed, it is the most important justification

1. Donaldson, p. 163.
2. Scheludko; Gay-Crosier.

the treatise presents for love between the sexes. Frequently Andreas's treatment of this theme shows much of the ambiguity observed in the troubadours. In certain passages, however, he displaces the emphasis toward a Christian interpretation of the courtly love ethic, sometimes going well beyond the Christianizing trend of the romances.

In discussing the effects of love in Book One, Chapter Four, Andreas exclaims: "O what a wonderful thing is love, which makes a man shine with so many virtues and teaches everyone, no matter who he is, so many good traits of character!" (*DA* 1.4.1 [38]). In naming "virtue" (*virtus*) as the principal effect of love, the Chaplain employs a term that is notoriously difficult and ambiguous. In its etymological sense, still current in the Middle Ages, it evokes manly virtues such as strength or courage. *Virtus* is often found in the *De amore* in this sense: to refer to the strength and courage of falcons and kestrels, symbols of military valor (*DA* 1.6.82 [62], 100 [68], 122 [74]); to indicate the same qualities in the footman bested by the Briton knight of the Arthurian tale (*DA* 2.8.28 [276]); to signify the strength of Samson, lost through the wiles of a woman (*DA* 3.88 [312]). On the other hand, the same term can also designate moral excellence in a more general sense, including specifically Christian virtues. These usages also occur fairly frequently in the treatise: for example, in a passage of Book Three (*DA* 3.24–25 [294]) that opposes systematically the antithetical notions of virtue and "vice" (*vitium*).

The moral thrust of Andreas's discourse is conveyed ambiguously by the frequent use of the term *probitas,* "goodness, worth, uprightness, honesty." Together with its opposite, *improbitas,* it occurs more than 150 times. Although the two expressions *nobilitas morum* and *probitas morum* are used by the Chaplain as more or less equivalent in their denotation, they carry very different connotations: the former emphasizes the concept's social aspect, while the latter stresses its moral dimension. Of the two expressions, the treatise gives much more relief to *probitas morum,* not only through its greater frequency, but also thanks to the strategic position that it occupies. At the beginning of Book One, Chapter Six, *morum probitas* is named among five ways of acquiring love, and in the subsequent discussion it is stipulated as the only one of the five ways really worthy of succeeding in this enterprise (*DA* 1.6.1

[40–42], 15 [44]). This principle is later formalized in the Rules of Love: "XVIII. Good character alone makes a man worthy of love" (*DA* 2.8.46 [282]).

The theme of moral amelioration through love, proclaimed especially in Book One, Chapter Four, can be interpreted first in terms of the secular social ethic examined in the last chapter. The term *virtus* is sometimes used with reference to the essentially social virtues composing that ethic: the virtues of generosity (*DA* 2.1.7 [226]), courtesy (*DA* 2.7.29 [260]), even nobility (*DA* 1.6.91 [64], 97 [66]) are all invoked in the course of the treatise. At the same time, such social virtues as generosity and service to others can also be assimilated to Christian charity. Andreas's principle of service to all women for the sake of one appears to be modeled on the Gospel admonition to serve one's fellowmen for the love of God. Even the notion of "good deeds" is not without Christian resonances.

One passage establishes an explicit parallel between the "good works" inspired by Christian charity and those springing from love between the sexes. Referring to I Corinthians 13.3, the woman of the Sixth Dialogue declares that whatever good a man may do in this world, it avails him nothing without charity. By the same token, she could devote herself to the acts and works of love, but this would not bring her love's rewards, because it would not come from the heart (*DA* 1.6.320 [132]).[3]

The Chaplain's efforts to Christianize the secular love ethic of the vernacular literature are most apparent in the lesson on the art of love proposed by the woman of the Third Dialogue. In several cases the point of departure for this development is one of the social virtues, but the treatment of the subject displaces the emphasis in the direction of a Christian interpretation. In other cases Andreas introduces matters decidedly Christian in origin, with no secular counterpart.

In advising the man to give generously, the woman discusses the appropriate recipients of his generosity, making two rather different recommendations: he should hasten to give to those who are noble or of

3. In his final summation to Walter, Andreas glosses the requirement to keep one's lamp always trimmed, like the wise virgins of the parable, in terms of charity and good works (*DA* 3.121 [322]), here the opposite of sexual love. These are the only two occurrences of *caritas* in the treatise.

good character, but the height of generosity consists in giving food to the poor (*DA* 1.6.149–50 [82]). The first criterion is distinctly social, the second more closely aligned with Christian charity. A similar shift can be seen in the discussion of the lover's service, which should have as its recipient all women according to one passage, all mankind according to another (*DA* 1.6.151 [82], 155 [84]). The most striking example concerns the lover's response to the *lauzengiers,* which embodies the Christian principle of "turning the other cheek": far from adopting the tactics of his disparagers, he should try to amend them with secret reproof and, reciprocating with kindness, force them to acknowledge their fault (*DA* 1.6.151–52 [82], 159 [84]).

Other elements of the woman's discourse adopt a conspicuous tone of piety, signaling a more fundamental recasting of the secular love ethic in terms of Christian morals. Included in the advice to would-be lovers is the recommendation to avoid uttering any word of blasphemy against God or His saints (*DA* 1.6. 151 [82]). Likewise, the lover should refrain from using insulting, base, or derisive language against God's clergy, or monks, or any person in a religious house; rather, he should render such people all possible honor for the sake of Him whose service they perform. Moreover, he should attend church frequently and listen gladly to those who are continually celebrating the divine service there (*DA* 1.6.160–61 [84]). Whether or not the following of such advice makes the man a more successful lover, it cannot help but make him a better Christian.

In Book Two Andreas follows up the Christianizing advice delegated to the woman of the Third Dialogue with similar comments of his own. Among the ways in which love may be diminished, he lists blasphemy against God or His saints, as well as mockery of the religion of the Church (*DA* 2.3.6 [230–32]). He also cites the withholding of alms (*elymosynum*) from the poor (ibid.), one of only two explicit references to this specifically Christian notion of generosity.[4] Love comes to an end, he later declares, if one of the partners is found guilty of error in the Catholic faith (*DA* 2.4.1 [232]).

---

4. The man of the Seventh Dialogue cites alms given to the poor out of hypocrisy or a desire for vainglory as an example of an entity whose character is altered by the surrounding circumstances (*DA* 1.6.380 [150]). See below, n. 20.

The pertinence of such observations, like the efficacity of the advice given in the Third Dialogue, will depend very much on the piety of one's partner. The woman of the Third Dialogue recognizes—and strongly condemns—the opinion of those who foolishly believe that they can please women by despising everything connected with the Church (*DA* 1.6. 161 [84]). Implicit in her argument is the assumption that those women who would be favorably impressed by such behavior are not the kind of women one should want to court. Whether through the woman of the Third Dialogue or in his own words in Book Two, Andreas is not content to describe objectively the psychological processes nor to offer practical advice; he also tries to influence attitudes and behavior, reorienting them in the direction of Christian values.

Andreas's efforts to moralize the vernacular love ethic take their point of departure in the troubadours' claim of moral improvement through loving. As with the troubadours, this thrust of the Chaplain's discourse remains vague and ambiguous throughout much of the treatise, finding expression in such general terms as *virtus* and *probitas*. It includes the promotion of certain secular social values, also promoted by the troubadours, such as service, courtesy, and generosity. Of obvious public utility, this social ethic does not conflict with Christian morality; on the contrary, certain of its principles are easily assimilated to Christian charity. Exploiting such similarities, Andreas subtly shifts the emphasis in certain passages in the direction of a Christian interpretation, in accordance with a practice already observable in some northern French romances. In a few cases he goes beyond this, charging love between the sexes with the paradoxical task of promoting exemplary Christian piety.

Love and chastity

The attitude of the troubadours toward physical love is among the most controversial questions in medieval literary studies. Some scholars have maintained that the conception of love proclaimed in the troubadour lyric is fundamentally platonic, with preference given to moral and spiritual perfection over physical gratification and consummation. Emphasizing the sensuality of the troubadours' poetic language and the abundance of erotic imagery in their work, others have argued that sexuality is of the essence in their poetry. Unfortunately, the issue has often been obscured by the practice of using the *De amore,* or certain parts of it, as a key to resolving the ambiguities of the poetic texts.[5]

The critical controversy surrounding the poetry of the troubadours is a reflection of the thematic complexity of their work. The most important of the lyric subgenres that they cultivated, the *canso,* or love song, is constructed around a dynamic, dialectical tension between two opposing impulses: that of the poet-lover who desires, and that of the lady who resists. Although the situation is described entirely from the first-person perspective of the poet-lover, the interests of the historical poet coincide only in part with those of his lover *persona.* As a poet his must maintain the tension, the careful balance between opposing forces, that allows the poem to exist.

The two opposing ideological tendencies that critics have detected in troubadour poetry both find their place and function in this poetic economy. The sensual language and erotic imagery constitute an expression of the lover's desire. They are generally muted, however, for reasons of rhetorical strategy, to avoid putting the lady off by a too direct approach. The lady's resistance can be expressed only indirectly, through the lover's complaints about her severity. It is also for rhetorical reasons that the lover often associates himself with that resistance, thus reassuring the lady of the purity of his intentions. This is the first, most obvious interpretation of the occasional manifestation of indifference to sexual gratification as well as the preference expressed for moral and spiritual improvement. It is possible, of course, to develop such declarations into something resembling a philosophical position, but that is a later phenomenon, to be found in thirteenth-century poets such as Guilhem de Montanhagol.

The Christian position on the subject of physical love has little of the ambiguity of the troubadours. For Christians sexual relations constitute a mortal sin except under very precise and limited circumstances. The reconciliation of the sensuality of the troubadours with Christianity's hostility to sexuality and prohibitions of sexual activity thus pres-

---

5. Monson, "L'amour pur.'"

ents the greatest single challenge in Andreas's project of mediation. In facing this challenge, the Chaplain calls on the spiritualizing tendencies in troubadour poetry, including the occasional expressions of indifference to physical gratification. He also exploits a much more widespread troubadour theme, that of fidelity to a single love partner.

Among the many virtues that love inspires, according to Book One, Chapter Four, one is singled out for special praise: the "virtue of chastity" *(castitatis . . . virtus)*. The term *castitas* is used with two quite distinct meanings in the *De amore*. In this passage it refers to fidelity to a single lover partner, as the discussion makes clear. In fact, the expression employed is *castitatis quasi virtus* (*DA* 1.4.2 [38]), "what is almost the virtue of chastity" (P. G. Walsh, p. 39) or "so to speak, . . . the virtue of chastity" (John J. Parry, p. 31). This relative use of the term also occurs twice in the dialogues. In Book Three, on the other hand, *castitas* is generally used in the absolute sense with which it is traditionally associated, that of sexual abstinence (*DA* 3.26 [294], 38[298]). In Book One it is *castimonia*, cognate and synonym of *castitas*, that conveys the latter meaning (*DA* 1.6.479, 482 [182]).

The two different meanings that Andreas assigns to *castitas* correspond to two separate undertakings evident in the treatise to limit sexual activity in love affairs. On the one hand, the Chaplain subjects love to a quantitative limitation, in terms of the number of sexual partners, restricted to one, or at least one at a time. At the same time, he also attempts to impose qualitative restrictions pertaining to the degree of physical intimacy engaged in by lovers. Support for both types of restrictions can be found in the troubadours, which probably accounts for the somewhat paradoxical fact that love itself is named as the source of chastity. The primary purpose of the restrictions, however, appears to be to make love more acceptable from the point of view of Christian morality.

The obligation of fidelity to a single love partner is an important theme in the *De amore*, evoked in numerous passages throughout the treatise. In addition to *castitas*, several other terms are called upon to express this notion. The most frequent of these are *fides*, "faith," and *fidelis*, "faithful," which occur more than sixty times with this meaning. *Constans*, "constant," and *constantia*, "constancy," along with their opposite, *inconstans,* are also found fifteen times in this sense. Finally, *firmus,* "firm," and *firmitas,* "firmness," as well as the antonym *infirmitas* and even the verb *firmare,* "to remain firm," are used all together ten times in this connection.

In Book One, Chapter Four, the paradox that the "quasi-chastity" of fidelity springs from love itself is explained in psychological terms, from the fact that someone in love with one person cannot even "contemplate" *(cogitare)* enjoying the embraces of another, however beautiful. This observation is repeated in Book One, Chapter Ten (*DA* 1.10.5 [220]), and codified in Rule XII of the Rules of Love, which states that a true lover does not desire the embraces of anyone except his partner (*DA* 2.8.45 [282]). The fidelity of the true lover is thus the converse psychological condition of the "excessive abundance of pleasure" that keeps some from loving.

Not just a psychological state, fidelity is presented more often as a moral obligation. The lesson on the art of love by the lady of the Third Dialogue stipulates that one should not be the lover of several women at the same time (*DA* 1.6.155 [84]). This principle is reiterated in the Precepts of Love: "II. You must maintain chastity for the beloved" (*DA* 1.6.268 [116]). That this is the relative chastity of fidelity is clear from the context in the Eighth Dialogue in which this precept is twice cited (*DA* 1.6.562, 564 [208]). The woman of the Eighth Dialogue sets an example in this regard by refusing, for reasons of fidelity, to hear the man's suit, being already bound by another love (*DA* 1.6.526 [196]).

Failure to observe the obligation of fidelity can have dire consequences for a love relationship, according to several passages. In Book Two, sexual intercourse *(commixtio)* with another woman, even when no sentiment is involved, is said to decrease love (*DA* 2.3.2 [230]). When one of the lovers breaks faith with the other, or tries to, Andreas later declares, love comes to an end (*DA* 2.4.1 [232]). Although the distinction is not entirely clear, the expression "to break faith" *(fidem frangere)* perhaps implies an effort to establish another love relationship, as opposed to merely engaging in sexual relations.[6] In Book Three the

---

6. In Book Two, Chapter Six, however, Andreas opposes the situations in which faith is broken with a view to winning a new love and without such an intention (*DA* 2.6.1, 10 [236–40]).

Chaplain argues that all women are by nature inconstant, and that they therefore cannot be reliable lovers (*DA* 3.70 [308], 83–88 [312], 105–6 [318], 110–11 [320]).

A corollary of the requirement of fidelity is the obligation not to undermine the fidelity of others. Precept III of the Precepts of Love states that one should not seek to seduce a woman who is suitably joined in love to someone else (*DA* 1.6.268 [116]). This precept is recalled by the man of the Eighth Dialogue, in reply to the woman's contention that she is already bound by another love. Although the man recognizes the general principle of not inciting infidelity, he tries to quibble about whether the woman is *suitably* bound by the other relationship (*DA* 1.6.527–29 [196–98]), hoping thus to keep his own chances alive. Later the man declares that, if a man seeks to undermine a woman's fidelity, she should try to repel him in a courtly way (*DA* 1.6.558 [206]). In Book Two Andreas extends the prohibition on subverting established love affairs to include the case in which one woman, presumably acting as a go-between, attempts to incite another woman to infidelity (*DA* 2.6.27 [246]).

In the dialogues several of the men protest their fidelity (*DA* 1.6.199 [96], 284 [120], 337 [136], 422 [164]), thus echoing the protestations of sincerity in troubadour poetry. In the Sixth Dialogue the woman challenges such a declaration, leading to a discussion of how someone's faithful intentions can be known to someone else. Only God can examine the human heart, the man declares, but the wise woman can judge inner thoughts by external deeds and actions. The faithful lover should not be rejected out of hand on the pretext that some lovers are insincere (*DA* 1.6.284 [120], 293, 296–97 [124], 301 [126]). As in the vernacular lyric, the falseness of the *lauzengiers* presents a potential threat to the relationship, but can also serve as a foil to underline the sincerity and fidelity of the lover.

The question of how to test a lover's fidelity recurs frequently in the treatise. In the introduction to the Third Dialogue the Chaplain declares that when a man of the middle class seeks the love of a woman of the higher nobility, his constancy should be tested by many trials before the hope of obtaining her love is granted to him (*DA* 1.6.121 [74]). The subject is taken up again in two passages of the Eighth Dialogue. The woman points out that even the most deceitful of lovers adopt the language of fidelity, making it very difficult to separate the good from the bad, especially for someone as young and inexperienced as she. A real lady should be capable of making such discriminations, the man replies, proposing that a man's fidelity be tested by the imposition of a delay in the granting of the woman's favors (*DA* 1.6.459–64 [176–78]). This principle of delay as a means of testing fidelity is repeated by the woman later in the dialogue (*DA* 1.6.520–21 [194]). Book Two, Chapter Five, "On Recognizing Reciprocal Love," is largely devoted to testing the fidelity of one's partner. This includes feigning infidelity to see whether the partner reacts with jealousy (*DA* 2.5.6–7 [236]). Book Two, Chapter Six, warns against deceitful lovers, who feign fidelity to arrive at their ends, and recommends delaying the granting of the woman's favors until the man's good faith can be ascertained (*DA* 2.6.8–9 [240]).

The problem of infidelity is a major topic of discussion recurring repeatedly throughout the treatise. A problem of casuistry in the proper sense, it includes an examination of the circumstances, extenuating or aggravating, surrounding various cases of infidelity, as well as the punishment appropriate to each case and the possibility of pardon.[7] This is the main subject of Book Two, Chapter Six, "If One of the Lovers Breaks Faith with the Other." It is also addressed in the Eighth Dialogue and in several of the Love Cases. Book Two, Chapter Six, establishes the main guidelines to be applied elsewhere to particular cases. The discussion is organized around a basic distinction between infidelity committed by men or by women, situations giving rise to very differ-

---

7. Casuistry is the application of general rules of conduct to particular situations, or "cases," especially to those in which there is a conflict between rules. See Jolles, pp. 137–57. It provided a fertile terrain for the application of the topoi of circumstances. See Gründel; above, Chapter 2, n. 30. The most striking examples of casuistry in the *De amore* are the Love Cases of Book Two, Chapter Seven, but the practice is already very evident in earlier passages, notably in the treatment of infidelity in Book Two, Chapter Six. Baldwin, *Masters,* 1:53, 252, stresses the role of Andreas's contemporary Peter the Chanter in the development of twelfth-century casuistry. Andreas shares Peter's propensity for the impersonal style, focusing on the judgment of the event itself rather than on the actors (cf. ibid., 1:252): the impersonal *quidam/quœdam,* "a certain . . ." (knight, lady, etc.) is used 18 times in Book Two, Chapter Seven to introduce the protagonists of 15 of the 21 Love Cases (plus 5 times in Book Two, Chapter Eight).

ent treatment. For men a further distinction is made as to whether the breach of faith involved the intention of establishing a new love relationship.

A man who is unfaithful with the intention of winning a new love deserves to lose completely the love of his first partner, unless perchance she graciously pardons him (*DA* 2.6.1–2 [236–38]). Andreas counsels against pardoning the man under such circumstances, however, for that would lead to a loss of worth for the woman (*DA* 2.6.3–4 [238]). Nevertheless, the Chaplain offers women advice on how to win back an unfaithful lover, including feigning interest in someone else to arouse jealousy (*DA* 2.6.5–7 [238–40]). If the man's infidelity is not aimed at starting a new relationship, it has less serious consequences. Under the impulse of an irresistible pleasure, he can seize an opportunity for a romp in the grass with an unknown woman, a prostitute, or a maid without being considered unworthy of his partner's love. If this happens too often and with several women, however, it will be assumed that the man suffers from an "excessive abundance of pleasure." And if he goes to some pains to seduce a woman with whom he is acquainted, it will be assumed that his intention is to start a new love affair, especially if she is of noble birth or otherwise distinguished (*DA* 2.6.10–12 [240]).

The woman of the Eighth Dialogue is somewhat sterner than Andreas on the subject of infidelity not aimed at a new love. At the very end of the dialogue, the man poses in the form of a disputed question the problem whether such behavior merits the loss of the first woman's love. Contrary to the usual practice, he volunteers immediately his own opinion, namely that a rebuke is sufficient, since the feeling of love was not diminished. The woman replies by citing the "rule" (i.e., Precept II) that one must remain chaste for one's partner, on the basis of which she argues that the man deserves to be punished by the loss of his love. She does hold open the possibility of a pardon, however. The man then reformulates the question, including the same circumstances, but with the additional stipulation that the attempted infidelity was unsuccessful. This detail does not alter the woman's condemnation, since the intent was to transgress the rule of chastity. The offender's only hope is to soften the heart of his partner by an affirmation of loyalty and contrition (*DA* 1.6. 561–64 [208]).

Book Two, Chapter Six, examines one possible extenuating circumstance regarding male infidelity, the fact of having requested and obtained prior permission from the beloved. The first point stressed is that such permission should never be accorded under any circumstances. Moreover, even with permission, an unfaithful lover should be deprived of his former love, because the beloved's wickedness in the granting of permission does not justify the lover's transgression. If, however, the man tries unsuccessfully to exploit such permission, he should be pardoned, because his fault and that of his too lenient partner cancel each other (*DA* 2.6.13–14 [240–42]).[8]

Regarding the infidelity of women, Andreas begins by denouncing an "old error," namely that women should be treated in this respect the same as men.[9] Infidelity committed by women is in all cases unpardonable, with no consideration given to intentions. The greater sexual freedom accorded to men is explained tautologically in terms of "prevailing custom" and the "privilege of the sex." On the other hand, because of the "modesty of the sex," women who serve the pleasure of several men are considered lewd prostitutes, unworthy of the company of respectable ladies (*DA* 2.6.15–16 [242]). It is a disgrace for a man to pardon the infidelity of his beloved, he continues. By contrast with the advice given to women under similar circumstances, Andreas refuses to

---

8. According to Love Case II, permission to commit infidelity does have a legitimate use as a means of testing fidelity. After having requested and obtained such permission, a man stayed away longer than usual, then returned with the explanation that he had not been unfaithful, nor sought to do so, but had only wanted to test his partner's constancy. The woman replied that the mere requesting and obtaining of such permission was enough to deprive the man of her love, but Queen Eleanor rules in favor of the man, declaring the measures taken to be necessary and appropriate (*DA* 2.7.6–8 [252]). The test in question is presumably the jealousy test recommended in Book Two, Chapter Five (*DA* 2.5.6–7 [236]). It may be that by refusing the man her love the woman showed appropriate jealousy and therefore passed the test, though this is not clear from the text.

9. Walsh, p. 243, translates *vetus error* as "the primeval sin," referring apparently to infidelity committed by women (and perhaps to Eve's "original sin"?). This is in keeping with the sentiments of the passage, but it is not a faithful rendering of the text. The *vetus error* is the *antiqua sententia* denounced in the next sentence, namely that women's infidelity should be treated the same as that of men. This is confirmed in the following sentence, in which the *sententia* in question is described as *vetus* and as leading to *error*.

offer any remedy to a man so base as to be unable to detach himself from an unfaithful partner (*DA* 2.6.17–19 [242–44]). This attitude also contrasts with that of Ovid, whose *Remedia amoris* was intended for just such cases.

Several potentially extenuating circumstances are examined in connection with the infidelity of women. The first concerns a woman whose transgression is limited to kissing and embracing. Such actions deserve appropriate censure, according to Andreas, because they are customarily the sign of future love (*DA* 2.6.20 [244]); whether they should be considered as serious as consummation is not specified. Another involves a woman who submits to another man's pleasure under the compulsion of force. She should not be repudiated, the Chaplain declares, unless she later consent to the act by repeating it (*DA* 2.6.26 [246]). A third possible extenuating circumstance is evoked in Love Case XIV, only to be rejected. According to the judgment of the Countess of Champagne, the prolonged absence of a lover does not justify his partner in abandoning him for another, unless there is clear evidence that he has been unfaithful (*DA* 2.7.31–34 [262]). The question of prior permission for women to be unfaithful in not discussed anywhere in the treatise.

Book Two, Chapter Six, raises the question whether a man or a woman can legitimately "seek a new love," that is, attempt to change love partners. Refusing to express an opinion on the legitimacy of such actions, Andreas observes that once one has been struck by the shaft of a new love, one is forced by the power of attraction to follow one's feelings. In any case, one cannot fall in love with someone else unless the first love is dead (*DA* 2.6.21 [244]). A special case can be made for seeking a new relationship when one's partner proves unworthy. In that situation, Andreas declares, one should first do all in one's power to improve the partner, making him or her worthy. If that fails, however, one is free to seek a new partner. This provision applies to men as well as to women (*DA* 2.6.28–29 [246]).

The changing of love partners is taken up again in Love Case XII. It tells of a man suitably joined in a love match who sought and won the love of a second lady, only to betray her by returning to the first. The Countess of Flanders rules that a man who practices such deceitful trickery deserves to lose the love of both ladies, and indeed never to enjoy again the love of any lady of worth. She adds, on the authority of the Chaplain, that the man appears to suffer from "uncontrolled pleasure" *(impetuosa voluptas)*, presumably the condition described elsewhere as "excessive abundance of pleasure." The second woman has nothing with which to reproach herself, however. Indeed, if the man remains faithful to the second woman, the first has no grounds for complaint (*DA* 2.7.25–27 [260]). The obvious conclusion is that changes of partner are permissible but irreversible.

Since the prescribed sanction for infidelity is the loss of the first love, anyone willing to make that sacrifice is free to change partners. What is apparently unacceptable, in Andreas's view, is any attempt to start a second relationship while still clinging to the first. Such a state of affairs would contravene two of the Rules of Love: Rule III, which states that no one can be bound by two loves, and Rule XVII, which states that a new love drives out an old one (*DA* 2.8.44, 46 [282]). With that provision, however, Andreas appears to be surprisingly open to the changing of partners. The "quasi-chastity" of fidelity must be understood in terms of a relative fidelity, limited to the duration of the relationship, which cannot be expected to last forever.

Beyond the question of fidelity, an effort can be observed in many passages of the *De amore* to limit sexual activity within love relationships. In such passages Andreas seeks to promote chastity in the proper sense of the term. This endeavor may take one of two forms, encouraging either the delaying of physical intimacy between the couple or its restriction to the preliminary stages. The distinction between these two strategies is more apparent than real.

Delay in the concession of sexual gratification is a subject frequently debated in the *De amore,* especially in the dialogues. It is intimately related to the question of favors too easily granted, which is the subject of Book One, Chapter Ten, and which Andreas associate with an "excessive abundance of pleasure." The too easy granting of favors is simply a failure to impose proper delay.

Near the end of the Fourth Dialogue, the woman claims that she needs time for deliberation to be able to choose the most deserving suitor. Suspecting a trick, the man voices the fear that joyless delay will cheat him of his hopes, thus bringing on his death (*DA* 1.6.190–93 [94]). Likewise, the woman of the Fifth Dialogue ends the discussion by requesting time for reflection. This time the man is less reluctant, however, expressing confidence that the results of her deliberation will be favorable to his cause (*DA* 1.6.277–79 [118–20]). In the Eighth Dialogue the man proposes delay in granting favors as a test of the lover's fidelity. He adds, however, that the woman's promises should not be postponed with lengthy delays, lest the suitor feel that he has labored for naught (*DA* 1.6.463–64 [176–78]). Later in the dialogue the woman accuses the man of being too hasty in his demands, and she invokes the same principle of testing fidelity by delay. Claiming that postponement will imperil his life, the man argues for a moderation of the delay. The woman replies that a more moderate delay is appropriate only if the woman decides to love, which is not the case with her (*DA* 1.6.520–26 [194–96]), thus putting an end to the discussion.

An intermediate position between delay and restriction is occupied by Andreas's exploitation of the commonplace of the five stages of love (*gradus amoris/quinque lineæ amoris*). This commonplace exercised an influence on Andreas's definition of love in the first chapter of the treatise, particularly in regard to the final cause of love. While the utilization of this theme remains implicit in the first chapter, it is developed explicitly elsewhere in the treatise, not without a certain ambiguity.

The stages of love are first discussed in the First Dialogue, in the debate on the relative value of loving younger or older men. The man, young and inexperienced, explains that his defense of youth applies only to the first three stages of the four stages of love, which he then describes (*DA* 1.6.59–64 [56]). In their classical formulation, the stages of love are five in number, with the first sometimes omitted: *(visus), alloquium, contactus, oscula,* and *factum;* ("sight"), "conversation," "physical contact," "kissing," and "consummation." Andreas's schema reducing the number of stages to four: "the giving of hope" *(spei datio),* "the granting of a kiss" *(osculi exhibitio),* "the enjoyment of an embrace" *(amplexus fruitio),* and "the yielding of the whole person" *(totius personæ concessio).*

Despite obvious points of contact, Andreas's adaptation of the stages of love presents several innovations. The first stage is omitted, as in a common variant of the classic formula, probably because "sight" already figures prominently in the definition of love. The second traditional stage, conversation, is already embodied in the situation of the dialogues; consequently, Andreas replaces it with the giving of hope, an additional concession by the woman. For the abstract, general "contact," Andreas substitutes the concrete and specific "embraces," which probably accounts for the fact that this stage now follows that of "kissing." The final stage—the "deed," in the traditional formulation; the "yielding of the whole person," here—remains, of course, the same, although Andreas's language is again more precise.

If she wishes to proceed at once to the fourth stage, the man of the First Dialogue argues, a woman should choose a man with many deeds to his credit, thus ensuring that her lover is a man of merit. By limiting herself to the first three stages, however, she can afford to take on an inexperienced man, and thus earn the honor of making a worthy man of him (§§ 61–62). The reason given for this diverse treatment is that up to the third stage a woman can withdraw without reproach from a love affair, but once the final stage is reached she must have a very good reason to do so (§ 64). It is not fitting for a wise woman to pass over the earlier stages, going directly to the fourth, the man adds; she would do much better to proceed slowly and by degrees (§ 63). Thus the argument from the stages of love serves simultaneously two functions, bolstering the man's case in favor of his own circumstances while reassuring the woman concerning his intention to exercise moderation in his demands.

The four stages of love come up again in the Eighth Dialogue, in a discussion as to whether a woman should prefer the love of a good man who asks first or that of a better man who asks later. Referring explicitly to the rule expounded in the First Dialogue, the man contends that, as long as the woman has not gone beyond the giving of hope, the granting of a kiss, and the enjoyment of an embrace, she can without blame deny the renewal of such concessions, and thus be free to accept the suit of the worthier latecomer (*DA* 1.6.438 [170]).

These affirmations by the men of the dialogues are contradicted by Andreas himself when he returns to the subject in Book Two, Chapter Six. There he raises the question whether, with a love that has advanced only through the first three stages, the denial of consummation constitutes a breach of faith. Unless the suitor has proven unworthy, the Chaplain declares, it is a grievous offense to deny him what he has long anticipated. A respectable woman should not postpone her promises without good cause; if she is not disposed to satisfy a suitor, she should not give him hope or other preliminary tokens of love. Such behavior is characteristic of the deceit of prostitutes (*DA* 2.6.34–35 [248]). These remarks are based on two assumptions encountered elsewhere in the treatise. The first is that the granting of preliminary favors constitutes a promise of subsequent consummation, an idea expressed implicitly by Andreas earlier in the same chapter, when he declares that kissing or embracing another is sufficient to be considered infidelity (*DA* 2.6.20 [244]). The other is that delay in the granting of sexual gratification is inspired by the greed of women, an accusation frequently repeated, though it conflicts with the advice to delay, lest love too easily granted be taken as a sign of excessive lasciviousness.

Regarding the granting of favors, the commonplace of the stages of love is ambiguous, allowing for different interpretations. In utilizing it in his definition, Andreas considers it objectively, as a means to describe and analyze the diverse components of a process. In the dialogues the distinction of various stages is regarded as a means of limiting, or at least retarding, the process, a view the men propose to the women with the obvious intention of reassuring them. In the eyes of the men themselves, however, the stages of love can be viewed only as steps in the progress toward their goal. This is the point of view that Andreas adopts quite frankly in Book Two, Chapter Six. From this perspective, any limitations in the granting of favors by means of the stages of love must be considered temporary.

Pure love

Not content to retard sexual activity in love relationships, Andreas seeks in a number of passages to restrict it to the preliminary stages. The motive generally alleged is "shame" or "modesty" *(pudor, pudicitia, verecundia)*. Altogether these terms and their derivatives occur fifty-five times in the treatise, although in a few cases, like *castitas,* they refer rather to fidelity (e.g., *pudicitia, DA* 1.6.562 [208]). The principle of limiting sexual activity in response to the promptings of modesty is formalized in Love Precept VIII, which states that in the giving and receiving of love's solaces the utmost modesty *(omnis verecundiæ pudor)* should be present (*DA* 1.6.269 [116]). It is implicated in the obligation, stressed in several passages, not to exceed the desires of one's partner.[10]

The most significant attempt in the *De amore* to restrict sexual activity between the couple is represented by the notion of "pure love."[11] The distinction between "pure love" *(amor purus)* and "mixed love" *(amor mixtus)* is developed by the man of the Eighth Dialogue in one of the most famous passages of the treatise. Many scholars have seen in this passage the foundation of a Platonic theory of love and a key to the interpretation of the love conceptions of the troubadours. Little attention has be given, however, to the rhetorical context surrounding it or to its thematic links with other parts of the treatise, including the discussion devoted to this subject in Book Two. When it is viewed in the light of these considerations, the discussion of pure and mixed love takes on a very different aspect.

The passage on pure and mixed love is part of the Eighth Dialogue, which opposes a man and a woman both of the higher nobility. In the introduction to the Eighth Dialogue, Andreas stresses the particular care that must be exercised in dealing with women of this class, for they are prompt and bold in refuting one's arguments, and they take great delight in ridiculing a man by turning his own words against him (*DA* 1.6.401 [158]). The astuteness of women of the higher nobility is illustrated by several of the comments made by the woman in the course of the dialogue. Even if a lover is of an utterly deceitful mind and strives to

10. In Book Two, Chapter Six, Andreas asks whether withdrawing from sexual activity in an already established relationship would constitute a breach of faith. Without answering the question, he declares that he would not want to discourage anyone form renouncing the pleasures of the world, for that would be contrary to God's teachings. Based on "the decision of the ladies," however, he adds that if the person later decides to resume lovemaking, he should return to the earlier partner, if she still wants him (*DA* 2.6.30–31 [246]). This is an apparent adaptation of the canon law on marriage, which allows married people to take monastic orders only as a final solution, not as a transition between marriages.

11. On this subject, see Monson, "L'amour pur.'"

dishonor Love's service with his cunning, she declares, under the impulse of desire he simulates the true lover in all his actions and attempts to beguile those who trust him (*DA* 1.6.459 [176]). A man will try by every argument to persuade an unwilling person to assent to what he himself desires and covets with all his heart, she later adds, but he is no true friend who neglects the interests of the other and seeks only his own advantage (*DA* 1.6.466 [178]). Clearly, the man must find some outstanding arguments if he wishes to advance his case with a woman of the higher nobility. This rhetorical background must not be forgotten is assessing the passage on pure and mixed love.

The passage is situated toward the middle of the dialogue, following a number of loosely related subjects. The Eighth Dialogue is the least consistent of any of the dialogues, portraying the woman successively as very young or very old, as a widow or a virgin, as bound by the love of another man or totally lacking in experience. Nevertheless, the passage on pure love represents a response to several of the earlier arguments. It is especially closely related to the subject of virginity that precedes it directly. Claiming to be a virgin, the woman expresses the fear that, if a husband later discovered a loss of virginity, this could bring her loss of reputation, repudiation, and general contempt. The man replies by citing a number of famous virgins who participated in love affairs. He adds that a good husband would appreciate the good qualities fostered in his wife by her prior love experience, whereas a bad husband would only damage his own reputation by raising a scandal about it (*DA* 1.6.452 [174], 466–69 [178–80]). Then follows the exposition on pure and mixed love (*DA* 1.6.470–75 [180]).

The man wishes to reveal a secret, he says, unknown to many: there are two types of love, pure love and mixed love. Pure love is defined as that which consists in the contemplation of the mind and the affection of the heart; it goes as far as kissing on the mouth, embracing with the arms, and modest contact with the nude lover, but omitting the final solace, which is not allowed to those wishing to love purely (§§ 470–71). Mixed love, by contrast, is that which results in every pleasure of the flesh and which culminates in the final act of Venus (§ 473). The man takes a firm stand in favor of pure love and against mixed love, enumerating the advantages of the former and the disadvantages of the latter, but without condemning it totally. Then he invites the woman to choose between the two.

Critics have sought the origin of the distinction between pure and mixed love in Plato or, more often, in the Arabian philosophers and poets.[12] In my opinion, however, it is not necessary to look so far away. The first, most obvious source of this doctrine is the classical and medieval commonplace of the five stages of love. Having already modified the stages of love with respect to their classic formulation, Andreas now presents yet another version combining elements of the two earlier versions. Once again, the steps are four in number: kissing on the mouth *(oris osculum)*, embracing with the arms *(lacerti amplexus)*, modest contact with the nude lover *(verecundus amantis nudæ contactus)*, and the ultimate pleasure *(extremum solatium)*.

This time the scale of four stages shifts noticeably in the direction of the goal. It begins with kissing, the next-to-last stage in the classic formulation. Kissing is followed by embracing, as in the Chaplain's earlier version. Between embracing and the final stage reappears physical contact from the classic formulation, but now subjected to two rather contradictory qualifications: it should be modest and it should be carried out with the nude body of the lover. The final stage, referred to as the ultimate pleasure or as the ultimate work of Venus, remains the same. The omission of this final stage is the only thing distinguishing "pure" love from that which is called mixed.

Why, we may ask, does the suitor introduce such a distinction at this point in the debate? The answer must be sought in the case that the man presents in favor of pure love (§§ 472–73). In fact, the suitor's speech answers point by point all the various objections that the woman has previously raised to loving—objections that apply, according to him, only to mixed love. Pure love never ceases to increase, the man argues, whereas mixed love ends rapidly and lasts only a short time. This responds to the fears expressed by the woman of being abandoned by an unfaithful lover (*DA* 1.6.459–60 [176]). Pure love causes no harm to those who practice it, the man claims, unlike mixed love, from which grave dangers arise. We have seen that the woman accused the

12. Parry, p. 11; Walsh, pp. 20–22.

man of seeking only his own advantage, to her detriment (*DA* 1.6.466 [178]). God sees very little offense in pure love, according to the man, but is offended by mixed love. This remark goes back to the beginning of the dialogue, where the woman claimed that love is a grievous offense against God (*DA* 1.6.411 [160]). Likewise, the suitor's affirmation that neither a wife nor a widow can receive any harm from pure love nor suffer any damage to her reputation answers an earlier passage in which the woman refuses love on the grounds that she is a widow, still in mourning for her deceased husband (*DA* 1.6.445, 449–50 [172]). Especially, the claim that no virgin can be defiled by pure love responds directly to the fears the woman expresses for the unfortunate consequences of losing her virginity (*DA* 1.6.466–67 [178]).

We can now see why the man takes such a strong stand in favor of pure love, rather than presenting a balanced, objective account of both types. By declaring a preference for a limited form of love, he apparently hopes to calm the woman's apprehensions while demonstrating his own good intentions. That is also doubtless the purpose of the term "modest" *(verecundus)* applied to physical contact with the nude body of the lover, a somewhat paradoxical situation rather difficult to imagine. The desire to reassure is again underlined at the very end of the passage by the suggestion that the woman should "put aside all fear of deception" (§ 475).

The man ends his speech by inviting the woman to choose between the two types of love. In light of his previous remarks, he can hardly expect her to choose mixed love. But even if she chose pure love, this would not leave him in such a bad position. At the beginning of the dialogue the man had not even obtained the granting to hope, and the woman has not offered him much encouragement in the course of the debate. If she now accepted his proposition of pure love, this would allow him to proceed directly to the next-to-last stage, physical contact with the woman's nude body, skipping over kissing and embracing. In fact, this next-to-last stage is an intermediary stage, a "stage three-and-one half," so to speak, with regard not only to the classic formulation but also to Andreas's earlier version.

Judging by her response, the woman is not at all taken in by the trap that has been laid for her. On the contrary, she demonstrates the astuteness that allows a woman of the higher nobility to ridicule her adversaries by turning their words against them. Rather than choosing between the two forms of love, she derides ironically the notion of pure love, calling it "unheard of, incredible, a prodigy." Resorting to an image previously used by St. Jerome and the Archipoeta, she asks: "Who can be placed in a fire and not be burned?" (*DA* 1.6.476 [180]).[13]

It is implicit in the commonplace of the stages of love that each stage leads more or less inevitably to the next. In particular, the tradition calls for a swift transition between the kiss and the "deed." Already in Ovid we read, "He who has taken kisses, if he takes not the rest, deserves to lose what has already been given."[14] Medieval examples abound.[15] In Book Two Andreas himself condemns any attempt to deny the final stage of love after having accorded the first three stages (*DA* 2.6.34–35 [248]). The woman's reply must be viewed in the light of this tradition. The distinction between pure and mixed love that the man tries to get her to accept is a false distinction, for the final stage, which theoretically differentiates the two types of love, is already implied in the first three stages.

The question of pure and mixed love is not formally resolved in this passage, but it comes up again in a different form later in the dialogue. This time it is the woman who poses the man a dilemma, in the form of a *quæstio disputata,* inviting him to choose between the sexual pleasures procured by the upper or the lower half of the body (*DA* 1.6.533–50 [198–204]). Without hesitating, the man chooses the pleasures of the upper half of the body, those associated with the first three steps of love. Some have suggested that the man is acting here as a spokesman for Andreas.[16] This is not impossible, for the woman also rallies to that position at the end of the debate. But on a rhetorical level, the man is chiefly concerned with advancing his own cause by reassuring the woman of the purity of his intentions. Likewise, the woman defends the pleasures of the lower half, those associated with the "deed," not

---

13. Jerome, *Letter to Eustochium,* 22.14; Archipoeta, 10.8.1; cf. Walsh, p. 181, n. 168.

14. *AA* 1.669–70: *Oscula qui sumpsit, si non et cetera sumet,/hæc quoque, quæ data sunt, perdere dignus erit.*

15. Friedman, pp. 174–75.

16. Lazar, p. 272.

only to oppose the man's arguments, according to the rules of the *jeu parti,* but also the better to defend herself against the man's advances, by making perfectly clear in advance the goal that is truly sought.

The man argues that the pleasures of the lower half are common to all the animals, whereas those of the upper half are specific to human nature. Unlike the solaces of the lower half, one never wearies of those of the upper half, he adds (§§ 536–37), repeating an argument from the discussion on pure and mixed love. The woman stresses the central role of the lower half as the ultimate goal of all amorous activity (§§ 538–43). The man replies that it is shameful to indulge in the solaces of the lower half without those of the upper half—a practice peculiar to prostitutes—and that those of the upper half can be enjoyed without violating the modesty of the lovers (§§ 544–46). He also adduces a number of analogies (sky/earth; heaven/hell; angels/men; head/body) to illustrate the general rule that things physically superior are also morally superior (§§ 547–48).

At the end of the debate, the woman takes the unusual step of accepting the man's position (§ 550). It may be that she has been convinced by the last of his arguments, especially those concerning shame and modesty. In any case, consensus is made possible by the fact that a hypothetical case is now being discussed regarding another couple, unlike the earlier discussion of pure and mixed love, and so the woman's acquiescence does not personally commit her to anything. This exceptional resolution prepares the position taken in Book Two by the Chaplain himself.

Andreas returns to the question of pure and mixed love in two passages of Book Two, Chapter Six. The first concerns the question whether a man can be joined simultaneously by pure love to one woman and by mixed love to another. The Chaplain is categorically opposed to such an arrangement, for these two types of love participate of the same essence, namely the same affection of the heart, although the manner of loving is different. Similarly, a man may quench his thirst with wine, with water, or with a mixture of the two, but the thirst remains the same (*DA* 2.6.23–25 [244–46]). Once again, the essentially psychological nature of love is stressed, with particular emphasis on the role of desire.

The other passage raises the question whether one partner, after having practiced pure love, has the right to resist the other's request to change to mixed love. While expressing a personal preference for pure love, Andreas declares that neither partner should resist the will of the other in this regard, unless there is a prior agreement not to practice mixed love except by express mutual consent. Even if such an agreement exists, he continues, a woman does not act properly in refusing to comply with her partner's will (*DA* 2.6.38–39 [248–50]), which seems to confirm the fears expressed by the woman of the Eighth Dialogue.

In effect, this opinion simply repeats Andreas's earlier remarks concerning the stages of love (*DA* 2.6.34–35 [248]). Nevertheless, the Chaplain's expression of preference for pure love is significant, especially in conjunction with the concession of the woman of the Eighth Dialogue on the pleasures of the upper and lower parts. Like the woman of the Third Dialogue—the only other woman of the higher nobility represented in the dialogues—it is the woman, rather than the man, who appears to speak for Andreas in the Eighth Dialogue, combining a preference for limiting sexual activity according to the dictates of modesty with considerable skepticism as to whether the practice of pure love could really have that effect.

We can now evaluate the significance of the passage on pure love in the overall context of the *De amore*. In view of the preceding analysis, this passage appears to deserve much less attention than it has generally received. Pure love is neither a philosophic position nor an original theory of love, much less a verifiable social practice. It is rather a courtly strategy, an argument in the rhetoric of love, designed to calm the woman's apprehensions. The very relative "purity" of this concept provides no satisfactory solution to the conflict between passion and morals. Pure love is just a stage—for the woman, a very compromising stage—in the lover's inexorable progress toward his goal.

Andreas's efforts to limit sexual activity in love affairs emerge from the preceding discussion as one of the most significant thematic clusters of the *De amore*. Indeed, this endeavor lies at the heart of the moral thrust of the treatise. Taking as his point of departure certain idealizing tendencies in the poetry of the troubadours, the Chaplain seeks to develop these suggestions into a conception of love that remains secular and profane but is more acceptable from the viewpoint of Christian morality.

Designated by the ambiguous term *castitas,* this undertaking is pursued along two separate axes, that of fidelity to a single love partner and that of restriction, or at least delay, of physical intimacy between the couple. The importance of fidelity is stressed throughout the treatise, including a prohibition on subverting the fidelity of others. Advice is given on choosing a faithful partner and on testing the partner's fidelity. Special attention is accorded to the casuistry of infidelity, with various cases adjudicated in terms of the accompanying circumstances and the appropriate punishments. Within the relationship, lovers are advised to restrict physical gratification to the preliminaries or at least to delay the granting of more intimate favors. The classical and medieval commonplace of the stages of love, in the particular variant developed by Andreas, is proposed as a mechanism to this end. The culmination of this tendency is the famous distinction between pure and mixed love.

Beyond the term that designates them, the "quasi-chastity" of fidelity and the somewhat more properly labeled chastity of (at least partial) abstinence have much in common. In fact, they intersect at several points in the course of the treatise, notably in the practice of delaying favors as a test of fidelity. Probably the most important feature that they share, however, is the failure of both these principles to provide a completely satisfactory solution to the problems posed. Sanctioned only by the loss of the first love, fidelity is a relative concept, limited to the duration of the relationship. As for the restrictions on intimacy, including the notion of "pure love," they must be viewed as temporary deferrals on the way toward the inevitable conclusion of total consummation. Having apparently set out to limit sexual activity, the Chaplain achieves the paradoxical result of illustrating the limitations of the limitations.

How can we account for this ironic outcome? Should we suppose an ironic intention on the part of the Chaplain, as do some critics? There is no reason to doubt either the sincerity of Andreas's expressed preference for pure love or his commitment to the principle of fidelity. The answer appears to lie not in Andreas's intention, ostensibly to promote these values as a means of accommodating secular love to Christian morality, but rather in the difficulties encountered in implementing this design. The troubadours' idealization of love, which provided the starting point for the Chaplain's project of reconciliation, occurs in a precise rhetorical context, that of the *domnejaire,* or courting discourse, and its treatment is conditioned by the laconic, allusive style characteristic of troubadour poetry. It is therefore impossible to develop in the poetry all of the implications and consequences of this thematic material. The systematic treatment proposed by Andreas, however, requires just such a development, with the result that the hidden contradictions of the troubadour discourse become fully apparent.

In the dialogues Andreas shows a keen awareness of the dynamics of troubadour poetry in passages such as the one devoted to pure and mixed love. By giving the woman the chance to reply, however, he dramatically alters those dynamics, transforming a rhetorical situation into a dialectical one, which casts the subject in a very different light. The same process is carried over into Book Two, where the Chaplain himself asks questions that are never asked, cannot be asked, in troubadour poetry: What happens after the lover has gained the concession that he is currently requesting? What becomes of his fidelity when he falls in love with someone else? An honest answer to such questions, in the light of the psychological principles developed elsewhere in the treatise, cannot fail to deliver a heavy blow not only to troubadour idealism but also to Andreas's project of moralizing love.

Love and marriage

The relationship of love to marriage in medieval vernacular literature is a subject as controversial as the troubadours' attitude toward sexuality. According to the theory promulgated by an earlier generation of scholars such as Gaston Paris and C. S. Lewis, adultery was an indispensable requisite of "courtly love." This view found support in a well-known feature of medieval society, the fact that among the nobility marriage was generally a matter of economic interests in which the sentiments of the participants played little or no role. It has been sharply contested, however, by some recent scholars, who have pointed to prominent examples not conforming to the classic pattern. Once again, the question has been obscured by reliance on the *De amore* for support.[17]

It seems appropriate to consider the vernacular poetry on its own terms, taking into account all the diverse attitudes toward the relationship between love and marriage expressed in the various authors, works, and genres that compose it. Adultery is an important theme in the poetry of the troubadours, but its function and significance vary from one lyric subgenre to another. It plays a fundamental role in the *gelosescas*, a minor genre closely related to the Old French *chanson de malmariée*, in which a woman complains of having been married to an unpleasant husband, vowing to avenge herself by taking a lover. Its role is equally pronounced in the erotic *albas*, or dawn songs, which relate the emotions of lovers forced to separate at dawn to avoid detection by the jealous husband. In the *canso*, or love song, adultery is present only sporadically and in a subordinate role, providing external, auxiliary support for the psychological resistance of the lady. It is reflected only indirectly in the *pastorela*, in which unmarried peasant girls are courted by knights, obviously an ironic inversion of the social configuration of the *canso*. Adultery is discussed in one dozen of the dilemmatic debate poems *(partimen)*, and it is the most important issue raised in the satirical poems of Marcabru, which may be seen as an exceptional critical reaction to the dominant trend.[18]

The theme of adultery also has an important place in the northern French romances, but with pronounced countercurrents. The myth of Tristan and Iseult, exploited by several writers, presents an archetype of adulterous love that exercised considerable influence on the entire literature of the North. A majority of the lays of Marie de France deal with adulterous situations; in several cases adultery is presented in a positive light *(Guigemar, Yonec, Laüstic, Chevrefeuille)*, though other poems appear to condemn adulterous relationships *(Equitan, Bisclavret, Lanval)*, and one attempts to reconcile such a relationship with conventional social norms *(Eliduc)*. Portraying the adulterous relationship of Lancelot

---

17. For a recent discussion skeptical of the centrality often accorded the *De amore* in the medieval debate over love and marriage, see Cartlidge, pp. 24–32.

18. Monson, "The Troubadour's Lady."

and Guenevere, Chrétien de Troyes's *Chevalier de la charrete* provided the starting point for Gaston Paris's theory of courtly love, but in other romances Chrétien attempts to combat or to surpass the adulterous love of the Tristan legend *(Cligés)* and to reconcile love with marriage *(Erec et Enide, Le Chevalier au lion)*. Clearly receptive to the influence of the troubadours, the northern French vernacular authors gave the theme of adultery a somewhat mixed reception.

The attitude of Christianity toward adultery could not be clearer nor more antagonistic. For Christians, any sexual activity outside of marriage is a mortal sin. Even within marriage sexuality is free of sin only to the extent that it is accomplished without carnal desire, being directed toward the goals of procreation or the payment of the marriage debt. At first glance, the reconciliation of this view with the troubadours' adulterous love conceptions seems an impossible task. Paradoxically, the very intransigence of the Christian position will provide the way toward a kind of solution.

The most substantial discussion of love and marriage in the *De amore* occurs in the Seventh Dialogue (*DA* 1.6.366–400 [146–56]). Occupying thirty-five paragraphs in Walsh's edition, it is among the longest debates in the dialogues. It is also exceptional in that the question is formally resolved at the end of the dialogue through a judgment by the Countess of Champagne (§§ 390–400). It thus anticipates the procedure later adopted in the Love Cases, which also devote considerable attention to the relationship of love to marriage.

After discussing several other subjects, the woman objects to the man's suit on the grounds that she is married to a worthy man, whose many qualities she enumerates, adding that they love each other with a reciprocal love. The "laws themselves" forbid her to love another, she argues (§ 366), referring either to the civil and canon laws on marriage or, more probably, to the laws of love concerning fidelity enunciated elsewhere in the *De amore* (Precept II; Rule III). Acknowledging the husband's qualities, the man is nevertheless surprised that the woman should confuse marital affection with love, which can have no place between husband and wife (§ 367), as he will try to show by three separate arguments.

The man's first argument relates to the definition of love, which he defines as nothing other than an immoderate desire to receive a furtive and secret embrace. What furtive embrace can exist between husband and wife, he asks, since they can fulfill all their desires together without fear of opposition? (§§ 368–89). The woman answers this with two arguments. In the man's definition the word "furtive" is equivalent to "secret," she claims, and so it does not exclude the legitimate embraces of married couples. She also offers her own definition of love, leaving out the "furtive and secret" clause on which the man's argument turns (§§ 374–76). The man makes no response to these arguments, so there the matter rests. Concentrating essentially on the final cause of love, neither of these definitions even approaches the precision or comprehensiveness of Andreas's own definition, but the woman's does have the advantage of not introducing extraneous matters.

A second reason why love cannot exist within marriage is based on an analogy with friendship. Citing Cicero, the man argues that, just as the mutual affection between father and son is not the same as friendship, so too the marital affection of spouses is not love (§§ 369–70). The woman does not bother to answer this argument, probably because its value is more illustrative than probative.

A final argument against love within marriage concerns the role of jealousy. Whereas jealousy is of the essence of love, the man argues, and true love cannot exist without it, between husband and wife it is universally condemned. Spouses should flee jealousy like the plague, he continues, although lovers embrace it as the mother and nurse of love (§ 371). This argument appears to combine two literary sources: the frequent association in Ovid of love with jealousy (*AA* 2.435–54, 539–54; *RA* 543–48, 767–94; *Amores* 1.4, 1.8.95–99, 2.5, 3.11a) and the strong condemnation of jealous husbands in the troubadours' poetry (especially the *gelosescas* and the *albas*).[19]

The woman responds with a general condemnation of jealousy, applicable not just to spouses but to everyone. In the course of her remarks she defines jealousy as nothing other than a base and evil suspicion *(turpis . . . suspicio)* of women (§ 373). To this the man replies with his own definition, in which he distinguishes three "aspects" of jealousy.

19. Ibid., pp. 271–72; cf. Köhler, "Les troubadours."

The crucial element in his definition, however, is the stipulation that the suspicion should be "without base thoughts" *(sine turpi cogitatione . . . suspicio)*. This condition cannot be met within marriage, he claims, because suspicion between marriage partners is always accompanied by base thoughts. This requirement thus provides the basis for a distinction between the "true jealousy" of the lover and the base suspicion of the spouse (§§ 377–82).

Although the man's definition of jealousy is essentially psychological, the provision concerning base thoughts adds an ethical dimension. As with the man's earlier definition of love, an element somewhat extraneous to the matter at hand is crucial to his argument. It would appear at first sight that the man has simply restated his previous argument about jealousy, combining a psychological observation, Ovidian in origin, on the frequent jealousy of lovers with a moral judgment, derived from the troubadours, unfavorable to jealousy in husbands. There is more, however. The underlying assumption of this argument is that infidelity in the case of a wife is "base" *(turpis)* in a fundamental sense that distinguishes it from the infidelity of a lover; this "turpitude" that is the object of the suspicion then acts on the suspicion itself, altering its nature.[20] Although the troubadours' distaste for jealous husbands is at the origin of the entire line of reasoning, here the argument is reinterpreted implicitly in Christian terms, emphasizing the sanctity of the sacrament of marriage.

Not content to counter the man's arguments, the woman advances a powerful argument of her own. The love that she enjoys with her husband is preferable to that which the man proposes, she says, because it can be practiced "without sin" *(sine crimine;* § 376). This argument cannot stand, the man replies, because whatever solaces married couples extend to each other beyond the desire for offspring or the payment of the marriage debt cannot be free from sin. Indeed, the punishment is greater when something holy is abused than for ordinary abuses. The matter is more serious in a wife than in another, because a too ardent

20. The man argues that a husband's jealousy is defiled by a defect of the subject itself. Two analogies illustrate this principle (§ 380), one physical (clear water that loses its clarity on passing through a sandy channel), the other moral (the giving of alms by a hypocrite or for vainglory).

lover is considered, according to apostolic law, an adulterer with his own wife (§§ 382–83). A commonplace among Christian canonists and theologians, this position goes back ultimately to St. Jerome.[21] It will be invoked again by Andreas in Book Three (*DA* 3.33 [296]).

Having failed to agree, the disputants appeal to the Countess of Champagne to decide a double problem: whether love can exist within marriage, and whether jealousy between lovers should be approved or censured (§§ 386, 392, 396). The countess finds in favor of the man on both counts, supporting her decision with several new arguments. Love can exercise no power over married couples, she declares, because lovers give each other everything freely and without compulsion, whereas spouses are obliged to comply with each other's wishes and to refuse each other nothing (§ 397). Moreover, spouses can increase neither their honor nor their worth by enjoying each other's embraces in the manner of lovers, since they have gained nothing to which they were not already entitled (§ 398). A third argument is constructed around two rules or precepts of love used as premises for a syllogism. A "precept of love" states that not even a married woman can be crowned with the reward of the King of Love unless she is enlisted in Love's army outside of marriage. Another rule teaches that no one can be wounded by love for two persons. Therefore, the laws of love cannot rightly be recognized between married couples (§§ 398–99).

Although the countess's position is clear, her reasoning is less so. Her first argument invokes the freedom of choice claimed by several women in the dialogues, opposing it to the legal obligations of marriage, but the characterization of love as "free and without compulsion" ignores the psychological compulsion of love illustrated in Rules IX and XXVI of the Rules of Love (*DA* 2.8.45, 48 [282]). The second argument refers to the principle that love is the source of virtue and hence of reputation, but it apparently requires the assumption, never clearly enunciated, that such moral amelioration comes about through striving to be worthy of the beloved, which striving is presumably not necessary within marriage because of the conjugal rights of the partners. The least satisfactory of these arguments is the syllogistic deduction. The second

21. Walsh, p. 20; p. 151, n. 133; Schnell, *Andreas Capellanus,* pp. 148–54.

rule cited is an easily recognizable variant of Rule III of the Rules of Love (*DA* 2.8.44 [282]), but the precept that precedes it is not found elsewhere in the treatise. It embodies the reasonable principle of no reward without service, but the crucial phrase on which the entire argument rests, "outside of marriage," appears to be extraneous with respect to this principle, recalling the man's equally questionable use of similar phrases in the preceding discussion.

The other question, whether jealousy between lovers should be praised or condemned, is answered by the countess only by implication. As a final argument against love within marriage, she repeats without further explanation the opinion expressed earlier by the man that true jealousy cannot be found between spouses. Yet without jealousy true love cannot exist, she continues, citing the "norm of Love himself," namely Rule II of the Rules of Love (§ 399).

The countess's decision establishes a precedent soon to be cited in others cases. The woman of the Eighth Dialogue rejects the man's suit on the grounds that he has a beautiful wife, and so must be suffering from an excessive abundance of passion to want to court someone else. According to the Countess of Champagne, the man replies, love cannot exist between husband and wife, and since no good can come in this life except through loving, he is forced to look for love outside of marriage (*DA* 1.6.443–44 [170–72]). Apparently accepting this argument, the woman drops the subject.

Three judgments rendered in the Love Cases by Ermengarde of Narbonne reinforce the countess's decision. In Case IX, the viscountess is asked to decide the abstract question, which is the greater affection, that which exists between lovers or that which unites spouses. After some "philosophical meditation" she answers that marital affection and true love are completely different in nature and so cannot be compared (*DA* 2.7.21–22 [258]). Case X concerns a woman, formerly married but now divorced, whose love was solicited by her former husband. The viscountess rules that love between former marriage partners is utterly wicked (*DA* 2.7.23 [258]). Case VIII tells of a woman bound in a love relationship to one man who, upon marrying another, denied her love to the first. Ermengarde censures the woman's improper behavior, declaring that the contracting of a marriage does not properly replace an earlier love affair (*DA* 2.7.20 [256–58]).[22] This decision is recorded as the first of the Rules of Love, which states that marriage is not a good excuse for not loving (*DA* 2.8.44 [282]). For not loving *someone other than the spouse*, must be understood in the light of Case VIII.

As a consequence of the incompatibility of love and marriage, Book Two lists the contracting of a marriage among the causes that bring love to an end (*DA* 2.4.4 [232]). Marriage *between the lovers* must be understood, as Love Case XVII makes clear. This case concerns a knight, in love with a woman already bound by another love relationship, who obtains from the woman the promise that she will love him if she ever stops loving the other man. When the woman subsequently marries her lover, the knight asks her to make good on her promise, but she refuses, claiming that the condition has not been met. The queen finds in favor of the knight, citing the judgment of the Countess of Champagne that love can exercise no power over married couples (*DA* 2.7.41–42 [266]).

Although the *De amore* generally condones and even encourages adulterous love, one of the principles enunciated could potentially serve as an argument against such relationships. Precept IV and Rule XI both state that one should not seek to love someone whom one would be ashamed to marry (*DA* 1.6.268 [116]; 2.8.45 [282]). Andreas himself invokes this rule as an argument against loving nuns (*DA* 1.8.1 [210]), but he apparently does not see it as applying to adulterous relationships. Of course, to marry someone already married would be to commit the sin of bigamy, so a strict application of the rule would also exclude loving married people.

Two other subjects closely related to marriage, incest and mourning, are discussed in the treatise in terms that illustrate once again the application to love of the canon laws on marriage. Case VII concerns a couple related by blood who, unaware of this fact, began a love affair. Upon discovering their error, the man wished to leave the woman, but she objected, claiming that their initial sin was excused by their ignorance. The queen disallows this excuse and expresses strong condemnation for

---

22. That is, unless the woman decides to give up loving entirely, the viscountess adds. This presumably entails renouncing all the good of this world, which can only come from love.

all acts of incest, which human laws oppose with the harshest punishments (*DA* 2.7.18–19 [256]). Significantly, that the appeal is not to the Rules of Love but rather to "human laws," whose condemnation of incest in marriage is transferred to the domain of love relationships.[23]

The discussion of widowhood and mourning is more developed, extending to several passages. In the Eighth Dialogue the woman claims to have some hidden griefs that prevent her from loving. The man does not know, he says, what those hidden griefs may be, but he recommends the solaces of love as a remedy to sorrow and a restorer of joy. If perchance the woman is grieving for a deceased lover, the precept of Love himself sets a limit of two years to such mourning (*DA* 1.6.434–36 [168]). The reference is to Rule VII of the Rules of Love (*DA* 2.8.45 [282]), which prescribes just such a limit. Assuming that the man has guessed correctly the nature of the woman's hidden griefs, her vagueness on the subject can be seen as an exemplary demonstration of the discretion required of lovers.

Later in the same dialogue, the woman raises explicitly the question of mourning. Her widowhood and her sadness at the loss of the best of husbands deny her all of life's solaces, she claims. The man responds with the same arguments advanced earlier, namely that love is a cure for sorrow and that mourning for the dead should be limited to the period established by the law. To continue mourning beyond the legal time period is to show contempt for the law and to oppose the divine will with a rebellious spirit. The woman contests this, arguing that the law has taken human weakness into account by prescribing a modest period of mourning and that to fulfill its commands beyond that minimum is to merit an ever greater reward. The legal period of mourning has been established not out of consideration for human weakness, the man answers, but to avoid the mixing of blood lines. When there is no possible confusion of descent, he continues, the "apostle" (cf. I Cor. 7.39) allows widows to remarry (*DA* 1.6.445–51 [172–74]). The woman then changes the subject.

The question of mourning returns briefly in a disputed question near the end of the Eighth Dialogue and in one of the Love Cases. The

---

23. Schnell, *Andreas Capellanus*, pp. 62–65; Brundage, pp. 191–95, 200–203.

"disputed question" concerns a woman whose lover, absent on an expedition, was reported dead. After making careful inquiry into the matter, the woman observed the reasonable and customary period of mourning prescribed for lovers, and then entered into another love relationship, at which point the first lover reappeared (*DA* 1.6.550–60 [204–6]). This case is not really about mourning, whose requirements have apparently been met, but rather about the unexpected reappearance of the lover thought dead, though it does illustrate, in passing, the application to love of the mourning customs of marriage.

Love Case XIV presents a similar situation, but with one important difference: the first lover is merely absent for a long time, with no presumption that he is dead. In fact, the woman argues that the two-year period of mourning observed upon the death of a lover should also apply to women "bereft" of a living lover by his absence. The Countess of Champagne rules against her, however, declaring that prolonged absence does not justify infidelity, unless there is evidence that the absent lover has himself been unfaithful (*DA* 2.7.31–34 [262]). This case illustrates the limits to be imposed on the analogical extension of the rules of mourning.

According to the documentation assembled by Rüdiger Schnell, mourning was a matter of dispute among the jurists.[24] Roman law provided for a period of mourning of one year, justified by the problem of the mixing of blood lines. The canonists generally followed St. Paul, however, who mentions no waiting period before remarriage. As Schnell points out, the man of the Eighth Dialogue is attempting to synthesize these two positions. The man's contention that the minimum mourning period—presumably one year for fecund women, but that is not specified—should also be the maximum has no basis in either civil or canon law. The argument is probably best understood in terms of the frequently repeated imperative that one should always be engaged in a love relationship unless prevented by a justifiable reason, since love is the source of all good things in the world.

The extension of the customs of mourning to the loss of a lover follows the pattern already observed in regard to incest. Here, however,

---

24. Schnell, *Andreas Capellanus,* pp. 108–12.

the mourning period is doubled to two years, with no explanation offered. Schnell (p. 110) sees in this entire discussion an ironic exaggeration of orthodox positions, but it is also possible that the longer mourning period for lovers is another reflection of the tendency to moralize love. By going beyond the minimum as the woman of the Eighth Dialogue advocates, Andreas sets a higher moral standard for lovers, thus creating an element of compensation for the scandal of love conceived as necessarily adulterous.

The position of the *De amore* on the relationship of love to marriage is among the most clearly enunciated and consistent of all those developed in the treatise: love and marriage are completely distinct and, in fact, incompatible. First underscored by the unusual intervention and judgment of the Countess of Champagne at the end of the Seventh Dialogue, this opinion is subsequently reinforced in the Eighth Dialogue, in several of the Love Cases, by Andreas himself in Book Two, and by the very first of the Rules of Love. The diversity and in some cases the obscurity of the arguments advanced in support of this conclusion do not detract from the clarity of the conclusion itself. The only potential conflict that arises with respect to this position stems from the principle of not loving anyone whom one would be ashamed to marry, but this conflict is never exploited in the treatise.

From a modern perspective, the Chaplain's position on love and marriage appears most baffling. By formally excluding the possibility of love within marriage, Andreas eliminates what many people today would consider the most promising compromise between the antagonistic claims of morality and sentiment, a compromise already envisioned, moreover, in certain of the romances of the Chaplain's contemporary Chrétien de Troyes. Indeed, Andreas's extreme position goes well beyond anything found in the troubadours, who developed the theme of adultery only sporadically, with varying degrees of emphasis from one lyric subgenre to another. It is doubtless a mistake to see his position as implicit in all twelfth-century vernacular love literature, as did an earlier generation of scholars, and it is not surprising that some recent scholars have been tempted to interpret it ironically.

A key to understanding the Chaplain's position can be found in the argumentation presented in support of it by the man of the Seventh Dialogue. In reply to the woman's advocacy of love within marriage as a way of avoiding sin, the man invokes the opinion of St. Jerome that the too ardent lover is an adulterer with his own wife, adding that the abuse of something sacred is more serious than an ordinary abuse (*DA* 1.6.383 [150]). This argument, which is repeated by Andreas himself in Book Three (*DA* 3.33 [296]), casts the question of marriage in a very different light. Far from championing profane, adulterous love at the expense of Christian morality—out-troubadouring the troubadours, as it were—the Chaplain appears to have adopted his extreme position on love and marriage with a view to protecting the sacrament of holy matrimony from the moral contamination of love.

This conclusion is reinforced by a close examination of the argument from jealousy, the principal argument advanced by the man in the Seventh Dialogue and the only one of his arguments retained by the Countess of Champagne. The only thing that separates the true jealousy of the lover from the base suspicion of the husband, according to the man's definition, is the relative turpitude of the supposed infidelity that is its object. The Chaplain has reinterpreted the troubadours' distaste for jealous husbands in Christian terms that emphasize the sanctity of marriage.

Once this distinction is firmly established, Andreas is free to pursue another important aspect of his project, the moralization of love. To become more acceptable morally, love must be subjected to regulation, for which the canon law on marriage provides a ready model. Love and marriage are thus presented as separate but parallel institutions, sharply differentiated but strikingly similar. An important element in the development of this view is the adaptation to love of various provisions of the canon law on marriage, from the rules concerning legal age or potency to those governing incest or mourning. The strong emphasis placed on fidelity in love relationships also makes an important contribution to this effort. This conception of love as a quasi-marriage lies at the very heart of Andreas's project of systematization and codification.

Love and the clergy

The celibacy of the clergy was a matter of discussion and conflict throughout much of the Middle Ages. Although the principle of clerical celibacy was ancient, the practice of marrying or maintaining a concubine was widespread among the clergy until the thirteenth century, when it was vigorously and successfully combated by several popes. In any case, marriage was permitted for the lower ranks of the clergy, with celibacy enforced only for the ranks of deacon or higher.[25] The matter was complicated by the inheritance customs of the lay aristocracy, based increasingly on the principle of primogeniture. To avoid dividing the patrimony, which was to be the sole inheritance of the eldest male, younger male children who reached maturity were often consigned to clerical orders, as were female offspring who could not be suitably married. In such cases, celibacy of the clergy reinforced the dynastic strategy of the great families by ensuring that the lateral branches would not produce future claimants to the patrimony. But this use of religious orders as an expedient to dispose of superfluous offspring presumably filled the ranks of the clergy with persons whose commitment to their ecclesiastical calling was somewhat marginal. Enjoying all the other privileges of their noble birth, many must have been reluctant to forgo the "pleasures of the flesh" that were theoretically denied them because of their ordination.

The anomalies and tensions in medieval clerics' relationship to sexual love are amply reflected in medieval literature. An especially important place is reserved for this topic in satirical literature, both in Latin and in the vernacular languages. In the Old French *fabliaux,* for example, the adulterous love triangles that constitute the most important single theme are frequently formed with a cleric in the role of lover. One genre is entirely devoted to this subject: the debates between knights and clerics, whose influence on the *De amore* is manifest.

Andreas first mentions the clergy in the introduction to Book One, Chapter Six, in expounding on the distinctions between social classes around which the dialogues are organized. For men there is one rank

25. Ibid., pp. 112–14; Brundage, pp. 150–51, 214–22, 251–53, 314–19.

more than for women, he explains, that of the "most noble" of men, namely the cleric (*DA* 1.6.20 [46]). The respect due the clergy is also emphasized in the lesson on love given by the woman of the Third Dialogue: a lover should utter no word of derision against clerics or monks, but rather show them all honor for the sake of Him whose service they perform (*DA* 1.6.160 [84]). These remarks prepare the treatment accorded the clergy in the chapter devoted especially to them.

The most extensive discussion of the clergy and love occurs in the Eighth Dialogue (*DA* 1.6.478–99 [182–88]). The woman refuses to choose between pure and mixed love, she says, because, as a cleric, the man should not be engaged in either (§ 478). In the long dispute that follows, the influence of the debate poems between knights and clerics is most apparent.[26] It begins with the moral issues raised by the love of clerics. The debates between knights and clerics touch only briefly on this subject, in the argument advanced in the Old French *Jugement d'Amours* (vv. 298–301) that clerics should pray rather than love, but in the *De amore* it receives considerable development. The woman argues that a cleric should devote himself solely to the service of the Church, renouncing all pleasures of the flesh and preserving his body spotless for the Lord, who has granted him the privilege of consecrating the Eucharist and absolving the offenses of sinners. If he were to see her inclined toward a lapse of the flesh, she continues, his duty as a cleric would be to recall her from her error, urging her to practice chastity and setting an example with his own conduct (§§ 478–80).

The man replies that, conceived in sin, clerics are prone like others to lapses of the flesh. They have no greater duty than others to preserve bodily chastity and to reprove the sins of others, commands enjoined on every Christian. Clerics do have a special obligation to declare the word of God and to strengthen the people in the Catholic faith; provided they discharge this duty with their words, however, the sins they commit through the weakness of the flesh are not punished more severely than those of others. The woman responds that the greater a man's dignity, the greater his fall if he sins (§ 489). This is true not in

26. Ed. Oulmont, pp. 93–100 (*Concile de Remiremont*); 107–21 (*Altercatio Phyllidis et Florae*); 122–42 (*Jugement d'amour*).

God's eyes, but only in the opinion of the slanderous crowd, the man answers (§ 492).

Not content to counter the woman's moral objections, the man advances a positive argument for loving clerics, presumably in the hope of shifting the discussion to a terrain more favorable to his cause. A cleric has knowledge of all things, he argues, and thus conducts himself with greater prudence and caution in love affairs (§§ 487–88). Although he cites the authority of "scripture" (Mal. 2.7), his argument is probably taken from *Phyllis et Flora* (vv. 157ff.) or from the *Council of Remiremont* (vv. 186–91). This shift to secular subjects provides him no advantage, however, for it allows the woman to deploy the anticlerical satire of the debate poems (§§ 490–91). Love requires pleasing and handsome physical adornment, she argues, but a cleric is dressed like a women and his head is hideously shorn (cf. *Phyllis*, vv. 113ff.).[27] A lover should be ready to bestow his possessions on all, but a cleric cannot aid anyone with his generosity, unless he steals the wherewithal from someone else (cf. *Phyllis*, vv. 76, 105ff.). A lover must be fearless in battle, but fighting is forbidden to the cleric (cf. *Phyllis*, vv. 121ff.). Known to be addicted to idleness and slaves to the belly, clerics deserve to suffer a humiliating and shameful rejection, if they dare mention love to a woman of character (cf. *Phyllis*, vv. 60ff.).

The man responds to each of these points in turn (§§ 493–99), although his arguments are not always convincing. Effeminate dress is ordained by the wisdom of the Fathers, to distinguish clerics from other men; if he were to transgress their injunction in this minor matter, he argues, there would be no reason to believe that he would be faithful to greater commands. Generosity is enjoined on all men, he continues, including clerics; the woman's argument applies only to those who have completely renounced the world, and not even to them. God has forbidden clerics from engaging in battle so that they might not be polluted by bloodshed and thus become unworthy to perform His service; if he were not prevented by this, he would gladly show his bravery in warfare. As for the accusations of gluttony and sloth, they apply more to women than to clerics, he claims, citing the example of Eve; the woman

27. In Book Two, clerics wishing to maintain love are advised not to adopt the behavior or dress of the laity (*DA* 2.1.11 [226]).

replies with a defense of her own sex (§ 500), thus abandoning the discussion of the love of the clergy.

Although clerics do not fare well in this passage, Andreas corrects the situation in Book One, Chapter Seven, "On the Love of Clerics" (*DA* 1.7.1–4 [208–10]). This chapter is formally presented as a complement to the sociological organization of the dialogues (§ 1) and was anticipated as such at the beginning of Chapter Six (*DA* 1.6.20 [46]). It takes up again several of the arguments advanced in the Eighth Dialogue, giving them a new twist more favorable to the clergy.

Chapter Seven stresses the cleric's status as "most noble" of men, according to the hierarchy established at the beginning of the dialogues. Bestowed on the cleric because of his sacred calling, this nobility comes from God (§ 1). By virtue of it, a cleric cannot love, but must renounce all pleasures of the flesh, preserving himself free of all bodily pollution for the Lord, whose service has been entrusted to his care (§ 2). It would therefore be foolish to discuss the love of clerics in terms of their nobility, for by loving, a cleric would deserve to be deprived of that nobility (§ 3). But since hardly anyone is free of sins of the flesh, and since clerics, because of their idleness and the plentiful abundance of food, are more exposed to temptation than others, if any of them should wish to enter the lists of Love, let him do so according to the rank of his birth, using the forms of address indicated in the dialogues (§ 4).

From old material Andreas has constructed a subtle dialectic to justify loving on the part of clerics. The moral objections developed near the beginning of the chapter are essentially those advanced by the woman of the Eighth Dialogue. To these objections is opposed the argument from original sin invoked by the man, the "weakness of the flesh" that clerics share with all human beings. Ironically, the accusation of idleness and gluttony that the woman brought against the clergy is now used as an extenuating circumstance in their favor. Taken alone, however, the sharp contrast between these two moral positions is not susceptible of resolution; hence the necessity of introducing another element, the so-called nobility of the cleric, a subject scarcely mentioned in the Eighth Dialogue,[28] although its inclusion is anticipated already at

---

28. The woman does mention the "dignity and rank" of clerics, but she defines this

the very beginning of the dialogues. The nobility of clerics is introduced only to be conceded: stressed early in the chapter, it is abandoned
in the end, thus creating a kind of artificial solution, at the level of social considerations, to an insolvable moral conflict.

Just as the chapter on the love of the clergy is appended as a supplement to the social schema of the dialogues, it is supplemented in turn
by Chapter Eight, "On the Love of Nuns" (*DA* 1.8.1–6 [210–12]). Andreas's approach to nuns is very different from that accorded their male
counterparts. Whereas the love of clerics is viewed primarily as a social
question, with the moral problem resolved at the social level, the love of
nuns is considered exclusively in moral terms. In fact, the nobility attributed to clerics does not apply to nuns, as Andreas makes clear when
first introducing the subject, in the comment that there is one class
more for men than for women (*DA* 1.6.20 [46]). Consequently, the
conclusion reached for nuns is the opposite of that proposed for clerics.

From the beginning of the chapter Andreas declares that the solaces
of nuns should be utterly avoided as a pestilence of the soul. The reasons given are four in number: the love of nuns is the cause of God's
greatest anger; the laws of the state sanction it with the severest punishment; from it springs an infamy that completely destroys one's reputation; and even the precept of Love warns not to choose the love of a
woman whom we could not properly seek to marry (§ 1).

The rest of the chapter is a long exhortation to avoid completely the
love of nuns, a scandal before God and men bringing the condemnation of death for both body and soul (§§ 2–3). Although Andreas himself is well-versed in the art of soliciting nuns, he refuses to share this
knowledge with his pupil, preferring that Walter remain perfectly ignorant on the subject (§ 4). The Chaplain does relate, as a cautionary exemplum, a personal experience in which he himself, despite all his
learning, nearly fell prey to the temptation of a nun (§§ 4–5). In light of
this incident, the chapter concludes, Walter should completely avoid
any situation where he is likely to be tempted by the love of a nun (§ 6).

In citing the authority of "both laws" (§ 2), Andreas indicates the

---

distinction in terms of the right to celebrate the Eucharist and to absolve sins (§ 478).
By another ironic twist, this detail from the woman's moral objections to the love of
clerics now becomes the principal mechanism for justifying their loving.

major source for his treatment of the love of nuns, the civil and canon laws on marriage, both of which strongly condemn the marrying of consecrated virgins.[29] The transfer of this principle from the domain of marriage to that of love is signaled formally by the injunction against loving anyone whom one would be ashamed to marry: twice repeated (Precept IV; Rule XI), this injunction finds no other practical application in the treatise than to support the prohibition on loving nuns, apparently the purpose for which it was invented. Another source for this chapter can be found in satirical poems such as the *Council of Remiremont,* in which the sexual appetite of nuns is a common target. This influence is reflected in Andreas's description of his own narrow escape and in his warning of the treacherous wiles that Walter must carefully avoid.

A relatively minor theme in the *De amore,* the love of the clergy is nevertheless important in several respects. Its development is confined essentially to three passages, but its significance goes beyond the modest space devoted to it. Combining synthetically material from the satirical debate poems between knights and clerics with arguments from Christian theology and canon law, the treatment of this subject is exemplary of Andreas's method. Much of the discussion is useless for Walter, the putative addressee, unless he happens to be a cleric, yet it is all useful for completing the sociological schema of the dialogues and the encyclopedic description of love. The conclusions reached are not profound, but the way in which they are derived is ingenious and also very revealing.

Andreas's approach to this subject is among the most personal offered by the *De amore,* not so much because of the pseudo-confessional account of his experience with a nun, but especially because he was himself a cleric. From this perspective, it is difficult not to see his pronouncements as interested and self-serving, like the pro-clerical debate poems from which he was inspired. The Chaplain's bias in favor of his own category is evident not only in his assignment of clerics to the highest nobility, but also in the special pleading by which he justifies their engaging in love. Even if a cleric decided not to avail himself directly of this facility, it would still serve to ensure him a greater reward

29. Schnell, *Andreas Capellanus,* pp. 36, 114.

for his abstinence, as Andreas explains to Walter at the beginning of Book Three (*DA* 3.2 [286]).

The woman of the Eighth Dialogue, often a spokesperson for the Chaplain, comes off much the better in the debate on the love of clerics. The theological arguments against the clergy's engaging in love are very strong, as Andreas himself acknowledges in the chapter later devoted to the subject; given the importance of imitation and example in the Christian tradition, the man's contention that it is sufficient for clerics to preach the word of God, without bothering to live it, is not at all convincing. As for the material from the satirical debate poems, it is reduced by half; deprived of the possibility of redressing the balance by scoring points against knights, the man is restricted to offering lame rejoinders to the much more engaging anticlerical satire.

Presented officially as a supplement to the dialogues, Chapter Seven serves especially to correct the impression left by the earlier debate. Himself a cleric, Andreas defends the erotic interests of his own category with a strong authorial voice and a tour de force of sophistic reasoning, for which the metaphorical "nobility" of the clergy provides the mechanism. If the strict separation of love and marriage is intended primarily to protect marriage from the corruption of love, the justification offered in Chapter Seven for moral laxity on the part of the clergy is the most significant departure in the treatise from the general and sustained effort to moralize sexual love in terms of Christian morality. Chapter Eight, the supplement to the supplement, compensates for this lapse by reintroducing a strongly moralizing tone. The very different treatment accorded the love of nuns provides yet another illustration of the marked gender bias permeating the treatise as a whole. It thus reflects a point of view that the Chaplain doubtless shared with many of his contemporaries, especially with many of his fellow clerics.

The rejection of love

To the first two books, devoted respectively to the winning and the keeping of love, Andreas appends a third book containing an impassioned plea for its rejection. This curious about-face has baffled scholars and is the single most important subject of discussion and controversy relating to the *De amore*. The explanations put forward include viewing Book Three as an imitation of Ovid's *Remedia amoris* or as an insincere attempt to appease Andreas's ecclesiastical superiors, seeing the first two books as an indirect, ironic condemnation of love, and seeing the entire work as embodying the Averroist doctrine of the two truths, to name only the most prominent. The number and variety of the solutions proposed bear eloquent testimony to the complexity and difficulty of the problem.

It seems likely that the existence and character of Book Three, as well as its relationship to the first two books, are not susceptible of a single, simple explanation, that they are rather the result of a convergence of several different factors.[30] That is one inference suggested by the numerous and diverse explanations that have been advanced. The same conclusion also emerges from some of the analyses developed earlier in the present study. Reexamining Book Three in their light, it is possible to reach several observations, diverse but convergent, concerning Andreas's final rejection of love. While making no claim to providing a definitive solution to the problem, these observations can perhaps contribute to a better understanding of Book Three and its place in the treatise.

If Ovid's erotico-didactic poetry served as a general structural model for the *De amore,* as seems likely, the existence of a third book, contrasting in content with the first two, is attributable first of all to the influence of that model. That appears to be the full extent of the Ovidian influence, however. If Andreas had been content simply to follow Ovid's example, Book Three would have presumably contained advice on how to stop loving, like that which Walter had apparently requested, according to the preface (*DA* 0.1 [30]). Far from offering such advice, the Chaplain refuses any such remedy to those most in need of it, men unable to forget an unfaithful partner (*DA* 2.6.18–19 [242–44]). It is curious to note, moreover, that the term *remedium* occurs sixteen times in the treatise, but not once in Book Three. Andreas may have been contemplating a *Remedia* modeled on Ovid's at the time he wrote the pref-

---

30. Schnell (ibid., p. 170) comes to a similar conclusion, although his analysis of the various contributing factors is somewhat different.

ace, but he had apparently abandoned that idea by the time he reached Book Two, and in the third book he doesn't even mention that possibility.

If the existence of a contrasting third book can be attributed to the influence of Ovid, other factors must be responsible for the specific content of the Book Three that we have before us. Of these other factors, two appear to me to be primordial. One, internal and substantive, concerns the results obtained in the moral discussions of the first two books. The other, external and methodological, relates to the dialectical method that informs the treatise as a whole.

The objections raised in Book Three with respect to love are predominantly moral objections. Other considerations, psychological, social, and practical, do come into the discussion, but in a completely subordinate role. The most important arguments are theological, and many of the others carry Christian overtones. The density of scriptural references is four times greater in Book Three than in the rest of the treatise. The predicatory tone of Christian exhortation established at the beginning of Book Three is sustained throughout the book and reemphasized at the end. Andreas finally rejects love because it conflicts with Christian morality.

The moral concerns so striking in Book Three are far from being limited to that part of the treatise. We have seen that the first two books undertake a multi-faceted effort to moralize the secular love conceptions of the troubadours, bringing them more into conformity with the requirements of Christian morality. Taking as its point of departure the idealizing tendencies apparent in the poetry of the troubadours, this endeavor includes several separate strands: the advocacy of love as a force promoting Christian and social virtues; the limitation of sexual activity in terms of the number of sexual partners and the degree of physical intimacy; and the regulation and codification of love in accordance with the model of Christian marriage. This complex undertaking lies at the very heart of the project of reconciliation and synthesis that is the *De amore*.

Obvious and hardly controversial, the moral thrust of Book Three requires no special emphasis, but that of the earlier books has not received from the critics the full attention that it deserves. Andreas's approach to the morality of love includes two separate and apparently complementary components: one positive, the effort to moralize love; the other negative, love's rejection. The relationship of these two components to each other is central to the entire problem of the place of Book Three with respect to the rest of the treatise.

We have no reason to doubt the sincerity of the moral convictions expressed in either part of the treatise. In the first two books, the attempt to moralize love is a phenomenon far too pervasive not to be taken seriously. In addition to the aspects examined above, it includes the preference expressed for moral worth among the means of acquiring love, as well as the strong condemnation of excessive lasciviousness, of venal love, and of love too easily granted, to name only the most obvious examples. In many respects, the moral declarations of Book Three are simply a prolongation of those contained already in the first two books, although they are expressed far more emphatically and systematically, and they are put to the service of different conclusions.

Beyond its apparent sincerity, the most striking feature of Andreas's moral endeavor in the first two books is the limited success that it encounters. This observation applies particularly, as we have seen, to the efforts to limit sexual activity in love affairs. Although there is no reason to question either the Chaplain's commitment to fidelity nor the sincerity of his expressed preference for pure love, neither of these moral precepts can stand up under scrutiny in the light of psychological principles enunciated elsewhere in the treatise. Since the fidelity of the true lover is a direct outcome of the intensity of his meditation and desire with respect to the love object, once his obsession with the beloved begins to wane, nothing prevents him from transferring his allegiance to another partner. And since physical consummation is, according to the very definition of love, the end toward which the entire phenomenon is directed, it is entirely unrealistic to expect lovers to limit themselves to some intermediate stage, except perhaps as a temporary expedient on the way to an inevitable conclusion. This incapacity of the troubadours' idealism to withstand closer scrutiny must surely be an important factor, perhaps the decisive factor, in determining the new direction taken in Book Three.

In Book One Andreas uses the word *castitas* to refer to one aspect of his effort to limit sexual activity in love relationships: the "quasi-chastity" of fidelity to a single partner. When he returns to the subject in Book Three, however, *castitas* takes on an absolute value much closer to its traditional meaning. It is now a synonym of "sexual abstinence" *(continentia corpis)* and is opposed to "lust" *(luxuria)*. Occurring only twice in the first two books, in the condemnation of venal love (*DA* 1.9.2, 6 [212–14]), the latter term and its derivatives are used eighteen times in Book Three to characterize love. Chastity is a virtue, and so its opposite, "lust" (i.e., love), is necessarily a vice, the Chaplain argues (*DA* 3.24–28 [294]). God is the source of the former, he later adds, and so the latter must come from the devil (*DA* 3.38–39 [298]). Bringing to bear the powerful tools of dialectic, Andreas polarizes the debate, thus underlining all the distance that separates the timid idealism of the troubadours from the stern dictates of Christian morality.

A similar conclusion emerges from the discussion of love and marriage. All of Andreas's efforts to regulate love as a kind of quasi-marriage are not sufficient to make it an acceptable substitute for marriage from the point of view of Christian morality. This point is underlined indirectly by the sharp distinction maintained between love and marriage. If the primary purpose was to protect marriage from the moral contamination of love, as I have argued, then it follows inevitably that love is morally inferior to marriage. Nor can the argument from jealousy lead to any other conclusion, for it too is based on a hierarchy of moral values that emphasizes the greater sanctity of marriage. Just as quasi-chastity is not chastity, so too quasi-marriage is not marriage.

Whereas Andreas is content in the earlier part of the treatise to stress the distinction between love and marriage, even as he revises the former on the model of the latter, in Book Three he presents them as totally antagonistic. Near the beginning of the book he declares that God hates, and in both Testaments prescribes punishment for, sexual activity outside of marriage (*DA* 3.4 [286]). If God has wished the act of fornication to be without sin, He would not have established the institution of marriage (*DA* 3.6 [288]). Even between spouses, the pleasures of the flesh are not without sin (*DA* 3.33 [296]). Among the accusations directed against love are those of breaking up marriages, separating husbands and wives, and producing illegitimate offspring (*DA* 3.44–47 [300]).

Starting once again from the limited results obtained in the moralization of love in the first two books, Andreas again polarizes the debate through the application of the techniques of dialectic, leading to the condemnation of love.

Despite the centrality of these moral considerations in Andreas's final rejection of love, they are not the only arguments put forward in support of that position. To bolster a conclusion reached essentially on moral grounds, the Chaplain takes up in turn most of the major aspects of love discussed in the first two books, contradicting systematically the opinions previously expressed, or at least giving them a new interpretation less favorable to love. Throughout the book dialectic plays a central role, polarizing the discussion toward an extreme position, that of a refutation in a disputation.

An obvious target for attack is the opinion, expressed in Book One, Chapter Four, and repeated in the dialogues, that love is the source of all virtue. Against that claim, Andreas now asserts that love is the source of all evil and that no good comes from it (*DA* 3.33 [296], 115 [320]). There is no crime that does not spring from love, be it murder, adultery, perjury, theft, incest, or idolatry (*DA* 3.29–32 [294–96]). And when a lover is reduced to poverty through his prodigality, there is no crime that he shrinks from committing to gain the riches with which to feed his love (*DA* 3.19–21 [292]). This extreme position is clearly intended to stand in antithetical opposition to the earlier claim.

No less effort is expended on combating the secular ethic of social virtues elaborated especially in the dialogues: it is now refuted point by point. Love's service is described as a harsh servitude (*DA* 3.14–17 [290], 36–37 [296–98]) and as a cause of deadly warfare (*DA* 3.43 [300]). Presenting his own version of the feudal metaphor, Andreas evokes the reward that will come to those who serve the devil: pain and suffering, in place of promised pleasure (*DA* 3.39–41 [298]). The encouragement to practice generosity now gives way to warnings that love leads inevitably to financial ruin and poverty, either indirectly, as a result of war (*DA* 3.43 [300]), or directly, through the lover's prodigality (*DA* 3.15–16 [290], 19–21 [292], 115 [320]). For young or old, cleric or layman, commoner or noble, man or woman, the Chaplain now argues, far from enhancing one's reputation, love leads to a major loss of reputation (*DA*

3.24–28 [294], 34–35 [296], 115 [320], 118 [322]). The most concrete, visible manifestation of the claim that love is a source of virtue, this social ethic is the major justification for love advanced in the first two books, hence the tenacity with which it is opposed in Book Three.

Although moral considerations, in the narrow or the large sense, are predominant in Andreas's rejection of love, their conclusions are reinforced by several arguments from practical prudence. Some of these are social in nature, and thus not without moral ramifications; they include the claim that love harms one's neighbors (*DA* 3.8 [288]) or that it destroys friendships (*DA* 3.9–12 [288–90], 17–18 [292]). Others are based on Andreas's earlier description of the psychological and physiological effects of love, often with a new admixture of Christian elements. Love is the only sin that stains both body and soul, the Chaplain argues (*DA* 3.13 [290]). It is responsible for unbearable pain, both here and in the hereafter (*DA* 3.22–23 [292–94]). Love weakens bodies through the loss of sleep and appetite, and through the effects of sexual intercourse (*DA* 3.57–61 [304]). Love damages the brain, leading to madness (*DA* 3.60–61 [304]), and it destroys wisdom, especially in the wise; witness the examples of David and Solomon (*DA* 3.62–64 [304–6]). These arguments illustrate the desire to respond from a Christian perspective to virtually all of the material of the first two books.

Among the most important arguments of Book Three is a long attack on women, which occupies nearly one-half of the book (*DA* 3.65–112 [306–20]) and which is organized around a catalogue of feminine vices inspired by antifeminist writings such as Juvenal's *Sixth Satire* or the *Adversus Iovinianum* of St. Jerome. This segment is the expression of a common medieval attitude of clerical misogyny already reflected in many passages of the first two books. That attitude alone is not sufficient, however, to explain the presence and function of an antifeminist diatribe in Book Three.

One of the most revolutionary aspects of the new love conceptions made fashionable by the vernacular literature of the period was the reversal of the traditional relationship of power between the sexes, a reversal exemplified by the humble submission before the lady of the troubadour poet-lover or the knightly protagonist of the romances. Love became the domain of women, to the extent that Old French *amours* and Old Provençal *amors*, derived from the masculine Latin etymon *amor*, are both feminine in grammatical gender. In the *De amore* this association is illustrated by the considerable authority accorded to women in several of the dialogues and especially in the Love Cases.[31]

From this perspective, it is clear that the antifeminist diatribe of Book Three stands once again in a relationship of dialectical opposition to the first two books. The refutation of love requires the refutation of the moral authority of women, who are not only the object of love, but also its arbiters. It is this dialectical function that explains the assertion, several times repeated, that the accusations leveled against women admit of no exceptions (*DA* 3.72, 73–74 [308], 79 [310], 106 [318]). If Andreas were content to argue that *many* women, or even *most* women, are greedy, inconstant, and so on, the reaction of the lover could well be to seek out the exceptional woman not corresponding to the general rule, as indeed the Chaplain advises Walter to do in the earlier part of the treatise. The extreme absolutism of the Chaplain's pronouncements is the result neither of personal animosity against women nor of a desire to satirize his own position by disseminating signals of irony throughout his discourse. It is rather a logical necessity stemming from the polarization of the discussion into positions of dialectical opposition.

Among the various accusations directed against women, one appears to assume a particular importance, the argument that women are incapable of reciprocating a man's affection, that they cannot truly love. This argument serves as an introduction to the antifeminist section, coming before the enumeration of feminine vices, and it returns at the end of the section to close it (*DA* 3.65–69 [306–8], 110–12 [320]). It is the innate venality of women, Andreas argues, that prevents them from truly loving, a contention developed in somewhat more moderate terms in Book One, Chapter Nine. The introduction of an Ovidian element of economic realism is a significant factor in showing the limitations of troubadour idealism, for though the troubadours were aware of eco-

---

31. Whether or not one accepts the contention of recent critics such as R. H. Bloch that "the depreciation of the feminine lurks just below the surface of the courtly idealization of woman" (p. 148), the surface idealization is a very real phenomenon whose influence is clearly perceptible in the first two books of the *De amore*, and perhaps more strikingly by contrast with its opposite, the blatant misogyny of Book Three.

nomic considerations, they generally managed to keep them separate from sentiment. That is not the entire explanation, however.

The problem of reciprocity returns in another form in the passage that follows immediately the antifeminist section. Love is not a just ruler, for he carries unequal weights (*DA* 3.113–14 [320]). This is the last argument presented before the final summation, a fact that underlines its importance. The image of unequal weights is also developed in several passages of the first two books, beginning with Book One, Chapter Four, which claims that love is the source of all the virtues. The fundamental pessimism that this image conveys about the chances of establishing truly reciprocal love relationships is closely related to Andreas's pessimism about the prospects for exercising modesty or fidelity in love affairs. Physical consummation, with the negative physical and moral effects that he attributes to it, is relatively attainable, but reciprocity of sentiment, which is the only source of true satisfaction for the lover and upon which the moral claims of love ultimately rest, is much more illusive. The Chaplain's moral objections to love are thus supported by a basic psychological attitude.

Andreas's rejection of love in Book Three appears to be the result of a combination of factors, none of which is alone sufficient to explain it. The Chaplain's point of departure may well have been the example of Ovid—not so much the Ovid of the *Remedia amoris,* who disclaimed any intention to make an all-out attack on love (vv. 1–40), but rather the Ovid of the medieval *accessus* tradition, whose *Remedia* was seen as a retraction of his earlier works. The specific content of Book Three should probably be attributed to other factors, however: the meager results obtained in the earlier attempt to reconcile secular love with Christian morality, as well as the polarizing power of dialectic. Underlying the Chaplain's superficial about-face, a fundamental pessimism about the possibility of establishing a truly reciprocal love relationship remains constant throughout the treatise.

Beyond any intention to rewrite Ovid, the rejection of love in Book Three constitutes the admission of a double failure: the failure of the idealism expressed by the troubadours to withstand closer scrutiny, and especially Andreas's own failure to achieve the synthesis between the secular and Christian traditions that he had undertaken in the first two books. Falling back on the dialectical method that formed the essence of his intellectual training, Andreas transforms this admission into an affirmation, drawing up a point-by-point refutation of the case for love previously presented. In so doing, he expresses not only a position of unimpeachable orthodoxy consonant with his ecclesiastical calling, but also a basic mistrust of women and of love endemic to his clerical caste.

As the preceding discussion demonstrates, the relationship of the troubadours' secular love conceptions to Christian morality is the most complex and difficult of all the subjects treated in the *De amore*. It is not at all surprising that this problem has received a major share of critical attention nor that it has given rise to the most heated controversies. Ultimately our assessment of the treatise and of its place in twelfth-century culture depends to a large extent on our conclusions in this domain.

Although the critics' attention has generally been focused primarily on the global contradiction between the first two books and the third, we have seen that the problem is much more complex than that simple opposition would suppose. Long before rejecting love in Book Three, Andreas had undertaken in the first two books a major effort to reconcile secular love with Christian morality. This enterprise includes several separate strands: the affirmation of love as a source of virtue, an attempt to limit sexual activity in love relationships in terms of both the number of partners and the degree of intimacy, and an effort to regulate and codify love on the model of Christian marriage, even while protecting the latter from the moral contamination of the former. This endeavor of reconciliation must be considered together with the later rejection of love as composing the moral dimension of the *De amore*, corresponding to the generic vector that we have called *sapientia*.

The moral discussions of the *De amore* involve materials coming primarily from two traditions: that of the vernacular love poetry and that of Christian theology and canon law. The secular love conceptions of the troubadours and trouvères appear at first glance to be totally antithetical to Christian morality, and yet they contain elements of idealization that furnished Andreas his point of departure. These include the notion of moral amelioration through love, occasional expressions of renunciation of physical gratification, and a strong emphasis on fidelity. Starting from these elements, the Chaplain attempts his customary reconciliation between traditions. For one relatively minor moral question treated in passing, that of love and the clergy, Christian morality is opposed not to the vernacular love poetry, but to the satirical debate poems, chiefly in Latin, between knights and clerics.

Despite striking differences in tone and in general thrust, we have no reason to doubt the sincerity of the Chaplain's moral commitment in either part of his treatise. Although it has been largely neglected by the critics, moralization is an extremely widespread phenomenon in the first two books, affecting nearly every aspect of the discourse. It is pursued with tenacity and a remarkable degree of consistency; the only major exception is a certain laxity concerning the love of the clergy, apparently a case of special pleading for the interests of Andreas's own caste. Many of the attitudes, opinions, and even specific arguments of Book Three have already been anticipated in the earlier part of the treatise: in the words of the women of the dialogues, who often serve as spokespersons for Andreas, or in the authorial voice of the Chaplain himself. Rather than stressing the discrepancies, we should perhaps see the two contrasting parts of Andreas's moral undertaking as complementary strategies directed toward similar ends.

However serious Andreas's commitment to moralizing love, the results that he achieves in this domain are limited and disappointing. The notion of love as a source of virtue concerns primarily the secular social ethic of the vernacular literature, with respect to which his efforts at Christianization remain rather marginal and superficial, certainly not sufficient to offset the moral implications of physical love. The crux of the matter is the attempt to derive from love itself a limitation of sexual activity, an attempt that proves largely unsuccessful. Andreas's expressed preference for fidelity and for what he calls "pure love" seems genuine, but he is obliged to recognize, on the basis of his own love psychology, that neither is a realistic long-term prospect. Motivated apparently by a desire to protect the sanctity of marriage from the contamination of love, the strict separation of love and marriage constitutes a tacit admission of the moral inferiority of love. With respect to that admission, the efforts to reform love along the lines of marriage appear as superficial and marginal as the attempt to Christianize the secular love ethic. Despite the promise held out by certain idealistic elements in the poetry of the troubadours, their profane love conceptions ultimately prove refractory to reconciliation with Christian morality.

The unsatisfactory results obtained in the moral discussions of the first two books go a long way toward explaining the change of direction evident in Book Three. Having failed in his efforts to reform love from within, thus making it more acceptable from the point of view of Christian morality, Andreas adopts the opposite tactic of attacking it from without in the name of those same Christian values. To this essential, internal motivation, two external factors must be added: the example of Ovid, as filtered through the *accessus* tradition, who had set a precedent for retraction in this delicate matter; and the polarizing power of dialectic, which transforms Andreas's retraction into a general refutation of his earlier discourse. Underlying the entire operation is a fundamental pessimism about the prospects for reciprocity in love relationships, a typically clerical attitude that remains constant throughout the treatise. This pessimism undermines the very elements of troubadour idealism that served as the point of departure for Andreas's abortive synthesis. Consequently, the final outcome was to a certain extent foreseeable from the beginning.

CONCLUSION

As *we approach* the end of our inquiry, we can return to the questions with which we began: Why are Andreas Capellanus and his treatise on love so controversial? What is there about the *De amore* that makes it the object of such intense interest and, at the same time, such diverse interpretations? To what extent do divergent accounts of the work's meaning stem from differences in scholarly methodology, and to what extent are they engendered by the work itself? Is there an explanation that would not only account for the controversy but also, perhaps, point the way toward its resolution?

Probably the most important single conclusion emerging from all the previous discussion is a recognition of the profound complexity of the *De amore*. An outgrowth of the Chaplain's synthetic, scholastic method, this complexity affects every aspect of his treatise. Most visible in several aspects of the work's form, it also extends to the cultural context in which Andreas wrote, and so it must be taken into consideration in any assessment of his intended meaning. More than any other factor, it is this multifaceted complexity that has rendered the *De amore* difficult of access, thus giving rise to a plethora of conflicting scholarly interpretations.

Beginning with questions of form, we observed complexity first of all in the generic identity of the treatise. Although the didactic character of the work is not in question, the specific nature of its didacticism is more problematic. From the outset the *De amore* presents a tension between description and prescription, a dual identity as both a scientific treatise on a natural phenomenon *(scientia)* and a practical manual on the conduct of an activity *(ars)*. This fundamental tension is further complicated by a third generic vector, theological and moral in character, that seeks to judge the phenomenon and the activity in the light of eternal principles *(sapientia)*. The intricate interweaving of these three generic strands, all of which correspond to standard types of scholastic didactic discourse, extends to every aspect of the treatise, complicating any assessment of the author's intended purpose.

The generic complexity of the *De amore* is intimately related to a tension between competing scholastic methodologies used to structure the discourse. The dialectical interweaving of the structuring principles of rhetoric and dialectic is most evident in the dialogues, but it extends beyond them to inform the treatise as a whole. Since the winning of love is very much a matter of persuasion, rhetoric provides the point of departure, but owing to its subordinate role in twelfth-century scholastic culture, it soon yields before the overwhelming power of dialectic. From rhetorical models for would-be lovers, the dialogues are transformed into veritable *disputationes,* and the dialectical, antithetic principles that they embody are extended to the entire treatise. The elaborate "disputed question" thus established is not susceptible of a solution at the level of human reasoning, however, hence the Chaplain's recourse to the sacred rhetoric of Christian exhortation to provide a kind of resolution at the end.

Whether rhetorical or dialectical in structure, scholastic discourse is always intertextual in character, a discourse on other discourses. The intertextual nature of the *De amore* is visible at both the "micro" and the "macro" levels, in terms of the authoritative opinions invoked in support of individual arguments and the literary models used to structure the entire discourse. The major conclusion that emerges from the examination of these features is, once again, the complexity of Andreas's inspiration. In addition to the standard scholastic authorities, the Latin authors of the classical and Christian traditions, the Chaplain extends his canon to include courtly vernacular poetry as well as the non-literary authority of feudal society. Starting from the overall framework of Ovid's didactic-erotic poetry, Andreas modified that design in several ways, calling upon various contemporary models of Latin and vernacular discourse to update and complete the work of his predecessor. Thus his medieval adaptation of Ovid reflects all the complexities and tensions of twelfth-century courtly and scholastic culture.

The modern debate over ironic intentions in the *De amore* is among

the most eloquent witnesses to the work's complexity. The ironic interpretations proposed, ranging from the Christian to the crypto-erotic,
often stand in sharp contrast to each other, yet each can find a basis of
support in the treatise itself. Together they illustrate our modern discomfort with the complexities of twelfth-century culture reflected in
the *De amore* and the attendant temptation to reduce those complexities to something more manageable. At the same time, they point to
ironic discrepancies within the treatise that are probably best explained
in terms of Andreas's inability to dominate all the heterogeneous and
contradictory material that he has assembled on this most complex aspect of the human experience.

The complexity so evident in several of the formal aspects of the *De
amore* also extends to its contents. Beyond the contradictions and tensions created by competing methods and models or by the citation of
authoritative opinions from diverse cultural traditions, much of this
complexity stems from the subject under investigation. Love between
the sexes is first of all a matter of human psychology and physiology,
but it also has profound implications for both the social and the ethical
realms, and all these dimensions are reflected in Andreas's comprehen-
sive treatment. In the interest of clarity we have considered separately
these various strands of the Chaplain's doctrine, but they are closely interrelated in many ways. The treatise itself makes no such distinctions,
constantly interweaving material of a psychological, social, and ethical
character. This integrated treatment is in keeping with the complex nature of the subject, but it has the effect of further confusing the work's
message.

The complexity characterizing the *De amore* is itself complex. It is
manifested on several levels: in the work's generic identity and form, in
the cultural context that it reflects, and in the subject that it seeks to investigate. This central characteristic of the treatise goes a long way toward explaining the controversy that has always surrounded it. In the
face of multiple, baffling complexities, scholars have always been
tempted to simplify, to reduce the *De amore* to something more manageable. The traditional view that sees the work as a key to understanding the vernacular poetry of "courtly love" is no less reductive than the
ironic interpretations that have more recently sought to replace it. At

the same time, the very complexity of the treatise means that several very different theories can find support in it. The challenge that the *De amore* poses to modern readers is to make sense of it while maintaining its complexity.

How can we dissipate some of the ambiguity surrounding the treatise without reducing its complex message to a fraction of itself? This requires, first of all, that we recognize the work's "constructedness." The *De amore* is not an innocent, neutral mirror of medieval social practice, nor is it the straightforward codification of a novel theory of love expressed more ambiguously in medieval vernacular literature. It is rather a highly artificial construction, incorporating courtly poetic themes and feudal social attitudes into a learned, clerical discourse with respect to which they are essentially alien. It subjects the vernacular thematic material to modes of thought and expression very different from those of the lyric poetry or the courtly romance, with the result that the courtly themes are inevitably altered in the process. In short, the meaning of the material in the treatise can not be separated from the manner of its treatment.

Another key to understanding the *De amore* is the recognition of its unique position at the intersection of very different cultural currents. In bringing to bear on the courtly themes the powerful tools of scholasticism, Andreas juxtaposes those themes to opinions and attitudes from other, very different traditions. The moral dictates of the Christian Church, the love writings of Ovid, even a certain social reality of the feudal courts contributed no less than the vernacular poetry to the Chaplain's inspiration. Book Three is not an afterthought designed to protect the clerical author from the scandal of a work promoting profane sexual love, for the Christian morality that it embodies runs throughout the first two books as well. Nor is it the straightforward statement of a message of clerical condemnation previously expressed ironically, for the earlier books present a serious attempt to reconcile secular love with Christianity, drawing on the idealism expressed in the vernacular literature. Book Three does signal a certain failure of synthesis, but it is a failure long resisted in the first two books, a failure rendered more or less inevitable by the heterogeneity of the material considered.

Why was such an enterprise undertaken in the first place? The question of authorial intentions that has aroused such controversy remains to a certain extent refractory to scholarly explanations. Certain of Andreas's intentions are obvious, such as that of rewriting Ovid in a medieval mode or that of subjecting the poetic theme of love to a systematic, scholastic treatment, but the spirit brought to the task remains elusive. Was the *De amore* originally conceived as a serious undertaking or as an elaborate joke? The treatise can lend support to both of these hypotheses, which are not necessarily mutually exclusive. If it began as a joke, it may have taken on the character of a serious project in the course of its elaboration. If the original project was a serious one, it may have uncovered paradoxes and discrepancies in the subject that can only be interpreted as comical or ironic. Whatever the Chaplain's initial intention, it may well have changed in the course of the project's completion, and in any case it is now irretrievably lost. What remains is the treatise itself, with all its complexities, tensions, ambiguities, and contradictions.

If the *De amore* is not a ready reference guide to the poetry of "courtly love," nor the clerical condemnation of such a social and literary fashion, what are its uses? What did Andreas achieve with his treatise, and why should we be interested in it? Without endorsing the sweeping claims that have sometimes been put forward as to the importance of this work for medieval culture, we can point to a number of achievements, more limited in scope but nevertheless substantial, that emerge from the second half of the present study.

High on the list of the Chaplain's achievements we can cite his definition of love. Despite minor problems in the use of terms, it is a rigorous, carefully constructed, elegant definition steeped in the tradition of medieval philosophy, though not without literary antecedents. Couched implicitly in the terminology of Aristotelian causality, it stresses the generic status of love as an "internal affect," or emotion, before going on to delimit it specifically in terms of the efficient causes of sight and meditation and the final cause of sexual union. It is not at all surprising that Andreas's definition enjoyed great popularity in the later Middle Ages, for it is arguably the best definition of love between the sexes produced in the entire medieval period.

Starting from an essentially psychological definition, Andreas goes on to develop a fairly elaborate and extensive psychology of love. The aspects of the subject considered include the role of sight and meditation in the generation of love, the function of desire and will in its subsequent development, the physical and mental aptitudes required for loving, the dynamics that the process generally assumes once it is set in motion, and the pain and suffering, fear and jealousy, that are the habitual result of those dynamics. Except in the early chapters, the treatment is somewhat fragmentary, but it is consistent in stressing the central role of meditation and desire in the psychological process of loving, while also expressing pessimism about the possibility of establishing and maintaining reciprocal love relationships. The concepts developed are not profound, but they have profound consequences for the social and ethical questions examined in the treatise. They also shed considerable light on the love psychology of the vernacular poetry, which constitutes a major source for this part of the discussion.

The Chaplain's treatment of the social ramifications of love is among the most solid of his achievements. In the dialogues and elsewhere he examines a number of interrelated social questions, including the competing claims of nobility of birth and of worth, as well as the roles of deeds and service, wealth and generosity, courtesy and reputation, in winning and maintaining love. Basing his discussion in large part on thematic material from the vernacular poetry, Andreas works out many of the social implications of the courtly themes, while also raising and attempting to resolve contradictions within the courtly tradition or, in some cases, between it and other traditions, such as the attitudes of northern French feudal society, the love writings of Ovid, or the dictates of Christian morality. He thus elaborates, from essentially literary sources, a kind of self-contained, secular social ethic based on the refinement and sublimation of sexual love.

The most ambitious dimension of the Chaplain's enterprise is its ethical component, but here his achievement is somewhat more ambiguous. The ethical thrust of the *De amore* includes two distinct, complementary elements: an attempt in the first two books to reconcile sexual love with Christian morality, followed by the rejection of love in Book Three on the grounds of their incompatibility. Taking as his point of departure the idealism expressed in the vernacular literature, Andreas deploys several strategies to make profane love morally acceptable from the point of view of Christianity: affirming love as a source of virtue, attempting to limit sexual activity in love relationships in terms of both the number of partners and the degree of intimacy, and attempting to regulate and codify love on the model of Christian marriage, even while protecting the latter from the moral contamination of the former. The radical rejection of love, largely on moral grounds, with which the treatise ends marks the ultimate failure of Andreas's project of reconciliation. Nevertheless, this essentially negative conclusion has the positive result of illustrating graphically the limitations of courtly idealism.

Although it is not a key to "courtly love," the *De amore* can contribute a great deal to our understanding of the nature and function of love in medieval literature. With its many psychological, social, and ethical ramifications, vernacular poetry contributes significantly to every aspect of Andreas's enterprise, making it perhaps the most important single source of material for the treatise. Nevertheless, the *De amore* occupies a unique position in the courtly tradition, which cannot be reduced to the simple question whether the Chaplain was for or against profane love. By subjecting the poetic themes to the powerful tools of dialectic, by juxtaposing them to material from other traditions, Andreas dissipates their ambiguities, makes explicit their implications, reveals their contradictions and ironies, their impossible idealism, their inadequacy as models of behavior in the real world—in short, their "poeticity." Thus the Chaplain's scholastic treatment of the courtly themes reaffirms them in the process of transforming them. Because of its unique approach to the subject, the *De amore* offers a privileged point of comparison and contrast with respect to other works of literature in the courtly tradition, but this requires a new, more nuanced use of it based on a full recognition of its anomalous place within that tradition.

The *De amore* is very much a product of its own time, but its implications extend well beyond any antiquarian concern for medieval culture, which may help to explain the sustained interest that it continues to arouse today. Not only did Andreas choose a subject of universal appeal, he also brought to its analysis a method singularly appropriate.

What better way to examine the complex, contradictory subject of love than with the antithetical tools of dialectic? What better way to investigate this most poetic of human experiences, with regard to which literary models have always played such an important role in forming perceptions and expectations, than by assembling the opinions of the authors? Perhaps the Chaplain's greatest achievement is his refusal to reduce the complexity of his subject. Thus, though he did not succeed in resolving all the problems, he continues to provide us with stimulation and insight, as we carry on struggling with all the complexities and contradictions of love.

BIBLIOGRAPHY

I. Reference Works

Deferrari, Roy J., and M. Inviolata Barry. *A Lexicon of St. Thomas Aquinas.* Washington: Catholic University of America Press, 1948.

Du Cange, Charles du Fresne. *Glossarium mediæ et infirmæ latinitatis.* New ed. 10 vols. Niort: Favre, 1883–87.

Gamillscheg, Ernst. *Etymologisches Wörterbuch der französischen Sprache.* 2nd ed. Heidelberg: Winter, 1969.

Grand Robert de la langue française. 2nd ed. 9 vols. Paris: Le Robert, 1985.

Grundriss der romanischen Literaturen des Mittelalters [*GRLMA*], 6: *La Littérature didactique, allégorique et satirique.* Ed. Hans Robert Jauss. 2 vols. Heidelberg: Winter, 1968–70.

Latham, R. E. *Revised Medieval Latin Word-List.* London: British Academy, 1965.

Lausberg, Heinrich. *Handbook of Literary Rhetoric: A Foundation for Literary Study.* Ed. David E. Orton and Dean Anderson. Trans. Matthew T. Bliss, Annemiek Jansen, and David E. Orton. Leiden: Brill, 1998.

Lewis, Charlton T., and Charles Short. *A Latin Dictionary.* Oxford: Clarendon Press, 1879; repr. 1984.

Manitius, Max. *Geschichte der lateinischen Literatur des Mittelalters.* 3 vols. Munich: Beck, 1911–1931; repr. 1964–65.

Niermeyer, J. F. *Mediæ latinitatis lexicon minus.* 2 vols. Leiden: Brill, 1976.

Oxford Latin Dictionary. Ed. P. G. W. Glare. Oxford: Clarendon Press, 1982.

Pillet, Alfred, and Henry Carstens. *Bibliographie der Troubadours.* Halle: Niemeyer, 1933.

Souter, Alexander. *A Glossary of Later Latin to 600 A.D.* Oxford: Clarendon Press, 1949.

Thesaurus linguæ latinæ. 10 vols. Leipzig: Teubner, 1900–.

Trésor de la langue française. Ed. Paul Imbs. 16 vols. Paris: Editions du CNRS, 1971–94.

Walther, Hans. *Lateinische Sprichwörter und Sentenzen des Mittelalters.* 5 vols. Göttingen: Vandenhoeck und Ruprecht, 1963.

Wartburg, Walter von. *Französisches Etymologisches Wörterbuch* [*FEW*]. 29 vols. Bonn: Klopp, 1928–.

II. Editions and Translations of Primary Sources

Abelard, Peter. *Dialectica.* Ed. L. M. de Rijk. 2nd ed. Assen: Van Gorcum, 1970.

———. *Sic et non.* Ed. Blanche B. Boyer and Richard McKeon. Chicago: University of Chicago Press, 1977.

Aelred of Rievaulx. *Aelredi Rievallensis, Opera omnia.* Ed. A. Hoste and C. H. Talbot. Turnholt: Brepols, 1971.

———. *Aelred of Rievaulx's Spiritual Friendship.* Trans. Mark F. Williams. Scranton: University of Scranton Press, 1994.

Alfarabi. *Über den Ursprung der Wissenschaften (De ortu scientiarum).* Ed. Clemens Bäumker. Münster: Aschendorff, 1916.

Andreas Capellanus. *Andreæ Capellani Regii Francorum, De amore libri tres.* Ed. E. Trojel. Copenhagen: Gad, 1892; new ed. Munich: Fink, 1972.

———. *Andreas Capellanus, De amore, libri tres: Text llatí amb la traducció catalana del segle XIV.* Ed. Amadeu Pagès. Castelló de la Plana: [Sociedad castellonese de cultura], 1930.

———. *Andrea Cappellano, Trattato d'amore: "De amore" libri tres. Testo latino del sec. XII con due traduzioni del sec. XIV.* Ed. Salvatore Battaglia. Rome: Perrella, 1947.

———. *The Art of Courtly Love.* Trans. John J. Parry. New York: Columbia University Press, 1941; new ed. 1969.

———. *André le Chapelain, Traité de l'amour courtois.* Trans. Claude Buridant. Paris: Klincksieck, 1974.

———. *Andrea Cappellano, De amore.* Ed. Graziano Ruffini. Milan: Guanda, 1980.

———. *On Love [DA].* Ed. and trans. P. G. Walsh. London: Duckworth, 1982.

Aristotle. *Aristoteles Latinus [AL].* Ed. Lorenzo Minio Paluello. 33 vols. Bruges: De Brower, 1951–.

———. *Art of Rhetoric.* Ed. and trans. J. H. Freese. Cambridge, Mass.: Harvard University Press, 1976.

———. *Categories, On Interpretation.* Ed. and trans. H. P. Cooke; *Prior Analytics.* Ed and trans. H. Tredennick. Cambridge, Mass.: Harvard University Press, 1962.

———. *Nicomachean Ethics.* Ed. and trans. H. Rackham. Cambridge, Mass.: Harvard University Press, 1960.

———. *Posterior Analytics.* Ed. and trans. Hugh Tredennick; *Topics.* Ed. and trans. E. S. Forster. Cambridge, Mass.: Harvard University Press, 1960.

[———]. *Problems.* Ed. and trans. W. S. Hett. 2 vols. Cambridge, Mass.: Harvard University Press, 1953–57.

Boethius. *Boethius's De topicis differentiis.* Trans. Eleanore Stump. Ithaca: Cornell University Press, 1978.

———. *In Isagogen Porphyrii commenta.* 2nd redaction. Ed. Samuel Brandt. Vienna: Tempsky, 1906.

Bouchet, Guillaume. *Les Serées* 1. Poitiers, 1584.

Boutière, J., and A. H. Schutz, eds. *Biographies des troubadours: Textes provençaux des XIIIᵉ et XIVᵉ siècles.* 2nd ed. Paris: Nizet, 1973.

Cicero. *De inventione; De optimo genere oratorum; Topica.* Ed. H. M. Hubbell. Cambridge, Mass.: Harvard University Press, 1949.

[————]. *Ad C. Herennium: De ratione dicendi (Rhetorica ad Herennium)*. Ed. and trans. Harry Caplan. Cambridge, Mass.: Harvard University Press, 1954.

Drouart la Vache. *Li Livres d'Amours de Drouart la Vache*. Ed. Robert Bossuat. Paris: Champion, 1926.

Faral, Edmond. *Les Arts poétiques du XIIe et du XIIIe siècle*. Paris: Champion, 1924; repr. 1962.

Gilbert of Poitiers. *The Commentaries on Boethius*. Ed. Nikolaus M. Häring. Toronto: Pontifical Institute of Mediaeval Studies, 1966.

Goddard, Alison, ed. "The *Facetus:* or, The Art of Courtly Living." *Allegorica* 2 (1977): 27–57.

Guillaume de Lorris and Jean de Meun. *Le Roman de la Rose*. Ed. Felix Lecoy. 3 vols. Paris: Champion, 1965–1970.

Gundissalinus, Dominicus. *De divisione philosophiæ*. Ed. Ludwig Baur. Münster: Aschendorff, 1903.

Halm, Carolus. *Rhetores latini minores*. Leipzig: Teubner, 1863.

Hartlieb, Johann. *De Amore deutsch: Der Traktatus des Andreas Capellanus in der Übersetzung Johann Hartliebs*. Ed. Alfred Karnein. Munich: Beck, 1970.

Huygens, R. B. C. *Accessus ad auctores: Bernard d'Utrecht; Conrad d'Hirsau, Dialogus super auctores*. Leiden: Brill, 1970.

Hugh of Saint Victor. *Hugonis de Sancto Victore, Didascalicon: De studio legendi*. Ed. Charles H. Buttimer. Washington: Catholic University of America Press, 1939.

————. *The Didascalicon*. Trans. Jerome Taylor. New York: Columbia University Press, 1961.

————. *On the Sacraments of the Christian Faith (De sacramentis)*. Trans. Roy J. Deferrari. Cambridge, Mass.: Medieval Academy of America, 1951.

Isidore of Seville. *Etymologiarum sive originum libri XX*. Ed. Wallace M. Lindsay. 2 vols. Oxford: Clarendon Press, 1911.

John of Garland. *Parisiana poetria*. Ed. and trans. Traugott Lawler. New Haven: Yale University Press, 1974.

John of Salisbury. *Ioannis Saresberiensis, Metalogicon*. Ed. J. B. Hall. Turnhout: Brepols, 1991.

————. *The Metalogicon*. Trans. Daniel D. McGarry. Berkeley: University of California Press, 1955.

Latzke, Therese. "Die Carmina erotica der RipollSammlung." *Mittellateinisches Jahrbuch* 10 (1975): 138–201.

McKeon, Richard. *Selections from Medieval Philosophers*. 2 vols. New York: Scribner's, 1929–30.

Migne, J.-P., ed. *Patrologiæ cursus completus, Series latina [PL]*. 221 vols. Paris: Garnier, 1844–1905.

Miller, Joseph M., Michael H. Prosser, and Thomas W. Benson. *Readings in Medieval Rhetoric*. Bloomington: Indiana University Press, 1973.

Minnis, A. J., and A. B. Scott. *Medieval Literary Theory and Criticism, c. 1100–c. 1375*. Rev. ed. Oxford: Clarendon Press, 1991.

O'Hara-Tobin, Prudence M., ed. *Les Lais anonyme des XIIe et XIIIe siècles*. Geneva: Droz, 1979.

Oulmont, Charles, ed. *Les Débats du clerc et du chevalier.* Paris: Champion, 1911.

Ovid. *The Art of Love and Other Poems.* Ed. and trans. J. H. Mozley. Rev. ed. Cambridge, Mass.: Harvard University Press, 1939.

———. *Heroides and Amores.* Ed. and trans. Grant Showerman. Cambridge, Mass.: Harvard University Press, 1914.

"Pamphilus." Ed. Stefano Pittaluga. In *Commedie latine del XII e XIII secolo.* Ed. Ferruccio Bertini. 6 vols. Genoa: Istituto di Filologia Classica e Medievale, 1976–98, 3 (1980): 11–137.

Peire Rogier. *Das Leben und die Lieder des Trobadors Peire Rogier.* Ed. Carl Appel. Berlin: Reimer, 1882.

———. *The Poems of the Troubadour Peire Rogier.* Ed. Derek E. T. Nicholson. Manchester: Manchester University Press, 1976.

Peter of Blois. *Un traité de l'amour du XIIᵉ siècle.* Ed. M. M. Davy. Paris: Boccard, 1932.

Philip the Chancellor. *Summa de bono.* Ed. Nikolaus Wicki. 2 vols. Berne: Francke, 1985.

The Prose Salernitan Questions. Ed. Brian Lawn. London: British Academy, 1979.

Li Proverbe au vilain. Ed. Adolf Tobler. Leipzig: Hirzel, 1895.

Pucci, Antonio. *Libro di varie storie.* Ed. Alberto Varvaro. Palermo: Academia di Scienze, Lettere e Arti, 1957.

Quintilian. *Institutio oratoria.* Ed. H. E. Butler. 4 vols. Cambridge, Mass.: Harvard University Press, 1920.

Remigius of Auxerre. *Remigii Autissiodorensis, In artem Donati minorem commentum.* Ed. Wilhelm Fox. Leipzig: Teubner, 1892.

Robert Grosseteste. *Die philosophischen Werke des Robert Grosseteste.* Ed. Ludwig Baur. Münster: Aschendorff, 1912.

Rockinger, Ludwig. *Briefsteller und Formelbücher des eilften bis vierzehnten Jahrhunderts.* 2 vols. Munich: Franz, 1863–64.

Sansone, Giuseppe E., ed. *Testi didattico-cortesi di Provenza.* Bari: Adriatica, 1977.

Schultz-Gora, O., ed. "Ein ungedruckter *Salu d'amors* nebst Antwort." *Zeitschrift für romanische Philologie* 24 (1900): 358–69.

Thomas Aquinas. *Commentary on the Posterior Analytics of Aristotle.* Trans. F. R. Larcher. Albany, N.Y.: Magi, 1970.

———. *Opera omnia.* 25 vols. Parma: Fiaccadori, 1852–1873.

———. *S. Thomæ Aquinatis, Opera omnia.* Ed. Roberto Busa. 7 vols. Stuttgart: Frommann, 1980.

———. *Summa Theologiæ.* Ed. Blackfriars. 61 vols. New York: McGraw-Hill, 1964–1981.

William of Auvergne. Guilelmus Arvernus, *Opera omnia,* 2 vols. Paris, 1674; repr. Frankfurt am Main: Minerva, 1963.

William of Conches. Guillaume de Conches, *Glosæ super Platonem.* Ed. Edouard Jeauneau. Paris: Vrin, 1965.

III. Secondary Studies

Adams, James N. *The Latin Sexual Vocabulary.* Baltimore: Johns Hopkins University Press, 1982.

Akehurst, Frank R. "Les étapes de l'amour chez Bernard de Ventadour." *Cahiers de Civilisation Médiévale* 16 (1973): 133–47.

———. "Words and Acts in the Troubadours." In Lazar and Lacy, pp. 17–28.

Allen, Peter. *The Art of Love: Amatory Fiction from Ovid to the "Romance of the Rose."* Philadelphia: University of Pennsylvania Press, 1992.

Amsler, Mark. *Etymology and Grammatical Discourse in Late Antiquity and the Early Middle Ages.* Philadelphia: Benjamin, 1989.

Auerbach, Erich. *Literary Language and Its Public in Late Latin Antiquity and the Middle Ages.* New York: Pantheon, 1965.

———. "Passio als Leidenschaft." *PMLA* 56 (1941): 1179–96.

———. "Remarques sur le mot 'passion.'" *Neuphilologische Mitteilungen* 38 (1937): 218–24.

Badel, Pierre-Yves. *Le Roman de la Rose au XIVe siècle: Etude de la réception de l'œuvre.* Geneva: Droz, 1980.

Baldwin, John W. *Aristocratic Life in Medieval France.* Baltimore: Johns Hopkins University Press, 2000.

———. "L'*Ars amatoria* au XIIe siècle en France: Ovide, Abélard, André le Chapelain et Pierre le Chantre." In *Histoire et société: Mélanges offerts à Georges Duby,* pp. 1–26. Aix-en-Provence: Université de Provence, 1992.

———. "Five Discourses on Desire: Sexuality and Gender in Northern France around 1200." *Speculum* 66 (1991): 797–819.

———. *The Language of Sex: Five Voices from Northern France around 1200.* Chicago: University of Chicago Press, 1994.

———. *Masters, Princes, and Merchants: The Social Views of Peter the Chanter and His Circle.* 2 vols. Princeton: Princeton University Press, 1970.

Bec, Pierre. "La Douleur et son univers poétique chez Bernard de Ventadour." *Cahiers de Civilisation Médiévale* 11 (1968): 545–71.

Benoit, Marie. "Le *De amore;* dialectique et rhétorique." In E. Ruhe and Behrens, pp. 13–21.

Benson, Robert L., and Giles Constable, eds. *Renaissance and Renewal in the Twelfth Century.* Cambridge, Mass.: Harvard University Press, 1982.

Benton, John F. "Clio and Venus: An Historical View of Medieval Love." In Newman, pp. 19–42.

———. "Collaborative Approaches to Fantasy and Reality in the Literature of Champagne." In Burgess, pp. 43–57.

———. "The Court of Champagne as a Literary Center." *Speculum* 36 (1961): 551–91.

———. "The Evidence for Andreas Capellanus Re-examined Again." *Studies in Philology* 59 (1962): 471–78.

Bergson, Henri. *Laughter: An Essay on the Meaning of the Comic.* Trans. Cloudesley Brereton and Fred Rothwell. New York: Macmillan, 1911.

Bloch, Marc. *Feudal Society.* Trans. L. A. Manyon. 2 vols. Chicago: University of Chicago Press, 1961.

Bloch, R. Howard. *Medieval Misogyny and the Invention of Western Romantic Love.* Chicago: University of Chicago Press, 1991.

Booth, Wayne C. *A Rhetoric of Irony.* Chicago: University of Chicago Press, 1974.

Bourke, Vernon J. *Will in Western Thought: An Historico-Critical Survey.* New York: Sheed and Ward, 1964.

Bowden, Betsy. "The Art of Courtly Copulation." *Medievalia et Humanistica* 9 (1979): 67–85.

Briscoe, Marianne G. *Artes prædicandi;* Barbara H. Jaye. *Atres orandi.* Turnhout: Brepols, 1992.

Brown, Catherine. *Contrary Things: Exegesis, Dialectic, and the Poetics of Didacticism.* Stanford: Stanford University Press, 1998.

Bruckner, Matilda T. *Narrative Invention in Twelfth-Century French Romance: The Convention of Hospitality (1160–1200).* Lexington, Ky.: French Forum, 1980.

Brundage, James A. *Law, Sex, and Christian Society in Medieval Europe.* Chicago: University of Chicago Press, 1987.

Bumke, Joachim. *Mäzene in Mittelalter: Die Gönner und Auftraggeber der höfischen Literatur in Deutschland, 1150–1300.* Munich: Beck, 1979.

Bundy, Murray Wright. *The Theory of Imagination in Classical and Medieval Thought.* Urbana: University of Illinois Press, 1927; repr. Folcroft, Pa.: Folcroft Press, 1976.

Burgess, Glyn S., ed. *Court and Poet.* Liverpool: Francis Cairns, 1981.

Buttruff, Douglas R. "The Comedy of Coquetry in Andreas' *De amore.*" *Classical Folia* 28 (1974): 181–90.

Cadden, Joan. *Meanings of Sex Difference in the Middle Ages: Medicine, Science, and Culture.* Cambridge: Cambridge University Press, 1993.

Cairns, Francis. "Andreas Capellanus, Ovid, and the Consistency of the *De amore.*" *Res Publica Litterarum* 16 (1993): 101–17.

Camargo, Martin. *Ars dictaminis, ars dictandi.* Turnhout: Brepols, 1991.

Campbell, K. S. "Irony, Medieval and Modern, and the Allegory of Rhetoric." *Allegorica* 4 (1979): 290–300.

Carlson, David. "Religion and Romance: The Language of Love in the Treatises of Gerard of Liège and the Case of Andreas Capellanus." In Lazar and Lacy, pp. 81–92.

Cartlidge, Neil. *Medieval Marriage: Literary Approaches, 1100–1300.* Woodbridge: Brewer, 1997.

Chadwick, Henry. *Boethius: The Consolation of Music, Logic, Theology, and Philosophy.* Oxford: Clarendon Press, 1981.

Chenu, M[arie]-D[ominique]. "Auctor, Actor, Autor." *Bulletin Du Cange* 3 (1927): 81–86.

Cherchi, Paolo. *Andreas and the Ambiguity of Courtly Love.* Toronto: University of Toronto Press, 1994.

———. "Andreas' *De amore:* Its Unity and Polemical Origin." In idem, *Andrea Cappellano, I trovatori e altri temi romanzi,* pp. 83–111. Rome: Bulzoni, 1979.

———. "New Uses of Andreas' *De amore.*" In Ruhe and Behrens, pp. 22–30.

Cherniss, Michael D. "The Literary Comedy of Andreas Capellanus." *Modern Philology* 72 (1975): 223–37.

Chydenius, Johan. *Love and the Medieval Tradition.* Helsinki: Societas Scientiarum Fennica, 1977.

Cline, Ruth. "Heart and Eyes." *Romance Philology* 25 (1971–1972): 263–97.

Crane, Ronald S. "On Hypotheses in 'Historical Criticism': A propos of Certain Contemporary Medievalists." In idem, *The Idea of the Humanities and Other Essays*. 2 vols. Chicago: University of Chicago Press, 1967, 2:236–60.

Cropp, Glynnis. "L'Expression de la générosité chez les troubadours." In *Studia occitanica in memoriam Paul Remy*. Ed. Hans-Erich Keller et al. 2 vols. Kalamazoo, Mich.: Medieval Institute, 1986, 2:255–68.

———. *Le Vocabulaire courtois des troubadours de l'époque classique*. Geneva: Droz, 1975.

Curtius, Ernst Robert. *European Literature and the Latin Middle Ages*. Trans. Willard R. Trask. Princeton: Princeton University Press, 1973.

Dahlberg, Charles. *The Literature of Unlikeness*. Hanover: University of New England Press, 1988.

Dällenbach, Lucien. *The Mirror in the Text*. Trans. Jeremy Whitely and Emma Hughes. Chicago: University of Chicago Press, 1989.

D'Alverny, Marie-Thérèse. "Translations and Translators." In Benson and Constable, pp. 421–62.

Delhaye, Philippe. "L'Enseignement de la philosophie morale au XIIe siècle." *Mediaeval Studies* 11 (1949): 77–99.

———. "'Grammatica' et 'Ethica' au XIIe siècle." *Recherches de théologie ancienne et médiévale* 25 (1958): 59–110.

Demats, Paule. "D'*Amœnitas* à *Déduit*: André le Chapelain et Guillaume de Lorris." In *Mélanges . . . Jean Frappier*, pp. 217–33. Geneva: Droz, 1970.

Denomy, Alexander J. *The Heresy of Courtly Love*. New York: McMullen, 1947.

De Paepe, Norbert. "'Amor' und 'verus amor' bei Andreas Capellanus: Versuch einer Lösung des 'reprobatio'-Problems." In *Mélanges . . . René Crozet*, pp. 921–27. Poitiers: Société d'Etudes Médiévales, 1966.

Donaldson, E. Talbot. "The Myth of Courtly Love." *Ventures* 5, 2 (1965): 16–23; repr. in idem, *Speaking of Chaucer*, pp. 154–63. New York: Norton, 1970.

Dronke, Peter. "Andreas Capellanus." *Journal of Medieval Latin* 4 (1994): 51–63.

———. *Medieval Latin and the Rise of European Love-Lyric*. 2 vols. Oxford: Clarendon Press, 1968.

Duby, Georges. *The Three Orders: Feudal Society Imagined*. Trans. Arthur Goldhammer. Chicago: University of Chicago Press, 1980.

Ferrante, Joan M., and George D. Economou. *In Pursuit of Perfection: Courtly Love in Medieval Literature*. Port Washington, N.Y.: Kennikat Press, 1975.

Fish, Stanley. *Is There a Text in This Class?: The Authority of Interpretive Communities*. Cambridge, Mass.: Harvard University Press, 1980.

Flori, Jean. *Chevaliers et chevalerie au Moyen Age*. Paris: Hachette, 1998.

Fortenbaugh, W. W. *Aristotle on Emotion*. New York: Barnes and Noble, 1975.

Frappier, Jean. *Amour et Table Ronde*. Geneva: Droz, 1973.

———. "Le Motif du 'don contraignant' dans la littérature du moyen âge." *Travaux de Linguistique et de Littérature* 7 (1969): 7–46; repr. in idem, *Amour et Table Ronde*, pp. 225–64.

———. "Sur un procès fait à l'amour courtois." *Romania* 93 (1972): 145–93; repr. in idem, *Amour et Table Ronde*, pp. 61–96.

———. "Vues sur les conceptions courtoises." *Cahiers de Civilisation Médiévale* 2 (1959): 135–56; repr. in idem, *Amour et Table Ronde,* pp. 1–31.

Friedman, Lionel J. "Gradus amoris." *Romance Philology* 19 (1965): 167–77.

Freud, Sigmund. *Jokes and Their Relation to the Unconscious.* The Standard Edition of the Complete Psychological Works of Sigmund Freud, vol. 8. London: Hogarth Press, 1905.

Gaffney, Barbara Marie. "Andreas Capellanus and the Myth of Courtly Love." Ph.D. dissertation, Arizona State University, 1977 (*Dissertation Abstracts International* 38:1408A).

Ganshof, F. L. *Feudalism.* Trans. Philip Grierson. New York: Harper Torch, 1961.

Gaunt, Simon. "Sexual Difference and the Metaphor of Language in a Troubadour Poem." *Modern Language Review* 83 (1988): 297–313.

———. *Troubadours and Irony.* Cambridge: Cambridge University Press, 1989.

Gay-Crosier, Raymond. *Religious Elements in the Secular Lyrics of the Troubadours.* Chapel Hill: University of North Carolina Press, 1971.

Genette, Gérard. *Palimpsests: Literature in the Second Degree.* Trans. Channa Newman and Claude Doubinsky. Lincoln: University of Nebraska Press, 1997.

———. *Paratexts: Thresholds of Interpretation.* Trans. Jane E. Lewin. Cambridge: Cambridge University Press, 1997.

Grabmann, Martin. *Die Geschichte der scholastischen Methode.* 2 vols. Freiburg im Breisgau, 1911; new ed. Darmstadt: Wissenschaftliche Buchgesellschaft, 1956.

Gravdal, Kathryn. *Ravishing Maidens: Writing Rape in Medieval French Literature and Law.* Philadelphia: University of Pennsylvania Press, 1991.

Green, Dennis H. *Irony in the Medieval Romance.* Cambridge: Cambridge University Press, 1979.

Grice, H. Paul. "Logic and Conversation." In *Syntax and Semantics, 3: Speech Acts.* Ed. Peter Cole and Jerry L. Morgan, pp. 41–58. New York: Academic Press, 1975.

Grimes, Margaret E. "Le Lay du Trot." *Romanic Review* 26 (1935): 313–21.

Gründel, Johannes. *Die Lehre von den Umständen der menschlichen Handlung im Mittelalter.* Münster: Aschendorff, 1963.

Haidu, Peter. *Aesthetic Distance in Chrétien de Troyes: Irony and Comedy in Cligés and Perceval.* Geneva: Droz, 1968.

———. "Au Début du roman, l'ironie." *Poétique* 36 (1978): 443–66.

Harvey, E. Ruth. *The Inward Wits: Psychological Theory in the Middle Ages and Renaissance.* London: Warburg Institute, 1975.

Highet, Gilbert. *Anatomy of Satire.* Princeton: Princeton University Press, 1962.

Hissette, Roland. "André le Chapelain et la double vérité." *Bulletin de Philosophie Médiévale* 21 (1979): 63–67.

———. "Une *duplex sententia* dans le *De amore* d'André le Chapelain?" *Recherches de théologie ancienne et médiévale* 50 (1983): 246–51.

Howard, Donald R. *The Three Temptations: Medieval Man in Search of the World.* Princeton: Princeton University Press, 1966.

Hunt, Richard W. "The Introductions to the 'Artes' in the Twelfth Century." In *Studia mediævalia in honorem . . . Raymundi Josephi Martin,* pp. 85–112. Bruges: De Tempel, 1948.

Hunt, Tony. "Aristotle, Dialectic, and Courtly Literature." *Viator* 10 (1979): 95–129.

Hutcheon, Linda. "Ironie, satire, parodie." *Poétique* 46 (1981): 140–55.

Jackson, W. T. H. "The *De amore* of Andreas Capellanus and the Practice of Love at Court." *Romanic Review* 49 (1958): 243–51.

Jacquart, Danielle, and Claude Thomasset. *Sexuality and Medicine in the Middle Ages.* Trans. Matthew Adamson. Princeton: Princeton University Press, 1988.

Jaeger, C. Stephen. *Ennobling Love: In Search of a Lost Sensibility.* Philadelphia: University of Pennsylvania Press, 1999.

———. *The Origins of Courtliness: Civilizing Trends and the Formation of Courtly Ideals, 939–1210.* Philadelphia: University of Pennsylvania Press, 1985.

———. "Patrons and the Beginning of Courtly Romance." In *The Medieval Opus: Imitation, Rewriting, and Transmission in the French Tradition.* Ed. Douglas Kelly, pp. 45–58. Amsterdam: Rodopi, 1996.

Jenny, Laurent. "The Strategy of Form." In *French Literary Theory Today.* Ed. Tzvetan Todorov, pp. 34–63. Trans. R. Carter. Cambridge: Cambridge University Press, 1982.

Joachim, H. H. *Aristotle, The Nicomachean Ethics: A Commentary.* Oxford: Clarendon Press, 1951.

Jolles, André. *Formes simples.* Trans. Antoine-Marie Buguet. Paris: Editions du Seuil, 1972.

Jonin, Pierre. "Le Vassalage de Lancelot dans le *Conte de la charette.*" *Moyen Age* 58 (1952): 281–98.

Karnein, Alfred. "*Amor est passio*—A Definition of Courtly Love?" In Burgess, pp. 215–21.

———. *Amor est passio: Untersuchungen zum nicht-höfischen Liebesdiskurs des Mittelalters.* Ed. Friedrich Wolfzettel. Trieste: Parnaso, 1997.

———. "Andreas, Boncompagno und andere; oder das Problem, eine Textreihe zu konstituieren." In Ruhe and Behrens, pp. 31–42; repr. in Karnein, *Amor est passio,* pp. 41–47.

———. "Auf der Suche nach einem Autor: Andreas Verfasser von *De amore.*" *Germanisch-Romanische Monatsschrift* n.s. 28 (1978): 1–20.

———. "*De amore* in volkssprachlicher Literatur: Untersuchungen zur Andreas-Capellanus-Rezeption in Mittelalter und Renaissance.* Heidelberg: Winter, 1985.

———. "La Réception du *De amore* d'André le Chapelain au XIIIe siècle." *Romania* 102 (1981): 324–51, 501–42.

Kaske, Robert E. "Chaucer and Medieval Allegory." *ELH* 30 (1963): 175–92.

Kasten, Ingrid. *Frauendienst bei Trobadors und Minnesänger im 12. Jahrhundert.* Heidelberg: Winter, 1986.

Keen, Maurice. *Chivalry.* New Haven: Yale University Press, 1984.

Kelly, Douglas. *The Arts of Poetry and Prose.* Turnhout: Brepols, 1991.

———. "Courtly Love in Perspective: The Hierarchy of Love in Andreas Capellanus." *Traditio* 24 (1968): 119–47.

Kelly, Henry Ansgar. *Love and Marriage in the Age of Chaucer.* Ithaca: Cornell University Press, 1975.

Kemp, Simon. *Medieval Psychology.* New York: Greenwood Press, 1990.

Kerbrat-Orecchioni, Catherine. "L'ironie comme trope." *Poétique* 41 (1980): 108–27.

Kertesz, Christopher. "The *De arte (honeste) amandi* of Andreas Capellanus." *Texas Studies in Language and Literature* 13 (1971–1972): 5–16.

Klinck, Roswitha. *Die lateinische Etymologie des Mittelalters.* Munich: Fink, 1970.

Klose, Friedrich. *Die Bedeutung von "honos" und "honestus."* Diss. Breslau, 1933.

Knox, Norman D. "Irony." In *Dictionary of the History of Ideas.* Ed. Philip P. Wiener. 5 vols. New York: Scribner's, 1973–74, 2:626–34.

———. "On the Classification of Ironies." *Modern Philology* 70 (1972): 53–62.

Köhler, Erich. *L'aventure chevaleresque: Idéal et réalité dans le roman courtois.* Trans. Eliane Kaufholz. Paris: Gallimard, 1974.

———. "Reichtum und Freigebigkeit in der Trobadordichtung." In idem, *Trobadorlyrik und höfischer Roman,* pp. 45–72. Berlin: Rütten und Loening, 1962.

———. "Les troubadours et la jalousie." In *Mélanges . . . Jean Frappier,* pp. 533–59. Geneva: Droz, 1970.

Kristeva, Julia. *Texte du roman; approche sémiologique d'une structure discursive transformationnelle.* The Hague: Mouton, 1970.

Lavis, Georges. *L'Expression de l'affectivité dans la poésie lyrique française du moyen âge (XIIe–XIIIe s.).* Paris: "Les Belles Lettres," 1972.

Lazar, Moshé. *Amour courtois et "fin' amors" dans la littérature du XIIe siècle.* Paris: Klincksieck, 1964.

Lazar, Moshé, and Norris J. Lacy, eds. *Poetics of Love in the Middle Ages.* Fairfax, Va.: George Mason University Press, 1989.

Leclercq, Jean. *Monks and Love in Twelfth-Century France: Psycho-Historical Essays.* Oxford: Clarendon Press, 1979.

Leff, Michael C. "Boethius' *De differentiis topicis,* Book IV." In Murphy, *Medieval Eloquence,* pp. 3–24.

Lejeune, Rita. "Formules féodales et style amoureux chez Guillaume IX d'Aquitaine." In *Atti del VIII Congresso internazionale di studi romanzi, Firenze, 1956,* pp. 227–48. Florence: Sansone, 1959; repr. in idem, *Littérature et société occitane au moyen âge,* pp. 103–20. Liège: Marche Romane, 1979.

Lerch, Eugen. "'Passion' und 'Gefühl.'" *Archivum Romanicum* 22 (1938): 320–49.

Liebertz-Grün, Ursula. Review of Alfred Karnein, *"De amore" in volkssprachlicher Literatur.* In *Mittellateinisches Jahrbuch* 22 (1987): 308–12.

———. "Satire und Utopie in Andreas Capellanus' Traktat 'De amore.'" *Beiträge zur Geschichte der deutschen Sprache und Literatur* 111 (1989): 210–25.

———. *Zur Soziologie des "amour courtois": Umriß der Forschungen.* Heidelberg: Winter, 1977.

Lyons, John. *Structural Semantics: An Analysis of Part of the Vocabulary of Plato.* Oxford: Blackwell, 1963.

McKeon, Richard. "Literary Criticism and the Concept of Imitation in Antiquity." *Modern Philology* 34 (1936–37): 1–35.

———. "Rhetoric in the Middle Ages." *Speculum* 17 (1942): 1–32.

Meyer, Paul. "Le salut d'amour dans les littératures provençale et française." *Bibliothèque de l'Ecole des Chartes* 28 (1867): 124–70.

Mickel, Emanuel J. "Marie de France's Use of Irony as a Stylistic and Narrative Device." *Studies in Philology* 71 (1974): 265–90.

Minnis, A. J. *Magister amoris: The "Roman de la Rose" and Vernacular Hermeneutics.* Oxford: Oxford University Press, 2001.

———. *Medieval Theory of Authorship: Scholastic Literary Attitudes in the Later Middle Ages.* 2nd ed. Philadelphia: University of Pennsylvania Press, 1988.

Moi, Toril. "Desire in Language: Andreas Capellanus and the Controversy of Courtly Love." In *Medieval Literature: Criticism, Ideology, History.* Ed. David Aers, pp. 11–33. New York: St. Martin's Press, 1986.

Monson, Don A. "L'amour pur' d'André le Chapelain et la poésie des troubadours." In Noble and Paterson, pp. 78–89.

———. "Andreas Capellanus." In *Dictionary of Literary Biography,* 208: *The Literature of the French and Occitan Middle Ages: Eleventh to Fifteenth Centuries.* Ed. Deborah M. Sinnreich-Levi and Ian S. Laurie, pp. 20–26. Detroit: Bruccoli Clark Layman, 1999.

———. "Andreas Capellanus and His Medieval Translators: The Definition of Love." *Mediaevalia,* 26 (2005), in press.

———. "Andreas Capellanus and Reception Theory: The Third Dialogue." *Medievalia et Humanistica,* n.s. 31 (2005): 1–13.

———. "Andreas Capellanus and the Problem of Irony." *Speculum* 63 (1988): 539–72; repr. in *Classical and Medieval Literature Criticism,* vol. 45. Ed. Elizabeth Gellert and Jelena O. Krstovic, pp. 133–53. Detroit: Gale Group, 2001.

———. "Andreas Capellanus's Scholastic Definition of Love." *Viator* 25 (1994): 197–214.

———. "L'Antonomase dans *Le Chevalier au lion.*" *Poétique* 133 (2003): 35–43.

———. "*Auctoritas* and Intertertextuality in Andreas Capellanus' *De amore.*" In Lazar and Lacy, pp. 69–79.

———. *Les "Ensenhamens" occitans: Essai de définition et de délimitation du genre.* Paris: Klincksieck, 1981.

———. "*Immoderatus* in Andreas Capellanus' Definition of Love." In *Etudes de langue et de littérature médiévales offertes à Peter T. Ricketts à l'occasion de son 70ème anniversaire.* 2 vols. Ed. Ann Buckley and Dominique Billy, 1: 293–302. Turnholt: Brepols, 2005.

———. "Les *Lauzengiers.*" *Medioevo Romanzo* 19 (1994): 219–35.

———. "La 'Surenchère' chez Chrétien de Troyes." *Poétique* 70 (1987): 231–46.

———. "The Troubadour's Lady Reconsidered Again." *Speculum* 70 (1995): 255–74.

Moore, John C. *Love in Twelfth-Century France.* Philadelphia: University of Pennsylvania Press, 1972.

———. "Love in Twelfth-Century France: A Failure in Synthesis." *Traditio* 24 (1968): 429–43.

Muecke, Douglas C. *The Compass of Irony.* London: Methuen, 1969.

———. *Irony and the Ironic.* London: Methuen, 1982.

———. "On the Communication of Verbal Irony." *Journal of Literary Semantics* 2 (1973): 35–42.

Murphy, James J., ed. *Medieval Eloquence: Studies in the Theory and Practice of Medieval Rhetoric.* Berkeley: University of California Press, 1978.

———. *Medieval Rhetoric: A Select Bibliography.* 2nd ed. Toronto: University of Toronto Press, 1989.

————. *Rhetoric in the Middle Ages.* Berkeley: University of California Press, 1974.

Muscatine, Charles. *Chaucer and the French Tradition.* Berkeley: University of California Press, 1957.

Nardi, Bruno. *Dante e la cultura medievale.* Bari: Laterza, 1942.

Neilson, William Allen. "The Purgatory of Cruel Beauties." *Romania* 29 (1900): 85–93.

Neumeister, Sebastian. *Das Spiel mit der höfischen Liebe.* Munich: Fink, 1969.

Newman, F. X., ed. *The Meaning of Courtly Love.* Albany: State University of New York Press, 1968.

Nitze, William Albert. "The Romance of Eric, Son of Lac." *Modern Philology* 11 (1914): 445–889.

Noble, Peter S., and Linda M. Paterson, eds. *Chrétien de Troyes and the Troubadours: Essays in Memory of the Late Leslie Topsfield.* Cambridge, Eng.: St. Catherine's College, 1984.

Nykrog, Per. *Les Fabliaux.* 2nd ed. Geneva: Droz, 1973.

Ogle, Marbury B. "Some Aspects of Medieval Latin Style." *Speculum* 1 (1926): 170–89.

Paden, William D., Jr. "The Role of the Jolgar in Troubadour Lyric Poetry." In Noble and Paterson, pp. 90–111.

Painter, Sidney. *French Chivalry.* Baltimore: Johns Hopkins University Press, 1940.

Paré, Gérard. *Les Idées et les lettres au XIIIe siècle: Le Roman de la Rose.* Montreal: Université de Montréal, 1947.

Paré, Gérard, A. Brunet, and P. Tremblay. *La Renaissance du XIIᵉ siècle: les écoles et l'enseignement.* Paris: Vrin, 1933.

Parkes, Malcolm B. "The Influence of the Concepts of *Ordinatio* and *Compilatio* on the Development of the Book." In *Medieval Learning and Literature: Essays Presented to Richard William Hunt.* Ed. J. J. G. Alexander and M. T. Gibson, pp. 115–41. Oxford: Clarendon Press, 1976.

Payen, Jean-Charles. "Un Ensenhamen trop précoce: L'Art d'aimer d'André le Chapelain." In Ruhe and Behrens, pp. 43–58.

Pellegrini, Silvio. "Intorno al vassallaggio d'amore dei primi trovatori." *Cultura neolatina* 4–5 (1944–45): 21–36; repr. in idem, *Studi rolandiani e trovatorici,* pp. 178–91. Bari: Adriatica, 1964.

Pratt, Mary Louise. *Toward a Speech Act Theory of Literary Discourse.* Bloomington: Indiana University Press, 1977.

Prior, A. N. *Formal Logic.* 2nd ed. Oxford: Clarendon Press, 1962.

Putanec, Valentin. "Un Second Manuscrit du *Livre d'Enanchet.*" *Romania* 70 (1948): 74–83.

Quadlbauer, Franz. *Die antike Theorie der Genera dicendi im lateinischen Mittelalter.* Vienna: Böhlaus, 1962.

Quain, Edwin A. "The Medieval Accessus ad Auctores." *Traditio* 3 (1945): 215–264.

Rajna, Pio. "Tre studi per la storia del libro di Andrea Cappellano." *Studi di filologia romanza* 5 (1891): 193–272.

Regalado, Nancy Freeman. "'Des contraires choses': la fonction poétique de la citation et des *exempla* dans le 'Roman de la Rose' de Jean de Meun." *Littérature* 41 (1981): 62–81.

Robertson, D. W., Jr. "The Concept of Courtly Love as an Impediment to the Understanding of Medieval Texts." In Newman, pp. 1–18.

———. "The Doctrine of Charity in Medieval Literary Gardens: A Topical Approach through Symbolism and Allegory." *Speculum* 26 (1951): 24–49.

———. *Essays in Medieval Culture.* Princeton: Princeton University Press, 1980.

———. "Historical Criticism." In *English Institute Essays, 1950.* Ed. Alan S. Downer, pp. 3–31. New York: Columbia University Press, 1951; repr. in Robertson, *Essays in Medieval Culture,* pp. 3–20.

———. *A Preface to Chaucer.* Princeton: Princeton University Press, 1962.

———. "The Subject of the *De amore* of Andreas Capellanus." *Modern Philology* 50 (1952–53): 145–61.

Rossman, Vladimir R. *Perspectives of Irony in Medieval French Literature.* The Hague: Mouton, 1975.

Rouse, Richard H., and Mary A. Rouse. "*Statim invenire:* Schools, Preachers, and New Attitudes to the Page." In Benson and Constable, pp. 201–25.

Roy, Bruno. "A la recherche des lecteurs médiévaux du *De amore* d'André le Chapelain." *University of Ottawa Quarterly* 55 (1985): 45–73; repr. as "Un art d'aimer, pour qui?" In idem, *Une culture,* pp. 47–73.

———. "André le Chapelain, ou l'obscénité rendue courtoise." In Ruhe and Behrens, pp. 59–74; repr. in Roy, *Une culture,* pp. 75–87.

———. *Une culture de l'équivoque.* Montreal: Presses Universitaires de Montréal, 1992.

Ruhe, Doris. *Le Dieu d'amour avec son paradis: Untersuchungen zur Mythenbildung um Amor in Spätantike und Mittelalter.* Munich: Fink, 1974.

———. "Intertextuelle Spiele bei Andreas Capellanus." *Germanisch-Romanische Monatsschrift* 37, n.s. 3 (1987): 264–79.

Ruhe, Ernstpeter, and Rudolf Behrens, eds. *Mittelalterbilder aus neuer Perspektive.* Munich: Fink, 1985.

Sargent, Barbara Nelson. "A Medieval Commentary on Andreas Capellanus." *Romania* 94 (1973): 528–41.

Schaerer, René. "Le Mécanisme de l'ironie dans ses rapports avec la dialectique." *Revue de métaphysique et de morale* 48 (1941): 181–209.

Scheludko, D. "Religiöse Elemente im weltlichen Liebeslied der Trobadors." *Zeitschrift für französische Sprache und Literatur* 59 (1935): 402–21; 60 (1937): 18–35.

Schmolke-Hasselmann, Beate. "*Accipiter et chirotheca:* Die Artusepisode des Andreas Capellanus—eine Liebesallegorie?" *Germanisch-Romanische Monatsschrift* n.s. 32 (1982): 387–417.

Schnell, Rüdiger. *Andreas Capellanus: Zur Rezeption des römischen and kanonischen Rechts in "De amore."* Munich: Fink, 1982.

———. *Causa amoris: Liebesdarstellung in der mittelalterlichen Literatur.* Berne: Francke, 1985.

Schoeck, R. J. "Andreas Capellanus and St. Bernard of Clairvaux: The Twelve Rules of Love and the Twelve Steps of Humility." *Modern Language Notes* 66 (1951): 295–300.

Schutz, A. H. "The Provençal Expression *Pretz e Valor.*" *Speculum* 19 (1944): 488–93.

Searle, John R. "A Classification of Illocutionary Acts." *Language in Society* 5 (1976): 1–23.

———. *Speech Acts: An Essay in the Philosophy of Language.* Cambridge: Cambridge University Press, 1969.

Sedgewick, Garnett G. *Of Irony, Especially in Drama*. Toronto: University of Toronto Press, 1948.

Seidler, Herbert. *Die Dichtung: Wesen, Form, Dasein*. 2nd ed. Stuttgart: Kröner, 1965.

Silvestre, Hubert. "Du Nouveau sur André le Chapelain." *Revue du moyen âge latin* 36 (1980): 99–106.

Sjögren, Albert. "Le Genre des mots d'emprunt norrois en normand." *Romania* 54 (1928): 381–412.

Sperber, Dan, and Deirdre Wilson. "Les Ironies comme mentions." *Poétique* 36 (1978): 399–412.

Stump, Eleonore. *Dialectic and Its Place in the Development of Medieval Logic*. Ithaca: Cornell University Press, 1989.

Sutherland, D. R. "The Love Meditation in Courtly Literature." In *Studies . . . Presented to Alfred Ewert*. Ed. Elizabeth A. Francis, pp. 165–93. Oxford: Blackwell, 1961.

Tacchella, Enrico. "Giovanni di Salisbury e i Cornificiani." *Sandalion* 3 (1980): 273–313.

Tobin, Frank. "*Concupiscentia* and Courtly Love." *Romance Notes* 14 (1972–1973): 387–93.

Toury, Marie-Noëlle. *Mort et "fin' amor" dan la poésie d'oc et d'oïl aux XIIᵉ et XIIIᵉ siècles*. Paris: Champion, 2001.

Trier, Jost. *Aufsätze und Vorträge zur Wortfeldtheorie*. Ed. Anthony van der Lee and Oskar Reichmann. The Hague: Mouton, 1973.

———. *Der deutsche Wortschatz im Sinnbezirk des Verstandes, von den Anfängen bis zum Beginn des 13. Jahrhunderts*. Heidelberg: Winter, 1931; 2nd ed. 1973.

Wack, Mary F. "Imagination, Medicine, and Rhetoric in Andreas Capellanus' *De amore*." In *Magister Regis: Studies in Honor of Robert Earl Kaske*. Ed. Arthur Groos, pp. 101–15. New York: Fordham University Press, 1986.

———. *Lovesickness in the Middle Ages: The "Viaticum" and Its Commentaries*. Philadelphia: University of Pennsylvania Press, 1990.

Wagner, David L., ed. *The Seven Liberal Arts in the Middle Ages*. Bloomington: Indiana University Press, 1986.

Wechssler, Eduard. "Frauendienst und Vassalität." *Zeitschrift für französische Sprache und Literatur* 24 (1902): 159–90.

———. *Das Kulturproblem des Minnesangs*. Halle: Niemeyer, 1909.

Weigand, Hermann J. *The Chapters of Courtly Love in Arthurian France and Germany (Lancelot—Andreas Capellanus—Wolfram von Eschenbach's Parsifal)*. Chapel Hill: University of North Carolina Press, 1956.

Weisheipl, James A. "Classification of the Sciences in Medieval Thought." *Mediaeval Studies* 27 (1965): 54–90.

West, Constance B. *"Courtoisie" in Anglo-Norman Literature*. Oxford: Blackwell, 1938.

Wolfson, Harry A. "The Internal Senses in Latin, Arabic and Hebrew Philosophic Texts." *Harvard Theological Review* 28 (1935): 69–133.

Worcester, David. *The Art of Satire*. Cambridge, Mass.: Harvard University Press, 1940.

Zumthor, Paul. *Essai de poétique médiévale*. Paris: Seuil, 1972.

CONCORDANCE AND INDEX

Passages Cited from Andreas Capellanus, *De amore*

De amore	Walsh	Trojel	Parry	Index
0.1–4	30	1–2	27	11, 20, 25, 63–65, 104, 117–18, 190, 257, 333
1.0	32	3	28	13, 18–20, 224
1.1.1–7	32–34	3–5	28–9	20–21, 35, 162, 171, 175–76, 179, 192–93, 208, 223–24, 230, 266, 278
1.1.8–13	34	5–6	29	21, 24, 105, 176–79, 204, 187–88, 190, 194, 205–6, 281
1.2.1–4	34–36	6–8	30	13, 22, 190–91, 208, 221–22, 231, 266–67
1.2.5–8	36	8–9	30–31	33, 64, 94, 211, 226, 266
1.3.1	36	9	31	22–23
1.4.1–5	38	9–11	31–32	13, 23, 59, 64, 84, 204, 224, 228, 232, 241, 251, 257, 264, 290, 295
1.5.1–8	38–40	11–14	32–33	24, 35, 163, 191–92, 200, 217–18
1.6.1–8	40–42	14–16	33–34	26, 34–35, 47–48, 82, 93–94, 203, 223, 268, 277, 290
1.6.9–15	42–44	16–18	34–35	26, 48–49, 64–65, 100, 203, 241, 245, 277, 285, 291
1.6.16–20	44–46	18–19	35–36	47–50, 82, 108, 249, 327
1.6.21–27	46–48	19–21	36–37	54–57, 102, 244, 247
1.6.28–39	48–50	21–25	37–39	82, 91, 94, 99–100, 102, 204, 241, 243–45, 259
1.6.40–54	50–54	25–30	39–41	62, 254–55, 259, 265, 275
1.6.56–67	54–58	31–36	41–44	71, 79, 91, 101, 193–94, 230, 253–54, 303–4
1.6.68–77	58–60	36–40	44–46	48, 54, 56, 58, 70, 82, 203, 209, 225, 232, 236, 242, 244
1.6.78–86	60–64	40–43	46–47	59, 225, 242–44, 259, 260, 264, 290
1.6.89–97	64–66	44–47	48–49	50, 52, 77, 241, 244, 259–60, 264, 278, 291

De amore	Walsh	Trojel	Parry	Index
1.6.99–106	68–70	48–51	49–51	94, 225, 232, 243, 278, 290
1.6.107–15	70–72	51–53	51–53	48, 226, 232, 242–43, 264
1.6.116–23	72–74	53–56	53–54	82, 91, 100, 219, 245–46, 275, 279, 290, 297
1.6.124–32	74–76	56–58	54–55	57, 109, 232–33, 244, 252–54, 271
1.6.134–44	76–80	59–62	55–58	76, 99, 241–42, 244, 276
1.6.145–47	80	62–64	58	25, 250, 259, 276
1.6.149–65	82–86	64–69	59–62	13, 36–37, 59, 203, 244, 251–52, 259–60, 262, 264, 280, 292–93, 296, 327
1.6.166–75	86–88	70–73	62–64	52, 56, 58–59, 64, 69,73, 230, 243
1.6.178–85	90–92	73–77	64–66	71, 98, 204, 228, 242, 244–45, 253–54
1.6.190–95	94–96	78–80	67–68	232–33, 251–52, 303
1.6.197–203	96–98	81–83	68–69	149–50, 200–201, 230, 232, 259, 276, 297
1.6.204–14	98–100	83–87	70–71	52, 77, 84, 149, 201, 232–33, 254, 257, 276
1.6.218–29	102–4	88–91	72–74	52, 99–100, 148, 152, 233, 257
1.6.244–47	108–10	97–99	77–78	94, 152
1.6.266–69	114–16	104–6	81–82	13, 28–29, 36, 71, 101, 211, 252, 259, 264, 280–81, 296–97, 306, 321
1.6.273–80	118–20	107–10	82–83	52, 151, 191, 253, 303
1.6.281–89	120–22	110–13	84–85	50, 53, 58, 191, 230, 233, 242, 245, 267, 297
1.6.292–98	122–26	113–16	86–87	59, 230, 242, 275, 279, 281, 297
1.6.299–307	126–28	116–19	87–88	59, 67, 78–79, 126, 259, 278–79, 297
1.6.310–20	128–32	120–23	89–91	69, 79, 210, 291
1.6.322–30	132–34	124–27	91–93	54, 56, 163, 191, 201, 244, 254, 259–60, 275–76, 280
1.6.332–38	134–36	128–30	93–95	48, 230, 244, 253, 280, 297
1.6.340–51	138–42	131–35	95–97	90, 252–53, 267, 280
1.6.353–58	142	136–38	97–98	25, 59, 232, 251, 254
1.6.359–65	142–44	138–40	98–100	80, 201–2, 219, 278
1.6.366–76	144–48	141–45	100–102	73–74, 191–92, 207, 234, 316–319
1.6.377–87	148–52	145–49	102–4	36, 59–60, 71, 74–75, 90, 100, 181, 201, 208, 234–35, 292, 316–319, 325
1.6.390–99	154–56	150–54	105–7	58, 68, 75, 112, 227, 234, 316–320

De amore	Walsh	Trojel	Parry	Index
1.6.401–05	158	155–57	107–8	50, 53, 58, 254, 276, 306
1.6.409–13	160–62	158–61	109–10	50, 83–84, 233, 257, 259–60, 276, 309
1.6.414–24	162–64	161–64	110–12	48, 68, 83–84, 261, 264, 297
1.6.425–38	166–70	164–70	113–15	60, 62, 90, 99–101, 193–94, 205, 230, 264, 276, 304, 322
1.6.443–51	170–74	171–74	116–18	59, 62, 91, 98, 101, 215, 218, 309, 320, 322
1.6.452–57	174	175–77	118–19	62, 215–16, 276, 278, 307
1.6.459–65	176–78	177–80	119–21	14, 33, 90, 207, 298, 303, 307–08
1.6.466–76	178–80	180–84	121–23	62–63, 69, 96, 193–94, 220, 230, 276, 307–10
1.6.478–99	182–88	184–93	123–28	35, 50, 62, 82, 90, 92, 112, 251, 265, 279, 295, 327–28
1.6.500–19	188–94	193–201	128–32	36, 48–49, 60, 68, 81, 90, 96, 99–100, 251, 261, 265, 329
1.6.520–32	194–98	201–6	132–35	68, 71, 100, 219, 224, 232, 261, 278–79, 281, 296–98
1.6.533–49	198–204	206–13	135–38	69, 81, 99–100, 185, 214, 220–21, 260–61, 310–11, 323
1.6.550–64	204–8	213–19	138–41	58, 68–69, 72, 90, 191–92, 205, 210, 224, 227–28, 230, 261, 278, 296–97, 299, 306, 323
1.7.1–4	208–10	219–21	141–42	13, 19, 50, 82–83, 241, 249, 329
1.8.1–6	210–12	221–24	142–44	25, 48–49, 64–65, 94, 104, 203, 233, 276, 321, 330
1.9.1–9	212–14	224–27	144–45	34, 207, 267–70, 276, 336
1.9.10–20	214–18	227–32	145–48	64, 264, 267–68, 270–72, 276
1.10.1–6	218–20	232–34	148–49	35, 218–20, 228, 296
1.11.1–4	222	235–36	149–50	13, 19, 212, 246–47
1.12.1–2	222	236–37	150	208, 273, 276
2.1.1–10	224–26	238–41	151–52	202–3, 205, 231, 249, 251–52, 259, 264, 277, 281, 291, 328
2.2.1–6	228	242–45	153–54	13, 48, 101, 202, 226, 234, 236, 277
2.3.1–8	230–32	245–48	154–56	25, 27, 48, 94, 114, 202, 208, 211, 213, 226, 231, 235, 251, 264, 266, 292, 296
2.4.1–6	232–34	248–50	156–57	64, 213–14, 223, 226, 228, 235, 269, 277, 292, 296, 321
2.5.1–9	234–36	250–54	157–59	13, 114, 224, 228, 230–31, 235, 268–69, 281, 298, 300

De amore	Walsh	Trojel	Parry	Index
2.6.1–9	236–40	254–58	159–61	191–92, 205, 226–28, 234, 296, 299
2.6.10–17	240–42	258–61	161–63	91, 220, 248, 296, 299–301
2.6.18–29	242–46	261–66	163–65	64, 90, 115, 228, 232, 297, 301, 305, 311, 333
2.6.30–39	246–50	266–70	165–67	64, 98–99, 211–12, 230, 270–72, 282, 305–6, 310, 312
2.7.1–5	250–52	271–73	167–68	191–92, 281
2.7.6–8	252	273–74	168–69	69, 300
2.7.9–12	252–54	275–76	169	269
2.7.13	254	276–77	169–70	68
2.7.14–15	254	277–78	170	191–92, 224
2.7.16–17	254–56	278–79	170	255
2.7.18–19	256	279	170	322
2.7.20	256–58	280	171	321
2.7.21–22	258	280–81	171	72, 320
2.7.23	258	281–82	171	70 320
2.7.25–27	260	282–84	171–72	69, 100, 302
2.7.28–30	260–62	284–85	172–73	255, 291
2.7.31–34	262	285–87	173	69, 282, 301, 323
2.7.35–36	262–64	287–88	173–74	256, 276
2.7.37–40	264	288–89	174–75	260, 283
2.7.41–42	266	290	175	164, 321
2.7.43–44	266	290–91	175	281
2.7.45–46	266–68	291–92	175–76	271
2.7.47–48	268	292–93	176	217
2.7.49–51	268–70	293–95	176–77	205, 270, 277, 282
2.8.1–11	270–72	295–99	177–79	28, 208, 255–56, 260–61
2.8.23–30	276–78	302–5	181–82	255–56, 260, 265, 290
2.8.40–43	280	308–09	184	28, 208, 255–56, 261
2.8.44–50	282–84	309–12	184–86	28–30, 36, 72, 190–91, 201, 205, 211–12, 216, 218–20, 226–31, 234, 255–56, 264, 277, 291, 296, 302, 319–22
3.1–8	286–88	313–16	187–88	33, 41, 64–65, 83, 118, 233, 332, 336, 338
3.9–18	288–92	316–20	188–91	13, 90–91, 94, 99, 230, 257, 267, 337–38
3.19–28	292–94	320–24	191–93	64–65, 94, 233, 266–67, 276, 290, 295, 336–38

De amore	Walsh	Trojel	Parry	Index
3.29–41	294–98	324–30	193–96	33, 84, 90, 232, 257, 276, 295, 325, 336–38
3.43–50	300–2	330–33	196–97	64–65, 208, 218, 232–33, 257, 267, 336–37
3.55–64	302–6	334–38	198–200	33, 90, 213, 231–32, 264, 338
3.65–79	306–10	338–44	200–203	33, 80, 85, 94, 99, 116, 203, 226, 270, 272, 277, 280, 297, 338–39
3.80–94	310–14	344–50	203–6	33, 92, 94, 97, 99, 116, 203, 272, 290, 297, 338–39
3.100–112	316–20	352–57	207–9	33, 64, 80, 85, 116, 218, 226, 270, 270, 272, 277, 280, 297, 338–39
3.113–19	320–22	357–60	209–11	11, 13, 25, 55, 64, 91, 103, 226, 267, 276, 337–38, 340
3.120–21	322–24	360–61	211–12	33, 64–65, 291

INDEX OF ANCIENT
AND MEDIEVAL AUTHORS
AND WORKS

INDEX OF MODERN
SCHOLARS

SUBJECT INDEX

378

Andreas Capellanus, Scholasticism, & the Courtly Tradition was designed and produced in Garamond by Kachergis Book Design of Pittsboro, North Carolina. It was printed on sixty-pound House Natural Smooth and bound by Sheridan Books, Inc., of Ann Arbor, Michigan.